A MINOR REVOLUTION

A MINOR REVOLUTION

HOW PRIORITIZING KIDS
BENEFITS US ALL

ADAM BENFORADO

CROWN
NEW YORK

Published in the United States by Crown, an imprint of Random House,
a division of Penguin Random House LLC, New York.

CROWN and the Crown colophon are registered trademarks of
Penguin Random House LLC.

Library of Congress Cataloging-in-Publication Data
Names: Benforado, Adam, author.
Title: A minor revolution / Adam Benforado.
Description: First edition. | New York: Crown, [2023] | Includes
bibliographical references and index.
Identifiers: LCCN 2022026405 (print) | LCCN 2022026406 (ebook) |
ISBN 9781984823045 (hardcover) | ISBN 9781984823069 (ebook)
Subjects: LCSH: Children's rights—United States. | Child abuse—
United States. | Child welfare—United States.
Classification: LCC HV741 .B443 2023 (print) | LCC HV741 (ebook) |
DDC 362.70973—dc23/eng/20220729
LC record available at https://lccn.loc.gov/2022026405
LC ebook record available at https://lccn.loc.gov/2022026406

Printed in the United States of America on acid-free paper

crownpublishing.com

2 4 6 8 9 7 5 3 1

First Edition

For all children

CONTENTS

INTRODUCTION

"When your children are swinging in the hammock, playing in the park, or hunting eggs down by grandpa's barn, stop and give a thought to the pale-faced factory boys and girls of the metropolis."

On a summer evening in 1906, readers of *The Spokane Press* received the charge on their porch steps. The story, bottom center, appeared on page four, the back page of the penny broadsheets.

Give a thought to the boy with "twitching, nervous hands rolling cigarettes all day long." Five inches short for the bench, his "emaciated legs do not touch the floor." They dangle like hung candlesticks, disturbed into motion by some erratic, soundless metronome. His body smells of his work—an acorned musk in his flesh and clothes. His widowed mother, with five younger mouths to feed, had no choice but to swear falsely to the age of her eldest. For this boy, there are no July vacations to "dream of." There are no hammocks. There is no play. Sunday is but "a day for sleep after the long, hard week."

Stop and give a thought to the girl with "weak, red eyes"—an apparition of the candy factory. Her eyes cast "an added pallor to her unhealthy skin." She arrives in the dark, she departs in the dark, blinking out of the gates in a perpetual moonlight. You could look through her, but she can be touched; there are scars to be found. "Her hands are thin and bony, with here and there a big, ugly water blister where the hot chocolate has spattered." All day, she stands "before a long wooden table dipping creams into hot chocolate coating." But she does not eat them: "Long ago her stomach revolted at the constant sweet smell. Candy to her is just bitter, miserable toil."

At the turn of the twentieth century, people in Spokane and around the country did stop to ponder "the hundreds of thousands toiling on for their pittance" in sweatshops, canning factories, and foundries. They considered the street children, the starved and battered waifs, the poisoned infants, the illiterate girls, the doomed boys destined for arrest and prosecution. They stopped to feel outrage. They stopped to despair. Their gaze was directed to the plight of children, near and far.

Sitting in the heat of a June dusk looking out on barley fields, a Spokane farmer read, on page three, about five English children trailing their mother in an indifferent London downpour. It was their scrape in this life to scrounge twenty-four cents each day to rent a room for the night. Chairs weren't included, so the family shared their supper, if they had it—condensed milk mixed with oatmeal, potatoes—sat upon soapboxes. The outside light was weak when it arrived, passed through brown paper windowpanes and "smoke from a foul chimney." If they came up short, the rent collector tossed the family out, and they went to a shelter: either the "Twopenny Coffin" or the "Penny Sit Up." For the Twopenny Coffin, each child lay down in a numbered casket on the floor and was covered with "a piece of oilcloth for the night." It stuck "to your skin unless you put newspaper over your face." As the mother explained, she'd had six children, but the baby had died when she was in the workhouse. They keep the little ones separate there and tell the mothers "it's a better system." The day her daughter was dying, they let her see her child, but they didn't let her nurse. That left the ashes of doubt: "My husband says I couldn't have saved her, but it has always been in my mind that perhaps I might."

The people of Spokane did not simply think of Mrs. John Mathews's dead child and what might have been. They stopped to consider what should be.

Above the fold on page four of the newspaper was a report out of Louisville, Kentucky, on the "annual convention of the National Children's Home Society" attended by "[m]ore than 100 men of national prominence in the field of child saving and general social problem work." Their aim was to promote children's welfare by en-suring that orphaned children languishing in almshouses and or-phanages were moved into family homes. And every week, *The Spokane Press* printed announcements of women's clubs, charitable associations, religious brotherhoods, academic conferences, and con-ventions keynoted by university presidents all working to better the lives of children.

There was nothing special about this Tuesday's edition—or the paper, in general. It carried the routine reports of an exceptional juncture, a zero hour. In 1906, there was a broad movement under way that championed and prioritized the rights of children, an ur-gent quaking felt by picking up any newspaper on any day in any town in America. The child savers—as reformers were sometimes known—had emerged in the late nineteenth century and by the early twentieth were forging ahead on numerous fronts. They gave us child labor laws and playgrounds. They helped marshal resources to protect children from abuse and neglect by their parents, and pushed for basic health measures, like ensuring clean cow's milk.

As supper beckoned, the Spokane reader might have wondered on the safety of the ground beef that awaited his children that eve-ning: page one noted that a state law introducing meat inspections had passed but not yet gone into effect. Tonight's hamburgers were still bacterial trust exercises. But progress was in process. By the end of 1906, Mrs. Winslow's Soothing Syrup, advertised at the foot of page four as a miracle cure "used by Millions of Mothers for their children while Teething for over Fifty Years," would be forced to disclose that its primary ingredients were morphine and alcohol. Mrs. Winslow's had long been a dark magic, so effective in calming cries, but always threatening a sleep too deep. For thousands of kids, the creeping shroud could not be lifted: each breath slower, the limbs growing cold and waxy, the pupils vanishing to pinpricks, until the ember was snuffed altogether. Regulation came because journalists, doctors, and coroners investigated, organized, and demanded changes to protect children from such "fraudulent and dangerous" nostrums—"Baby Killers," as the *Journal of the American Medical*

Association warned in no uncertain terms. They pressed on until Mrs. Winslow's removed morphine from its formula and "soothing" from its name.

Reformers were following a similar course in reorienting the criminal justice system and their initial rewards were already evident around Spokane. On page one of the newspaper was a story about fourteen-year-old Frank Hogedon. The previous night, around eleven o'clock, Patrolman Willis had caught him and his friends, Max Berry and George Skine, both fifteen, stealing flowers from the lawns of the neighboring houses on Frank's street. The young teens had admitted to it straightaway and, just a year earlier, armed with the confessions, prosecutors would have proceeded to trial in adult court. As a Spokane prosecutor bemoaned in 1904, "Without any exception the most disagreeable duty of this office is the prosecution of young boys on petty offenses." But in 1905, the state legislature had created a separate Spokane juvenile court. They'd remodeled rooms in the basement of the county courthouse and Judge Kennan had given up his divorce and insanity cases to hear juvenile matters on Fridays. In his words, it was a "court for correction, not for punishment."

The transformation had materialized from the relentless "agitation"—to quote *The Spokane Press*—of activists in Washington and around the country who organized meetings and circulated petitions to demand a new approach to child offenders. The legal system should be rebuilt around "reformation and character building," keeping children separate from adults and showing them care and respect. Newspapers amplified the message. *The Seattle Star* arranged to have an expert write four articles to help readers understand "the origin, growth, development and purposes of the 'juvenile court idea.'" *The Spokane Press* published three profiles of Ben Lindsey, the "father" of juvenile justice and "a peach" of a judge to the erring boys who received his empathy and trust. The standout in the series described Lindsey recessing a two-million-dollar civil trial after spotting a "freckled face" street urchin who'd appeared before him months earlier. The boy had been making "50 cents a day with which he had kept his mother" by selling newspapers—"honest business," the article reported. But "a new cop [who] thought he owned the town" had been harassing the boy, ordering him off his favorite corner. He'd come to the judge for justice. Lindsey listened patiently to the facts, as the waiting attorneys glowered and reshuffled their papers, and then wrote the boy an "injunction" to deliver to the officer. "A live boy is worth more than a dead man's millions," the judge concluded. It was, to the paper, "a remarkable and altogether unusual thing," but a vision of our brighter future: "a court worthy of a republic" in which "a boy of the streets in his rags has as good a footing as the cause of men clothed in broadcloth and represented by high-priced lawyers."

The new structures and mindset made a real difference for a Spokane child like Frank. His youth was suddenly salient. The other forces in his life were now relevant: it mattered that his mother was "aged and widowed;" it mattered that she was "ill at the hospital" when Frank set off with Max and George and their shovels. It changed his present and his future. Rather than being sent to a jail cell with men, the newspaper reported, "[t]he Hogedon boy was allowed to go home."

A separate juvenile justice system, though, was never the principal plot for the child savers. As the editors of *The Spokane Press* proffered the previous year, "[I]s it not better to get hold of the young delinquents before they reach the court stage?" On the same page as Frank's story, there were two separate articles on primary education in the city, one celebrating a "great increase" in pupil attendance in the Second Ward and another reporting a call for additional school construction before the First Ward Improvement Club. The paper had warned its readership to think proactively and they had taken the message to heart: "The state makes a great mistake when it puts the future citizen into a gloomy, ugly school house. . . . Some day, when society learns how to utilize what it has, the school house will be the center of culture, and music, and art and literature, and good citizenship, and humanity; in short, the center of commercial life. Some day society will learn that money spent to promote these things is money spent better than for juvenile courts and truant officers."

Across fields, reformers offered a new vision: many societal problems originated in the poor treatment of children, but with proper interventions, young people once destined for lives of desperation could be steered toward health and success. Saving children from harm and nurturing their potential meant ensuring a better future for all of us. By 1912, President William Taft had been convinced to create a federal agency, the Children's Bureau—the first of its kind in the world—focused solely on improving the welfare of young Americans. As the bureau's first director explained, the core mission was to "serve all children, to try to work out standards of care and protection which shall give to every child fair chance in the world."

There was a brave new era on the horizon. True advancement was imaginable—inevitable even—like technological and scientific progress: in a hundred years, children would lead far better lives.

So what care, what protection, what chance do we give to a child born a century after the child savers?

In those hundred years, we have built nuclear submarines, self-driving cars, and rockets to take tourists to space. Acknowledging the tremendous work still to be done in achieving equality, women have nonetheless secured seats on the Supreme Court, Black Americans have won the presidency and vice presidency, and openly LGBTQIA+ leaders are now prominent in business, entertainment, and politics. We have learned to transplant faces and hearts. We have mapped the human genome. In our pocket, each of us carries a device that can play any song we want to hear, show us rain clouds moving eastward a hundred miles away, bring us Grandma laughing in her kitchen as if standing in ours.

In nearly every domain, we have made miraculous strides. But not with children. Against all reasonable expectations, in the quest to better their lot, we have slowed to a trudge. Return to the pages of *The Spokane Press* from June 19, 1906, and our lack of progress is stark.

A hundred years on, children still go hungry. Children still end up on the street when their families can't make rent. Not a handful of children—millions. In America today, one in six kids grows up in poverty. In our largest cities, one in seven has experienced eviction by the age of fifteen. And, on any given night, one in five people experiencing homelessness is a child. The agonizing decision whether to feed your brood or shelter them is no entombed relic of Edwardian England; it is a modern American tragedy. One in eight households experiences food insecurity each year—a number that skyrocketed to one in three during the COVID epidemic. Without adequate care leave, we still separate poor working mothers from their infants, reassuring them that it is a "better system."

A hundred years on, children are still laboring under appalling conditions so that we can buy cheap candy and cigarettes. Nearly a million children under the age of twelve work on the West African cocoa plantations that support our chocolate bar cravings. Tens of thousands of those kids are literal slaves—young boys trafficked from Burkina Faso and Mali to work long, dangerous hours spraying chemicals and swinging machetes. They drink polluted water in stolen moments unwatched. They are locked up at night in shacks. We may have barred American children from our cigarette factories, but they work on in India. And they work on in American tobacco fields. Children as young as seven pick tobacco in North Carolina today. It is legal: with parental permission, a child of any age can begin working on a small farm, and by age twelve, that child can work an unlimited number of hours on any farm.

What has changed since 1906? Not the toil—dawn to dusk, six days a week. Not the reasons—in sixteen-year-old Elena's words, "With the money that I earn, I help my mom. I give her gas money. I buy food from the tobacco work for us to eat." And not the cost of that labor—"I get headaches and my stomach hurts," Elena explains. At night, "I try to sleep and I just can't."

More than a hundred years after *The Spokane Press* warned about the boy with the "nervous hands," child laborers are still suffering from acute nicotine poisoning. They are still breathing in pesticides that will stunt their development and give them cancer. They—thirty-three each day—are still being injured in farm accidents.

Aware of the threats to children's health, we choose inaction or retreat. In 2018, the Department of Labor sought to remove protections that have long kept sixteen- and seventeen-year-olds from hazardous jobs. In 2020, the Environmental Protection Agency reversed course on banning chlorpyrifos—a pesticide that harms developing brains—part of a Trump administration rollback of more than one hundred environmental rules protecting children. A child born today will die, on average, 2.6 years earlier because of the small particulate that enters their lungs from car exhaust, coal-fired power plants, and other human activity. This year, roughly half a million children will experience lead poisoning.

A hundred years after the alarms echoed in newspapers across the country, we are restaging our greatest blunders upon children's bodies—the choreography hideously familiar. Mrs. Winslow's Syrup may be long gone, but morphine is still swirling in infants' veins and the prologue is the same: companies aggressively marketing dangerous products indifferent to their impact on our youngest citizens. As Mallinckrodt, the largest manufacturer of oxycodone, told its sales team in 2013: "You only have 1 responsibility. SELL BABY SELL!" So, today, every fifteen minutes a real baby is born in the United States with the telltale symptoms—the tremors, the clenched muscles, and agonized breaths—of neonatal abstinence syndrome. How is it possible that one in five children is obese—three times the prevalence in the 1970s? Count the number of spots for fast food and sugar-sweetened drinks the next time your child sits down to watch cartoons. The average American kid sees over thirteen thousand television ads per year.

Once in the vanguard, we have fallen behind other advanced nations on protecting children at every stage of development. Among the twenty richest countries in the world, America is dead last on childhood mortality. An American kid is 70 percent more likely to die before adulthood than a child living in one of our peer nations. That wasn't true fifty years ago: in the 1960s, American children were safer than kids in other wealthy, developed countries. But while our peers worked hard to provide health insurance to all pregnant mothers and kids, we have pursued policies that leave millions without coverage. Even today, more than 10 percent of children in Texas do not have health insurance. Car crashes and firearm injuries persist as the leading causes of child fatalities because we've vigorously blocked gun and vehicle safety laws that our peers passed years ago without controversy.

The protective institutions the child savers bequeathed to us have grown derelict, been taken over by squatters, or expanded, favela-like—terrible, sprawling, and essential. We've somehow ended up with a child welfare system that both fails to protect hundreds of thousands of children from abuse and neglect by their parents each year and actively harms hundreds of thousands of kids by taking them away from their parents and placing them in worse conditions. We've somehow ended up with a justice system that treats kids as adults when it comes to policing and punishment but not when it comes to basic rights.

It is 2022 and poor boys on city street corners are still being harassed and abused by police officers. Since 2002, one in five pedestrians who were stopped by New York City police were eighteen or younger. And two out of three civilian complaints filed against New York City police officers in 2018–19 were by or on behalf of Black children, eight to eighteen. The youngest are not spared: more than thirty thousand children under ten were arrested in the United States between 2013 and 2018. And, overall, roughly seventy-six thousand children are prosecuted as adults each year.

And, yet, they are not adults when they seek the privileges of that status. In the later part of the twentieth century, children gained important rights under the Constitution to privacy, to free speech, to racial equality, and the like. But, in recent decades, the Supreme Court has ignored children's pleas for protection from unreasonable searches, corporal punishment, and censorship. When minors have sought equal treatment to adults, they've mostly lost: the legal establishment has decided that it's generally okay to lump all children together and disqualify them from freedoms adults take for granted, even if the rationale for exclusion doesn't apply to many individual children, who are just as capable as the average voter, juror, or patient. Today, *The Spokane Press*'s hope that a boy of the streets would soon be on as good footing in court as "men clothed in broadcloth and represented by high-priced lawyers" is preposterous.

So, too, is their vision of the schoolhouse "as the center of culture, and music, and art and literature, and good citizenship, and humanity." Against their expectations, we have not learned that "money spent to promote these things is money spent better than for juvenile courts and truant officers." We have let our public schools crumble. In my well-off neighborhood in downtown Philadelphia, the dog park is far closer to the paper's vision of a "bright, cheerful, cozy, home-like, inviting, refined" space than the cracked asphalt public school play yard that sits directly next to it. The school no longer has a library. Its windows have bars. When the coronavirus pandemic hit, that elementary school immediately shut its doors, but the bar down the block stayed open. The city government's logic was economic necessity.

Overall, where once we led the world in investing in our children, we now lag behind most of our peers. That matters in the present: American kids are now more likely to drop out of high school than kids in other advanced democracies. And that matters in the future: today's young people are likely to face significantly worse financial prospects—more debt, more unemployment, less homeownership, and lower wages—than their parents. Because of our actions, our children will experience an adult life that is far less certain and more fraught with peril in numerous other domains. In the coming years, the devastating harm from climate change—wildfires and flooding, food and water shortages, forced migration and political instability, pandemics and wars—is going to accelerate and expand because of our selfishness and inattention. We are giving our children a worse life than our parents gave us.

What is particularly infuriating is that a century after the child savers movement, we have a much greater capacity to better children's lives. We have bountiful wealth, technology, medicines, and other tools that we could marshal at any moment to boost the welfare of kids. And advances in psychology, neuroscience, sociology, and public health have provided us with an ability unparalleled in human history to understand and protect children. We know so much more about what is good and bad for young people, but we do so much less about it.

What led us to this stagnation on children's rights?

Progress often turns on how subsequent generations respond to the failures and blind spots of the pioneers. For all their promise, it was not inevitable that the gliders of 1900 would evolve into transatlantic passenger jets. The aeronautical successors had to build upon what the forefathers got right and fix what they got wrong. They had to figure out that expanding the vision—adding pilot control and self-propulsion—didn't imperil flight but rather made it more certain.

Early-twentieth-century progressives did not provide a complete structure for the realization of children's rights but merely the beginning of one. It was flawed—like the rickety engineless flying machine the Wright brothers pulled along Kitty Hawk beach. Even as they professed a universality, the child savers were largely focused on white immigrants in the big city, not Black children in the rural South or indigenous children on reservations out West. Even as they spoke broadly, the child savers were responding to a particular set of horrors coming out of the industrial revolution—ten-year-old mine workers with black lungs, bright young minds dimmed in the factory, kids sucked into the morass of adult prisons—and so they focused on protection from harm and rehabilitation, not on personal freedoms. Viewing children more as *future* persons—to be shaped into productive, sociable, assimilated adult citizens—than *existing* persons worthy of being listened to and respected in the present, the institutions they created were often highly paternalistic and authoritarian. The early juvenile justice system, for instance, largely overlooked children's perspectives and due process rights.

The breath of social activism that animated the 1960s and 1970s presented an opportunity to address the pioneers' oversights: to extend protection and investment to nonwhite children and to ensure the long-neglected liberty of our youngest citizens. But the new generation of reformers became convinced that the project to advance children's status as full human beings worthy of voice, power, and dignity could not be reconciled with the coercive and dehumanizing social welfare and protection framework the child savers had provided. Their forbears' work had to be razed, not redeemed. With ensuring children's health and safety cast as the enemy of securing children's freedom, the opportunity for progress was squandered. The new blueprints were never realized—the public rejected the notion that children were deserving of inclusion in the broader civil rights movement as a distinct class subject to oppression and deserving of equality—and the old structures that treated kids as a distinct class needing greater care and understanding were left crumbling. Faced with the challenge of adding autonomy to protection, we settled on doing neither.

Under the auspices of securing children's liberation from the biased discretion of despotic juvenile judges, we turned back to treating boys like men, rejecting rehabilitation for punishment, and sending more children than ever to adult prisons. With lip service to upholding their inherent liberties, we permitted children to be removed from public schools to be homeschooled by their parents. Eager to exploit the autonomy rhetoric, business entities welcomed children as full citizens of the marketplace, proclaiming them rational consumers to be listened to and served—not patronized with nanny state regulations—while actively shaping children's behavior through aggressive marketing designed to maximize profits from cigarettes, fast food, and other harmful products.

Indeed, the second half of the twentieth century saw a growing challenge to the very principle that state intervention to ensure the rights of children was the best way to secure their welfare. The animating idea of the Children's Bureau—that a government entity ought to be attending to the interests of the "whole child"—lost out to those who argued that agencies should be organized around function—health, labor, and the like—not the constituency that they served. And, more important, it lost out to those who argued that it wasn't the state's responsibility at all to look out for kids: it was the duty of parents. Infant mortality, poverty, low test scores? Those were the result of poor choices by parents—a matter of individual, not collective, responsibility. By the end of the century, it was accepted wisdom for many Americans that "welfare mothers" and "deadbeat dads" were the problem. Bad parents should be blamed, good parents should be empowered, and the state should butt out.

Correspondingly, if anyone were to be given rights, it was mom and dad, not kids.

These undermining dynamics are conspicuous in matters big and small, in our many failures and our rare victories. They have derailed the efforts of lone social workers trying to better the life of one boy. And they are reflected in the greatest achievement of child rights advocates on the global stage: the United Nations Convention on the Rights of the Child.

By the 1970s, many in the international child advocacy community had reached the same conclusion as their peers in the United States: the efforts of the forebears, embodied in the League of Nations' Geneva Declaration of the Rights of the Child in 1924 and the UN's Declaration of the Rights of the Child in 1959, had largely cast children as passive objects to be protected and that dependency frame had facilitated their continued second-class citizenship. With distance from the world wars, it was now apparent that young people needed more than "special safeguards and care." With the UN designating 1979 as the International Year of the Child, the Commission on Human Rights seized the opportunity to begin a decade-long process to create a more complete instrument.

Adopted by the General Assembly in 1989, the treaty establishes that all children are due basic protections and entitlements, but it also declares that they have agency rights to expression, association, and participation. It combines freedoms *from*—torture, exploitation, and discrimination—and freedoms *to*—education, play, and knowledge. It is as close as the world has come to an inclusive and comprehensive vision, providing a shared framework to assess each nation's progress on ensuring the welfare of children. And the United States has refused to ratify it. We are the sole holdout of the 193 UN member states—defiant and alone.

Although the convention had a number of powerful backers in the States, like the National Parent Teachers Association and the American Bar Association, ratification was derailed by those who saw the document as a grave threat to parents' child-rearing rights—an invitation for the international community to invade the privacy of the American home. Champions of the fundamental sovereignty of parents not only doomed passage in the United States, they also shaped the convention for everyone else. Their fear of strong intervention on behalf of children is evident in the treaty's deliberate vagueness and weakened language, in its lack of teeth, and in its ultimate deference to mom and dad, who are empowered with "the primary responsibility" in upbringing, development, and care. Moreover, an unwillingness to upset the privileging of adult interests and preferences is apparent in many of the declarations, reservations, and objections that other countries included in signing on. Iran, for instance, reserved "the right not to apply any provisions or articles of the Convention that are incompatible with Islamic Laws." Indeed, even as the convention admirably asserted the agency of children—that they were capable of having beliefs and opinions and worthy of being listened to—it did not guarantee that they be given meaningful political power, only that they be consulted and their views be taken into consideration.

So, while the convention stands as a remarkable accomplishment and has prompted countries to incorporate aspects of the treaty into their domestic law—like providing greater access to healthcare and banning child labor practices—it has not ushered in a bright new era for kids. Rights violations remain pervasive around the world. And the treaty has generally worked best for those who need the least help—wealthy white children in wealthy white countries. For most children—whether they live in Yazd, Iran, or Bellamy, Alabama—the convention is a list of empty promises: they have no voice unless their parents speak for them, they have no toys unless their parents buy them, they have no classroom, no friends, no doctor unless their parents provide them.

The puzzle of incorporating autonomy rights into basic protections has continued to evade us. But that need not be true. Empirical research into child psychology and biology can help us resolve the conflict between advocates pushing for children to be given the full rights of adults and advocates arguing that children must be protected from societal and environmental forces. The latest scientific evidence on children's capacities and vulnerabilities provides the means for reaching a basic consensus on what is best for children. It can act as an objective arbiter over disputes characterized, for decades, by gut intuitions and biased risk perceptions. And it can reveal that many seemingly intractable clashes between extending autonomy and ensuring protection—that have stymied progress—have no basis in fact. Psychology and neuroscience provide a coherent account of why, for example, a sixteen-year-old should have both a right to vote just like an adult and a right not to be treated like an adult when it comes to the criminal justice system. Adopting a data-based approach can help us see that ensuring developmentally appropriate rights to self-determination can be a path to securing children's protection.

The research provides a powerful case for urgent intervention. Our children are what we make them. Their bodies, their actions, and their futures are determined by our choices. A child may end up speaking seven languages or unable to utter a single word, deft at back handsprings or struggling to grasp a pencil, a murderer or a saint. And the earlier we intervene, the more potential impact we can have. The first years of life are a time of rapid brain development—with each second that ticks by, more than a million new neural connections form. But as time passes, the basic architecture takes shape and the focus shifts to refinement: the brain connections are reduced, pruned back to improve efficiency. The bottom-up nature of the process means that as we age, it becomes harder and harder to fix cognitive, emotional, and social deficiencies. Moreover, the capabilities that children gain early in life provide the foundation for future development. Strengthening infant health means increasing the potential benefit of investing in pre-K education. Providing a safe and stable home environment in elementary school provides the basis for more effective interventions in adolescence on habits—eating well, exercising, avoiding drugs, nurturing relationships—that will last a lifetime. And every year we learn more about how traumas and deprivations experienced in childhood can adversely affect a person's children and grandchildren. If your goal is to foster healthy, successful, productive human beings, the data is unambiguous. Don't wait and remediate. Childhood is the window of opportunity.

Our inattention and inaction, then, are not simply a moral problem; they are also an economic and social one. By failing our children today, we doom ourselves in the years ahead. The root cause of nearly every major challenge we face—from crime to poor health to poverty—can be found in our mistreatment of children. But in that sobering truth is also the key to effectively changing our fate as a nation.

The premise of this book is that the best way to address society's major challenges is to put children first. When we invest in the welfare of children—protecting them from harm, ensuring their needs, granting them standing and voice—the profits compound over their entire lives. They accrue to their kids, to strangers, to generations to come.

Focusing on the broad benefits to *all of us* from prioritizing children's interests makes this an unconventional book about rights. But the standard model—declaring rights to be inherent and worthy of respect even if the rest of us got nothing from the deal—hasn't worked for kids, in part because many people view children's subordinate status as justified by the obvious differences between children and adults. To many, it is the condition of control—not rights—that seems natural for children. Another frame is needed: the reason that children deserve rights is not because they have equal capacities to those who already have rights. It is because of the benefits that flow to all of us from ensuring their rights. So, while I sometimes offer evidence on the unappreciated competence and potential of kids to refute those whose basis for denying children a seat at the table is that they lack some prerequisite that adults possess, the main purpose is to make the case for why ensuring their liberty and protection has such value.

When I asked Sidney, a six-year-old from New Jersey, what all kids needed, she said, "Water. Food. Sunlight. And a bed to sleep in." That, in a nutshell, is the minimalist approach of the mainstream human rights movement—embodied in some of its most venerated institutions and core agreements. It is a claim to granting the barest materials of life, enough to allow a person to survive. We may sometimes assert more, as in the Convention on the Rights of the Child, but we always settle for less in practice. The barest materials of life are not nearly enough for children.

We must ensure this most basic set of rights—and confront the fact that we are failing even in America, as our children drink contaminated water, go hungry, and lie upon shelter mats. But we must also pursue a more expansive vision—and not simply in replacing a human rights of sufficiency with one centered on material equality. I propose something seemingly more radical: prioritizing children's rights, granting young people more than we allow ourselves. What children are due is not sufficiency—nor even equality—it is a prioritizing. When genuine conflicts arise, the default should be to privilege their rights over the rights of others. We must work to understand that our fates are entwined with those of children, and challenge ourselves to feel more responsibility to future generations.

That ties into another way this is a different type of rights book. It's not focused solely on constraining or tasking the government. It asks us all—the state, businesses, private institutions, parents, and nonparents alike—for a commitment to ensuring the rights of children. We all need to heed the scientific evidence that supports the value—to all of us—of putting children first, rethinking how we bring children into the world, how we organize our families, and how we care for and educate our young people.

To advance this children's revolution, I identify six core rights that all children possess—organized chronologically, in the book, in terms of a child's maturation:

1. The First Years: The Right to Attachment
2. Early Childhood: The Right to Investment
3. Late Childhood: The Right to Community
4. Early Adolescence: The Right to Be a Kid
5. Late Adolescence: The Right to Be Heard
6. On the Cusp of Adulthood: The Right to Start Fresh

In the chapters, I'll provide the latest scientific evidence—from biology, psychology, sociology, and other fields—that shows how children's interests are particularly imperiled at each stage of development and why ensuring a specific right will benefit both children and society at large. To better illustrate the themes, I'll share the stories and voices of children and adults looking back on their early lives. When considering the research on a child's cognitive capacity to make independent decisions, handle controversial material, or serve on a jury, it can be helpful to hear what it is like to be a kid navigating a city alone, interviewing a white supremacist for the school newspaper, or getting locked up in an adult prison.

I've chosen to focus on rights—rather than capabilities, well-being, or other promising avenues—because I think rights are particularly powerful in advancing change. And I've identified these six rights because I believe they are especially important. But they aren't the only ones that matter. I hope the book will prompt you to consider your own list and how you might open new fronts in this collective endeavor to advance children's interests. In the conclusion—chapters 7 and 8—I'll argue that recognizing a set of core rights is ultimately a means to a more fundamental reorientation as individuals, groups, and institutions: adopting a children-first mindset in everything that we do.

For me, this is a deeply personal book. I've been thinking about children's rights my whole life. From an early age, I was keenly attuned to injustice. I didn't think it was right when I learned that my friend's dad spanked him. I thought I should get to vote as a sixth grader. I noted the powerful mark of wealth as I switched elementary schools. I was shaken watching the cruelty of junior high schoolers as they bullied boys who must certainly bear those scars today, but more by the indifference of the adults who saw exactly what I saw and did nothing.

It was this concern with unfairness that brought me to law school and later shaped my perspective as a student, lawyer, and law professor. Sitting in family law, I saw the way children were ignored even in moments in which the law purported to be looking out for their best interests. And I saw that same blindness when I argued in court for the first time, representing a woman in a custody and support battle with her ex-husband—as the children's interests were debated, their voices were absent. Investigating the causes of the childhood obesity epidemic in my first law review article, I was shocked to learn about the complex ways that fast-food companies have targeted and exploited children—and the failure of our legal system to protect them. And I was shocked, later, running psychological experiments exploring human intuitions about punishment to see how ready people are to jettison notions of the blamelessness of youth. In the classroom, I've come to feel responsible for drawing attention to the mistreatment of children, not simply when I teach a course called The Rights of Children, but also in the courses where kids don't make it onto the standard syllabus, where their interests are deemed irrelevant, indistinct, or *de minimus*—Criminal Law, Contracts, Business Organizations.

I am grateful that as my earliest memories begin to fade, I get to see childhood again through the lives of my own children. And I'm grateful to know fatherhood—it has enriched my perspective on the best path forward. My experience with the realities of modern parenting—the weight of it, trying to figure out what advice to take, which battles to fight, which sides to support, when to sit back, and whom to trust, all while keeping up on the everyday rites of packing preschool lunches, shuttling to swim practice, and washing favorite dresses—has led me to the firm conviction that the general problem for children is not one of affection or commitment, but of where we focus our efforts.

There's no question that we love our kids, that we want what's best for them. We are tireless and fearless in what we will do for our children—in our battles with toothbrushing and sorry-Mom-I-forgot bake sales and travel-team soccer practices. We invest far more in our children—in terms of both time and money—than parents did back in the 1970s. And we are constantly trying to improve with tips for a better breastfeeding latch, a better night's sleep, and better homework habits. We open our wallets for the latest child-optimization gadgets: immersion blenders for preparing healthy baby food, light-up rattles to encourage developmental growth, and educational apps to boost creativity, vocabulary, and mathematical proficiency. We spend billions of dollars trying to figure out the secrets to mastering child-rearing and "guaranteeing" the success of our offspring. Amazon has over fifty thousand parenting books.

The problem is that a lot of what we are doing—the items we are buying, the endless fretting about the right way to potty train and introduce solid foods—is useless. And, looking at the uninspiring data on various individual parenting interventions, some well-meaning people conclude that nothing matters and that we should just relax and stop worrying about our kids. But that's misguided: children can be powerfully influenced by their environments, and attention and investment matter a lot. Our "intensity" is admirable—and could be an incredible force for improving the welfare of children—if only it were properly directed. In general, when it comes to helping children reach their potential, it is our broad societal policies, not our individual choices, that matter most. But the business of raising kids is atomized: each family is left on its own to sink or swim. So, we spend our energy trying to figure out when we should stop breastfeeding and how to ace baby-led weaning. We stress over what version of the "cry-it-out" method to use. Thousands of anxious parents will spend millions of minutes this week reading and trying out largely worthless child-rearing tips. Meanwhile, some two million American children live in families with income and benefits below half the poverty line, 2.7 million minors have a parent currently locked away in jail or prison, and twenty million teenagers are denied any say in choosing their government. We don't need to stop worrying about children; we need to stop sweating the minutiae and channel our efforts to the big questions.

And that leads to one final point. This book is filled with big ideas, but it is not a radical book at all. It's not about changing our values; it's about better upholding them. It was "self-evident"—nearly 250 years ago—that "all men are created equal" and "endowed by their Creator with certain unalienable Rights." The Universal Declaration of Human Rights, adopted by the United Nations General Assembly in 1948, echoes that same basic sentiment: "All human beings are born free and equal in dignity and rights." We do not need new words; we need to follow the ones we have. There are so many frameworks for prioritizing children's welfare that already exist, that reflect the society we want to be, and that we have forgotten, neglected, or misused. The "best interests of the child" is still the guiding standard in family law. We still have a separate juvenile justice system. We even still have that first federal agency, the Children's Bureau, though it's now an office within the Department of Health and Human Services focused narrowly on abuse, neglect, adoptions, and foster care.

What I am calling for is not upheaval—some risky social, political, and cultural disordering. It's the opposite. It is the status quo that is dangerous. Those who assail the recognition of a child as a full human being—worthy of respect, protection, and autonomy—are the same who denied personhood to Black people, who laughed at the idea of women being able to attend college, who told us that the institution of marriage would crumble once gay people were permitted to wed. But kids aren't the same, you say. Perhaps. But, then, second-class citizenship always seems natural, obvious, and justified to the privileged. We will not reach our destination if we leave the kids behind. Their march is our march. We cannot progress alone.

A MINOR
REVOLUTION

PART I

RIGHTS

CHAPTER 1

THE FIRST YEARS

The Right to Attachment

The boy was put out with the chickens. He wasn't yet two. The reasons remain hidden in the past. Sujit's mother killed herself. His father was found stuffed in the trunk of a taxi. There is not anyone left to ask, though there were witnesses. In the rural village outside of Suva, Fiji, the neighbors noticed the boy from time to time, penned in the coop, underneath the house out of the sun, tied up with the hens. But, for years, he was left there.

When social workers finally intervened, Sujit was eight. He could not speak. And he didn't move like a boy. He would hop, perch. When food was brought to him, he'd knock over the plate and peck at the meal on the floor. The sounds that emerged from his mouth were like bird calls. He didn't want to sleep in the bed they made for him at the Samabula Old People's Home. He set down to roost on the stone.

There are animals that do not require caregiving when they emerge into the world. Megapodes are like that. The stocky, chicken-like birds do not parent. They spend their days on themselves: stalking the wooded landscapes of the Pacific islands kicking up leaves in a search for centipedes, lizards, termites, shoots, and seeds. While most birds incubate their eggs with their own bodies, megapodes lay theirs inside warm mounds of decaying vegetation or in sand piles naturally heated by the sun. Their offspring dig themselves out when they are ready. The youngsters emerge with eyes open, able to run and forage. Within an hour, they can fly. They aren't taught; they aren't nurtured. Even in their first day of life, megapodes are completely independent, off to explore without mom or dad. One chick, only a few days old, was spotted flying twenty-five miles out at sea.

We are not like that. We need our people from the moment we are born. And when we do not have them—when we are denied those nurturing bonds—the consequences can be devastating and permanent. The tragic experiences of profoundly neglected children like Sujit—those locked in basements alone, forgotten in institutions, lost to regular human contact—reveal just how essential our human connectivity is for development.

That was not at all clear to experts a hundred years ago. As the Children's Bureau's 1914 publication *Infant Care* exhorted, "The rule that parents should not play with the baby may seem hard, but it is without doubt a safe one." The influential psychologist John Watson echoed the sentiment in his 1928 book *Psychological Care of Infant and Child:* "Let [the child] learn to overcome difficulties almost from the moment of birth. . . . If your heart is too tender and you must watch the child, make yourself a peephole so that you can see it without being seen, or use a periscope . . . and, finally, learn not to talk in endearing and coddling terms." Be a megapode parent, in other words.

It was not until the middle of the twentieth century that we began to rethink the value of detachment, prompted in large part by our primate relatives. While rhesus monkeys share roughly 93 percent of their DNA with humans and demonstrate similar behavior, they develop roughly four times faster. They can also be randomly assigned to particular early-life conditions in a controlled laboratory experiment. When, in the 1950s, Harry Harlow showed that orphaned baby monkeys preferred a terry cloth "surrogate" with cradled arms over a wire mother that offered milk but no surface to cling to, it suggested that we'd been overlooking something critical in early development: for primates, comfort might be a greater necessity than food. And in numerous subsequent experiments, we've gotten a picture of just how important parental attachment is to the life course.

In one recent study, researchers tracked generations of rhesus monkeys over three decades. When they were born, each monkey was either raised by its mother or placed in a nursery. The nursery conditions were designed to be enriching, with plenty of nourishment, human care whenever needed, and playtime with other baby monkeys—just no mom. At eight months, all monkeys were brought together and reared in identical conditions. Each generation that followed was subject to the same protocol.

What researchers found is that early-life attachment between a child and their mother yields significant health and social benefits, not simply to the child but to subsequent generations. Monkeys allowed to develop a strong attachment to their mothers and descended from a lineage of monkeys bonded to their moms had the best health and rose the highest up the monkey hierarchy as they aged. They had the strongest chance at securing the rhesus good life, as measured in access to choice food items and grooming from the most coveted partners. The intergenerational benefit of being from a line of mother-raised monkeys, though, didn't accrue to those who were themselves reared in the nursery. As the authors concluded, "[P]arenting is the primary channel of intergenerational transmission of early-life advantage." And if you're denied that special bond at the very beginning, it doesn't matter that things get better later. After just eight months, the monkeys were all treated the same, but they were indelibly, forever different.

Unfortunately, the research on human children paints the same picture. Young people deprived of nurturing attachments in the first years of life miss out on an essential basis for their healthy development intellectually, emotionally, socially, physically, behaviorally, and morally. Secure bonds are the foundation for learning about and exploring the new world. It is within these vital relationships that we gain our sense of self, how to navigate the social landscape, how to learn, how to trust, how to control ourselves, and how to love. The costs of isolation manifest in learning disabilities, interpersonal struggles, and poor physical and mental health decades into the future.

Seventy-six years ago, Dr. Benjamin Spock published *The Common Sense Book of Baby and Child Care*, indelibly reshaping the way we raise our children. Though it is often described as the bible of child-rearing, it's really more of a user's manual: a how-to guide, marrying the logic of a Vulcan with a down-to-earth empathy. I was a Spock baby, as were my parents before me. Spock, a Yale-trained pediatrician, didn't buy the conventional wisdom of his time that warned against excessive affection. He wanted parents who were involved with their kids. For him, the equation was simple: "Useful, well-adjusted citizens are the most valuable possessions a country has, and good . . . care during early childhood is the surest way to produce them." But there was more standing in the way than the scowls of elderly neighbors who thought children were best neither heard *nor* seen. Indeed, in Spock's view, the biggest problem was a quite modern development: the rise of families where both parents worked outside the home. While Spock couldn't rise above the cringe-worthy sexism of his time, he recognized the fundamental dilemma that posed: "It doesn't make sense to let mothers [or fathers!] go to work making dresses in a factory or tapping typewriters in an office, and have them pay other people to do a poorer job of bringing up their children." As he reasoned, "It would save money in the end if the government paid a comfortable allowance to all mothers [and fathers] of young children who would otherwise be compelled to work."

Today, we know that there are many positives that come from having parents successfully pursuing careers outside the home. But Spock's core claim remains true: it makes sense for parents to spend more time with their kids, particularly when they are very young, and investing in giving parents time to do that makes sense for society.

Especially in the early years of life, the research is clear that greater parental investment makes a significant difference. Paid childcare leave is linked to reduced mortality and better health. With time off from work, women are able to breastfeed longer and infants get more one-on-one attention. Paid leave also supports parent-child bonding, which is associated with improved physical and cognitive development.

The benefits of increased parental involvement in early child-rearing appear to extend far into the future. When researchers looked at what happened after Norway changed its maternity leave policy to guarantee women four months of paid leave in 1977, they found that the increased time mothers spent with their kids correlated with reduced high school dropout rates and higher incomes at age thirty. The effects were largest for mothers who had the least education.

Part of the reason may be that early bonding promotes later connectedness between children and their parents. In one study of 1,319 mostly socioeconomically disadvantaged families, fathers who took two or more weeks of leave had children who, at age nine, reported greater closeness, communication, and engagement with their dad. And the children of engaged fathers demonstrate numerous advantages as they mature, from superior language development to more advanced social and cognitive skills.

Scientists have begun to explore how being with our young children primes us for more interactions. And it seems that we've been thinking about things backward: as the psychologist Alison Gopnik has written, "We don't care for children because we love them; we love them because we care for them." Spending time touching, talking to, and playing with your baby raises oxytocin levels—and, in men, lowers testosterone. In fact, caregiving appears to change parents' brains.

In a recent study, new fathers were given either a baby seat to place in their home or a baby carrier to wear. After three weeks, the scientists looked at the fathers' brains as they heard an infant's cry. The men who'd carried their babies around with them, for twelve hours a day on average over that period, showed a much stronger response in the amygdala, an area of the brain involved in processing emotionally relevant information. Moreover, the effect was most pronounced in dads who suffered adverse childhood experiences and who were, therefore, most at risk of struggling to bond with their children.

Against this overwhelming evidence, we do not guarantee Americans any paid time off to care for a newborn or adopted child, so nearly half of parents report taking less than three days. If your two-year-old gets leukemia, there is no national right to paid leave to take her to her medical appointments. There are no federal laws stopping an employer from requiring a mom to work every day of the week or denying a dad any vacation days. In other advanced nations, paid time off to care for infants and sick children, paid vacation, and a guaranteed day of "rest" each week are standard. Indeed, America is one of only seven countries—along with the Marshall Islands, Micronesia, Nauru, Palau, Papua New Guinea, and Tonga—that doesn't have any national paid leave.

In November 2014, then vice president Joe Biden sat down to write a note to his staff. He wanted to "make something clear to everyone." It concerned "an unwritten rule since [his] days in the Senate":

> I do not expect nor do I want any of you to miss or sacrifice important family obligations for work. Family obligations include but are not limited to family birthdays, anniversaries, weddings, any religious ceremonies such as first communions and bar mitzvahs, graduations, and times of need such as an illness or a loss in the family. This is very important to me. In fact, I will go so far as to say that if I find that you are working with me while missing important family responsibilities, it will disappoint me greatly.

The memo was later shared with the media and went viral. The sentiment ought to be entirely unnoteworthy, obvious. But, in America, it's not.

Even when employers talk about the importance of prioritizing family, family is rarely privileged in practice. If you're a member of the working poor and have a kid with health problems, you are 36 percent more likely to lose your job than a parent without a sick child. If you are in a high-powered position, no one may ever say it out loud, but just look around the office and the norm is clear: the client, the deal, the case, the project, the firm come first. In a recent survey, half of fathers and a third of mothers admitted missing key events in their children's lives because of work.

While Biden's enumeration of family obligations seems to address the problem, it inadvertently reinforces a damagingly narrow understanding of working parents' responsibilities to their children. Make it to the once-a-year candle blowing and you are an A+ dad—no bother that you leave before your daughter wakes up and get home after she's asleep most days of the week. Be there for the birth, sure, but decline the weeks of paternity leave.

If we care about a right to attachment, we must ask for more for children. In a 2016 interview, Biden actually identified the dilemma: "In the mid-sixties, early seventies, it was: *You know, you have to spend quality time with your kids.* Well there's no such thing as quality time. It's all quantity. It's all *quantity.* Every important thing that's ever happened to me with my children has been on unscheduled time."

We need a strong national care leave policy that's generous and inclusive. By generous, I mean that it ought to offer enough leave to meet the needs of young children and provide a high level of wage replacement. By inclusive, I mean that it should cover all workers, offer a broad definition of family care that reflects the many important attachments that people can have, and promote maximum participation.

A good place to start is simply looking to match our peers. Roughly three quarters of developed nations offer at least six months of paid leave to mothers and roughly three fifths offer that to fathers. Many of our close peers are far more generous: Austria, Japan, Norway, and South Korea all provide more than a year of paid maternity leave. Roughly three quarters of developed nations have a wage replacement rate of at least 80 percent for mothers and more than two thirds provide that for fathers.

When researchers looked at the countries with the most successful economies and low unemployment rates, they found that the policies that supported working families did not hamper competitiveness. Of the thirteen low-unemployment countries in the study, all but one—the United States—replaced wages at a level of at least 80 percent and seven offered 100 percent replacement. Full cover appears to be particularly important for getting men to take the leave they are given. And the data suggests that if you want new parents not to take a career hit, you need to ensure that people mostly all participate.

Like three quarters of the countries with paid leave, we could adopt a social insurance model with a new payroll tax, along the lines of Social Security. This could help change the perception of care leave from a "gift" we give new parents—like a wedding present—to part of the basic social contract: the means to ensure stability and prosperity across generations.

While the details of any new child leave policy are important, in some ways, it is the changed cultural mindset around care and work that is more critical.

What made Biden see things differently?

It was tragedy.

In December 1972, a week before Christmas, Biden's first wife, Neilia Hunter, took their three young children out to run some errands. A tractor-trailer plowed into their car. Neilia and one-year-old Naomi were killed. Hunter and Beau, two and three, were badly injured with multiple broken bones. Biden had just been elected to the Senate and suddenly he was on his own with two toddlers. As his son Hunter describes, "After that, we had a rule, with Beau and I, which was that no matter what, as long as we were sincere about it and not trying to get out of something—but even sometimes if we were—if we wanted to go to work with Dad, we could go with him." "Anywhere," Joe Biden explains. "They could pick a day. They didn't have to explain. Just say, 'Dad, I want to go with you today.' They could miss school, travel with me to Washington, be in the office." So many of us say family comes first, but so few of us live it.

Today, many of us push hardest at work when our children are young—the years when they need us most are the years we are striving to make partner, establish our business, gain tenure, make a name for ourselves. We buy into the model that says sacrifice now—in your late twenties, thirties, and forties—so that you can rest on your laurels later.

It feels like the natural way of things—an inescapable aspect of the human life cycle—but that's only because we're so used to it. We're inured to family disunion in the realm of work and everywhere else. We oversee an array of systems, rules, and procedures that act to separate young children from their guardians. And they are reinforcing. The pervasiveness of separation masks its perversity: that so many young children are kept from their parents is taken as proof that they must not actually need them.

For Ariel and Adam, three and six, the partition came like an eclipse.

In that bright before, they were playing in the hayloft, exploring the woods, taking out the horses. There was a pond, an Easy-Bake Oven, a large picture window with a seat. Ariel liked to dance there. When I spoke to Adam about the first years of his life, he used the words "fondest memories" twice as he thought back on it.

They loved their parents and, suddenly, they were gone. Everything was gone—the farm, the animals, all of it. A sheet had dropped over them as they slept. Kenny and Jackie, their parents, had been arrested in a drug conspiracy. Awoken to darkness, Ariel and Adam found themselves in an orphanage with, in Adam's words, "a lot of really angry children," "shuffled from room to room."

Jackie had thought the orphanage would be the best of bad options: the only way to keep the kids together. She had thought they would bring Ariel and Adam to visit her, but they didn't.

Entering first grade, Adam discovered what it was to be "miserable all the time." Ariel's memories are filtered through the stories of others, infused with the bitter contradiction of institutionalization: oppressive abandonment—to be deserted and coerced in the same moment.

One day, their extended family came to check on them. As Ariel recounts, "They had showed up just to visit and they had parked and they saw me walking from the orphanage to a building next to the orphanage, by myself, with no adults escorting me. They went into the orphanage and were fussing at them, like, 'Why is she alone? Why is she walking down the sidewalk by herself?'" It was not a mistake, though. It was neglect by design. The orphanage "said I had to get vaccinated: 'She knows where she is going.' They just sort of blew it off: 'She can get there by herself, she knows where to go.'"

Adam and Ariel might easily have been lost for good. Their parents were both given long sentences—Kenny, more than four life sentences for his part in a scheme to distribute marijuana and cocaine; Jackie, six and a half years, a third of what the prosecutor had sought. None of their relatives, struggling with medical and other problems, could take them in. But a couple from their parents' church heard about their plight and reached out. It was a moment of profound generosity, but it was a blue moon event.

For so many other children, there is no rescue. One in five kids who enter the child welfare system has a mom or dad in jail or prison. And incarcerated parents are more likely to have their kids permanently taken away than people who physically or sexually assaulted their children. That's largely down to a federal law that requires a state to seek to terminate parental rights whenever a kid has been in the foster system for fifteen out of the last twenty-two months. The problem, of course, is that many parents, like Adam and Ariel's, are locked up for longer than that—and cannot check the boxes to put them in good standing, like having stable employment and housing, paying child support, attending parenting classes, and spending time with their kids. While terminations frequently occur before children have the opportunity to form new bonds with other adults, they are often barred from contact with their parents or siblings, regardless of whether a judge thinks it's in their best interests.

Even in circumstances where new devoted caregivers step forward to fill the hole of parental incarceration, the negative consequences of separation are immense. Adam does not mince words: the outcome for him and Ariel was the "best-case scenario for kids with two parents getting incarcerated at the same time." The couple who took them in "saved us from a system that was guaranteed to allow us to fail." But they could not protect Adam and Ariel from the lasting harm exacted by our criminal justice system: "Even with these super loving people who bent over backward for our education, it was still a struggle."

The U.S. Department of Health and Human Services recognizes having a parent incarcerated as one of nine Adverse Childhood Experiences, along with having a parent die and living with someone with an alcohol or drug problem. These experiences are notable in leading to trauma and stress, which can affect brain development and produce lifelong tolls on mental and physical health. Indeed, the

children of incarcerated parents face an array of negative consequences: higher rates of smoking, asthma, HIV, depression, and
PTSD. In one recent study, young adults whose mothers were incarcerated when they were kids were three times as likely to have ex-
changed sex for money and twice as likely to have used the ER rather
than a primary care physician for their healthcare needs. In another
study, the children of incarcerated parents were six times more likely
to acquire a substance use disorder, five times more likely to become
a teenage parent, and twice as likely to suffer from anxiety.

One of the reasons that the impact can be worse than other adverse childhood events is because parental incarceration is uniquely
stigmatized and because the experience touches so many aspects of a
child's life. If your mom dies, you can expect sympathy; if your mom
is locked up, you may get jokes and scorn. As Ariel explains, "I felt
very different than everybody else . . . I didn't have a lot of childhood
friends because I didn't like talking about [the fact that my parents
were in prison] and I didn't want anyone to know." Many children
suffer alone. And that can leave enduring emotional scars. As Adam
points out, "Kids are malleable. They are really tough, but at the
same time you are going to leave permanent marks on them, on their
minds, on their development."

The effects of parental incarceration are also financial. When you
take a father away from his kids, you increase the probability that the
family will be plunged into poverty by 40 percent. The loss of family
income—an average decrease of 22 percent when dad is imprisoned—
can set off a downward mobility spiral in which families, who can no
longer pay the bills, are forced to move into poorer neighborhoods,
with worse schools, more unemployment, and higher crime rates.

You might expect the outlook for kids to suddenly improve when
their parents are released, but research on the challenges of reunifi-
cation suggest that's often not the case.

Adam and Ariel both mentioned how much of a struggle it was
when their mom got out of prison. They'd spent years dreaming of
the day she'd finally come home and "expecting everything to be
perfect." But, as Adam recounts, the whole situation was set up for
failure: "She gets out and works minimum-pay-type jobs wherever

she can find, comes home super tired, and has to deal with us wanting to catch up on [the missed moments]." She was simmering with
anger.

Adam remembers thinking, "I just want to die." Ariel felt "invisible": "I used to hide until she said, 'Where's Ariel?' and she never
would."

Being a ghost might be the most apt metaphor for the child of the
returned prisoner—out of place between worlds. Who are you and
where do you truly fit? Ariel highlighted that question: today, if she
has an issue with her son, she'll call the mom who took her in when
her parents were incarcerated, not her biological mom. "But it's hard
because we don't spend Christmas with them, we don't plan family
vacation with them, so we are kind of in this weird limbo because we
are close to them because we spent those important years, but at the
same time we are not their family. There is that line, you know. My
son will probably never call them Grandma and Grandpa."

Even economically, parental release frequently fails to improve
the outlook for children. Paroled parents can struggle to find employment because many businesses conduct background checks and
don't hire people with criminal records. Those who find work make
10 to 40 percent less than those who've never been locked up.

The fallout is widespread and penetrating. Almost half of U.S.
kids have a parent with a criminal record. And there is a cascade effect. If you've been incarcerated, it is going to be harder not only to
land a good job but also to secure an apartment, go to college, and
accumulate the savings necessary to withstand hardships—the pre-
cise things that can help facilitate the upward mobility of your children.

Is it any surprise then that so many kids follow in their parents'
ankle-chained footsteps? An adolescent boy whose mother is locked
up is at a significantly increased risk of both dropping out of high
school and ending up in the system. In each turn of the jailer's key,
we set off an intergenerational cycle of harm.

The destructive pattern we get when we incarcerate parents is not
unique. It's predictable and reproduceable—it's what you get with
the standard deprivation condition in a human extension of those

monkey attachment experiments. We replicate the trauma in our child welfare system and in our immigration system.

In America, we address concerns over the safety and well-being of children—she has lice, he is always hungry, they are withdrawn—by taking children away from their caregivers. On any given day in the United States, there are over four hundred thousand kids in the foster care system. The vast majority of those children are not removed from their families because their parents abused them. Most investigations and removals involve allegations of neglect stemming from poverty. As law professor Dorothy Roberts has described, "If an outsider looked at the American child welfare system, she would likely conclude that this is not a system designed to promote the welfare of America's children. Rather, it is a system designed to regulate, monitor, and punish poor families, especially poor Black families." One in ten Black children is placed in foster care at some point in their early life.

Even short periods of separation can produce serious trauma, as when police on a domestic call find a roach-filled pantry and empty refrigerator and decide to take a three-year-old away from his mom. Young children often have no idea why they are being pulled out of their mother's arms and placed in a squad car, and can view the separation as their fault or rejection by their parents. They are suddenly thrust into a foreign environment, away from all of the sources of reassurance and stability they have ever known—their caregivers, siblings, toys, pets, and crib—without explanation, unsure where they are or how long they will be there. It can be utterly debilitating.

Longer removals often produce tails of destruction decades into the future. One in five people raised in foster care will end up homeless at some point; one in four will be incarcerated within just two years of departing the system. By age twenty-five, fewer than 3 percent of people who were in the foster system will have a college degree.

In 2018, the public's attention was drawn to President Trump's "zero tolerance" family separation policy at the southern border, which tore thousands of children away from their parents. But breaking the parent-child bond has been a standard part of immigration enforcement for years. Since 2009, more than five hundred thousand children who are U.S. citizens have had their parents deported. And the experience for a young person is often very similar to when a parent is imprisoned, from the immediate agony of witnessing your mom or dad being dragged away to the enduring economic hardship from losing a breadwinner.

We've become adept at justifying separations—as inevitable, as necessary for deterrence, for children's own good—because we've had so much practice over the centuries. It was okay to sell slave children at the auction block because they were property. It was right to send hundreds of thousands of Native American children to boarding schools to "civilize the savage." To remove poor city children from their parents and ship them on trains to midwestern farms was to end a cycle of failure. As American businessman and philanthropist William Pryor Letchworth explained in 1877, "If you want to break up pauperism, you must transplant."

We need to end this legacy. Stable, quality relationships in childhood have an impact on nearly every facet of a child's development, and when parental attachment is compromised, it can produce lifelong cognitive, social, emotional, and physical problems. Recognizing a right to attachment for all children would align the United States with international norms articulated in the UN Convention on the Rights of the Child, which provides that "State Parties shall ensure that a child shall not be separated from his or her parents" unless it "is necessary for the best interests of the child." That promising language, though, is immediately swallowed up by a formal recognition of the power of states to detain, imprison, exile, deport, kill, and otherwise separate a parent from their children, with the child entitled to nothing more than "information concerning the whereabouts of the absent member(s) of the family." To secure a right to attachment, we need a more substantial commitment to preserve existing bonds, strengthen weak ones, and support the creation of new desired relationships between loving caregivers and kids.

Let's consider what that would look like.

To better preserve current attachments, we could start small by working within the present system to improve contact between children and incarcerated parents. Respecting a right to attachment, there would be no ban on toys in the prison visiting room, as in New Hampshire, or shirts containing logos with pictures, as in Tennessee. We would never prohibit breastfeeding during prison visits, as New Mexico recently tried to do, or eliminate in-person family contact in favor of video chats, as roughly one in ten local jails has done. We would not charge kids $11 to talk to their locked-up dad on the phone for fifteen minutes or move him to a prison six hours away from their home.

The research on the value of visitation between incarcerated parents and their children is clear: such contact is a key factor in reducing the harm children experience when their mom or dad is locked up. Yet, shockingly, more than half of all incarcerated parents are never—not once—visited by their young children. That's often because the parents end up housed so far away—160 miles, on average, in the federal system.

As Ariel recalls, when she was little, "my mom was in Lexington, Kentucky, and my dad was in Atlanta and we saw them about once a year." Kenny was then transferred to Kansas, West Virginia, and, finally, South Carolina.

With a focus on ensuring a right to attachment, we would mandate that parents be placed in prisons that were as close as possible to their children. And a concern with keeping inmates nearby their families would drive decisions about the location of new prisons and the closure of old ones. We would increase in-person visitation hours, not decrease them, as the Florida Department of Corrections recently proposed. Talking to your incarcerated mom or dad would be free and encouraged. You could talk every day.

When Ariel recalled her saddest moment as a kid, it "was when my mom recorded reading a story to us—*Green Eggs and Ham*—and they mailed a video to us of her reading it in prison clothes and we watched it over and over to hear her voice. . . . At that time, I was so broken and felt so alone and just wanted my mom."

When you focus on ensuring a right to attachment in setting prison policy, the main arguments in favor of decreasing in-person contact between inmates and their children suddenly seem weak.

Does physical affection between children and their incarcerated parents increase the risk of drugs or weapons coming into the prison? Perhaps, but the problem can be addressed in other ways that don't harm kids, and the cost of a marginal increase in contraband pales in comparison to the toll on children from restrictive policies. The truth is that we should encourage physical contact between parents and their kids—especially for infants for whom touch is so critical. Both Adam and Ariel mentioned how good it felt, how needed it was, sitting on their dad's lap, falling asleep on him. At seven, Ariel remembers, she was told that such contact was now prohibited and "that was really hard." Why should we make life any more difficult for a first grader whose dad is locked up for the rest of his life?

We should encourage the sharing of letters, drawings, and keepsakes, not discourage them under the vague auspices of "prison security." Anyone who has a child knows how important special objects can be, how meaningful letters received in the mail are, how children want you to hold their work in your hands. Ariel emphasized how critical the mementoes she received from her parents were: "My mom would crochet us angel bookmarks and even in the orphanage I had a picture of my parents and those little things meant so much to me." When other children "borrowed" them, it was devastating: having them "taken away from me was like my life is going to end." So why does Pennsylvania require kids' homemade birthday cards to be sent to Florida to be scanned and then sent back as black-and-white copies—weeks late—at a monthly cost of $376,000 to taxpayers?

In 2019, New York became the first major city to make jail phone calls free. Overnight, call volume at Rikers jumped 30 percent. All it took was people in power noticing and caring about the problem. But taking the research on the importance of attachment seriously, you realize how much more ambitious we ought to be.

In Norway, incarcerated mothers are often allowed to keep their babies with them, weekend leave to return home is common, and guards help prisoners to maintain and improve family ties. For correctional officials over there, it makes perfect sense: strong families help people not end up back behind bars.

There is no reason we couldn't go even further. Adam is right: "It is inexcusable for perfectly good parents to be removed from their kids' lives." Allowing women to raise their babies behind bars is a lot better than our status quo in America, but babies don't belong in prisons. So why not take their mothers out instead? Of course, some parents clearly pose such an ongoing threat to society (and their kids) that allowing them to interact with other people makes no sense. But for most parents who have committed crimes, monitoring is likely to be equally effective as incapacitation in prison, without the corresponding harm to children.

Whatever the context—at the border, after a 911 call or a concern at school, at the close of trial—we just shouldn't separate kids from their parents if it's not in their best interest to do so. Making foster children should be our last resort, yet it's often the standard protocol in our wars on crime, drugs, terror, poverty, and everything else.

Since the 1970s, for example, we've focused on addressing poor living conditions for children by taking more and more kids away from their parents and placing them in the welfare system. But it would be much better to just address the challenges poor parents face by providing them with cash assistance, food security, stable housing, substance-abuse treatment, and other support—a topic we'll explore in more detail in the next chapter. Instead of pouring billions of federal dollars into foster care, we should put it into improving existing parent care.

One of the things that prevents us from changing course is not simply the inertia of the massive foster industrial complex we've strapped ourselves to, but the profit motive that guides it.

For private entities, "stable, loving, forever families"—in the lingo of reformers—are the enemy. When Congress passed the Family First Prevention Services Act of 2018, the purpose was to boost funding for programs to help parents struggling with mental illness, addiction, and other issues and therefore keep kids from falling into the foster care system. But for-profit group homes were dead set against these modest, sensible measures for the simple reason that it meant they'd have fewer filled bunks.

Indeed, private agencies' power in the foster system helps explain the persistence of institutions and group homes—where more than forty thousand children are currently placed—in spite of the overwhelming data on their negative impact on kids. Children raised in institutions are at a greatly increased risk of psychosocial neglect: they get less adult attention, they get less stimulation, and they experience greater instability in important relationships because staff don't tend to stick around. This, in turn, drives deficits in the cognitive and self-regulatory abilities that predict academic attainment, income, and mental health into adulthood.

If you are raised in an orphanage that's got its eye trained on the bottom line or if your foster mom only signed on for the $22 a day she gets from a company seeking to make money from your care, you are going to miss out on what the renowned development psychologist Urie Bronfenbrenner identified as the most essential need for normal development: "progressively more complex joint activity with one or more adults who have an irrational emotional relationship with the child." For a young human to thrive, there must be, well, love—special and strong: "Somebody's got to be crazy about that kid. That's number one. First, last, and always."

There are foster parents who meet that bill—who ache with love for children they've only recently met and who can provide essential support to the small number of kids who simply cannot remain with their parents because that presents an obvious and unmitigable danger. We need to do a better job of identifying these essential caregivers and confirming that we've made the right call by attending carefully to the feedback from children in their care. When a child tells us that a foster placement is bad, we must listen. And when they are desperate to stay attached, we should attend to that love.

An implication of love's necessity is that we need to help people who don't want kids to avoid becoming parents. Part of the solution is ensuring that everyone has access to free, safe, reversible, long-acting contraception, so that people can decide if and when they are ready for parenthood. Nearly half of all pregnancies are unintended in the United States each year, and it's not hard to understand why that's a huge threat to promoting devoted, stable bonds.

Recent state-level initiatives have demonstrated the power of supporting reproductive choice. When Colorado launched a pilot program, in 2009, offering to cover long-acting birth control, the results were stunning. Over the next five years, the unintended pregnancy rate dropped nearly 50 percent for teens aged fifteen to nineteen, and by 20 percent for women aged twenty to twenty-four. With the highest rate of unplanned pregnancies in the country, Delaware teamed up with a nonprofit, Upstream USA, with a simple mission: ensure that any woman can access whatever birth control she wants in a single visit to her healthcare provider, at low or no cost. As a result, between 2012 and 2017, the state saw an 18 percent drop in the unintended pregnancy rate—more than double the decline seen in all other states collectively.

Those who count themselves as "pro-life" ought to think hard about their oppositional instincts. Expanding contraception access is a pathway to greatly reducing abortions that does not require punishing women or doctors, overturning precedent, or fighting endless battles with fellow Americans. In the first five years of the Colorado pilot, the teen abortion rate plunged nearly 50 percent. If you believe that the stable, loving family forms the basis of society, you ought to care about securing a right to attachment against the threat of unintended pregnancies, for it is the bedrock of the foundation.

To give people control over the decision to have kids, we also need to address a culture that pushes procreation. Many of the top factors people identify for spurning parenthood—like desiring more leisure time and having no desire for children—are entirely valid. Parents today have very little time to themselves, particularly in comparison to previous generations. Research consistently shows that having children tends to make people less happy. And it is a myth that if you forgo having kids, you'll end up feeling unfulfilled. Yet, that is the relentless message sent to childless young adults. "You're overthinking this." "You'll regret not having kids the rest of your life." "You don't know how you'll feel until you have them." "The clock's ticking." The singer Adele struck a chord when she told *Vanity Fair*, "I think it's the bravest thing *not* to have a child; all my friends and I felt pressurized into having kids, because that's what adults do."

One of the great benefits of disrupting the cultural expectation of reproduction is that it can help us appreciate that parenthood isn't the only option for people who want children in their lives.

Anne and her husband thought they'd end up on the traditional path: "We always assumed we'd have kids. A dog. A white picket fence, if lucky. That's what people did where we were from. But as time went on, we never felt the urge." At the point most of their hometown friends were starting families, they moved to New York and that opened up a world "that didn't involve children." Anne realized that the way to *have* it all was to not try to *do* it all. "Women who have children are supposed to maintain a career, friendships, and a marriage. And be a Pinterest mommy. But it's not possible. I can't travel nonstop for my job (and pleasure), maintain long working hours, be a wife, a caretaker to my own mom, *and* be a parent." But rejecting parenthood didn't mean rejecting kids. "I love children," she explains. For her, the solution was to embrace "aunting"— a term that's come to encapsulate the act of deeply caring for and engaging children that are not your own.

As Anne puts it, "'Aunting' gives me the time I want with children without the commitment. . . . My niece and nephew mean the world to us, and I adore my friends' children, too." So, she has cultivated relationships with them that are independent from the ones she has with their parents. She and her husband, for example, have taken their niece on international trips and plan to do the same with their nephew. One of the great aspects of "aunting," as Anne notes, is that it can allow you to engage with children in a different—and sometimes better—way because you don't have the responsibilities and constraints of a parent. The research is clear that these other meaningful relationships with adults are greatly beneficial. They don't sap the strength of the primary attachment a child has with her parents; they supplement it.

If it is essential to ensure that adults are not pushed into parenthood when that's not what they want, it is also important to make it easier for eager, loving caregivers to take on that special role. Yet we often put up incredible barriers to the formation of new nurturing attachments.

Derek, like Anne, expected to get married and have children. "I grew up in a very conservative part of Mississippi and . . . that's kind of the goals that everyone has there, and I had them too, even though I was gay." But, as he admits, "how I was going to get there was a little confusing in the 1980s and '90s and 2000s."

By 2014, though, the route forward seemed clearer, enough so that, on his second date with Jonathan, he felt sufficiently confident to say it out loud: "Look, if you're not looking to get married and have kids, you probably shouldn't be barking up this tree."

As Derek recalls, Jonathan had "the other gay experience": he had the same dreams "for himself, but because it looked hard and society said you shouldn't do this, he just put it away as something that he would never do." Derek's boldness made Jonathan think maybe he could be a father after all.

Still, they didn't jump into things. "We did things in the Mississippi way," explains Derek, "got married, spent a year honeymooning, and I spent a year intentionally not talking about it. But as soon as we hit that year mark, I said, 'All right, this is the deal.' "

The first step was to look into their options. As Derek and Jonathan quickly discovered as they met with friends who had adopted, the process can be daunting. Indeed, 83 percent of people considering a foster care adoption cite concerns about paying for the adoption and 74 percent cite concerns with the paperwork and bureaucracy as a reason for not moving forward. Yet foster care adoptions are relatively inexpensive in comparison to the tens of thousands of dollars people spend working through a private agency or international organization. Just the price of a home study—like the one Derek and Jonathan completed—assessing a family's ability to meet the needs of a child based upon interviews, observations, and background checks can be three or four thousand dollars.

That said, the biggest obstacle for Jonathan and Derek was a cultural one. "As gay men wanting to become parents, I think we battle feeling illegitimate, feeling like we don't belong in the institution, feeling like people are going to judge us, feeling like people will try to take our children away." As Derek explains, adoption "felt scary, because there were always going to be these birth parents who were always going to be more straight than us, more normal than us, more attractive than us."

That made surrogacy seem like a better option: "We felt like having some biological connection to the child would make us more legitimate. It wasn't about vanity. It wasn't about re-creating our genetic child; it was . . . about securing our family." But they "couldn't afford it in the commercial way that it's done in the U.S. . . . where you sign a contract and you pay a lump sum of money to someone you don't know." In an amazing act of generosity and love, an old friend of Jonathan's offered to help.

The fact that she was British added a bit of complexity, certainly, but finding the right person to carry their child for forty weeks seemed paramount. Here was someone they trusted and knew, acting purely out of affection for them, someone they could count on for the journey ahead. They'd figure it out. Plus, they had strong connections to England. Although Jonathan's mother was American and he had American citizenship, he'd spent most of his life in the U.K.

So, they began jumping through the various regulatory hoops to begin the gestational surrogacy process. As required, Derek and Jonathan met with psychologists and lawyers, as did the surrogate and her partner, to make sure that everyone was prepared and that "no one was being coerced." They had the mandated blood tests to screen for diseases; they answered various questionnaires. Derek recalls it "took the better part of a year to do all those things," but then they were through. They received eleven eggs from the anonymous donor: "We split them, six and five."

On the second try, the surrogate got pregnant. Derek went to live in the U.K. to help, and Jonathan arrived for the last five weeks. "Jonny and I never missed an appointment. We never missed a scan." They were there at the house, when the surrogate went into labor, and there in the room, as she underwent an emergency C-section. They watched Simone come into the world: "They handed her to me, and I held her, and Jon cut her umbilical cord."

But then, despite all of this, despite being the ones in the hospital learning to swaddle and change diapers, the ones waking to soothe

the crying baby, they were not yet—officially, legally—Simone's parents.

In England, six weeks after a baby is born through surrogacy, a couple like Derek and Jonathan can apply for a "parental order" naming them on the birth certificate. They were at the court with the paperwork, six weeks and one day after Simone came into the world. The additional process is meant to ensure that the parents have the necessary qualifications and meet the requisite standards. As Derek explains, U.K. officials "reviewed our financial records, they visited our home, we met with social workers, social workers went to [the surrogate's] house." Eight months after Simone was born, in March 2019, the U.K. court granted the order.

They'd made it: child and parents. Yet when they went to return to their life in Atlanta, they discovered there was a hitch. Applying for a passport for Simone, they were told by the U.S. Department of State that Simone—despite having two American citizen parents—was not a U.S. citizen.

According to State Department policy introduced in the 1990s, a child born to same-sex parents through gestational surrogacy or some other assisted reproductive technology was born "out of wedlock"—even if the parents were wed. And if you were born "out of wedlock" to two men, like Derek and Jonathan, you were not an American unless the American citizen father you were biologically related to had been present in America for at least five years prior to your birth. Jonathan hadn't been—and, through pure chance, it had been one of his assigned embryos that had been successfully implanted. If they stayed in the United States, Simone could potentially be taken away and deported; if they went to visit her aunt, cousins, and grandparents in the U.K, she wouldn't be let back in.

When I asked Derek what made him Simone's parent—why she was his daughter and not the surrogate's or the egg donor's—he thought back over the long journey. "If there is a child whom you would put before yourself in every situation, who you would take a bullet for, who you would spend all your money for, who you would go to the end of the world to make happy, then you are that child's parent." "So, when Simone was born," he continues, "this is a real story, I'm not just being dramatic—when Simone was born, I was sitting right there and I was rocking back and forth with anxiety, and when she came out of the womb and I saw her face for the first time I literally said, quietly but out loud, I said, 'I am going to protect you for the rest of your life.'"

That, in a nutshell, is the attachment that we need to respect and privilege. Everything else is noise.

Derek, Jonathan, and Simone's story has a happy ending. In 2020, a judge in Atlanta declared that Simone was a United States citizen by birth and, in 2021, the State Department finally agreed to grant citizenship to infants born overseas to married couples with at least one American parent—regardless of whether that parent shared DNA with the child. That is meaningful progress.

But there is much work left to change laws, practices, and wrong-headed beliefs that impede the creation of strong, lasting relationships between primary caregivers and children. A narrow view of parenthood continues to isolate too many kids. In a 2017 survey, only 41 percent of Americans agreed that same-sex parents can definitely provide a healthy and loving environment for their children. And other legal developments show just how threatened familial bonds still are for LGBTQIA+ parents.

Eleven states currently permit religious foster care agencies to bar LGBTQIA+ parents. And, in 2021, the Supreme Court offered support to faith-based bans even in jurisdictions that require non-discrimination, declaring that Catholic Social Services didn't have to follow Philadelphia city rules and could reject same-sex couples applying as foster parents. Should the political winds shift even slightly, it is entirely possible that there will be another push to allow adoption agencies to deny children a right to be adopted by same-sex couples, as occurred under the Trump administration.

That's particularly damaging because between a quarter and a third of all foster children are LGBTQIA+. Many of those kids ended up in the system as a direct result of disclosing their sexual identity to their birth family. And there is growing evidence that LGBTQIA+ foster and adoptive parents often provide the strongest attachments because they've lived through similar experiences, they know what it is like, and they have built connections to supportive communities. They accept and love LGBTQIA+ children fully as they are.

Again, in seeking to ensure children's rights, the quality of the bond ought to be our touchstone—and we must end policies of categorical exclusion. As Derek points out, "there are aunts and there are grandparents" who have that same intense connection to a child that he does for Simone. There are kids who want to recognize a formal parental relationship with three parents—not just the two who are allowed in most jurisdictions—because they love these three caregivers equally. There are siblings whose close bonds are often broken without any thought at all as families are moved into the welfare system. There are godparents, family friends, and former stepparents who are entirely ignored in making foster care placements despite the robust positive connections they have—or are eager and ready to have—with children.

As Sixto Cancel explains, she entered foster care when she was "11 months old because of [her] mother's drug addiction and poverty." For the rest of her childhood, she bounced around, separated from her siblings, never making the forever attachments she desperately needed. But that's not because those attachments didn't exist to be made. At the age of twenty-seven, she was invited to a reunion in New York City: "I was introduced to family I had never met and discovered that four of my aunts and uncles were foster and adoptive parents." One of those aunts had adopted four siblings and had been fostering for the entire time Sixto had been alive, just fifty-eight miles away. "That's how close I'd been to family members who would have taken me in, who I would have loved to have lived with. But the system never thought to find my family."

Sixto has founded a nonprofit, Think of Us, dedicated to changing the process that failed her, and one step is broadening "the legal definition of kinship to encompass more of the loving adults who are in youths' lives already." Derek echoes the point: "I actually don't think the rules need to be changed. In our legal system, we provide a lot of protections . . . to families. I just think we need to understand differently what families are, we need to expand that definition." He draws an analogy to Simone's favorite song, "Baby Shark": "We want Simone to sing that song in the same way everybody else does. But we just want her to know, and everyone else to know, that not everyone has a mom, not everyone has a dad, not everybody has a grandma or grandpa. There are certain parts of this song that apply to you and certain parts that don't. That doesn't mean you're any less or more."

A legacy of labeling, excluding, and punishing "illegitimate" bonds has only hurt children—and society. On the most basic level, we need to get out of the business of policing family relationships and get into the business of supporting them.

CHAPTER 2

EARLY CHILDHOOD

The Right to Investment

When did you first notice the gap between rich and poor?

For Harold, it was a specific moment. He was six years old. "This is right after my family lost our house, and we're standing downtown."

Everything to that point had been "okay": "My mom has a security job. Her kids are in school. The neighborhood isn't that bad. I play football. I'm really good in school."

But then the fourth kid arrives—a little brother. Harold's mom loses her job while she's pregnant, and they are suddenly sinking.

In the two years that follow, they will be homeless, "moving from shelter to shelter." There will be fights and domestic violence. There will be substance abuse. There will be depression and chaos.

That's the future to come. But in this moment, Harold is at the crossroads, a six-year-old boy standing on a corner in downtown Philadelphia. "I vividly remember looking at my mom and my mom is in tears because she's trying to figure out what we are going to do. My older sister and my older brother are trying to console my mom. And my little brother is just in the stroller being a baby. I looked at my family and I turned around and the first thing I saw was a white man with the cleanest black suit I've ever seen in my life: he had this decked-out Rolex, and he was carrying his briefcase."

As Harold recalls, it wasn't some intellectual epiphany; it was more like a sucker punch or ice water poured down your shirt. It was stark and raw: "Something in my head was like, 'Yo, he obviously knows something we don't.' This man looked like he never had to worry about anything in his life and here we are with no idea where our next meal is going to come from."

Reflecting back now, it is defining to Harold: "That was the first moment when I thought, okay, something fishy is going on around here. How can it be that we are in the same city, on the same day, at the exact same time—I can touch you—and my family has nothing and you look like you have everything. How can it be that these polar opposites can coexist right next to each other?"

In the country with the most billionaires—724—11.6 million children live in poverty. Based on the 2020 census, that works out to roughly one in six American kids. And while we say, no matter, just pull yourself up by your bootstraps, in this land of opportunity, any poor six-year-old can close the gap with hard work and grit, we do not deliver on our rags-to-riches promise. If you are born to a New Orleans family in the bottom 25 percent of incomes, your chance of moving up to the top 25 percent is 5.1 percent. In Atlanta, it's 4.5 percent. And the dynamics that lock children into impoverished destinies appear to have gotten worse over time. A son born in 1940 had a 95 percent chance of earning more than his dad; a son born in 1984 had only a 41 percent chance. There is, indeed, something "fishy" going on.

The travesty of being born poor is not simply that it is correlated with depressed educational attainment, worse employment outcomes, and, therefore, lower lifetime earnings. As we saw in the last chapter, poverty is a major reason that kids end up in foster care on the grounds of "neglect." And there is an abundance of research exploring how early destitution may compromise your health throughout the life span. A recent study showed that children from poor families were 2.5 times more likely to die before the age of five than children from wealthy families. And the threat did not dissipate over time: poor school-age kids were more at risk of dying of preventable illnesses, and adults who'd been poor in their youth were more likely to die of heart disease and cancers that had their origins in the childhood environment.

When researchers analyzed data from a diverse set of over nine thousand young Philadelphians, living in the city at the same time

Harold was, they found that growing up in poverty was associated with significant cognitive deficits, particularly in executive functioning and complex reasoning. The brains of children from depressed socioeconomic backgrounds also looked different: structurally, they were more likely to have lower volumes and lower gray matter density, and, functionally, they were more likely to exhibit reduced cerebral blood flow and coherence. Other studies have identified similar deficits in areas of the brain related to language, impulse control, learning, and memory.

Scientists have now begun to trace how changes in the brain mediate the relationship between childhood poverty and negative outcomes in early adulthood. In one example of this work, researchers recruited a group of preschoolers and then assessed their development and experiences over the next thirteen years. Controlling for factors like maternal mental health and adverse life events, they found that being poor in preschool was associated with worse cognitive function, more high-risk behaviors, and worse social and educational results. And the pathway appeared to be through the brain. Those experiencing poverty between ages three and five showed less subcortical gray matter initially and less growth over time. That, in turn, mediated the relationship between early deprivation and detrimental outcomes more than a decade later, including depressed memory, attention, and verbal IQ scores and problem behaviors, like lying, fighting, substance abuse, and criminal offending.

Yet, we need more research to piece together what particular aspects of poverty pose the greatest risk to children. Poor kids' experiences and environments are different from rich kids' in countless ways. Poor kids are less likely to go to the doctor or dentist than rich kids. When they fail to crawl or speak, therapists are less likely to be brought to the house to help them reach developmental milestones. In 2020, 9.3 percent of children living in poverty had no health insurance at any time during the year. Affluent parents are more likely to enroll their children in high-quality preschool, take them to art classes and music lessons, and encourage volunteer work. Poor children have different diets from rich children. And they are exposed to chemicals and heavy metals that rich kids don't have to worry about because they are not living in rentals with peeling lead paint or next to superfund sites or freeways. Parents in families earning less than $30,000 are roughly five times as likely as parents in families earning more than $75,000 to call their neighborhood only a "fair" or "poor" place to raise kids, and roughly twice as likely to worry about their child getting shot. Every night, rich kids fall asleep in the same bed, in their own room, in the same house. Poor kids bounce around: evicted, off to dad's, on a couch at grandma's, into a shelter, into a group home, off to foster care, back to mom.

"I kept switching schools throughout my childhood," Harold remembers. "In sixth grade we moved to West Philly," from a project complex in the north of the city. At this point he was "sick of moving." He begged his mom to take the bus back to his old school. But it wasn't as if the last school was somehow better than the new one, Belmont Charter. Each school he'd attended was fundamentally the same: poor, predominately Black, run-down, ranked near the bottom on whatever state metric you wanted to consult.

It was only when he started wrestling that Harold saw that schools weren't all like that. He was big for his age, and when the wrestling coach approached him, he dove in: "Once that ball got rolling, I was like I can really take off with this thing." The next year, he joined Beat the Streets, a nonprofit focused on helping to "positively alter 'life's trajectory'" for student athletes in Philadelphia. He began traveling to tournaments: "It was these poor Black and Brown kids going up to wrestle these suburban all-star teams." We'd "get absolutely smacked in these tournaments," he recalls. But it was "wonderful" and eye-opening. And it led to a scholarship to Penn Charter, a "college preparatory school committed to enlivening the spirit, training the mind, cultivating the aesthetic, and developing the body," which, as its promotional materials note, was "established in 1689 by members of the Religious Society of Friends in response to a charge by William Penn."

Harold's initial visit had a strange effect on him, as if he were standing again on that Center City corner with his family: it was "the first time I reflected back on that moment," he recalls. The prompt, what caught his eye, as he pulled up to campus, was something so mundane that it is both tragic and comic. I laughed when he told me. "They had grass, *for no reason*—a big-ass lawn of grass for absolutely no reason. I was like, 'Yo, again, these people know something we don't know,' because we don't even have grass growing out of our sidewalks. There is no life whatsoever surrounding Belmont Charter."

And as he looked around, the whole landscape was foreign: here was a fellow Philadelphia school that had a climbing wall, a swimming pool, and a performing arts center with a hydraulic orchestra pit lift and a spring dance floor. Everything was ordered, edged, curated. Everything was scaled up: "I can look at Belmont and I can see all of Belmont from one position. You can't do that with Penn Charter." It's forty-seven acres. "There's a building across the street. There's fields that stretch back there. They had an upper school. They had a middle school. They had a lower school. They had a damn recording studio at the damn school. I'm like, we are *high school students:* this is ridiculous."

But as he discovered upon enrolling, what was "ridiculous" to him wasn't to the kids who'd grown up with wealth. "It was obvious who this space was created for because they regularly tapped into everything that was on offer without even thinking about it—it was just normal that you did those things—and for me, I'm like, 'What? There's a music studio here? You have a field for every sport? What the fuck is squash?'"

The kids here had "been living a completely different life." It was not simply that they had different possessions and experiences; it was that those elements had altered their very outlook on life. "People who have been able to grow with wealth," Harold explains, "can think as a human being and not think like someone who is just trying to survive every day." Growing up destitute gives you "a different mindset: You are not worried about what you are interested in, you are not worried about your passions, you are not worried about the next new thing, you are not worried about inventing some shit. I need food tonight. I'm not worried about building the next app."

By the beginning of high school, these divergent paths have already left their mark. It's not a matter of being smart. Harold had that covered. But he could not unlive what he had lived to match his classmates. "You are able to think outside the boxes in ways that I could never think of because I didn't grow up with that. I didn't grow up thinking, 'Hey, if there is a hole in the ground, how can I fix it? What can I do to patch this? We might even take the ground out and put new ground in.' I grew up thinking, 'There's a hole in the ground. This hole has been here for ten years. There's always going to be a hole in the ground. There's nothing I can do to fix this hole. No one is coming to fix it. This hole isn't even a problem.'"

In America, we talk big about our casteless society, won with a revolution and refreshed with a civil war, but in many ways our tiers are as trenchant as ever. They can feel inevitable and organic. Yet, they are only maintained through relentless efforts to protect the elite strata: to retain privilege and deny new entry.

Bussing or redrawing school districts to bring more poor elementary students into high-achieving wealthy schools is met with vehement resistance in nearly every jurisdiction. When poor inner-city students try to attend the coveted public schools in the suburbs, slipping across the county border each morning, districts hire private detectives to follow the children home and threaten lawsuits for "stealing" an education. Just propose altering the entry process for the magnet school or eliminating the gifted and talented program for the benefit of poor children of color and watch the engine of outrage roar to life.

Privileged parents are no less vigilant on the personal level. If your kid starts to slip, you pay for the tutor, the test prep, you juice the extracurriculars. Fork over $10,000 for neuropsychological evaluations to secure a coveted 504 plan—under a federal law meant to assist students with impairments that substantially limit learning—and your son will get extra time on tests and other accommodations, which research shows can boost scores regardless of whether he suffers from a disability or not. Roughly one out of seventeen students in the top 1 percent of public high schools by median household income have a 504 plan, while just one out of sixty-seven students in the bottom 1 percent do.

What is squash? Squash is a currency given to and traded by those at the top. It is one of the many tokens bestowed by rich parents to ensure that their offspring will not disappoint, will not fall, will always have enough. When you start your seven-year-old on lacrosse, sailing, or fencing—sports favored by elite colleges—you are capitalizing him for the journey ahead. Experts recently calculated that recruited athletes with high academic scores had an 83 percent chance of getting into Harvard, sixty-seven points higher than non-athletes.

How can it be that a greater proportion of students in the top 0.1 percent went to an Ivy or other elite university than students in the bottom 20 percent went to any nonprofit two- or four-year college? The system was built to produce this outcome and the wealthiest parents work hard to make sure that it continues to serve their children.

At three years old, Donald Trump was already getting roughly $200,000 a year (in today's dollars) from his dad's businesses; by his twenties, he'd received around $9 million. But that, of course, is not the story Trump tells. "I built what I built myself." In this version, his incredible wealth was earned by being smarter, working harder, never settling. It's a fairy tale but it resonated with many Americans in the 2016 presidential election, who waved their red hats at the restoration of a Horatio Alger America before affirmative-action line-cutting and government handouts to the losers and suckers destroyed the meritocracy. Trump didn't win because he lied, he won because he told the people what they knew to be true.

In many ways, the most powerful tool for maintaining the status quo in which the children of the rich are destined to succeed and the children of the poor are locked into poverty is our own psychology. As numerous experiments have shown, in the United States, when people go to make sense of someone's current circumstances, they tend to place too much causal emphasis on an individual's disposition—his personality, character, and preferences—while neglecting far more influential forces in his surrounding environment. When we pass a man sleeping on the sidewalk, for example, we tend to see personal failure. We don't consider all of the deprivations he experienced as a kid—his terrible public school, his absent father, the tainted water in his public housing complex—or the constraints he faces in the present—racism, a slowing economy, an arrest record. Overestimating the ability people have to influence events—what psychologists refer to as "the illusion of control"—we assume he could simply choose to set his life on course at any time.

Survey data backs this up. Sixty percent of Americans believe that poor people "are lazy or lack willpower"—by comparison, only 26 percent of Europeans think that. And just 29 percent of Americans think that destitute people are trapped in poverty.

In addition, psychologists have documented that we are all driven to believe that our world is just and that people get what they deserve. Good things happen to good people, and bad things happen to bad people. That's how our system works. When you fail in America, you fail because you had it coming. And when you are rich, you should be celebrated. In the laboratory, even when people know that a fellow participant has been *randomly* assigned the largest payment, they still chalk it up to the participant's—nonexistent—greater talents.

It makes sense that a strong belief in the righteousness of current conditions would increase the self-esteem and relieve the consciences of the wealthiest members of society, as psychologists have shown. But the motivation to justify our existing system is so powerful that it can also lead poor people to view their lowly state as the product of their own personal shortcomings. In essence, it can be more cognitively reassuring to believe that you are destitute because you made foolish life choices—that you could turn around at any time—than to believe that you have been kept down by colossal structural forces over which you have little or no control.

These findings fit with other work that shows that the areas of the country with the least actual intergenerational economic mobility—in particular, southern states—tend to have the highest perceived mobility. Alabamans estimate that a person born in the poorest quintile has a 16.2 percent chance of reaching the top quintile by adulthood when the actual chance is just 5.2 percent.

Faith that a good disposition always triumphs over a bad situation fits most snuggly within conservative ideology, but Americans of all stripes are raised on the idea that with grit and determination, anything is possible. And the strength of that conviction has an impact on our motivation to intervene on behalf of poor families. Indeed, recent research shows that people who attribute poverty to bad personal choices and flawed character tolerate a significantly higher level of income inequality than people who attribute poverty to situational factors. What's more, in experiments, while liberals express greater support for public assistance after being told that they've overestimated the odds of upward mobility, when conservatives learn that their projections were too optimistic, they are even less likely to support government intervention. It's hardly surprising, then, that disadvantaged children are often left to fend for themselves.

Harold noticed the pernicious sweep of the fairy tale in his own life. "Growing up I would hate when people would praise me." It felt like "being paraded around as some unicorn"—"this mythical creature." He always had this sinking feeling that even those who helped him so much—the mentors, coaches, and teachers—"weren't happy or here for 'Harold the human,'" but for "Harold the middle schooler who escaped the jungle and was a Beat the Streets wrestler and went to Penn Charter and now is a Wharton student." They seemed proud only of "what I overcame."

When he was in eleventh grade, a local news station did a short segment on him and it had that same up-by-your-bootstraps spin: this poor kid was born into a violent, drug-filled neighborhood "and he made it out because he's not like those other savages you see there." As Harold points out now, they never asked the real question: "Why are we even calling this a success story? Because if we were to go to an affluent neighborhood where this is more common, there is no cameraman showing up at my door." What makes it a "feel good" story is, quite perversely, our failures. Harold was homeless at six years old. Harold's public schools were crumbling. There was a shooting on Harold's street and he watched the man's blood creep toward the drain from his bedroom window. We made Harold's struggle. And for every Harold who has "beat the odds," there are countless others who did not and will not.

That's behind the conflict Harold feels looking back: on the one hand, incredible gratitude, to those who "pushed me to be better, recognizing what I had that other kids didn't to do the work and get good grades," and, on the other hand, sadness and exasperation, at always being "put on a pinnacle in front of those peers," at it always being "a comparative thing, where you have to strive to be like Harold because Harold is better than you."

No one ever seemed to frame things the right way: "We are failing you all as a system and Harold just happened to get lucky. . . . We just got it right with Harold." Even as he was being celebrated, Harold wondered: "Why am only I going to Penn Charter, and fifty of my other friends are going to Overbrook High School," where one out of two students doesn't graduate in four years, and less than 1 percent goes to college? "It became increasingly frustrating for me to even be in these positions . . . and [be] in direct contact with people who can help. It's like, why hasn't this been done? What's the holdup?"

As perhaps Harold always sensed—and feared—it has to do, in part, with the celebration of "Harold the unicorn." For all the benefits they bring to the chosen few, the scholarships, the diamond-in-the-rough programs, the talent scouting, the diversity outreach efforts at elite schools, and even affirmative action efforts have often functioned as a means to maintain the status quo that privileges the wealthy, not to dismantle it. Every rich kid, no matter how naturally talented, can have a great education. Only the very brightest poor kids get the same privilege—and only sometimes.

What a scholarship to an elite school, like the one Harold received to Penn Charter, does is lift that one kid over the wall that was created to protect the upper class; it doesn't remove the wall. What it removes is the impetus to get rid of the wall—and all the systemic problems that hold back poor children. It's a safety valve: proof that with a couple of minor "adjustments," the meritocracy machine works just fine; the "good ones" are succeeding, the diamonds are being picked out. With Harold in the glossy brochure, how can anyone argue that the competition is rigged?

I asked Harold how he'd respond to a critic who said that he was proof that the American dream works. His answer was blunt: "The concept of the American dream is B.S." "It puts people in this competition where someone is going to win and someone is going to lose." It "tells people that things like access to food, access to housing aren't human rights, that people just don't deserve those things." It tells a poor child that to be a success at even the most basic level, they must "grind themselves into the dust," they must never err, and that that is fair. If you come up short, that is on you and you alone. If you don't get a scholarship, you are rightly left in the underclass. If you fail to thrive when you arrive at a place like Penn Charter, you weren't meant to be here. But, as Harold points out, his daily experience as a poor student granted entry into the elite realm has been "trying to navigate spaces that weren't created for me," while being told, "Hey, we got you in the door, now you guys handle everything else." With the entire landscape "catered to white rich kids, that results in a lot of troubles, physically, mentally, spiritually for poor students of color." And over time that "starts to trickle into grade results, depression, anxiety, drug abuse," which are treated as dispositional problems and worse: evidence that "inherently these kids themselves just aren't smart enough or aren't good enough."

As Harold's experience suggests, there are other critical constraints besides parental wealth that unfairly limit a child's future: the legacies of racism and gender discrimination, for example, also place young people at different starting points before they've even taken their first step.

A recent study of 195 countries, for instance, showed that girls' biological advantage in health may be stifled by sexist norms. The higher the gender inequality in a country, the higher the death rate for girls under five. Likewise, troubling new data shows that parents with male children—and no girls—tend to save more money for education, be more likely to prioritize educational savings over their own retirement, and be more likely to say they will cover the entire cost of college than parents with only female children. We must commit ourselves to addressing these biases as well.

Yet, there's a compelling argument for giving economic inequality particular attention. Targeting poverty can be an effective path to addressing some gender- and race-based disadvantages. Give all children access to health resources and you'll greatly reduce mortality rates for girls, even without addressing sexist ideology. Use public funding to ensure that access to quality education does not turn on family wealth, and parental sexism won't have the same power to hold girls back.

That said, we cannot understand the drag of being born poor—why it weighs so heavily on some and not others—without reckoning with race and gender. If you are Black, you are far more likely to be born poor, and more likely to stay poor, than if you are born white. A Black child with a household income in the bottom quintile—like Harold—has just a 2.5 percent chance of moving into the top quintile by adulthood, compared with a 10.6 percent chance for a poor white child.

Even more troubling, though, is that, if you are a Black boy, being born to a wealthy family isn't enough to ensure your success. While a rich white boy is likely to stay that way—63 percent of such boys become rich or upper-middle-class adults—a rich Black boy is more likely to lose his position than retain it. In 99 percent of neighborhoods, Black boys end up with lower incomes than white boys when they reach adulthood. The same is not true for Black girls: indeed, as adults, they end up earning slightly more than their white peers with parents at the same income level.

When researchers looked for an explanation for why Black boys were struggling, none of the common theories—lower education attainment for Black parents, greater prevalence of single-parent households, or depressed test scores for Black children—held much water. A Black boy and a white boy, who went to the same school, lived on the same block in a two-parent college-educated household, nonetheless ended up at different points by their mid-thirties.

What seemed to prevent that divergence? The few neighborhoods where Black boys weren't pulled down shared a set of common characteristics: low poverty, low levels of racial bias among white people, and a high presence of Black dads. Having a large proportion of Black male role models and mentors appears to make a difference for Black boys even if their own father isn't around.

Unfortunately, most Black boys don't live in areas like that. They live in places where they face discrimination every time they step out of their house, which is a big reason why a Black boy raised by parents in the top 1 percent of incomes is as likely to end up in prison as a white boy whose parents made roughly $36,000 per year. While 63 percent of white kids grow up in a neighborhood with over 50 percent of white fathers around and a poverty rate under 10 percent, just 4 percent of Black kids enjoy the same advantages.

That's reflected in Harold's experience. He describes his father as "a shadow figure"—appearing and disappearing, "a menace" one day, offering anger and derision, then gone, then back to put Harold on a bicycle, offering intense joy, then gone again. With his mother's struggles, there were voids in the early years of his childhood, like someone had taken an eraser to his life and rubbed people away, but that loneliness seemed common in the project where he lived. As he reflects now, if you are poor and Black, "no one growing up tells you how you are supposed to regulate your thoughts and emotions, and how you are supposed to carry yourself as a human being. . . . And I think there are too many situations where kids who come from backgrounds like mine are sent on emotional roller coasters throughout the day and we just have to figure it out. . . . You have kids who are dealing with frustration from parents fighting at home, or frustration from food and social insecurities at school, or frustration from the teacher calling them a bad student, and then you have no oversight from the people we are looking up to for answers." So where do children turn? "We have to look back down and look at each other. And we go outside and the older kids on the corner are selling drugs and they may not look perfect in our eyes, but they are still here and in these moments of intense emotional stress and abuse and neglect, we are looking for ways to survive."

The lack of role models within a community can alter the way children come to view themselves. "You are a product of your environment whether you like it or not," Harold explains. "I would look around and see that everyone who looked like me was poor or they were always angry, or always upset, or always doing something bad. . . . [And] I subconsciously started to associate those bad things with who I am as a person." As he recalls, "A lot of my low points came from me saying to myself, 'You are meant for this, this is your environment, you are built to be here.'" He supposed it was in his destiny: "I'm struggling because I was born to struggle. As a poor Black person you are going to struggle in this life. Period." "I would feel bad, and I would feel upset, and I would cry my eyes out, but I would never look forward to better days. I didn't even know better days existed."

Harold's struggle was not coded in his DNA. But it was preordained. It's written into our laws, it's woven into our practices, it is built into our institutions. But that struggle can be unmade.

To address the stratification of opportunity and provide all children with the means to reach their potential, we need to recognize a right to investment. From the perspective of basic fairness, all kids deserve a claim on societal wealth regardless of whether the rest of us earn a return. But the investment frame is fitting because capitalizing children is one of the surest means to profit as a nation.

The first step is to address the way we pass wealth between generations. We need to shift from a model of inheritance based on ensuring family dynasties to one based on collective investment. The benefits are twofold: removing a source of unfair advantage for wealthy children and generating the means to remedy some of the sources of unfair disadvantage for poor children.

"We think we have found the true path," Louise Carnegie wrote to Prime Minister William Gladstone in 1889. She enclosed her husband Andrew's article. And much to their delight, the prime minister read it and wrote his review for the British public. It seemed "like a dream" that Gladstone—"who was to the little Scotch Lad, something beyond human"—might take interest, although Andrew hardly resembled that bobbin boy, working for pennies in a cotton mill, anymore. With grand ambition and a merciless drive, he was on the cusp of becoming the richest man in the world. And what he was shouting from the steel pulpit he'd built was a wake-up-and-stand sermon.

"Why should men leave great fortunes to their children?"

Carnegie saw a new way forward to a better future: "Wise men will soon conclude that, for the best interests of the members of their families and of the state, such bequests are an improper use of their means."

Provocative as it was, the prime minister had his answer: "Hereditary transmission of wealth and position" was "a good and not an evil thing."

And although Carnegie would offer a striking example to his fellow titans of industry, giving away the vast majority of his immense fortune in the decades that followed, in many ways, it's been the prime minister's gospel that's won out.

For most of us, the intergenerational transfer of capital is an uncontestable part of the eternal cycle. When we think about taking care of our children, we think about the assets that we will pass to them—in our life and at our death—to ensure their futures.

Bloodline inheritance seems natural, fair, and beneficial. But Carnegie was right: it is none of those things.

On average, 40 percent of household wealth is inherited, not earned. That's just an average, though: many people have no inherited wealth and some people have vast portfolios made up entirely from what they were gifted. If you are in the latter category, your children gain an enormous financial advantage both when you pass on that wealth to them and when you use it to invest in the things, like elite education, that boost earnings in adulthood. Over time, inheritor families gain more and more over non-inheritor families because wealth generally grows faster than the economic output from work, and because we tax wage income at a higher rate than investment income.

Moreover, the preservation of dynastic wealth helps entrench other unjust disparities. It is one of the reasons that Black children face worse prospects than white children. Today, 41 percent of white, college-educated families receive an inheritance from the previous generation of more than $10,000—a gain, on average, of $150,000. By contrast, just 13 percent of Black, college-educated families stand to receive more than $10,000—and, on average, less than $40,000.

A norm of inheritance passed by blood hampers the long battle for racial equality, but it also throttles our economic prosperity. Carnegie was worried about encouraging sloth among the sons of privilege. As he exhorted, "I would as soon leave to my son a curse as the almighty dollar." But there's another problem with privileging heredity over merit. In the words of Warren Buffett, when you allow "an aristocracy of wealth" to "pass down the ability to command the resources of the nation," you're not going to have the best and the brightest leading the way. It's akin to "choosing the 2020 Olympic team by picking the eldest sons of the gold-medal winners in the 2000 Olympics."

That's backed up by research showing how the distortionary effects of family wealth lead us to miss out on potentially critical scientific and technological breakthroughs. By combining tax returns, census data, and childhood test scores, economists discovered a terrible truth: a poor third grader who scored in the top 5 percent of all standardized test takers had roughly the same chance of becoming an adult patent holder as a wealthy third grader who scored in the bottom 25 percent. If your parents were in the top 1 percent of earners, you were ten times more likely to become an inventor than a kid whose parents were in the bottom 50 percent.

Race, gender, and geography also mattered: a wealthy, white boy from the Northeast was several times more likely to become an adult patent holder than a poor, Black girl from the South. As the researchers concluded, if women, people of color, and people born to poor families filed for patents at the same rate as white men from wealthy backgrounds, we'd have roughly four times the rate of innovation. We are missing out on a huge amount of potential. Indeed, in a separate recent study, economists found that the genes associated with academic success are distributed fairly evenly across family income levels, but their impact is dwarfed by the role of wealth. Wealthy children with the least genetic potential—those in the bottom quartile of the scale—were as likely to graduate from college as children with the greatest genetic potential who were born poor.

Renouncing dynastic privilege and committing ourselves to establishing a true meritocracy isn't abandoning American principles; it's returning us to them. Our nation was founded on the rejection of hereditary power. And we've made brave changes to the norms of inheritance before.

In the late eighteenth century, the stewards of the new republic abolished the feudal inheritance laws that had enriched firstborn sons and left everyone else to scrounge on the crumbs. Thomas Jefferson was particularly proud of his efforts in Virginia, "abolishing the privilege of primogeniture, and dividing the lands of intestates equally among all their children." "These laws, drawn by myself, laid the axe to the foot of pseudo-aristocracy." As he wrote to James Madison in 1789, "[T]he earth belongs in usufruct to the living; the dead have neither powers nor rights over it. The portion occupied by any individual ceases to be his when he himself ceases to be, and reverts to society."

More than one hundred years ago, we were the ones who ushered the world into an era of progressive taxation—what Carnegie called "the wisest" approach. And it was Teddy Roosevelt, not Franklin, who argued, "as a matter of personal conviction," for a levy "on all fortunes, beyond a certain amount, either given in life or devised or bequeathed upon death," not to raise money for the government but to ensure our core identity as a country.

We have since lost our way so that our system now appears designed to maintain and grow family wealth across generations. The total tax liability for the top 0.1 percent amounts to 3.2 percent of their wealth, but the bottom 99 percent have a total burden of 7.2 percent. We've hacked away at the federal estate tax, so it now only applies when you bequeath more than $12.06 million individually or $24.12 million as a married couple. And we've riddled our code with holes, so that those with larger estates can minimize their tax burden by setting up a trust or engaging in any number of legal dodges.

But the good news is that Americans generally support hefty taxes on inherited wealth and the accumulated evidence offers a strong retort to the critics. Historically, the U.S. economy has grown more quickly during periods with higher taxes on the wealthy and less inequality. And research shows that taxing the transfer of wealth does not have a big impact on reducing how much people work, save, or engage in entrepreneurship. In fact, inheritance taxes appear to promote work by heirs.

To move forward, there are multiple promising avenues. We ought to reform rules that the wealthy use to shield their legacies from taxes and raise the tax rate on investment income. We might consider an annual wealth tax for multimillionaires and billionaires or simply increase estate taxes. A related idea is to institute a federal inheritance tax, aimed at heirs rather than estates, which some scholars argue would be more politically palatable and more difficult to evade. A tax of 40 percent on cumulative inheritances of over $1 million and annual gifts of over $16,000 would result in over $1 trillion in the next decade.

How much we can accomplish will depend a lot on whether we can change our notion of what inheritance means. Right now, baby boomers and the Silent Generation are sitting on $84 trillion in wealth. And most of them plan, one day, for that money to go to *their* heirs: *their* children, *their* grandchildren, *their* great-grandchildren. But what if we thought about the wealth we accrued as something meant to enrich the lives of *all* children, to help them *all* achieve their potential? What if we saw all children as our heirs?

This brings us to the second step of ensuring a right to investment—focusing our societal resources on children. We are ranked third from last among developed economies in the percentage of federal government spending that goes to kids. Today, we expend far more of society's funds on bettering the last years of old people's lives than on ensuring that young people have what they need at the beginning of life to develop their potential. On average, the federal government spends more than six times as much on each senior citizen as it does on each child. That must change: we need to shift societal resources forward in the life span.

It's not a trade-off, though, between the young and the old. Children who receive early enrichment and preventative care lead better adult lives. As we touched on in the introduction, one of the reasons that early interventions produce much greater returns than spending on remediation later in life is that establishing strong capabilities and health in the first years of childhood provide a solid foundation for later development in middle childhood and adolescence.

As a society, it costs money to ensure that people are healthy, successful, and safe. The only question is when to take out the checkbook. If you wait until bad outcomes occur in adulthood, you are going to pay far more—with respect to law enforcement, courts, prisons, jobs programs, hospitals, and drug treatment—and you are going to miss out on the big upside of investing early: years of increased productivity, stronger families and communities, and a healthier, happier citizenry.

To get a better sense of the advantages of shifting resources forward in the life span, let's look at three areas where there is strong empirical support for early childhood intervention: education, health, and housing.

If you want to see what a lack of child-centered investment looks like, walk into a public elementary classroom in the poor part of town. It does not look like Penn Charter. There is no school library. The pages of fifteen-year-old textbooks pull away from their bindings like faded petals. There are lead water pipes, broken desks, and peeling paint. Mold constellates asbestos ceiling tiles and mouse droppings aren't noticed. The heat fails in winter, and there's no air-conditioning to turn on when the temperature pushes into the nineties. According to the American Society of Civil Engineers, more than half of public schools need repairs, renovations, and modernization to be considered in "good" condition.

In a recent survey, 94 percent of public-school teachers reported paying for school supplies out of their own pocket during the last academic year, at an average cost of $478. These are people who earn far less than their peers with similar educational credentials—the salaries we provide to teachers don't even keep up with inflation. One in five takes a second job during the school year to get by.

The picture for pre-K is just as bleak. As a percentage of GDP, we spend less than half of what our peer developed countries do on early childhood education. In the United States, the status of many childcare centers is abysmal—a 2007 review conducted by the National Institutes of Health found that only 10 percent of daycares provided high-quality care. And only about a third of American four-year-olds attend a state-funded preschool—with fourteen states offering none at all. With a median salary of just $15 an hour, it's no surprise that preschools struggle to attract the most-qualified teachers: a majority of staff only have a high school degree.

Improving school outcomes is far more complex than just increasing teacher salaries, fixing pipes, and providing adequate learning materials, but the basic lesson from decades of research is simple: skimp on the front end and you'll pay on the back end. We now have compelling evidence of the long-term value of investing in childhood education, and the benefits seem to be particularly profound for children who start life with the least.

In 1962, disadvantaged children living in Ypsilanti, Michigan, were randomly assigned to two years of high-quality early education, with a curriculum focused on the development of cognitive and emotional skills through intensive interactions between children and teachers. Each school day was only two and a half hours, but once a week a teacher would make a home visit to help parents figure out stimulating projects to do with their kids. The researchers supposed that, as the children continued into elementary school, this might permanently raise the rough IQ measure they'd employed, and that didn't happen. But the researchers kept watching as the participants became adults and entered middle age. And, at that point, five decades later, those who'd received the preschool enrichment appeared significantly different from those who'd missed out. They were, on average, more educated, more highly paid, more likely to be in a stable marriage, and less likely to have a criminal history than those in the control group. Moreover, they had higher levels of executive function, stronger cognitive skills, and better health.

The more stable, positive home environments of those who had received early enrichment seemed to benefit their children, too: their offspring were 17 percent less likely to have been suspended at school, 26 percent more likely to be employed, and 11 percent more likely to be in good health than the children of the control group. Just as we saw in the last chapter with the study showing the intergenerational benefit of strong maternal attachment in rhesus monkeys, the positive impact of high-quality early childhood education seems to be passed down to the next generation.

All of this means that when we spend a dollar on high-quality early education, we can expect, down the road, to save several dollars we otherwise would have had to expend on drug treatment, incarceration, and welfare, and to collect several dollars in profit from increased tax revenue generated by better employment outcomes. When economists ran the numbers for a study of disadvantaged children in North Carolina who participated in birth-to-five programs designed to provide comprehensive developmental resources, they estimated an annual return of 13 percent from the initial investment.

Every child should enjoy a federal guarantee to free public education with top-quality facilities, a strong research-based curriculum, highly qualified engaged teachers, and small classroom sizes.

The same pattern emerges for health: invest in early prevention and you save tremendously later on. Heart disease, cancer, and diabetes eat up 75 percent of American health spending and sap economic output by many billions of dollars through missed days of work, but the risk of chronic diseases like these can be drastically reduced. That's particularly true if you intervene in childhood, establish healthy lifestyle patterns, provide routine screenings, and ensure necessary inoculations. Experts estimate that each dollar invested in childhood vaccines, for example, provides a return of $44.

And we should think about health broadly because early interventions targeting mental health disorders, promoting good eating habits, and reducing toxins in the home all promise significant returns into adulthood. When researchers considered the benefits of preventing kids from ingesting lead paint in old buildings, for instance, they found that each dollar invested in remediation resulted in gains of at least $17. The upside came from reduced healthcare and special ed expenditures, increased lifetime earnings and tax revenue, and lower costs arising from criminal activity. One of the great things about investing in health is that it can help boost the yield on other child-focused investments: ensure that children aren't hungry and they will be in a better position to succeed in school. Poor children who had access to food stamps in the 1960s and '70s grew up to be more educated, healthier, and more productive.

Again, it's not a matter of choosing the young over the old. Nearly half of healthcare expenses accrue during people's senior years, but it doesn't need to be that way. Pay for great healthcare for children and when they are eighty, they won't need costly heart procedures or bariatric surgeries.

It's hard, though, to look at kids and feel the urgency to intervene when the really bad thing isn't going to show up on the horizon for years, when the threat is dust on a chipping windowsill, a plate without any vegetables, when the kid in front of you seems basically okay.

But that's not the case with housing insecurity. Homeless children—like six-year-old Harold—suffer as children, unmissable, before us. In shelters in New York City, the most common inhabitant is a child under six. The Big Apple—the only place in America with a guaranteed universal "right to shelter"—has more than one hundred thousand homeless children. And, although there are numerous adverse consequences of housing insecurity that may take their toll over time—like malnutrition and developmental problems—there are often immediate impacts, too—like toxic stress and physical abuse. In New York City, 43 percent of homeless students are chronically absent from school.

The benefit of investing in stable, long-term housing for every child should be obvious even without confronting the evidence. What happens to kids who miss school because the shelter where they are living is across town, because they are too exhausted to go after a night sleeping on the floor in an aunt's crowded apartment, because their mom is worried that their unwashed clothes will be taken as neglect? They fall behind—only 15 percent of New York City students in grades three through eight living in shelters were deemed proficient in reading. And many won't ever catch up. Just 62 percent of homeless students in the city graduate from high school, which is, itself, a strong predictor of whether a person will experience homelessness as an adult. Without a diploma, you're 4.5 times more likely to not have secure housing in the years ahead.

As a society, there is no free option: you pay less now or more later. Yes, ensuring that a kid has good housing costs money. But it is far more expensive to wait. It is estimated that a chronically homeless person costs taxpayers $30,000 to $50,000 a year, tallied up in emergency room visits, detox programs, prison stays, and the like.

And there is plenty of start-up cash hiding in plain sight if municipalities prioritize at-risk children by requiring wealthy universities and other "nonprofits" to pay the property taxes they currently avoid, ending tax abatement giveaways to developers, ensuring that property assessments keep up with market values, and raising rates on business properties and second homes.

Investing in good housing means building low-income units in cities that have far too few and offering financial assistance to ensure that kids aren't evicted from their homes, but it also means providing subsidies so that kids can move to homes in neighborhoods where they have a better shot at success—like the ones we discussed earlier in the chapter where Black boys bucked the downward mobility trend.

When economists looked at the 2010 census, they found that a Black man who grew up poor in the Watts neighborhood of Los Angeles had a 44 percent chance of being listed as incarcerated, but a man who also grew up in the lowest-income bracket in Compton, roughly 2 miles away, only had a 6 percent chance. There are poor city blocks that will sink you and poor city blocks where people rise. And every year a child spends in a neighborhood with better outcomes, the more likely they are to avoid prison and teen pregnancy and experience upward mobility.

You can try to identify the factors that set a place like Compton apart from a place like Watts: perhaps better schools, more two-parent families, and stronger community organizations. And you can invest in reviving neighborhoods. But the authors of this research have argued that a better approach is just to help poor parents move. Within the same metropolitan area, relocating at birth from a below-average neighborhood, in terms of upward mobility, to an above-average neighborhood increases a person's mean lifetime earnings by more than $200,000. Environments of upward mobility aren't always the most expensive neighborhoods. Researchers have already begun to pinpoint "opportunity bargains"—places like North Quincy in Boston, Oxford Circle in Philadelphia, and Alhambra in Los Angeles. And there is work under way to subsidize these local population shifts.

Given that the investments in health, education, and housing we've discussed have been largely aimed at changing the trajectories of poor children, a simpler possibility might have occurred to you: Why not just give poor families money? In 2021, America had the opportunity to test out that idea.

As part of the federal response to the pandemic, the Child Tax Credit was temporarily expanded, giving poor and middle-class families $300 per month for each child under six and $250 per month for each child between six and seventeen. The money was fully refundable, meaning that low-income families could still claim it even if they were paying no taxes, and there was no paperwork: you just received a direct deposit or a check.

The program was a swift and undeniable success: belying the cynics, the initial payments were used on necessities—like clothes, food, school supplies, and utilities—and produced a 25 percent decline in food insufficiency for poor families.

Economists estimated that were it to be extended through 2025, it would reduce the child poverty rate by 40 percent, with poverty for Black children cut in half. And looking at returns for the country as a whole, the case for long-term funding seems even stronger: for an annual net cost of just $16 billion, the child payments would produce roughly $794 billion in societal benefits each year, from increased future earnings, improved health, and reduced crime, among other things.

We need to use our money more intelligently. But there are other ways that we can meaningfully invest in children, too. As we've touched on, nonparental engagement can make an incredible difference in helping children to achieve their potential.

A growing body of research shows that such mentoring and support can counter adverse childhood experiences—like abuse, abandonment, addiction, and divorce—that imperil physical and mental health years into the future. Indeed, it appears that missing out on these positive childhood relationships may actually result in greater harm than the adverse childhood experiences themselves. And the benefits of strong bonds with coaches, youth leaders, and teachers come in many forms, from reduced suicide risk to better eating habits in adulthood. In one study, researchers followed kids over a sixteen-year period and found that mentors outside a child's family who stayed close played a significant role in reducing delinquency and other dangerous behavior. A basketball coach, a dance teacher, or a Big Brother or Sister can make kids feel like they matter and belong, which can provide crucial psychological cover as they face the threats and temptations of adolescence.

Even when kids aren't struggling, mentoring can help foster their potential. Other research shows that kids who grow up exposed to inventors are significantly more likely to hold patents as adults—and the effects are highly specific. A girl's likelihood of becoming an inventor is influenced by the presence of female inventors in her neighborhood, but not by male inventors. And the type of innovation also matters: a girl is more likely to go into biotech if the women around her are in biotech.

This suggests that financial incentives to adults, like tax cuts and intellectual property protections, may not be the best way to breed invention, as we've long assumed. Rather than using our resources to try to squeeze a bit more juice out of the apples we've already pressed, we ought to focus on all of the seedlings left to wither in neglected orchards: the incredible potential we fail to nurture. Researchers have estimated that if we increased the engagement between girls and female innovators to the same level as between boys and male innovators, the gender gap in patent holding would drop by half.

Even with his frustration at being celebrated for the wrong reasons, Harold is unequivocal on the importance of the mentoring he received. When he began wrestling, the contrast between the darkness of his home life and the bright afternoons he spent with Beat the Streets was stark: "I would have the most amazing time around people I just met, with coaches I've only known for one or two weeks, and I would go home and I would experience the worst feelings ever with people who are my family, people who I grew up with."

As he explains, "Aside from actually wrestling, it was being in an environment where I felt loved and supported constantly in a genuine way." Part of that was being challenged and pushed to go beyond what he thought was possible for himself. As Harold points out, wrestling is intensely individual. "There's no one on the offensive line next to me. There's no point guard I can pass the ball to. It's just me and that guy." But to be successful, you need other people helping you "break down the chinks and weaknesses that are in your armor," showing you how to be better, telling you that you are better than you think you are, and ensuring that when you reach for something, you never "fall too far." That changed Harold's life: "Having that genuine support gave me the opportunity to develop in ways that my peers didn't have."

And it instilled in him a deep commitment to helping the next generation of children: "If I can go through a door and open it, I'm going to do everything in my power to keep a door open." There was a point in his life that giving back began to feel like a huge weight: "I felt that pressure and responsibility that you have to be doing those things because you are in this position, because you are who you are and you come from where you come from." He began to wonder if some of his friends were right—that he was focusing too much on others. "I started to think, I need to be looking out for myself. . . . [But] when I did that, I felt so detached from who I was and who I am as a human being." The doubts ultimately helped strengthen his conviction: "I'm not wrong for knowing that this life, our culture, our society, is bigger than any one individual. Once you are in the ground, that's it. Your legacy, what you are going to leave behind, is always going to be attached to another person."

CHAPTER 3

LATE CHILDHOOD

The Right to Community

Daniel Stoltzfus told the police he'd googled it. He wanted to make sure that the "transaction" was legal. Lee Kaplan had been a savior for Daniel and his wife, Savilla. Blacklisted by the Amish community in Lancaster, Pennsylvania, after leaving the church, their metal scrapping business had collapsed. They were being evicted from their house. At the darkest moment, Kaplan had offered help. They'd been able to keep afloat. Now they were paying him back. They gave him—"gifted" him—their nine-year-old daughter.

The idea that children are parental property has a long history. More than two thousand years ago, Aristotle argued that "a man's chattel, and his child until it reaches a certain age and sets up for itself, are as it were part of himself"—his to direct, his to use, according to his will. A father in the early Roman republic could sell his children in an open market—even kill them on a whim. For centuries, under English common law, a dad could legally go after his young daughter's lover or a peddler who enticed his son to leave home on the grounds that such miscreants deprived him of his children's work and earnings.

The currents that carried men to the New World did little to dilute these notions of paternal ownership—something quite apart from the coexistent horror of slavery, not comparable to that, and yet a property interest, nonetheless. Across the colonies, children were subject to the powerful control of their fathers: their labor was a commodity that belonged to their begetter. It could be used, sold, or hired out. By the age of ten, many children in colonial America had been apprenticed or sent out to work for another family. At age twelve, Benjamin Franklin was apprenticed to his older brother in a nine-year contract, and he credited the "harsh and tyrannical treatment" he received with engendering his deep "aversion to arbitrary power."

But in the decades that followed the Revolution, little changed. Children who ran away—as Franklin had done, bribing and lying his way onto a sloop sailing out of Boston—could be tracked down and returned to their parents by force. Assailants who assaulted or raped a child could be made by a court to pay damages, but only to the child's father, because it was against his interests that their body was abused. Their body was his to discipline when necessary. Even at death, they remained his: by will, it was the paterfamilias's prerogative to transfer his progeny to whomever he chose—their mother, or not.

When women were finally able to break paternal control over the family, in the later part of the nineteenth century, it was not to turn over the table but to gain a seat at it: their own right to consent to apprenticeships and to receive their children's wages. In fact, opponents of the child labor laws that followed often chose to focus on the harm to parents' liberty. In 1924, Columbia University's president railed against newly introduced legislation that "would empower Congress to invade the rights of parents and to shape family life to its liking." And, over the next century, that came to be a common refrain in broadsides against all sorts of government efforts aimed at protecting, empowering, or enriching children.

When the Texas GOP announced its platform in 2016, the sentiment was front and center: "Local, state, or federal laws, regulations, or policies that limit parental rights in the rearing of both biological and adopted children shall not be enacted. Parents have the God given right and responsibility to direct and guide their children's moral education." Today, you can find the same language in Supreme Court opinions and podcasts alike. In 2019, the rapper T.I. had no compunction in explaining to the host of *Ladies Like Us* that he takes his daughter on "yearly trips to the gynecologist" to ensure that she remains a virgin. "So I say, 'Look doc, she don't ride no horses, she don't ride no bike, she don't play no sports. Just check the hymen please and give me back my results expeditiously.' " *His* results.

In this country, parents are still cast as all-powerful deciders, guardians of what is ours. We may tweet our outrage at T.I. and shake our heads as picketing parents get *The Bluest Eye* pulled from the school library. But the evidence is all around us. It's in the way we talk to our children when frustrated: "Because I said so, that's why." It's in how we respond when a stranger suggests that our son could use a hat on a cold day: "Mind your own business; it's *my* kid." It is there in how thoughtlessly we deny our children a say in family matters—a topic we'll return to in chapter 5—and how guiltlessly we invade their privacy. We share their secrets, read their diaries, monitor their texts, listen to their calls, and post photos they don't want us to post, for all to see, forever, on the internet.

The idea of parental ownership is reflected in our everyday language—how we talk about a boy "becoming his own man"—and our most vital rituals—how fathers "give away" their daughters at the altar.

In an ever-changing America, the ownership model has remained resilient, surviving in disparate cultures. You can flip open a tome by the esteemed Harvard philosopher Robert Nozick and read that kids are "part of one's substance . . . part of a wider identity you have," or you can flip on Bravo. The same conviction is there in the opulent wealth of the Real Housewives of Beverly Hills: the ladies who lunch with their accessory children, treasured like the pet Shetland pony and purse dog, to be dressed up in fancy clothes, cared for by the hired help, and brought out when desired by mommy. But it's also there in the poorest neighborhood, where having a baby may be the surest way to, in the words of the sociologists Kathryn Edin and Maria Kefalas, "make life more meaningful": a rare opportunity for self-actualization and control in a world in which you are denied power and agency at every turn. Sonia, a young Philadelphia mother with a four-year-old son, explained it this way to Edin and Kefalas: "[My son is] my heart. [When I have hard times] I always tell myself I wanted him. Even if I get that rock on my finger, that white picket fence, and that deed that says the house is mine, [I'll still have my son] just in case anything goes sour. I'll say to my husband, 'You leave! This boy is *mine*.'" Our sense of ownership does not mean that we do not love our children genuinely. In fact, that sense of personal ownership may make us love them more intensely.

But "you are mine" love reflects a certain type of relationship. We could easily speak and think about children differently: not as our things, not in relation to ourselves, but as entities with their own standing in the world. And, if we did, our interactions with our children would suddenly seem very strange.

We'd notice, for example, how much our exchanges are defined by orders, by force, by threats. We determine what our children eat, when they eat, what they read and watch, where they go and don't go. We set the rules. And when the rules are broken, perhaps we see the ownership model most clearly. We can speak harshly to our children, as if they deserve no respect. We pick them up against their will, pull them along, hold down their arms, lock them in their rooms, ground them for weeks. We take away their property—their phones and gaming consoles—as punishment because we own it *all*, it would seem.

As Janusz Korczak, the pediatrician, writer, and director of a Jewish orphanage in Warsaw, recorded in 1928, "A beggar can dispose of his alms at will. The child has nothing of his own and must account for every object freely received for his own use. He is forbidden to tear, break, or soil; he is forbidden to give anything away as a present; nor is he allowed to refuse anything with a sign of displeasure. The child has to accept things and be satisfied. Everything must be in the right place at the right time according to his regimen."

You can watch videos for hours on YouTube of parents destroying their children's Xboxes and PlayStations. People record themselves smashing their children's favorite toys with sledgehammers, as their children watch, sobbing in indignation. We're meant to laugh.

If you struck a nonconsenting stranger on the street, you'd be arrested. But if you are disciplining your child, you are protected—in every single state in the Union. In Oklahoma, you can use a switch. In Texas, it's legal as long as you don't cause "substantial harm" to the child. We've banned the corporal punishment of adult inmates—

condemning it as cruel and unusual—but not for children. That's baffling, until one realizes that children belong to their parents, and, as Aristotle put it, "[t]here cannot be injustice . . . towards that which is one's own."

So, what about Daniel and Savilla Stoltzfus?

When Daniel met Lee Kaplan, he was in crisis, having accidentally killed his fourteen-month-old son while using a forklift. He was losing faith, picking a hole through the tight-knit Amish community. Lee offered redemption: a man who communicated with God through dreams, willing to help him and his family chart a new course. Whatever they needed—business advice, money, housing, marital guidance, spiritual counsel—Lee was there for them. Savilla, too, married at nineteen with only an eighth-grade education, found Lee an intoxicating presence. They were desperate and vulnerable, and they believed everything he said. They were grateful for what he had done and what he promised to do. Eventually, they gifted nine of their daughters to him.

When the authorities arrived at Lee's white clapboard house with the royal blue door, the grass was high and yellow, gone to seed, in the front yard. The daughters were all there, aged three to seventeen, along with two babies. Not one of them was enrolled at school. None had ever gone to the doctor. A detective testified that he'd found no toys and no toothbrushes, although there were musical instruments and an avocado tree under grow lamps. The children slept on air mattresses. Only Lee had a real bed. They did not know what a birthday cake was.

It is understandable to want to minimize all of this as a strange and awful anomaly, to feel distant from it. Daniel, Savilla, and Lee are aberrational people, yes. And egregious abuse like this is not lurking behind the pulled curtains in every unkept yard. But there is no making sense of this great wrong—why it happened and why it was not discovered sooner—without grappling with our history and our present. This tragedy is a product, in no small part, of a culture that vests incredible authority in parents and demands great deference to their decisions.

Daniel and Savilla may have been impressionable and naïve, but they believed that their children were theirs to give away, that it was their right, and high duty, to direct their children's better destinies. From that perspective, they were simply exercising, in the words of the Supreme Court, their fundamental liberties "in the companionship, care, custody, and management" of their daughters. They loved their children and thought they were acting in their best interests.

Lee may have been a deluded monster, convinced he was a prophet entitled to half a dozen child wives, but when the police arrived to investigate, he sounded no different from the Texas GOP, telling Sergeant Shane Hearn that he worried that the day would soon arrive when "society would crash in on what he was trying to do with his family." When he chatted in town with the owner of Lenny's Hot Dogs, explaining that he was homeschooling the girls out of a desire to keep them from the "evils of the world," it raised no flags.

We might never have discovered the depth of abuse. A neighbor had thought "something wasn't right" about the children "all in blue dresses." They were "never outside the house regularly." She thought they looked "scared." But there was no allegation of physical abuse. And, as the authorities acknowledged, they wouldn't have followed up further, but for one mistake Lee made in speaking with the Children and Youth Service workers who made the house call. He told them there were only five children living on the property, but they found eleven.

One of the most significant effects of casting children as belonging to their parents is that parents become the gatekeepers for all outside contact. Everything that connects a child to his community goes through his parents, and if they want to filter out elements or close the gate completely, that's up to them. Once the doors are shut, there's often no way to know how kids are doing. Are they safe? Are they learning to read? Are they sick? Are they happy? What do they want to do when they grow up? What do they need that they don't have?

When parental rights are invoked in this country today, it is often centered on keeping the community out, to bar people, ideas, and scientific progress, and that imperils us all.

To understand the threat, let's look at three of the most critical areas where community is excluded: personal relationships, education, and medical care. As we'll see, behind the blanketed windows of 428 Old Street Road, the Stoltzfus children were isolated on all of these fronts.

If the last chapter was about reshaping the meaning of "inheritance," this chapter is about "belonging." We need to stop thinking about kids belonging to their parents. Instead, we need to cultivate every child's sense of belonging—of being connected to the broader community and benefiting from the personal relationships, knowledge, and services that come from inclusion.

Before the accident that killed Daniel and Savilla's son, they had been close to their families. They lived next door to Daniel's mother, and Savilla's sister Sarah was directly across the street. "They shared the children with us," Sarah explains, "because we could not have any of our own." Whenever a new baby would arrive—every thirteen months or so—Sarah would take care of the youngest and help out with the rest of the growing brood. She felt bound to the children, sewn forever to them, but then Daniel changed.

One day, Sarah remembers, "his mother walked in my door crying." "He asked to be excommunicated." Breaking with the church, Daniel barred Sarah and her husband from spending time with the kids. "It was the hardest thing I've ever gone through." She kept trying to gain access to her nieces and nephews, but it was futile. When the Amish community sought to reach the kids—filing complaints with the police and child services—they lost, too.

In America, parents are empowered with deciding whether grandparents, aunts, and friends can associate with their children. As the Supreme Court has explained, "the interest of parents in the care, custody, and control of their children"—including the right to exclude others from access—"is perhaps the oldest of the fundamental liberty interests recognized by this court." It does not matter what evidence a grandmother can produce on the benefits of maintaining a relationship; normally, a fit parent's determination is not to be second-guessed.

As we will discuss in more detail in chapter 5, younger children often have little say in the matter, even when the question is about who will have physical custody of them.

When I enrolled in Family Law as a student, I expected to hear a lot about children's perspectives and rights. But kids, I found out, were not the protagonists in the course; they were often treated as passive objects.

And when I entered practice, I saw firsthand how they ended up cast as bargaining chips after parents separated: access traded for money. Dad's lawyer agrees to pay more child support; mom's lawyer agrees to more visitation. Dad doesn't keep up on his payments; mom asks the judge to cut back how much he can come around. You don't ask a chip where it wants to land. The word "custody" is particularly apt: we use it for children, property, and prisoners.

As a child, your personal relationships are subject to the whims of your custodians. They can be paused, altered, erased in an instant, without regard for what you want or need.

In every state, the birth mother and birth father (who has properly established paternity) must consent to the adoption of their child. But, in forty-five states, a child under twelve does not need to consent for the adoption to go through.

Each year, tens of thousands of parents transfer control of their children to residential centers to address various behavioral issues, real or perceived—using drugs, acting up, coming out, having sex, losing faith, being depressed. As Paris Hilton explains, "When I was sixteen years old, I was awakened one night by two men with handcuffs. They asked if I wanted to go 'the easy way or the hard way' before carrying me from my home as I screamed for help. I had no idea why or where I was being taken against my will." Mom and dad sign a form and the kids can be legally kidnapped and isolated from all friends and family, with no ability to contact them.

Even in more mundane, day-to-day interactions, parents act as a supreme filter for children's relationships. If you want to socially isolate your child, you can. Move in the middle of sixth grade. Take away their phone for being disrespectful. No internet for a month for getting a C in math. It's widely accepted that parents have near-total control over their children's freedom of association in any form.

For many kids, this parental prerogative may matter very little—they live with their parents, see their grandparents and cousins all the time, have friends in the neighborhood they've known since birth, talk and text until they fall asleep each night. But for those who are not so lucky, this power of parents can come at a tremendous cost.

As we've already seen, stable relationships are an essential basis for healthy development, and losing friendships and connections with extended family members can be disastrous for young people. We are beginning to understand the importance of community engagement in children's health, as well. Community ties can promote children's sense of belonging—of fellowship and shared experience. And they can also be important in ensuring that kids have extra people looking out for them. The routine interactions that many children take for granted—talking to neighbors in the backyard, seeing teachers every day at school, playing over at a friend's house—are all small opportunities for people to notice that a child might not be okay and intervene. Take children away suddenly—as happens when parents send their kids off to boot camps and religious treatment courses—and the risk of abuse spikes.

On every front, the Stoltzfus children were cut adrift. The girls did not have any friends. They did not see relatives, coaches, or guidance counselors. Even if they had been permitted to leave the house on their own, they were now far from the Amish community where they grew up.

Of course, if we are to realize a right to community, it's vital to understand that the state can isolate children from their communities, too. We touched on that, in chapter 1, with the modern child welfare system, restrictive immigration policies, and our ugly history of removing Native American children from their tribes to place them with white families or in boarding schools. We have not properly reckoned with our past harms: what it meant to strip away from indigenous children the very things that rooted them—their language, their clothes, their special objects, their names—and how those wrenched from their communities still struggle to make sense of who they are. We have failed to address the wounds we inflict by severing children from communities that lie across the border. And we have much work to do to ensure that foster children do not lose the valuable connections with their extended networks when there are no options but to remove them from a dangerous home.

Yet we can take some optimism from recent efforts to amend laws requiring closed adoptions: a system designed to protect the privacy of biological and adoptive parents. For decades, we proclaimed parents' wishes to remain anonymous as sacrosanct while never asking whether children wished to be kept in the dark. Pam Hasegewa, who led the New Jersey Coalition for Adoption Reform in its successful campaign to open up records in the state in 2014, explained how that ignored kids' essential needs: "If you're adopted it's just a natural thing to want to know where you came from."

Children deserve to be shown the tree from which they are branched. And they should not have to wait until they are adults to learn the truth. Yet, today, only ten states offer adoptees unrestricted access to the records of their birth—and in nearly all of them you must be at least eighteen to exercise your rights. While a changing culture means that a majority of domestic adoptions today are open, more progress is needed internationally and what "open" means can vary considerably within the United States.

We ought to heed the research on the developmental value of establishing strong kindship networks in which birth parents, adoptive parents, children, and their communities are linked in meaningful ongoing collaboration. To promote a sense of belonging in adopted children, they need the chance to access and explore their full identity and heritage. We should not fear greater knowledge.

That principle carries weight in the realm of education, too. But, unfortunately, parents are granted the same supreme powers as gatekeepers. Today, across the United States, we allow parents to opt out of numerous school lessons and activities: field trips, state testing, sex ed. We empower parents to decide what their children know (and don't know).

In 2009, the River of Life Church in Niceville, Florida, provided form letters online to its parishioners to direct school officials to remove their children from discussions about subjects like homosexuality, tolerance, and saving the environment. If you checked the online box for "evolution," you got a made-to-order note to print out and slip into your kid's backpack:

> While many of our local teachers seek to be sensitive to this topic, the text books and materials [*sic*] often pertrayed [*sic*] it more as fact, rather then [*sic*] popular scientific theory. This presentation is often a biased one, refusing to look at even the possibilities that other views present. And it is biased even in the face of evidence [*sic*] to the contrary. I do not want my child to be apart [*sic*] of such discussions. Please provide an alternative activity for my child.

Just like that: your child would not learn about Darwin, dinosaurs, or finch beaks. We make it easy to control your child, to shape his beliefs to suit yours.

As the Wisconsin Assembly committee advanced a bill to ban public schools from teaching students about implicit racial bias and systemic racism in 2021, Republican Representative Donna Rozar explained her support: "I don't want school professionals to make decisions about teaching and learning. I want parents to be in charge of teaching and learning that their children and students go to." The bill passed, and now students in Wisconsin—the state measured to have the worst disparity on life outcomes between Black and white children in the entire country—will not learn that our "meritocracy" does not work for everyone, unless their parents provide their own lessons on the impact of race.

The Supreme Court has been a powerful player in promoting the message that mom and dad are the gatekeepers to knowledge. As they explained in 1925, the "liberty of parents and guardians" includes the right "to direct the upbringing and education of children under their control." If it is your child, you have a right to "direct his destiny." In general, parents' preferences trump what experts say is best for a kid. They trump what the kid himself wants. They trump what a state—that is, all the rest of us—deems optimal. Yes, the court has affirmed the "paramount responsibility" of the state in the "education of its citizens," but that authority must "yield to the right of parents." Deference to parents is the norm.

When Beatrice Weber got divorced, part of the agreement was to cede her right to control her son's education to her ex-husband. Her son is now eight and she is worried. "He tells me he wants to be a scientist when he grows up. But his ultra-Orthodox Jewish school doesn't offer any sciences. Even the math and English, it's only four hours a week."

In New York, there are basic minimum educational requirements that all kids in the state are meant to receive in these subjects and others, including geography, history, and art. But, for years, that has not happened at many Hasidic yeshivas, where the focus is instead on Talmudic discourse and Jewish law. English is considered profane, so most instruction is in Yiddish. As the Satmar Rebbe Aaron Teitelbaum, the leader of Kiryas Joel, a Hasidic enclave north of New York City, put it in a rare moment of candor: "We all know the truth, that in our primary Torah schools for boys, they studied [nonreligious subjects] at most an hour and a half, and in the advanced yeshivas, there were no secular studies at all." Despite a 2019 New York City report showing that just two out of the twenty-eight ultra-Orthodox yeshivas met the basic state requirements, lawmakers and regulators have looked the other way. In part, they've been wary of offending an extremely unified voting bloc. But, on a deeper level, New York's neglect of Hasidic kids is a reflection of our acceptance that parents are the deciders. It is a shrugged shoulder—"Sorry, kids, but you are not ours."

So, how do those children—the tens of thousands denied a secular education—fare? Quite simply, many end up unprepared for life outside of the Hasidic community. If, at eighteen, an ultra-Orthodox yeshiva graduate wants to leave, what options does he have? Many are unable to write or read English beyond a rudimentary level. Most lack the basic requirements to get into college. It can be a struggle to find even a minimum wage job.

Kiryas Joel is the poorest place in the entire country: the median family income is $17,929. Half of the twenty-one thousand residents get food stamps. Many others are on Medicaid or receive housing vouchers. It is not simply the Hasidic children who are harmed by our deference to their parents' preferences; it is all of us. Hundreds of millions of state and federal dollars go to yeshivas through Title I, Head Start, universal pre-K, and the like, and then hundreds of millions more go to public welfare when the ill-prepared graduates of those schools struggle to get by.

What Beatrice is asking for is not a lot: "I want my son to be able to fill out a job application, write a college essay, just the basics." And she is eager to point out that it "is not about suppressing the religious education." It's about ensuring that kids aren't isolated from other essential knowledge. "Many yeshivas offer a Judaic study curriculum and an academic study curriculum—math, science, history, geography. The modern Orthodox schools, the Catholic schools, the Quaker schools—there are so many schools that do this really successfully."

The truth is that yeshivas and other religious schools can provide a wonderful environment for a child to maintain and develop a sense of community. It just ought not to be at the exclusion of fostering other vital connections. Whether New York is able to ensure that the education of Hasidic yeshiva students is "substantially equivalent" to public school students will depend on whether those in power can stick up for children against their parents' preferences.

But we do not have a strong record on that front. We write laws that grant parents incredible discretion, we provide weak oversight over how it's exercised, and then when there's a rare challenge in court, our precedent ensures that any progress in reducing the authority of the parent is heavily constrained.

Home schools present a prime example. In thirty-one states, if you want to homeschool your children, you have to notify the state annually, but that often just means providing the name of the home school and basic details about the kids. In the other nineteen, registration is either a onetime deal or no notice is needed at all. Critically, in every jurisdiction, except Massachusetts and Rhode Island, approval is automatic.

What about teaching credentials? In forty-one states, there is no requirement that a homeschooling parent hold a college degree, or even have graduated from high school (and in the other nine, a GED tends to be sufficient). For the most part, in the United States, you decide yourself whether you are up to the task and that's it.

But there's a lot of evidence that the qualifications of teachers matter. In one recent study, high school students who received instruction from people who had majored or minored in the subjects they were teaching were significantly more likely to graduate from college than those who received instruction from adults with general teaching degrees. Imagine how things turn out when your teacher—the only one you have—dropped out of school in eighth grade.

Before Lee took over, Savilla was homeschooling her children. She readily acknowledged her limitations: that's one of the factors that made moving the girls to Lee's house seem so wise.

In many jurisdictions, we never learn how homeschooling students are performing. There are no assessment requirements in the majority of states. There are no curricula, lesson plans, or records of any sort. No one ever checks what you are taught—or if you are taught anything at all. In America, our old cars are scrutinized far more than our young homeschoolers.

About a year before Lee was arrested, a neighbor had called the police to complain about him burning trash. When the police arrived and inquired about the children, Lee told them the girls were being homeschooled and they got back into the squad car and drove away.

None of this is to suggest that the experience of the Stoltzfus girls is somehow representative of homeschooling—it absolutely is not—or that homeschooling cannot be far superior to public school education—it absolutely can be.

Indeed, we need to face the reality that public schools often fail to measure up in ensuring a right to community: much of the time, they do not sufficiently introduce students to a diversity of ideas and experiences, or help students feel connected and supported. Making an eight-year-old sit at a desk for hours each day doing multiplication problems and taking spelling tests is not the best way to enrich his mind and character.

And we cannot ignore the fact that public education in the United States was indelibly shaped by men, like Woodrow Wilson, who had no interest in developing every child into a creative, broad-minded citizen. As he told the New York City High School Teachers Association in 1909, "We want one class of persons to have a liberal education, and we want another class of persons, a very much larger class, of necessity, in every society, to forgo the privileges of a liberal education and fit themselves to perform specific difficult manual tasks." The critic H. L. Mencken was equally blunt: "The aim of public education is [not] to fill the young of the species with knowledge and awaken their intelligence, and so make them fit to discharge the duties of citizenship in an enlightened and independent manner. . . . It is simply to reduce as many individuals as possible to the same safe level, to breed and train a standardized citizenry, to put down dissent and originality."

In that light, it is entirely reasonable that, in a modern America with very imperfect public schools, some people would make the rational decision that homeschooling was a better option for developing the full potential of their child.

Yet, it does not follow that parents should have total control, discretion, and privacy over their child's education. We don't imperil the benefits of homeschooling for the many children currently thriving by protecting the few suffering outside our view. The problem with homeschooling is that it all comes down to luck. You could get gifted educators who spend hours each week working with you on a tailor-made curriculum designed to expose you to a broad range of ideas, nurture your independence and creativity, and support your intellectual and social development, or you could get someone who doesn't teach you at all or feeds you a stream of half-truths and lies.

Young children's good sense can be corrupted by the false ideas they are exposed to. When psychologists looked at South African children's beliefs about AIDS, they found that, at first, kids put more credence in biological explanations for the disease—for example, that it was caused by a virus. But as both urban and rural children grew up exposed to widespread myths, they became more accepting of the notion that AIDS was a result of witchcraft. Think about the implications of that for a country with the world's largest epidemic. Nearly one in five South Africans, between fifteen and forty-nine, is living with HIV or AIDS.

In 2018, a mother of a student at Spanish River High School in Boca Raton, Florida, sent a note to Principal William Latson asking him if the Holocaust was taught to students. Principal Latson wrote back that there were optional educational activities related to the Holocaust but that study was "not forced upon individuals as we all have the same rights but not all the same beliefs." The mother was confused—the murder of six million Jews was not a belief. She shot off a follow-up email thinking he'd misstated what he meant, to which Latson replied: "I can't say the Holocaust is a factual, historical event because I am not in a position to do so as a school district employee." As he explained, "Not everyone believes the Holocaust happened and you have your thoughts but we are a public school and not all of our parents have the same beliefs." His role, he explained, was to be "politically neutral": "Not all parents want their student exposed so they will not be and I can't force the issue. One must understand that in a public school setting the school can't take a position but provide information and allow parents to work with their students on what they want their children to understand." He pointed out that he did "the same with information about slavery": "I don't take a position but allow for information to be presented and parents to be parents and educate their students accordingly."

In a culture that empowers parents, and not schools, as the arbiters of truth, it is a predictable position but an unconscionable one, with devastating consequences for society. In a recent survey, one in eight Americans between eighteen and thirty-nine wasn't familiar with the Holocaust and one out of four believed it to be a myth or exaggerated or just wasn't sure. One in two reported coming across Holocaust denial or distortion posts online. Information—true or false—drives behavior. In 2021, one in four Jews disclosed being the target of anti-Semitism over the last year.

The education of children is not a private matter. What a child learns or does not learn will affect the lives of many other people. We need to instill a sense of those communal consequences. Our laws and practices should stop fueling the damaging expectation that kids will emerge from the cocoon of childhood as fully realized replicants of their parents' beliefs and values. The education of our children should not be dictated by what parents believe—or want—to be true about the world, but by what is actually true. Evidence ought to drive education, just as in medicine.

But, then, currently, evidence doesn't even drive decisions about children's health—parents do. In most of the United States, medical treatment for someone under eighteen is controlled by mom and dad.

In June 2021 in Delray Beach, Florida, just north of Spanish River High School, COVID vaccines had finally been approved for kids as young as twelve and Charisse was on the fence. After an early summer dip, the coronavirus cases in Palm Beach County had just begun to creep back up. But Charisse had heard that the shot could damage her daughter's reproductive system.

Public health officials had been doing their best to knock down that baseless theory, but it hadn't gone away. Isabella, Charisse's daughter, was pushing back. She didn't agree with her mom's fears; she was ready. As Charisse explained to a *New York Times* reporter, "Isabella wants it because her friends are getting it, and she doesn't want to wear a mask."

Charisse was listening, but it was her decision: in Florida, as in most states, the law requires parental consent for all vaccinations of minors. As Charisse explained, "Isabella said, 'It's my body.' And I said, 'Well, it's my body until you're eighteen.'"

In certain states, even after a child gets gravely—and obviously— ill, a parent is permitted to decide against medical care.

Arrian was a typical teenager. She ran track at Parma Middle School in Idaho. She loved snowboarding and her friends. One day, she got sick—food poisoning. It was bad. For three days she vomited, so violently that she ruptured her esophagus. But her family didn't take her to the doctor. Even as she fell unconscious, they elected not to call an ambulance. They were members of a Pentecostal Christian group, Followers of Christ, that believes that professional medicine is a tool of the devil. So, instead, they prayed for Arrian. When the coroner arrived, he elected to postpone a physical examination due to the number of family and friends in the house.

Arrian's death was not an anomaly. In the largest Followers of Christ cemetery, 204 of the 592 graves are those of minor children. Many of these children could have been saved; they died of untreated complications from diabetes, pneumonia, intestinal blockages, and other conditions we know how to manage.

But no charges were brought against Arrian's or any of these children's parents because the state's "Child Protective Act" states that "no child whose parent or guardian chooses for such child treatment by prayers through spiritual means alone in lieu of medical treatment shall be deemed for that reason alone to be neglected or lack parental care necessary for his health and well-being." What, in any other circumstance, would be deemed a homicide is accepted as sound parenting.

Although Idaho takes an especially ardent position on parental faith, thirty-four states and D.C. currently have laws designed to protect parents who refuse to give their children medical treatment on religious grounds, and six offer exemptions for manslaughter. As Idaho state representative Christy Perry explained, it comes down to the rights of the parents: Followers of Christ members "have a clear understanding of what the role of government should be [and that] it isn't how to tell me how to live my life."

That's a sentiment echoed in many quarters. As Senator Rand Paul put it, in arguing against vaccinating children over their parents' wishes, "The state doesn't own your children. . . . Parents own the children, and it is an issue of freedom and public health." What is amazing about his statement is not simply how explicit it is in acknowledging the notion of children as property, but that Paul is arguably the most prominent libertarian in the country. You'd think that the freedom of a human being to be free from control would trump the freedom to be able to control another human being, but then Paul doesn't see kids like that: they are things to be owned. It's not that he's against vaccines or that he thinks they don't work. He's a doctor, after all, and he vaccinated his own kids: "I'm not arguing vaccines are a bad idea. . . . I think they are a good thing." It's purely that he is blinded by parents' liberty interests and cannot see beyond that.

But there is much to see. When we allow parents to close the gates, we frequently find children in need when we reopen them. As investigators walked through Lee Kaplan's house, after removing the Stoltzfus children, they noticed that there was no soap or other toiletries in the bathroom. When they spoke to the girls, they learned that they had never received medical care. They did not know how to wash their own hair. Two of the girls had Lyme disease. Nearly every child needed to have rotten teeth removed and the oldest daughter needed oral surgery because tooth decay had caused a bone infection.

There is a broader lesson here: if we provide children with rights, but allow parents total discretion over whether children can utilize or even know about the rights, for many children, it will be as if they had no rights at all. Rights—to healthcare, excellent public education, free breakfast and lunch, counseling and mentoring, good housing, and the like—are meaningless if you cannot access them.

No children should be deprived of the incredible advances we have made in medicine over the last decades. They deserve to benefit from our progress. When a child like Isabella wants to get inoculated, she is not on her own—she is backed by a vast community: the scientists who developed the vaccines to fight COVID, the people who participated in trials, the regulators who carefully sifted through the data to ensure effectiveness and safety, and her own pediatrician.

As the coronavirus pandemic made clear, we all pay when children are blocked by parents from receiving safe and effective vaccinations. And empowering them with an unchecked veto makes no more sense than allowing parents to decide whether to buckle their kids in when they go for a drive. Of course, we could leave it to parents to assess the relevant research on their own and come to their own conclusions on the merits of seatbelts for kids. But thousands more children would end up dead or badly injured in car accidents. And we would all pay for that, just as we do today when we fail to reach herd immunity against terrible viruses. Our major infectious disease victories in keeping measles, mumps, rubella, pertussis, and diphtheria at bay have all come from school mandates that limit parental dominion.

Promoting the best medical outcomes for children—and society—by hemming back parental rights is not anti-autonomy. Quite the opposite. It's about understanding that the patient is the child, not the parent, and that a child's interests can be different from her parents'. It's about seeing a child as a distinct individual.

Your child's life is not your own. That's hard to comprehend when your child is made from your body and when you invest so much—and sacrifice so much—for her. And it is particularly hard when our culture is relentlessly pushing you in the direction of doing more gatekeeping, not less.

By casting parents as the directors of their children's destinies—the all-powerful deciders to the exclusion of other stakeholders, including children themselves, extended family, experts, and the state—parents become responsible for the "success" or "failure" of their kids. In this light, to not exercise your parental rights to the fullest extent—to forgo filtering every school lesson, social media interaction, and medical recommendation from the pediatrician—is to be a bad parent. It is to be negligent. For the most part, we are all helicopter parents because that is what our culture demands.

Yet a lot depends on exactly what our "hovering" entails, and the evidence suggests that the version of helicoptering most consistent with a notion of children as parental "property" is also the version most harmful to kids.

To conservative commentators, coddling parents—always there to lend a hand, to offer encouragement, to meet with teachers, to shuttle from dance recital to math club to soccer practice—are the villains because they breed dependency and weakness. However, researchers have found that this type of helicoptering—associated with what psychologists term "authoritative parenting"—can actually be beneficial. When your mom and dad spend time with you, when they engage with you, when they invest in your education and offer you varied enriching experiences, you tend to do better.

Many facets of authoritative parenting are in direct opposition to a parental ownership model: authoritative parents don't offer directives without explanation—they reason with children to persuade them; they don't demand that their kids strictly toe the line—they encourage creative problem-solving and independent thinking; and they don't chastise or hit their kids when they come up short. The payoff isn't just better academic performance. Across cultures, the children of authoritative parents also tend to have better mental and physical health.

The damaging version of helicoptering is the one associated with authoritarian parenting, with its strong connection to treating children as property: think of the mom or dad who gives strict orders, who expects them to be followed solely because they were given, who grants no privacy and offers no voice, and who enforces the rules with harsh punishments. Authoritarian parents are far more likely to support exercising their parental rights to keep their children from being exposed to people, ideas, and services they deem wrong or dangerous.

But even those of us who would never consider spanking for speaking back or grounding for a poor grade can find ourselves exerting greater control over our children's lives in an attempt to optimize outcomes.

Despite the research suggesting that children learn far more through watching, listening, and imitating—and much less through structured teaching—many of us end up feeling compelled to do more "school" at home. We're not proper parents if we don't have our daughter doing problems from the supplemental STEM workbook in the evening, if we don't seize every quiet moment for observation to explicitly teach, if we aren't always assessing where she isn't quite measuring up and designing interventions, extra lessons, more instruction.

We feel obliged to manage our children's social lives, too. As they attempt to venture out in the world, we seek to impose order, maximizing productive and positive exchanges. We shuttle them from structured activity one to structured activity two. We set up playdates with the children we think are best, screening out interactions unlikely to be constructive, and carefully listening in to refocus play in the right direction. It is just easier to feel like an engaged, invested parent who is preparing his daughter for success when you are actively shaping her experiences.

Even if we are not slamming gates shut, all of this gatekeeping—relentlessly filtering, monitoring, and steering—can come at a significant cost.

If you do not have two actively involved parents looking after you, you are instantly at a disadvantage in realizing the *upsides* of an intensive parent-centric model—enrichment, engagement, and deep commitment. This is one of the reasons that even the beneficial authoritative helicopter parenting can be harmful to society as a whole. As researchers have documented, it can promote inequality. In some cases, parents can become so driven to ensure their own children's success that they fall into "opportunity hoarding": taking up a disproportionate amount of teachers' time, spots in special programs, and other public resources.

Furthermore, parents' manic gatekeeping is often unnecessary or outright counterproductive. Parents feel compelled to scour the internet and come up with their own tailored vaccine schedule for their infants rather than just going with the one carefully crafted by doctors on the Advisory Committee on Immunization Practices at the CDC—experts who have spent their entire professional lives figuring out how to protect kids' health. Other times, the normalization of helicoptering seems to take pressure off trained professionals to do their jobs ensuring children's healthy development. Parents end up sending their third graders to school with portable carbon dioxide monitors to assess whether their classrooms are sufficiently ventilated to minimize the spread of coronavirus, trading tips on Twitter on how to interpret the data.

Tasked with making the final call on every matter affecting our child—being the last line of defense—we convince ourselves that we must gain expertise on everything and make our own independent assessment. And it is miserable and exhausting, leaving us constantly feeling as if we have come up short.

When scientists looked across forty-two countries, they discovered something odd: rich Western nations, where people had fewer average children, had the highest parental burnout.

Why?

"Our individualistic countries cultivate a cult of performance and perfectionism," explains Professor Isabelle Roskam, one of the researchers who initiated the study. "Parenthood in these countries is a very solitary activity, unlike in African countries, for example, where the entire village is involved in raising children." People there may have more kids on average and far less money, but they don't have the same unreasonable expectations put on their shoulders. And they are supported in numerous ways as they guide their children into adulthood. Our stress and disillusionment, though, is not inevitable, Roskam suggests. "The first [step] would be to revive in our cultures the dimension of sharing and mutual aid among parents within a community." And, she adds, "abandon the cult of the perfect parent."

You cannot protect your child from every harm—every upsetting book, every illness, every rejection and failure. You cannot manage all their relationships. You cannot be everywhere. You cannot know everything you need to know. It takes a community.

But with raising children cast as the prerogative of parents alone, our culture absolves everyone else from responsibility for their welfare. It tells us that the suffering of other people's children—in front of us, that we could do something about—is not our problem. It tells us to forget about what we saw and what we felt when we saw it.

That is not who we were made to be. We evolved to be cooperative breeders. We could not have come this far separate and apart. And the path to restoring that identity is for each of us to adopt a simple mantra: accept help and give help.

If you are a parent, resist the urge to go it alone. When you face an important question about your child, rely on our collective wisdom. Lean on experts and other professionals who have done the hard work for you. You don't need to be your kid's teacher, doctor, coach, and librarian when there are already people in those positions who know what they are doing. And when the invite says you can leave your seven-year-old at the birthday party or a neighbor offers to carry your stroller up the stairs as you struggle with grocery bags, say yes and return the favor down the line.

Volunteer in your community. Always give a bit more than your instincts tell you. And watch out for other people's children, when their parents turn their backs. What cultures that embrace sharing and mutual aid have found is that you are not losing anything at all when you attend to the welfare of other people's children, because everyone else is looking out and giving to your children.

In 2018, in a scene reminiscent of the Stoltzfus rescue, Argentinian police found six siblings in dire conditions inside a home in La Plata, southeast of Buenos Aires. Taken to the hospital, the youngest child—a seven-month-old infant—was sobbing uncontrollably. "I noticed that he was hungry, as he was putting his hand into his mouth," officer Celeste Ayala recalled. She had a sixteen-month-old daughter at home. "I asked to hug him and breastfeed him." The nurses warned her that he was dirty and smelled bad. But "I didn't doubt it for a second," she explains.

In the photo that her colleague posted on Facebook, she is seated in a chair against a cinder-block wall, still in her uniform. The boy's head fits in the turn of her arm. His face is pressed against her breast, along with his small hand, which holds her finger.

"I want to make public," her colleague wrote, "this great gesture of love you had with this baby, whom you treated like a mother without a second thought, even though you didn't know him."

The post was shared more than a hundred thousand times around the world.

This is who we want to be.

We are in this together. Let us think of all children as *our* children.

CHAPTER 4

EARLY ADOLESCENCE
The Right to Be a Kid

The policy was for all prisoners to be in restraints while inside the courtroom. It was Christmas Eve, but there weren't exceptions. So, when D.C. Public Defender Andrew Crespo's first client was brought in, he wore handcuffs, a waist chain, and shackles. The fetters make it difficult to walk properly, and the client shuffled as best he could up to the defense table.

He was eight years old and weighed less than fifty pounds. His feet didn't touch the floor when he sat in his chair. Prosecutors alleged that he'd inappropriately touched a girl at his birthday party earlier that day. Police had arrested him for sexual assault. And now the scared and confused third grader kept whispering to Crespo: "My mommy said I can still have my birthday cake. I can still have my cake, right?"

When is a child an adult?

Where we set the dividing line matters immensely because we see children as possessing unique characteristics that require different treatment than adults. Children are more vulnerable and more impressionable. They are less developed and less capable. So, they require far greater protection, understanding, leniency, and forgiveness.

That's why the child savers set up a juvenile justice system back in the early twentieth century. They grasped that children lacked the culpability of adults and were more capable of rehabilitation. That made the existing criminal framework of blame and punishment seem unfair and unproductive. Decades later, the same basic notion motivated the Supreme Court to ban the death penalty for young offenders.

Yet, we treat children as if they were adults all the time. Each year, more than one hundred thousand kids under the age of fifteen are arrested. Prosecuting minors as adults is routine and several states have no minimum age for transfer. Each day, about ten thousand kids are locked up in adult jails and prisons.

On his sixteenth birthday—July 14, 2020—William marked his 511th day in an adult jail in Lexington, Mississippi, for an alleged aggravated assault of another teen. Though presumed innocent, he was out of school and locked away, fighting men, just waiting for the local district attorney to bring the indictment or let him go. The accuser no longer wanted to pursue charges, but the prosecutor did not flinch on her continued opposition to release: "If that person gets out and offends somebody else, the first thing the community is going to say is he has already been deemed a threat." Asked to comment on the effects of placing a child in adult pretrial detention for so long, she pointed to the upside: "I hope that he will be a better person. I hope that for all defendants."

When judgment finally comes to the young, it can be just as heavy a blow as a man's punishment. It can be heavier. Bryan Stevenson, founder of the Equal Justice Initiative, noticed the strange phenomenon early in his career as a defender: "The children I was representing, [in] places like Florida, who had been convicted were getting harsher sentences than adults who had committed the same crime, because we were fascinated with this idea of a super predator child."

You cannot kill a boy, the justices have told us, but you can lock him in a nine-by-seven-foot coffin until he dies. Roughly three thousand children have been sentenced to life in prison without parole.

That was the deal for Ghani. He ran away from home when he was fifteen years old with his pal Dameon: they hopped the train down from Brooklyn to Philly. They wanted to be men: "I didn't want to take a half step—I wanted to plunge myself all the way, to force myself to be independent, to be free." Less than a year later, the two boys were locked in a house, dealing drugs through the mail slot.

"We were in captivity," Ghani remembers—a nightmare come to

life—"the ash and undead, scurrying about, the new walking death, emaciated people addicted to crack cocaine." His previous existence had no relevance here: "Everything my mother had worked so hard to instill in me and my grandmother and my grandfather and my whole family in Trinidad had tried to instill, all these classical principles, family values, none of that stuff mattered. It was a new situation: new rules applied, and I didn't even know the rules. I was a house kid doing good in school and I plunged myself into a situation without any street smarts whatsoever, drawing my own conclusions, coming up with my own strategies. . . . It was madness that, one day, culminated in an explosive act of violence."

Anjo Price was two years older than Ghani—a fellow runaway. To look at Anjo was to look into the future: "Before he became a courier, driving around and picking up the money, and the supplies, he worked in my position." "He was an artist." Ghani had noted "his artwork around the drug house": "I saw pencil sketches of gorillas and tigers—even after they were crumpled up, you spread them back out and it still was amazing, the details drawn in pen, you couldn't erase it."

In a terrible moment, Ghani and Dameon killed Anjo. They were arguing, they were suddenly fighting, and then Anjo was bleeding out: "I left a tear in the fabric of life, a hole in the cosmos that will never be filled—that was Anjo Price. And whatever purpose he was put on this earth to fulfill, that only him and nobody else was supposed to fulfill, I interrupted that and I robbed the world of that and quite frankly robbed myself of whatever he was supposed to give to the world. Who knows how I would have benefited from his life? But these are things, as children, of course, we didn't think about."

Ghani and Dameon were tried as adults and sentenced to life in prison without the possibility of parole. Before society deemed them responsible enough to have a beer or cast a ballot—in the same breath it called them minors—it condemned them as men, held them to the same standard as men, said that you shall suffer in cages with men until you die.

In drawing our lines between childhood and adulthood, we are wildly inconsistent. In Texas, you can go hunting alone when you are nine years old, but you'll have to wait eight more years before you can watch an R-rated movie by yourself. In Mississippi, with parental consent, a girl can get married at fifteen, but if she wants to sell her bicycle instead, any agreement she makes is voidable until she turns eighteen, the year she stops being an "infant" for purposes of contract law. At your Passaic, New Jersey, bar mitzvah, we proclaim you a man but maintain the right to imprison you for up to six months should you buy a can of spray paint at any point in the subsequent half decade. We celebrate your independence as a woman at your quinceañera, but don't dare try to vote in the local sheriff's election in York County, Maine, or go to the dentist on your own.

Whether we treat someone as an adult is meant to be based on objective, pertinent factors, but the best evidence suggests our assessments are frequently influenced by things we consider irrelevant, like race. In one study, people were asked how old a child was after being presented with his photograph and a description of a crime. On average, they overestimated the age of Black boys by 4.5 years—an astonishing discrepancy, given that all of those pictured were between ten and seventeen. Participants also perceived the Black boys to be more culpable than the white and Latino boys they viewed. Other research suggests that people view Black girls through a similarly distorted lens, regarding them as more independent, more knowledgeable about sex and other adult topics, and less in need of nurturing, protection, comfort, and support than white girls.

How does this translate to the real world? Black kids, like Ghani, are 40 percent more likely to end up charged as adults than white kids accused of the same crimes. And prosecutors are far less likely to dismiss their cases or offer them diversion than their white peers. They are also more likely to be pulled from their homes and more likely to receive harsher sentences.

The disparate treatment is evident in school as well. A Black girl who is disruptive, engages in bullying, or gets in fights is three times more likely to be disciplined than a white girl who acts out. And schools are roughly four times more likely to give a Black girl an in-school suspension—and two times more likely to give her an out-of-school suspension—as a white girl. When Black kids misbehave, they get immediate consequences; when white kids misbehave, they get second chances. In a recent study of North Carolina middle schoolers, a Black boy was 95 percent less likely to receive a verbal warning from a teacher than a white boy. With a Black boy, the impulse is to jump to exclusion: kick him out of the class, out of the building, out of the system.

When teachers, police officers, and members of the general public see Black children as adults, those kids' very lives can be in danger. As twenty-eight-year-old George Zimmerman explained at his bail hearing after shooting Trayvon Martin, "I thought he was a little bit younger than I am." Trayvon was still in high school—a mere seventeen.

Trayvon's case is particularly revealing because it shows how race can even encourage us to recast a child *victim* as an adult *criminal*. That has special relevance in cases of sexual trafficking and statutory rape. When the protective label of "child" is removed from a Black girl—when she is mistakenly viewed as more knowledgeable about sex simply because of the color of her skin—her actions take on a very different meaning. They suddenly reflect agency and culpability. A Black girl is more likely to be seen as complicit in her rape, a willing partner in her sex trafficking, and as "asking for it" when she is beaten by an older man. A Black girl ends up dismissed as a prostitute by cops who see no reason to investigate.

But race is only one of the factors driving inequality and inconsistency in how we classify children in our criminal justice system. Take the role of luck. When you intentionally threw a bottle off an overpass, did the bottle—through pure chance—shatter harmlessly or did it cause an accident that killed a young family? When my colleague Geoff Goodwin, a cognitive psychologist at the University of Pennsylvania, and I ran a study asking people how much a child should be punished for such a transgression, the actual age of the child mattered far less than whether he ended up being lucky or unlucky. In fact, on average, an eight-year-old whose bottle ended up killing a woman and her young daughters was assigned more than twice as much time in a detention facility as a twenty-year-old whose bottle—again, through pure chance—caused no loss of life.

This may help explain why we routinely bypass the structures and rules we set up to protect children from the harshness of adult criminal justice. The default in place was to try Ghani as a minor, but prosecutors pushed the case into adult court and successfully pressed for a life sentence without parole.

When the Supreme Court, in 2012, announced that such mandatory sentences were unconstitutional for people under eighteen because the "imposition of a state's most severe penalties on juvenile offenders cannot proceed as though they were not children," Ghani was resentenced and released at the age of forty-five. But Dameon's parole board couldn't bring themselves to do the same: they told him to try again in another five years.

Denials like this are routine for juvenile lifers, even those who appear to pose little continuing threat to society. And, around the country, the response of many states has been to undermine the Supreme Court's ruling by exploiting loopholes and dragging their feet to ensure that juveniles still end up locked up in prison for their entire lives.

Even as we appear to make progress, it may be limited and ephemeral because of our underlying psychology. When no one has been hurt or when we are talking in the abstract, we can acknowledge that a fifteen-year-old is not as culpable as an adult and is far more amenable to rehabilitation. But when something really bad has happened, such lenience conflicts with our moral expectation that harms originate in the intentional actions of evil people who, consequently, deserve punishment. This cognitive need for closure and drive to blame may lead us to view the "unlucky" child as possessing far more adult motives and capacities than would seem realistic to us if nothing had happened—as with the "lucky" child.

That failure to distinguish children from adults—properly and consistently—can lead to profound harm at every stage of the criminal justice process. Research suggests that interactions with police may be far more psychologically traumatic to children than adults, yet they are commonplace for many city kids. In one recent study of urban youth, more than one in four kids had been stopped by police by the age of fifteen, and those stopped more often by cops were more likely to suffer from subsequent post-traumatic stress. When officers use force, children's bodies are far more vulnerable. But, in the heat of the moment, police fall back on the same tools and approaches they use with adults. So, we get an eleven-year-old shoplifter tased in the back by a pursuing officer, a sixteen-year-old student beaten and punched for "resisting," a twelve-year-old's arm bent painfully behind his back after he was caught selling CDs of himself rapping.

The one-size-fits-all approach colors investigations as well: detectives commonly use the same flawed interrogation approach they use with adults, despite evidence that young people are particularly sensitive to the coercive conditions that can lead to false confessions. In one study of DNA exonerations, 42 percent of exonerees who were juveniles at the time of the crime falsely confessed. Overall, minors appear to be more than three times as likely to confess to a crime they didn't commit than an adult—with the very youngest suspects most at risk.

An initial problem is that roughly two out of three young people aged twelve to nineteen don't adequately understand at least one Miranda right. Those under fifteen are particularly likely to think that they need to cooperate with authorities and waive their rights, and they tend to focus on immediate rewards rather than long-term costs. As a result, young suspects frequently end up in an environment fraught with consequence with no one to offer them counsel or protect them.

Once an interrogation has begun, innocent minors appear to be especially susceptible to what psychologists refer to as "the illusion of transparency"—they overestimate the extent that detectives grasp what they know to be true about themselves: most notably, that they didn't commit the crime in question. Combining the deceptive, high-pressure tactics the police use on adults with adolescents' high suggestibility and impulsiveness is a great recipe for extracting a confession—just not a reliable one. The wrongful convictions of the Central Park Five—four of whom falsely confessed to participating in the rape of a jogger—remain a warning of the threat to young suspects, but its lessons have largely gone unheeded.

We still don't think much about the special risks young people face in talking to the police as suspects or negotiating with prosecutors as defendants. And we do little to protect them from making wrong decisions likely to devastate their futures.

Ghani and Dameon "had already been in county jail for a year" when their "lawyers and the DA sat down" and spelled out the deal: they'd been charged with first-degree murder, but the prosecutor was offering third-degree, which "at that time was ten to twenty" years in prison. As Ghani recalls, "Me and Dameon, we looked at each other and they said think about it and let us know. We went back to the holding cell and true to form we poisoned each other—the blind leading the blind—the same way we poisoned each other when we ran away together." "They say two minds are better than one, but not when it comes to he and I. We both were like, man, I can't do ten to twenty. If we do a minimum of ten years, we'll get out when we're twenty-five. Oh, no, that's too long. And if we do the whole thing, we'll be thirty-five—man, we'll be old as hell! Oh, no, we can't do that."

So, they convinced themselves they could beat the case: "We started working out our strategy, even though we were guilty." "There was no sense of accountability," Ghani explains. "We were sixteen years old. And this is what my lawyer would later point out as immaturity, impulsiveness, lack of appreciation for the gravity of the situation—the hallmarks of youth." They "went back to the lawyers and said, no, we're not taking the deal."

The knockout of Ghani's account—the lights-out, floor-hitting calamity of it—is what he told me next: "We had already confessed . . . I gave two statements saying that I did it." As I teach my Criminal Law students, that's as close to a sure conviction as a prosecutor can get.

But Ghani's and Dameon's lawyers and the system let them go to trial. As Ghani reflects, "If I had taken the deal, our minimums would have been in 1997. With parole, we'd have been home twenty-something years ago. . . . We'd have maxed out in 2007. . . . We thought we were going to be old at thirty-five. Now looking back as a forty-six-year-old man, that's so young. At sixteen years old, we couldn't see that."

Even minor contact with the criminal justice system can lead to major life consequences for young people because of cascade effects. Kids who end up suspended are significantly more likely to drop out of school and end up arrested. Once you are arrested and enter the formal system, it can be extremely difficult to get back on a productive path. That has led certain cities to focus their attention on simply keeping kids out.

In Philadelphia, for instance, the district attorney, Larry Krasner, launched a new program in June 2021 to divert children who have committed robberies, assaults, and burglaries to a restorative justice program that pairs juvenile offenders with caseworkers who help them meet with their victims and plan a path forward. The charges are then dropped. As Krasner explains, this is not being soft on crime; this is research-backed best practice for reducing crime because it keeps young people from slipping off the track. We all lose when we take a fifteen-year-old who has broken into an apartment and "permanently mark [him] as someone who cannot own a home, and cannot be a provider and cannot go to school and cannot get a loan."

It is no surprise that the end point of landing in adult prison can be profoundly damaging to juveniles. A child placed in an adult prison or jail is five times as likely to be sexually assaulted and eight times as likely to commit suicide as an adult. And young people face particular psychological stress and lasting damage from solitary confinement. That's led to important recent reforms at the federal level—most notably the First Step Act and the reauthorized Juvenile Justice and Delinquency Prevention Act—to greatly limit the use of solitary for juveniles. However, at the state level, children are still routinely placed in isolation for days on end, often for just acting like normal adolescents: talking back, being messy, passing notes, swearing.

Of course, our flawed categorizations cast a shadow far beyond the criminal justice system. Across contexts, we often treat kids as adults when that leads to blame and harsh consequences they don't deserve, and when that exposes them to dangers they are ill-equipped to handle. Children deserve a right to be judged based on their unique capacities as children and to be safeguarded based on their unique vulnerabilities. That means granting children the right to make mistakes but also ensuring that they are safe.

To start, we need to understand the ways in which children have truly different capacities and vulnerabilities from adults.

Throughout history, people have noted the behavioral changes that occur at the transition from childhood to adulthood. In a passage from *The Winter's Tale*, written in 1611, Shakespeare laments: "I would there were no age between ten and three-and-twenty, or that youth would sleep out the rest; for there is nothing in the between but getting wenches with child, wrongdoing the ancientry, stealing, fighting." But it has only been in recent decades that biologists and anthropologists have provided the cross-cultural and cross-species evidence that adolescence is a shared, biologically distinct stage of development. That work has been complemented by research from psychologists and neuroscientists that has allowed us to move beyond an account of "hormones gone haywire." What we know now is that adolescents don't have addled adult brains; they have brains undergoing critical changes.

And that ought to influence how we view the same action taken by a fifteen-year-old and a forty-year-old. As Ghani explains, "Children can do some heinous things. Children are capable of great harm." But it doesn't follow that they are equally blameworthy. We must, in Ghani's words, "understand the lives on fire that teenagers live" and the fact that "children are not able to perform executive functions totally, keep impulses in check, control emotions, [engage in] foresight, anticipate consequences." In searching to understand his young self, Ghani spent long days in prison reading deeply into the mind sciences, and it influenced both his understanding of where youth criminal behavior comes from and how best to address it.

Modern statistics back Shakespeare up: unsafe sex, dangerous risk-taking, and law breaking all peak in adolescence, and adolescents really do forsake the guidance of their elders in favor of their peers.

Experts point to several key differences between adults and young people that seem to drive this dynamic.

First, adolescents appear to perceive risks similarly to adults—they get that there is a cost to trying drugs or jumping into bed with someone—but they are more sensitive to rewards, particularly immediate ones. So, they may overestimate the upside of getting high, driving fast, or leaping into a quarry pond to the cheers of their pals. The area of the brain involved in sensation seeking—the limbic system—develops early with the onset of puberty and it's far more active in adolescents than young children or adults.

Second, it's not just that adolescents experience a stronger drive to take risks, it's also that they are less capable of keeping their urges in check and less oriented toward the future consequences of their actions. The prefrontal cortex—the area of the brain most critical to impulse control, mood regulation, and sober judgment—is not fully developed until people enter their mid-twenties. That means that the spike in risk-taking may have a lot to do with a discrepancy between when different areas of the brain mature. In this light, castigating a young person for making what seems to us to be a clearly foolish mistake—breaking into a public pool to skinny-dip or posting an offensive limerick about the algebra teacher on TikTok—is as unfair as indicting a tadpole for spending too much time in the water where it can be eaten by fish. Yes, fully grown frogs are less at risk of being snapped up by a hungry bass, but you can't get an adult frog without the tadpole stage. And, to draw upon a personal example, maybe you don't get a (generally upstanding) forty-three-year-old law professor without the ordered-to-go-to-traffic-school-with-mom stage at age sixteen.

Third, adolescents are significantly more attentive to their peers than adults are. Approaching the teen years, young people become particularly self-conscious of how they appear to their classmates and are strongly motivated to fit in. The heightened desire for peer approval appears to relate to changes in the brain and may be a product of evolutionary pressures to avoid costly social exclusion at this age.

In light of the research, it doesn't seem a coincidence that Ghani and Dameon were together when they killed Anjo. And, much less consequentially, it doesn't seem like a coincidence that the night I got pulled over for speeding, I had two of my best friends in the car.

In the latter case, researchers have actually tracked how the presence of peers can influence risk-taking by teen drivers. In one study, scientists had people of different ages race a car around a track in a computer simulation. Sometimes the drivers came upon a yellow light, at which point they had to choose whether to sail through or hit the brakes. It was a significant risk: if they made it, they gained time; if the light turned red, though, they suffered a "crash" and lost time.

For adults, having friends in the car had no impact on how safely they drove, but for adolescents it had a huge impact. They took nearly three times as many risks when their peers were sitting alongside them compared to when they were driving solo.

Ghani notes how much a desire for acceptance and approval drove his behavior: "All children want respect and dignity amongst their peers." I certainly did. I was desperate to be cool. I acted differently when none of my friends were watching. I drove more like my parents did. And that aligns with the experimental findings. In the driving simulation, without friends in the car, adolescents and adults were almost identical in their risk-taking.

Adolescents don't take risks indiscriminately. In fact, they can be more risk averse than older people in certain contexts, like speaking in class. That's because they are powerfully shaped by their situations—whether they are alone or in a group, whether they are in a hot or cold state, whether they have to react immediately or have time to ponder. It depends on what's at stake.

That malleability makes blaming and punishing kids seem inappropriate; indeed, if anyone is responsible for bad outcomes, it is those who have the most control over the situations in which young people find themselves: adults. As Ghani points out, placing blame entirely on a fifteen-year-old offender is "an easy way of not having to deal with the role that each of us play in that one crime . . . all of us are guilty by omission or commission of some role that we played or didn't play." Instead of condemning teenagers for making the exact bad decisions we would predict they would make under the conditions we created, we ought to change the conditions to protect them.

If the last chapter underscored how *all* people—not simply parents—should help protect children, the rest of this chapter focuses on *what* we should protect kids from. Despite our great concern with keeping our kids safe, we end up protecting them from the wrong things—swear words, country mud, library books—while leaving them exposed to significant dangers: pollution, guns, bullying.

At its core, our failure to attend to the true threats comes down to flaws in how we think about risk. This is an area where our intuitions often mislead us. When I asked six-year-old Sidney from New Jersey what things she thought kids needed to be protected from, she didn't hesitate: "Sharks. Alligators." Listening back to the interview, I laughed—when I pressed her for additional risks, she doubled down on the sharks: "Sharks' teeth are very pointy; they have three hundred sets of teeth, I think." But I shouldn't have laughed because adults are just as focused on low-probability threats, while ignoring serious dangers to their kids. Why are we so irrational?

The more readily an incident comes to mind, the more frequently we think it happens—psychologists refer to this as the availability heuristic. But harms that are more common may fade into the background as a result of "psychic numbing," or because they're not treated as newsworthy. An alligator attacking a child or a pedophile serial killer gets huge media attention. When a child drowns in his backyard pool, it might not even get written up in the local paper. Yet, the risk of your kid getting abducted and killed by a stranger in any given year is less than 1 in 1.4 million. By contrast, drowning is the leading cause of death for those aged one to four.

Because our assessments are often guided by fear rather than facts, our attention tends to be drawn to threats that are dramatic, unfamiliar, and uncontrollable. We worry about our kids walking by sex offenders' houses on the way to school, but we don't even think about the danger when we drive them. In a national study from 2018, half of parents reported talking on their cellphone, one third reported reading texts, and one seventh reported using social media when their school-age children were in the car. That is despite the fact that one in four motor vehicle crashes today is caused by distracted driving. Just as concerning, 14.5 percent of parents didn't consistently use the child restraint systems in their cars—and those who used their smartphones were particularly likely to forgo that critical safety measure.

Other significant threats to children—like poor nutrition, indoor air pollution, and stress—end up ignored because they take their toll gradually or wreak havoc only years later. We can be particularly inattentive when the danger doesn't come in the form of a bogeyman. We are on high alert for murderers, dealers, pimps, Peeping Toms, and general bad seeds, but tend to miss the menace from omnipresent, nonhuman threats, most notably commercial entities.

When parents fret about substance abuse, they imagine a guy in an alley selling heroin or a dropout friend offering a cigarette behind the bleachers. But the most significant threat to young people is not illegal drugs. It's legal pharmaceuticals relentlessly marketed by companies to help address the things they tell us are holding our kids back: an inability to focus at school, anxiety and depression, and chronic pain. Roughly one in three teens and young adults reported misusing a prescription psychoactive drug they had been given by a doctor. The reason that nearly a million fewer high schoolers used Juul-type e-cigarettes in 2021 than 2020 wasn't that our kids stopped running with the "wrong crowd." It was that new regulations banned Juul from selling the fruit- and candy-flavored pods that kids prefer.

It is sobering to think that many of us spend more time fretting about sociopaths injecting grapes with cyanide or adulterating Tylenol bottles than we do about the poisons that companies knowingly—and legally—spray onto the fruit kids eat, mix into the products kids use, and expel into the environment where kids live. Few of us make the connection between the thousands of advertisements the average young person sees for high-calorie food and the fact that childhood obesity has tripled since the 1970s. We worry about binoculared perverts spying on our children from the bushes when our kids' images and data are constantly being collected, from their watches and phones, smart speakers and videogame systems, and the websites they visit. The average child between five and fifteen spends more than two hours online each day and by age eighteen may have posted tens of thousands of times on social media.

While we may fail to understand how young people think, feel, and act differently from adults, corporations spend billions of dollars educating themselves on children's psychology and then designing marketing efforts to exploit their unique vulnerabilities. They are well aware, for example, that young people are highly susceptible to peer effects, so they rely on ads that feature children and invest heavily in kidfluencers—child social media stars who peddle products on the most popular platforms. Children's malleability presents an incredible corporate opportunity to use kids to steer their parents' spending and—even better—to create brand loyalty that will last a lifetime.

Given that children aren't allowed to purchase alcohol, why do so many beer ads reflect strategies, like comedy, animation, animals, and special effects, that have been shown to draw children's attention? Because alcohol companies are eager to capture long-term customers when they are most impressionable. Recent research shows that teens' favorite commercials are alcohol-related, and the amount of money companies spend on advertising strongly predicts the percentage of young people who have drunk particular brands of beer.

We cannot continue to sit back and rely on our existing threat alert system. Our gut instincts just weren't designed to deal with the complex risks—like those posed by corporations—that our kids face today. We need to lean on the expertise of those who spend their lives understanding young people, not to profit and manipulate them but to ensure they successfully navigate to adulthood. So, let's look at three examples in light of the evidence: a significant risk we often ignore; something we worry about but misdiagnose; and finally, an area where we need to relax.

One of the surprising research findings is that a lot of harm to our kids happens right under our noses. Take bullying. "Safe" in their rooms, in homes secured by cameras and alarm systems, our sons and daughters receive texts, Tweets, Snaps, and TikToks telling them that they are sluts, worthless, hated; saying "Kill yourself." "Safe" at school, they are mercilessly teased, threatened, dehumanized.

I witnessed it every single day in junior high school. Eric, stripped down to his boxers and thrown in the girls' locker room. David, gouged by a pencil stuck in the basketball bench as he sat down. Fights scheduled at "the Pit" for Tuesday; fights started with a bleary-eyed bump as the buses dumped us into the 7 A.M. cafeteria. I heard racist terms that I'd never heard before and gay slurs I'd heard a thousand times.

Bullying is prevalent: according to a 2016 National Academies of Sciences, Engineering, and Medicine report, between 18 and 31 percent of American school-aged children had been bullied in the previous year. And it is far from benign. Kids often suffer significant physical injuries: in a recent study of three American cities, 22 percent of seventh-grade victims of bullying had been violently injured. Even when they escape bodily harm, victims regularly experience emotional trauma, psychological problems, and poor academic performance that can reverberate for the rest of their lives.

Bullying in childhood has been linked to harmful adult behaviors like binge eating and smoking, and a significantly reduced quality of life—similar to that of people living with chronic diseases. Moreover, witnessing bullying can sometimes be just as damaging as being bullied. In one recent study, researchers looked at exposure to violence—ranging from threats and insults to actual assaults—for students in eighth grade. It didn't matter much whether you were a bystander or a target: two years later those who had been exposed to bullying showed increased mental health problems, antisocial behavior, drug use, and struggles with schoolwork.

In spite of the evidence, adults often let bullying happen, as if it were a harmless and inevitable by-product of adolescence along with acne and period cramps. If they intervene, it's often to reshape the victim's behavior rather than the bully's. We tell our bullied kids: Don't give him the satisfaction of knowing that he got to you. Don't be so sensitive. Sticks and stones. For some parents, "toughening up" amounts to lessons in fighting: Here is how you make a fist. If he hits you, you hit him back—even harder.

All of this reflects a false belief that "name-calling" doesn't matter and that physical bullying makes people stronger. Today, parents adapt the traditional character-building rhetoric to fit into the current child pop psych landscape, conflating battling bullies with developing "grit." In fact, many accept bullying as a necessary part of getting the most out of young people: football players, dancers, pianists, mathletes, beauty contestants.

One study of American children found that roughly half had been called a name, insulted, or otherwise verbally abused by their coach. And another study showed that one in five high school athletes dropped out due to a coach's bullying toward them or a teammate. Elite child stars are not immune. Mary Cain was the fastest girl in America, but under constant berating to drop weight by Nike's star track coach, Alberto Salazar, and his team, her body gave out: she lost her period, she broke five bones, she developed suicidal thoughts. Likewise, verbal and emotional abuse under the eye of Bela and Martha Karolyi may have produced numerous medals for USA Gymnastics, but it also left numerous girls with injuries, anxiety, and eating disorders that plague them to this day. We celebrate bully coaches like these. And the message to children is clear: it's not bullies that we hate, but weaklings.

Our bullying culture played a powerful role in Ghani's strange fall from gifted student to dropout to lifer. He didn't realize it then: "I just started spiraling into something I couldn't put my finger on at that age. But years later in prison, when I sat on my bunk in the cell, or pacing the floor of my cell at night, asking myself over and over, How did I end up here? How could I have done something like that? . . . I was able to go back and unpack some of the things about myself, and I realized I was a very insecure little boy . . . because of poor showings in situations that required courage—I'm talking about dealing with bullies especially. And I think, in those moments, it started a certain kind of thinking in me that I had to be tough."

Arriving in Brooklyn at age seven, he stood out. In Trinidad, all the kids had worn a uniform, but in his new environment, clothes mattered and his single mother just didn't have any money for that. His voice, too, made him different: "I got an accent that I couldn't hide and it led me into a lot of situations with other kids that I had problems navigating . . . I wasn't used to confrontation with other kids. I was used to mango trees in the yard." He didn't have siblings to protect him; there was no "older male figure" of any kind: "I didn't really have a model of how to deal with certain situations." His mother's unwavering love held no magic on the schoolyard. "I got picked on and so . . . I started overcompensating for these inadequacies. I started taking risks, starting fights, starting trouble, just to plunge myself into dangerous situations, to prove myself."

He ran away, not with dreams of being a drug dealer—"I was so averse to drugs that even though I worked inside crack houses, I never used, never got high"—but of being a kingpin: the type of person who no one messed with, someone with status. Sifting through these memories, reading and learning about the world, Ghani came to realize the problem "was toxic masculinity": "We are fed, as young boys growing up, that the way we prove ourselves and feel good about ourselves and have respect, dignity among our peers, is by being alphas and sometimes that's expressed through how violent we can be."

Ghani is driven to help other children not succumb to the same mindset: "I feel now it's my responsibility to run interference on that in the most positive way. That's what I owe to the world for taking something that I had no right to take: Anjo Price." But we all owe a debt because it is our culture that created and fed Ghani's "inner demons."

And the solution, then, is not to come down harshly on children who bully—to treat them as adults—but to address the conditions that create and facilitate bullying. We can help young people recognize bullying behavior as unacceptable by rejecting bullying in our families, in our schools, and in our extracurricular activities. Research reveals that children who witness and experience abuse at home demonstrate a significant increase in aggression and callous unemotional traits. But a recent study showed that sixth and ninth graders with strong family relationships were more likely to reject bullying and more likely to intervene to stop it.

Understanding the importance of peer influence on adolescents, it's easy to grasp why youth interventions may be even more effective. In a real-world experiment, researchers assigned a small number of students at New Jersey middle schools to learn about the harms from bullying and to initiate anti-bullying activities, like handing out orange wristbands to students they saw being friendly to other kids. Those small peer interventions had a huge effect, corresponding to a 30 percent drop in reported incidents. And when popular students—as measured by the extent of their social interactions—were the ones publicly rejecting bullying, the effect was significantly larger.

If bullying is an example of a serious threat to children that we ignore, sex is an example of a threat to which we are rightfully attuned. Yet our faulty risk assessments still get us into trouble, causing us to misdiagnose the nature of the threat and to mishandle our response. We assume that the best way to avoid unwanted pregnancies, STDs, assaults, and reputational damage is to create a sexless environment for children. That justifies R ratings for nudity in movies, weighty criminal charges for teen sexting, and the elimination of sex ed in schools, as a majority of states have now done. And it helps to explain parents' reluctance to talk to their kids about sex. For more than half of families, that amounts to a single, awkward "birds and the bees" exchange.

Unfortunately, censoring sexuality doesn't prevent sex. There is little or no evidence that abstinence-only programs in school have any sustained impact on restraining sexual behavior. And worryingly, there is data that links them to decreased contraceptive use and increased STD risk. Moreover, the sexual abuse of young people remains commonplace: 43 percent of Illinois middle schoolers in a recent study reported that they had been the victims of verbal sexual harassment, and roughly half as many had been subject to physical sexual assault.

With parents and educators vacating the space, teens' main source for learning about sex is pornography. While defenders of the don'task-don't-tell approach shout down the "agendas" of academics pushing for comprehensive sex education, our children are quietly being taught about sex by people who aren't thinking about children at all—just money. The result is a near-endless stream of videos that depict women as subservient objects, there to pleasure men, and where consent is treated as irrelevant or worse—a turnoff. One recent study of thousands of online heterosexual pornography scenes showed people—mostly women—being physically or psychologically harmed in one out of three scenes.

If we want to protect our kids—to help them develop into people who practice safe sex, who feel comfortable with who they are, and who are respectful of their partners' desires and needs—we need to prepare them for the hot-cognition moments where their adolescent brains can lead them astray. Research shows that when there are more conversations about sex between adolescents and their parents, those adolescents feel better approaching their parents with concerns about sex and they are more likely to take precautions that reduce the risk of disease and unwanted pregnancy. As with anti-bullying efforts, peers can be an incredible force in creating norms of behavior that prioritize consent, but that's not going to happen if less than half of young adults continue to recall ever talking to their folks about the importance of unpressured consent or how to avoid sexually harassing someone.

It's also not going to happen if we don't commit to creating a less pernicious culture around sex, including holding business entities who profit from sexualizing children accountable. Within days of Nicholas Kristof writing a single column in *The New York Times* about videos of the sexual exploitation of children on a popular porn site, U.S. senators introduced legislation to make it easier for rape victims to sue companies that monetize their victimization and the Canadian government began developing new regulations for internet pornography. We can make big changes quickly, but it requires a different perspective.

Again, our societal instinct is often to treat children as adults when things go wrong: they send a nude photo to their boyfriend, have sex after getting really drunk, get pregnant. But these are the foreseeable results of teenage cognition in the culture we curate. One of the victims Kristof profiled made naked videos of herself in eighth grade at the request of a fifteen-year-old boy whom she had a crush on. The videos ended up on the internet and the fallout sent her into a spiral of drugs, homelessness, and suicide attempts. "I was dumb," she told Kristof. "It was one small thing that a teenager does, and it's crazy how it turns into something so much bigger. A whole life can be changed because of one little mistake." We can never hope to prevent all of our children's missteps, so we must also strive to ensure that the mistakes kids make are not ruinous.

More broadly, we must accept that trying to protect our children by cutting off all avenues of exploration is not only doomed to fail but can also threaten their positive development.

Growing up, my mom describes wandering the woods, parks, and streets of Webster Groves, Missouri, unrestricted by parents. "We could go anywhere," she recalls. Three decades later, I explored the suburban landscape outside Washington, D.C., with similar freedom: my younger brother, our two best friends, and I would hop on our bikes and disappear for hours. That's unthinkable for many parents today.

Did the world get more dangerous?

In the 1970s, psychologist Roger Hart mapped the range of school-age children—where they were allowed to go—in a particular New England town. When he returned forty years later, the crime rate hadn't budged, but the average ten-year-old child, who had once roamed wherever he wanted, was now barred from going much beyond his own yard.

A more likely explanation for the shifting geography is that parents view the risks to their children through the lens of their values, and our values have changed in recent decades. That's one of the reasons that the experience of elementary school students is so different in many of our peer countries, like France, Japan, and the Netherlands, where kids routinely walk to school, go to the park, run errands, or attend a birthday party alone. It is a tradition for small groups of Dutch preteens to be dropped in the woods at night and then find their way back to base on their own. They are given a cellphone for emergency use and must wear reflective vests. But that's it. Parents in the Netherlands care about their children's welfare just as much as we do; they just view the risks differently.

It's not simply that modern Americans overestimate the prevalence of kidnappings because of outsize media coverage of rare horrific abductions; it's also that we have come to view leaving children alone as *wrong*. Drawing back to chapter 3, as helicopter parenting has become the norm, it's engendered an implicit code that stigmatizes those who fail to be vigorous guardians. That moral intuition can drive our perception of the danger.

The process seems backward: we think our disdain for parents who allow their elementary schooler to walk unaccompanied to get ice cream must be motivated by our understanding of the risk. But, as scientists have discovered, it's often the opposite: our gut tells us that it's "bad" to allow your kid to be so "vulnerable" and we justify that gut instinct by overestimating the threat.

In a clever set of studies, researchers described a scenario in which a child was unsupervised for a period of time, varying only the reasons why the parent left the kid alone. The scientists then asked participants to rate the level of danger the child faced. When the parent left the child on purpose, the child was viewed as significantly more at risk than when the parent left the child alone by accident. And the more morally objectionable the purpose—leaving your kid to pursue a sexual affair versus leaving your kid to do volunteer work—the more dangerous the exact same situation appeared.

So, what is it actually like to be a modern kid untended and out in the world? Andre is eleven and lives in downtown Philadelphia. He gets himself up at 6:30 A.M. and walks to the bus stop. But he doesn't wait for a school bus. It's a regular city bus, which takes him to the subway, which he rides four stops, before a short walk to school. Andre explains that the school is "on the edge between the good neighborhood and the bad neighborhood." And he admits that he's missed his stop before and "ended up in the bad neighborhood." So, what happened? I ask him. "I just went to the other side and hopped right back on the subway and went back." And how does he deal with the general grittiness of the Philly underground? He laughs: "I probably stepped in pee this morning walking down the stairs to the subway. It's fine—I'm used to it. I'm in the city." He feels bad for his suburban peers: "They can't do anything until they're sixteen because they can't drive a car until they are sixteen. Right now, I get to go anywhere I want after school. The rule is that I have to be home by six. We get out at three-nineteen."

One of the things that is frustrating to Andre, though, is that while his parents trust him and provide him with great freedom, the rest of Philadelphia does not. The other day, he wanted to do something new after school, so he tried to go to the Philadelphia Museum of Art. "I didn't even get past the security guard," Andre recalls. "He was like, 'You have to be with an adult.'" Andre, though, had already called customer service before making the trek up the famous "*Rocky* steps" to the summit of the museum. "I asked them, 'So, I'm eleven and I can just get in, right? No strings attached?' and they said, 'Yes, no strings attached.'" So, in front of the security guard, Andre called up again and a different person picked up and once again confirmed: Andre could get in free, "no strings attached." But the guard wouldn't budge, so Andre called a third time and that's when he learned the truth: "There is one string attached . . . you have to be with an adult."

To some, that may seem a reasonable compromise: after all, the museum welcomes many young people every day, for chaperoned school field trips and art classes, Boy Scout troops and Christian youth groups, with parents and grandparents charting the path to the gallery highlights. But what is lost is significant. Organized activities and outings mediated by adults are not the same as Andre's walkabouts.

The research is clear that, throughout childhood, independent unstructured play and exploration is critical to developing into a well-adjusted adult capable of navigating our complex social world. But somehow, we've convinced ourselves that if our kids are to turn out well, they must spend their afternoon and weekend hours on homework and at practices, tournaments, performances, tryouts, and clubs. Since the 1970s, kids have lost some twelve hours of true free time—including a 50 percent decrease in their time spent outdoors engaged in unstructured play and exploration.

Likewise, rather than addressing the dangers children face when alone in public, we've simply restricted their ability to be alone in public. Under the guise of protecting them, children like Andre face a curfew year-round in Philadelphia—barring them from being out in the evening. And if they dare venture beyond their front door, many city rec centers and playgrounds have installed devices—modeled on those used to repel rodents—that emit a high-pitched noise after dark that only children can hear.

It's not too late to change course. We can take inspiration from the UN's foresight in recognizing "the right of the child to rest and leisure, to engage in play and recreational activities" in the Convention on the Rights of the Child. We can commit ourselves to fostering safe environments where children can explore, learn, and interact on their own.

But it requires giving up a black-and-white world, where everything can be classified as good or bad for children. Hanging out with other kids on a summer evening can be incredibly beneficial, but if society has done nothing to address bullying, guns, gangs, drugs, and the like, a lack of any adult supervision may make the potential costs too great. Appreciating the nuance of risk often means rejecting the type of all-or-nothing response to which we gravitate: completely free-range kids or Tiger-mom-all-in-directed-enrichment, an iPad in every student's hand or no screens at all, life in a Purell bubble or let them eat dirt and no baths ever.

No parent wants to hear that the answer is "some screen time, in certain contexts, with some engagement from caregivers" or "organisms in soil can be beneficial to our microbiome but that can be outweighed if the soil contains the by-products of industry" but that is where the growing body of evidence is pointing. If you try to impose an on-off approach to a situation of gradations, you're going to get it wrong, and that's particularly true with age cutoffs. No alcohol at all—not one drop—until you are twenty-one, then as much as you want, whenever you want, is a recipe for disaster. If we are going to permit a person to do something eventually, gradualism tends to make a lot more sense.

That's what the research suggests when it comes to driving. It's appealing to say, okay, it's your birthday, you are now sixteen, you are completely free to drive wherever you want with no oversight at all. It felt like a breakout moment to me and my friends, fantastical and fantastic: to be able to suddenly go anywhere, miles away from home, to go a hundred miles an hour after walking for years, to be at the wheel. But in all the euphoria, I sensed then, and I know now, that the over-the-waterfall approach is dangerous: in the first three months after getting their license, teens are eight times more likely to have an accident or near miss than they are in the three previous learner's permit months. And simply raising the driving age by a couple of years doesn't make much of a difference because it doesn't address the core issue: stark transitions don't provide young brains with the necessary practice and preparation to be successful. Gradually phasing out adult supervision and gradually phasing in driving with friends is likely to drastically reduce risky behaviors.

So, the opening frame of this chapter—when is a child an adult?—was a bit of a trick. It doesn't appear, like magic, after the birthday candle smoke dissipates. It's not a switch flicked on when you do something very good or very bad. Growing up is a process, filled with expected mistakes and progress, fast and slow. When we protect it and help young people navigate it, we ensure a future with happier, healthier, more capable adults.

CHAPTER 5

LATE ADOLESCENCE

The Right to Be Heard

Wylie had worn his grandfather's old National Guard jacket to school. He had added buttons to it, outward signs, perhaps, of his own political awakening.

As a junior, his government and history classes had stirred something—a welling up of ideas and beliefs. He'd begun to test them with friends and family, pressing and being pressed back. He'd sought out books and articles. But the most defining influence on Wylie's political identity was the Pulse nightclub shooting in Orlando that summer. Forty-nine people lost their lives in the deadliest attack on the LGBTQIA+ community in American history. "I'm gay so that hurt me a lot and made me scared for the first time." The vacuous "thoughts and prayers" response of politicians and much of the public was maddening to him: "This sort of thing is happening and the most we're getting is a general 'Oh well, that's the way it is in a free democracy.'"

The Parkland massacre—midway through Wylie's senior year—came as a sick, rasping reprise. Another Floridian had walked into Marjory Stoneman Douglas High School and murdered seventeen more people. Where was the reaction? Who was moved? It was as if everyone was walking around with toilet paper jammed into their ears, and wrapped around their eyes, and cocooned up their arms—as if the whole country were mummified. The "paranoia and fear of tragedy," it seemed to Wylie, were becoming normalized: his brother's cohort, four years younger, who'd grown up "sheltering in place," had resigned themselves to it all. No adult was going to make it better—a realization both shattering and empowering. As Wylie suddenly understood, it was very much up to him: "I can't have these beliefs and not do anything about it except bring it up occasionally in class. I've got to actually do something. I've got to put practice to my belief."

Wylie had hoped the jacket would give him "some comfort and confidence." It was a month after Parkland, a Wednesday, and he was in East Program, a computer business application class. He was watching the clock, waiting for it to tick to 10 A.M. That's when students around the country were meant to walk out—a mass protest against gun violence, a public vigil, seventeen minutes to reflect, one for each victim. When time finally aligned with the moment, Wylie stood. The rest of the class stared. One kid said, "They're gonna suspend you." Wylie said, okay, and opened the door. When he got outside, he was all alone. That, he said, was the most unnerving part, thinking: I'm the only one.

Wylie's hometown of Greenbrier, forty-five miles north of Little Rock, is not activist country. You head in, north on US 65, giving up farmland and billboards for a few low strip malls, a Walmart, a Shell, a McDonald's, and then you're back up to fifty-five miles per hour, driving past flat farms. It's a tight-knit community of around five thousand, conservative and white, with a clean-cut law-and-order bent. A large American flag flies at First Service Bank on 65. A smaller one is raised at the Immanuel Baptist Church, across from Greenbrier High. When the Panthers play, there is no kneeling.

And, so, it was a bit of a surprise, when two other seniors joined Wylie on the bench in front of the school, beneath the gaze of their own Stars and Stripes. Two police trucks slowly rolled by. "We couldn't see through the windows," Wylie recalls, "but we knew they were glaring at us." The boys wondered if they might get arrested. But it was the principal who came out first and, then, the dean of students.

"Boys, what are you doing?" the dean asked in his thick southern accent. He warned them there would be punishment. Wylie explained they were protesting gun violence in schools and that they were willing to accept the consequences. The principal was exasperated—he'd assured the school board there wasn't going to be anything like this—but he and the dean went back in and the boys spent the rest of the seventeen minutes on their own.

When they returned to school, the air had thickened. The other students were talking. Wylie was volunteering in the library during the next class period and the librarian was worried about him. What, precisely, was next?

The boys were called back one at a time.

To his surprise, Wylie was given a choice: a suspension or two "swats."

Under Greenbrier Public School policy, such corporal punishment is officially sanctioned. It's right there in the rules. Children can be struck.

Wylie didn't hesitate: he'd "take the violence"—he thought that would send a "stronger message." It seemed "nobler, in a way." The other boys had chosen the swats as well, but they were eighteen. Seventeen-year-old Wylie had to call his dad to come sign a consent form.

Wylie describes the wooden paddle as a "small one-handed cricket bat." It's "all marked up" and has the words "Board of Education"—a pun—written on it. There's a ritual to the swats—a procedure to be followed. After the dean pulled the paddle out of his drawer, he called in the assistant principal as a witness and read out the "crime" and "sentence." Wylie put his hands on the wall and the dean hit him with the paddle, twice on his thighs.

Violence for protesting violence. Wylie doesn't suppose the irony was "lost on any of us, even the school board," although he's certain "that plenty of people in the community thought they were too lenient on us."

Indeed, there were many people around the country who looked at the Parkland students and other young protesters with anger, frustration, and condescension. Survivors like David Hogg, who began publicly speaking out against gun violence following the attack on Stoneman Douglas High School, were immediately derided as attention-seeking, hysterical, and unwittingly manipulated by adults. Rumors circulated that David was a child actor hired by left-wing activists or controlled by his father. When David and his sister, Lauren, proposed wearing protest armbands, the actor James Woods derided them on Twitter for historical ignorance: "You might have a little trouble getting Jewish Americans to embrace this look. Do you have some shiny jackboots and brown shirts to go with it? Guessing maybe you skipped history class while you were shilling for the @DNC." Never mind that the actual historical reference was the armbands Mary Beth Tinker and her brother wore to school, fifty years earlier, to protest the Vietnam War. Never mind that David and Lauren's initial social media post made that connection clear: citing the resulting Supreme Court case upholding student speech rights by name and including matching photographs of the sibling pairs, dressed in identical clothes, with their peace sign bands held just so.

According to the conservative radio host Erick Erickson, David was a clueless "bully" taking cheap shots at the NRA while using "what happened to him as a shield to avoid criticism." As Erickson concluded, "High school kids are not people we should take seriously on any subject." Bill O'Reilly offered a similar take: "The big question is: should the media be promoting opinions by teenagers who are in an emotional state and facing extreme peer pressure in some cases?" As Parkland students petitioned Florida lawmakers to enact more restrictive gun legislation, Todd Starnes, another conservative commentator, wondered, "Do the kids speak to their parents and teachers with the same level of disrespect?"

Given the context, the harshness of the attacks on the Parkland protesters seems noteworthy, but what is particularly revealing is how inapt they seem. In many ways, it was the child protesters—not their critics—who appeared to be the "adults" in the room. Emma González came off as heartfelt and brave as she spoke at a rally in Fort Lauderdale just days after her classmates were gunned down. On television and social media, David Hogg and Cameron Kasky showed poise and savvy. In conversation, Wylie struck me as thoughtful, knowledgeable, and unnecessarily respectful to those who had disrespected him—emphasizing to me that the dean and principal had been entirely professional, that he bore them no ill will, and that he did not want to slam his hometown. Far from attention-seeking, these seemed to be young people thrust into the spotlight against their will, their courage reflecting desperation, reflecting our failure as adults to protect them and look out for their interests. Wylie didn't walk out because he wanted his name in the newspaper; he walked out because no one else was stepping up. As he explained, "It really is important for us as young people to not shut up about it and just assume that it will be all right because for a lot of people it won't be. Hundreds of children have been killed and we're doing a whole lot of nothing about it."

One of the most remarkable things about the Never Again kids is how quickly they built a movement that managed to be both coherent and inclusive. Hundreds of thousands of people turned out for the March for Our Lives—just six weeks after Parkland—and what they saw was a sharp rebuke to all the pundits who claim that political strength comes in homogeneity and narrowness. The march called Americans to action against a common threat, besetting affluent suburban schools, poor city street corners, and middle-class bedrooms. Alongside David Hogg and Emma Gonzáles, eleven-year-old Naomi Wadler spoke to "represent the African-American women who are victims of gun violence" and seventeen-year-old Edna Chavez spoke to "uplift" her "South Los Angeles community." "I learned to duck from bullets before I learned how to read," she recalled. She asked the crowd to imagine what it is like to watch your brother die, as she did, to "see the melanin on your brother's face turn gray."

In the weeks and months that followed, youth activists of color—including those involved with Black Lives Matter—helped focus attention beyond mass shootings. In Florida, hundreds of students at Miami Northwestern Senior High School staged a walkout against gang violence—the very act of protest putting their lives in danger—as they "trespassed" gang territory to reach the spot, marked with teddy bears and balloons, where two of their former classmates were gunned down the previous month. As Ricky Pope, a junior, explained, it was worth the risk: "Everyone got to see that the children from Liberty City who see these tragedies on a daily basis are not just silent."

In Nashville, six young women—Nya Collins, Jade Fuller, Ken-

nedy Green, Emma Rose Smith, Mikayla Smith, and Zee Thomas—
ages fourteen to sixteen, organized and led a march of ten thousand
people against police brutality and racism. "No justice, no peace,"
they chanted, as blistering midsummer heat gave way to a torrential
downpour. "Change is coming," the group posted that evening on
Instagram. "We see it we feel it, we know it."

These broad efforts have produced concrete results and have laid
the foundation for future reform. In the first six months after the
shooting at Stoneman Douglas, there was a huge spike in gun control
legislation, with fifty new laws enacted across the country, including
fourteen laws in states with Republican governors. For the first time
in a quarter century, the House passed a gun control measure, requiring background checks for almost all firearm purchases. And
lawmakers have been encouraged to challenge the NRA in a way that
has been unheard of in recent decades. Youth protests against police
violence have prompted states and municipalities to ban choke holds,
adopt body cameras, and shift resources to other public safety interventions.

This is no anomaly. Young environmental activists—like Greta
Thunberg and Autumn Peltier—have been at the forefront of sustainability efforts, pressing countries to combat climate change and
protect indigenous water rights. Youth movements have successfully
pushed for greater traffic safety in Bangladesh and free public education in Chile. Argentinian vice president Cristina Fernández de
Kirchner explained the impact of adolescent protests in favor of reproductive rights on her own position on abortion: "If you want to
know who it was that made me change my mind, it was the thousands
of girls who took over the streets. It was seeing them become true
feminists."

Look back through history and you will find numerous instances
where adolescents have been catalysts for important social change:
the young protesters in Mexico, Paris, and Berlin pressing for their
voices to be heard in 1968; the public-school kids in Soweto, South
Africa, marching against apartheid in 1976; the pro-democracy student demonstrators in Tiananmen Square and Prague, both in 1989.
The members of the Greensboro Four, whose 1960 Woolworth lunch

counter sit-in would alter the course of the civil rights movement, were all teenagers. A year later, Freedom Rider Hezekiah Watkins was in ninth grade at Rowan Junior High when he was arrested for protesting segregation in his hometown of Jackson, Mississippi.

Mary Beth Tinker was thirteen when she and her brother put on their black armbands. As she recalls, "I didn't feel that kids should be left out of the direction and decisions that were going to be made about the country and the world. I didn't feel like I shouldn't have a part in that." The brave, defiant acts of teenagers helped end a war that seemed unending.

When I spoke to Mary Beth recently, she marveled at how young people, across generations and movements, have taken inspiration from other youth: "The Parkland kids are standing on the shoulders of Black Lives Matter in the way we stood on the shoulders of the civil rights youth who came before us."

And, yet, the substantive victories have often been smaller than hoped, tenuous, requiring unsustainable grit, bravery, and unity— and lost with a changing wind. For all the effort of child activists, America has not gotten rid of guns, acted to stop global warming in its tracks, or meaningfully changed policing practices. And the reason is simple.

In 2019, when a group of young students pressed eighty-five-year-old California senator Dianne Feinstein on her lack of support for the Green New Deal, she told them they were naïve and that it was not their place to question her—rather, they "should listen." When sixteen-year-old Isha Clarke pushed back, "You're supposed to listen to us. That's your job," Feinstein brushed it off: "Well, you didn't vote for me." It was a stunning admission, but only for its brutal directness. It's always been true, discovered by each hopeful upstart: you are nothing to those in power without power yourself.

Sixteen-year-old Benjamin Brown Foster had his Feinstein moment in 1848. By his mid-teens, Foster had made himself into an ardent abolitionist, reading essays and books on the subject, and even publishing an anonymous article in the *Bangor Gazette* advocating the creation of an anti-slavery political party. On election day in

Maine, he spent his time trying to convince voters of the evils of slavery. His arguments were strong, and his position would be borne out by history. But, as he recorded in his diary, many of the adults he encountered laughed at "[my] childish enthusiasm and coolly reminded me that I was a boy." The truth was that he had no say in the matter. And, so it was that he wished—because that was all he could do—"that I was for one year, and on this one topic, a man, a voter." As Susan B. Anthony would explain, twenty-five years later, "The moment you deprive a person of his right to a voice in the government, you degrade him from the status of a citizen of the republic to that of a subject . . . [a person] helpless, powerless, bound to obey laws made by superiors."

So, what if we changed course? What if we made children citizens? What if they had power, too?

"[B]aby boomers have messed things up for us again." On June 23, 2016, the vote had come in: the United Kingdom was leaving Europe. And nineteen-year-old Elizabeth Mayfield was infuriated. As she told the BBC, "They've voted for something that's not going to really affect them. They're not going to have to deal with the consequences."

Elizabeth, a Staffordshire University student, knew exactly what she and her fellow young people had lost. As a member of the EU, an English teenager could look forward to a future of incredible freedoms. On a whim, she could pick up and move to Barcelona or Oslo or Budapest. She could walk into a coffee shop in Paris, get a job, and begin that afternoon. She could take up graduate study at the University of Zagreb, buy a flat in Amsterdam, and marry a Slovenian, as easily as an American conducts his affairs across states. And as she moved between the EU's twenty-eight member countries, she'd have her same health insurance and enjoy the same rights that all EU citizens enjoy.

With the referendum, those possibilities vanished. The door to cosmopolitanism—to a world of exchanges with diverse peoples in diverse places—was shut and along with it the economic and political benefits of European engagement. Elizabeth wasn't wrong when she pointed her finger at older voters. Sixty percent of those aged sixty-five and older voted to leave the EU. By contrast, 73 percent of those aged eighteen to twenty-four voted to remain.

The perversity, as Elizabeth recognized, is that the Brexit vote—like most elections and referendums—was far more consequential for the young than the old for the simple reason that the young will experience the effects over a much longer period of time. In America, the next presidential election matters a lot more to someone who is fifteen than someone who is eighty. If a president starts a war, that kid could be drafted halfway through that president's term; his grandfather could not be. And that fifteen-year-old will end up paying far more in taxes over his lifetime to pay for it than the eighty-year-old. A newly appointed Supreme Court justice will likely serve for decades, most of which grandpa will never see.

The truth is that the elderly voters who came out for Trump won't experience the harshest realities of climate change. They could cheer his warm embrace of the coal industry and cold shoulder to the Paris Climate Agreement knowing they will be long dead when any true reckoning comes. But a sixth grader has no such luxury. No one asked her what she thought or wanted. But she will be there to watch the worsening floods, feel the droughts, and worry for *her* children. Senator Feinstein's "wait your turn" response to the climate activists in her office—"I think one day you should run for the United States Senate and then you do it your way"—only makes sense if you get a turn. In sixty-five or seventy years, when Isha Clarke is Feinstein's age, the window of action will have passed to avoid environmental catastrophe.

It is revealing that many of the arguments against allowing young people to vote are familiar in the annals of American history. More than a century ago, women were told that voting was irrelevant to their lives, that their experiences and natural abilities left them unprepared for the task, and that their interests were adequately represented by others: husbands and fathers. Then, as now, there was a sense among many that there was simply no need to rock the boat. As one pamphlet circulated by the National Association Opposed to Woman Suffrage in the early twentieth century explained, "90% of the women either do not want it, or *do not care.*" "You do not need a ballot to clean out your sink spout." California state senator J. B. Sanford put it more bluntly, "Politics is no place for a woman," driving the point home with a cavemanesque flourish: "Woman does not have to vote to secure her rights. Man will go to any extreme to protect and elevate her now."

Today, the biggest objection to extending the franchise to children is that they simply lack the requisite intellect. But the latest research from psychology and neuroscience contests the idea that young people don't have the necessary cognitive capacity to vote.

Many of us think of our brain as a generalized organ: a sort of balloon filled with the uniform matter of thinking. Brain development, in this light, is a matter of inflation: an overall expansion of capacity. So, a five-year-old isn't as adept at decision-making as a twenty-five-year-old because his "balloon" is only partially full. It's an appealing analogy, but it's just hot air.

As we touched on in the last chapter, different areas of the brain are involved in different functions and develop at different rates. And the areas implicated in voting mature much earlier than you might assume. Once a person reaches her mid-teens, her capacity to understand and reason her way to a decision is comparable to an adult's ability in situations that allow for coolheaded deliberation. In the voting booth, a sixteen-year-old and an adult aren't distinguishable: both are equally proficient at comprehending relevant information, gathering facts, weighing the pros and cons, and applying the accumulated evidence in a logical manner to reach a conclusion. It's not that once people are in high school, they stop making bad choices; it's that they don't make them any more than adults do. And neuroimaging studies back up what we see in laboratory experiments showing comparable performance on logical reasoning, memory recall, and other cognitive tasks: the brain regions involved in cold cognition look the same in teens and adults.

But, you might be wondering, what about the slower-developing areas of the teenage brain? Well, these late-blooming sectors can leave young people at a disadvantage when they are in a group, pressed for time, or emotionally taxed. In such a "hot" state, adults tend to make better decisions because the self-regulation systems in our brains don't appear to mature until a person is in his early twenties. As we've already discussed, teenagers have more trouble resisting peer pressure, turning down immediate rewards that entail major risks, and keeping their impulses in check, among other things. But, in the seclusion of the voting booth, having had months to consider the options and with no immediate payoff on offer, young people don't have to worry about all of that—and neither do the rest of us.

This account of brain development also allays the fear that if we lower the voting age, we have to lower every other age limit in lockstep. It is entirely consistent with the scientific evidence to argue that we should both lower the voting age and end the practice of trying juveniles as adults.

All that said, focusing on the age at which the average young person is indistinguishable from the average adult in terms of voting competency doesn't actually make much sense, given that we don't hold adults to this standard. Many existing voters have below average intelligence and compromised cognitive functioning. Many others are ill-informed or irrational, swayed to cast their ballot in favor of the taller candidate, the candidate appearing first on the ballot, the candidate with the snappier nickname. One in three American adults can't name a single right guaranteed by the First Amendment. Just one in four can correctly identify the three branches of government.

Indeed, in deciding when a child is competent to vote, it's more pertinent to ask when an adult is deemed incompetent. To remain enfranchised, the bar is very low: if you have some idea of what voting is and how it works, you are generally free to proceed behind the curtain. In other words, we are utterly inconsistent. A ninety-five-year-old is presumed competent and, before his right to vote can be denied, in much of the country, he is entitled to an individualized assessment focused narrowly on voting, not on general cognitive capacity. He may struggle to control his impulses or be unable to dress himself properly but still be deemed qualified to vote. By contrast, the smartest, most responsible, most knowledgeable seventeen-year-old in the country is lumped in with every other person under eighteen and barred from the franchise based solely on her status as a minor, with no opportunity to prove her competence.

But, still, you say, even if many of those under eighteen are "smart" enough to vote, they still lack valuable "life experience," right? Well, test it out.

Do fifteen-year-olds really possess less personal knowledge about the major issues facing our nation: Whether it is acceptable for society to discriminate against transgender people? How we should regulate social media? Whether we should build a border wall or welcome migrants from Central America? Whether racial bias in policing needs to be addressed? How we ought to balance Second Amendment rights with ensuring a safe and comfortable learning environment for students?

My father-in-law is eighty. He doesn't know anyone who is transgender, nor does he have any close friends who are gay, Black, or Hispanic. He hasn't been inside a high school in two decades. My grandmother is ninety-seven. She types me wonderful letters on a typewriter and has only ever had a landline.

Contrast their experiences with the teens and preteens I talked to writing this book. Gen Z is the most diverse generation in American history. Ninety-four percent of children between thirteen and seventeen use social media and virtually all of them own or have access to a smartphone. So, when the FCC moved to repeal net neutrality rules that prevented service providers from slowing or blocking access to certain websites, it was middle and high schoolers who were among the most vocal critics, organizing protests, writing letters, and participating in campaigns to pressure the FCC commissioners.

Maria, a high school sophomore from Palo Alto, California, put it well: "People don't realize how capable and smart people my age are. They think we're still little children who don't understand politics, or any issues, like gun control." But Maria knows what a lockdown feels like at a public high school—what it's like to "make a barricade and hide behind it and wait for the police, sitting there in silence when you don't know what's happening." They'd practiced the drills and then one day it was real. "You're not supposed to text, [you're meant] to stay off the phone lines, but everyone was on the phone with their parents and friends to say goodbye."

Listen to young people and you begin to realize how much we underestimate them. When I asked Andre, an eleven-year-old sixth grader from Philadelphia, what the age limit on voting should be, he suggested "thirteen, even ten. I've had political opinions for a while." And while he acknowledged that he might be unusual, he explained that his friends are both knowledgeable and competent. Speaking with him for an hour, as he offered up insights on conservative policies, Sixth Amendment rights, and the juvenile justice system, I found it hard to disagree.

All of this calls into question the argument that young people are apathetic, so it's pointless to give them the vote. The oft-cited proof of disinterest—low election turnout in the eighteen to twenty-four age group—is worthy of note: just 51.4 percent of the youngest voters participated in the 2020 presidential election, as compared with 76 percent of those aged sixty-five to seventy-four. But it tells us less about the dispositions of younger Americans and more about the choices of the old guard that suppress the youth vote. Eighteen, for example, turns out to be a really poor moment to extend the franchise because it's a time of incredible disruption and activity, when many Americans graduate from high school, leave home, and start a new chapter at college or in the workforce. If you want more eighteen- to twenty-four-year-olds to vote, a surefire way to do that is to lower the voting age so people learn the ropes at a moment that is less chaotic, register them automatically, and make it easy to cast a ballot.

Instead, since 2020, we've let older adults push us in the opposite direction, with an array of new laws designed specifically to hinder young people from voting, by prohibiting the use of university buildings as voting sites, banning online voter registration, and barring the use of student IDs at the polls.

The architects of these tactics are right to worry. Young people vote differently from old people—and adding even younger voters to the rolls holds the potential to significantly change the direction of our country.

Young people, for example, are far more likely to be concerned about climate change and inequality. While 60 percent of U.S. adults under thirty believe in man-made climate change, just 31 percent of those over sixty-five do. Likewise, 59 percent of those between eighteen and thirty-four believe that the government should redistribute wealth through heavy taxes on the rich versus only 47 percent of those over fifty-five.

But it's not simply that young people tend to be more liberal than older people; it's also that they are more open to holding positions inconsistent with their ideology. So, if you are sixty-five and identify as a conservative Republican, you are significantly more likely to be against universal healthcare and fighting climate change than a twenty-five-year-old conservative Republican. In recent elections, this has translated into sharply divergent voter behavior based on age. There was a 26 percent gap in the 2016 presidential election between voters under thirty and those sixty-five and over. In the 2018 midterms, those young voters skewed Democrat by a 35-point margin. Consistent with all of this, the available evidence confirms that teens do not just vote the way mom and dad say, as some critics of youth enfranchisement warn. In the vote for Scottish independence in 2014, for example, researchers found that only about half of sixteen- and seventeen-year-olds were planning to vote in alignment with their parents.

Skeptics of extending the franchise tend to cast the different preferences of young people as proof of their naïveté and bias. In this view, young voters lean to the left because liberals offer handouts—reduced student loan debt, single-payer healthcare, and the like—and young people don't know any better. As Tyler, a seventeen-year-old from Kansas, put it, "I think the older generation, especially Republican politicians, they believe young people are lost, that they don't know what they're doing, that they're out of touch. . . . Essentially that means that our opinions on certain subjects aren't as legitimate." He notes how older social conservatives tend to cast young people's support for transgender rights or gun control as evidence that they have been "subverted" or "tricked into submitting to liberal pedagogy." Allowing young people to vote, then, is putting a finger on the scale.

But it's the opposite: we are currently skewing elections in favor of conservatives by excluding young voters. And the condescending stance of the critics is itself a reflection of cognitive bias. One of the major insights from psychology over the last two decades is that all of us view the world filtered through the lens of our backgrounds and identities, but we believe we see matters objectively and expect other reasonable people to share our perspective. When they don't, we tend to dismiss their beliefs as a product of some character flaw, like stupidity, selfishness, or narrowmindedness. Young people, as a group, view the issues differently from older people, not because they are unreasonable but because they are wearing different lenses— ones shaped by a different set of identities, challenges, and experiences. The motivation to exclude them from political participation isn't driven by any actual deficiencies that young people possess. It's driven by who they are. That's antidemocratic and it leaves us weaker as a country.

To make good policy, we need children's valuable perspectives and insights. On many issues, young people may encourage us to rethink long-held assumptions, reform antiquated practices, and seize opportunities.

Research shows that as people get older, they tend to become more risk averse across domains. This increased cautiousness appears to reflect a number of factors, from cognitive decline, to shifting motivations, to changed circumstances that may make potential losses more costly. Part of the reason older people reject beneficial risks may simply be that they have less capacity to properly assess them, with age-related reductions in key brain areas. Other studies have linked the natural decline in dopamine in the brain to the rise in risk aversion as people get older: when levels of the neurotransmitter decrease, people become less receptive to the prospect of big rewards that can come from risk-taking behavior.

Obviously, being cautious can be a good strategy or a bad strategy, depending on the specific context, but being too cautious too much of the time can be devastating at the societal level, and that's exactly what is likely to happen when the people with power—that is, voters—are disproportionately older.

When it comes to choosing elected leaders, researchers have shown that risk averse voters are drawn to support incumbents even when challengers are far better matched to their particular ideological preferences. And this irrational privileging of the status quo carries through to other domains, with obvious implications for policy choices: the most risk averse consumers, for example, have been shown to stick with their existing brand even when they were aware that there is a superior alternative. In an era of rapid change, staying the course is often not the safest option.

The costs of ignoring young people's input is not just a story of risk perceptions, it's also that by having far shorter time horizons than younger people, older voters may lead us to underinvest in the future. Andre was quick to highlight the connection between students' disenfranchisement and the poor state of Philadelphia schools: "Since kids don't have a voting right, schools don't get that much funding. In our school, in the boys' bathroom, we have two faucets with spray painting on the walls 'do not drink from sinks,' . . . and the bottom part of the window is broken so you can see directly in." As he points out, his is "one of the nicer schools in Philly, some schools have rats, peeling [lead] paint." "Why do we have to have thirty-three kids to a class without air-conditioning and . . . textbooks from 2003?" It's a rhetorical question.

If children like Andre could vote, public education and so much else would be different. It's not a daydream. The seeds of change are already planted. Today, a sixteen-year-old can vote in a growing number of countries, including Argentina, Austria, Brazil, Cuba, Ecuador, and Nicaragua. And, as predicted, voter turnout of those under eighteen is generally higher than older age groups in these countries. When Scotland lowered the franchise to sixteen for people to vote in a referendum on Scottish independence, a staggering 80 percent of eligible young people under eighteen signed up.

As Tommy Raskin, a high school student in Takoma Park, Maryland, explained as his city became the first in the United States to allow people over fifteen years old to vote in local elections in 2013, "We cultivate interest in democracy by giving people opportunities to participate." Four other municipalities in the state have since followed suit. And a similar measure in San Francisco would have passed in 2020 with a swing of just four thousand votes. Today, the march continues, with other localities considering expanding the franchise and a growing number of states permitting seventeen-year-olds to vote in primary elections.

At the federal level, Representative Ayanna Pressley of Massachusetts has been urging her colleagues to think about reform at the national level, not out of some sense of charity but because it is what young people are due: "They have earned their right at the table." In March 2021, 125 members of the U.S. House of Representatives voted in favor of a measure to lower the voting age to sixteen in all congressional and presidential elections.

This recent progress suggests that a gradual lowering of the voting age is the most realistic avenue to extending the franchise in America. States and localities are generally free to drop the minimum age, and there is a history of localities acting as a catalyst to the eventual state and national expansion of voting rights—including eliminating property requirements and extending the franchise to women. In the near future, we'd expect to see larger progressive cities welcoming sixteen- and seventeen-year-olds to the polls, followed by an opening of state elections and finally federal ones. That process might, then, be repeated with fourteen- and fifteen-year-olds and so on, as the benefits of greater participation became clear and the imagined carnage failed to materialize. That would bring meaningful change over a period of time, but there are alternatives worth considering.

We could embrace the ideal of "one person, one vote" and fully enfranchise every citizen, regardless of age. For very young children, we could charge other people with casting the ballot until the child was able to take over, requiring the proxy to act in the child's best interests and consult with the child, once that was possible. Over the last century, a number of countries—including France, Germany, Japan, and Hungary—have considered, and even voted on, that basic model. It has an intuitive logic. As Andre pointed out in our conversation: "A family of five should get five total votes; a family of five should not get two votes, the same as an eighty-year-old retired couple."

The proposal introduced in Germany in 2008 would have allowed all children a vote from birth but would have granted control to parents until they determined that the child was competent. Others have suggested it would be better to leave it to the child herself to determine when she is ready—competency being demonstrated by the very act of registering—although the most straightforward approach would be to simply set a default age—say, twelve—of transferring formal control to the child. One of the most significant criticisms of a proxy system is that parents are likely to vote their own interests in the early years of their child's life. But even if that were true, it would surely be more just than the status quo, given the close alignment of many interests between parent and child during this period.

A related idea is to draw from the general principles of disability law and consider how we might make reasonable accommodations to permit even very young children to vote knowledgeably and intelligently. The Americans with Disabilities Act and related legislation already requires states to provide reasonable accommodations to allow people with cognitive disabilities an equal opportunity to vote, including having someone explain the ballot instructions in more basic terms at the polls, read out the contents, and assist the person with filling out an absentee ballot. We could consider similar adjustments for children, from simply offering special help and explanation, to developing special child ballots, to having each candidate for office prepare age-appropriate materials describing their beliefs, background, and ideas. We take a similar approach with kids in numerous other contexts, allowing them to have autonomy but simplifying and explaining things to help them make a decision. When I go to a restaurant with my four-year-old, for example, I read him the menu, explain words he doesn't know ("fettuccine is like a thicker spaghetti"), describe what certain dishes are likely to taste like ("that is going to be very similar to the rotolo you get at Pizzeria Vetri"), and then I let him choose.

If such accommodations were too ambitious in the current political climate, we might consider granting young people partial suffrage, either limiting them to issues of particular relevance—as Oakland did, in opening school board elections to sixteen-year-olds in 2020—or weighting children's votes based on age. California legislators introduced a bill along these lines in 2004 that would have granted fourteen- and fifteen-year-olds a quarter vote and sixteen- and seventeen-year-olds a half vote. It was approved by two committees before eventually losing steam. One of the most appealing aspects of the idea is that it acknowledges that competency isn't an on-off switch. Young people's public voice would grow in stature as they matured.

To some, these proposals might seem to upset the cart, but the cart has never been set right. We have never been a functioning democracy with a government of, by, and for *all the people*. Extending the franchise to everyone is part of ensuring our ideals, but we ought not stop there.

Wylie was firm: "Young people should be allowed to vote," and, he quickly followed up, they should also be allowed to "run for office." Sure, some will be impulsive or naïve, but as Wylie points out, "that's also going to be true of adults." "If your system fails when more people get involved, maybe it's not the people that are the problem."

We have blindly accepted rule by the old. But is it really optimal for the average age of a member of the House of Representatives to be 57.6 and the average age for a member of the Senate to be 62.9—roughly two decades older than the median American? Are we well served by seniority systems that give the most power—plum committee assignments, leadership positions, and the like—to the very oldest members of the legislature? Has it benefited our country that the average age of a U.S. president has been fifty-five, despite the fact that the average life span in the country didn't hit forty-nine until 1900?

In 2018, we got a glimpse of what might happen if we opened things up because some enterprising high schoolers in Kansas noticed a hole in state law: there was no age restriction on running for governor. So, six teens decided to enter the race.

To some, it was a sign of America's political collapse. As Monica Hesse summed up in *The Washington Post,* the reaction of many on-lookers was dismay: "the candidates we deserved"—"a passel of hor-monal teenagers . . . clog[ging] the ballot," "reflect[ing] the morass of the country." Legislation was quickly introduced to close up the "loophole" that had allowed them to run in the first place. And the Republican Party of Kansas took the unprecedented step of creating a new rule that required candidates to have voted in the 2014 guber-natorial election to participate in the Republican debates.

But the young candidates did not turn out to be embarrassments: in interviews and the events open to them, they often came off just like their adult counterparts, or better. They had good ideas to re-form Kansas. Democrat Jack Bergeson's core platform included raising the minimum wage, supporting the "Medicaid Buy-In" passed by the Nevada legislature, demilitarizing the police, increas-ing teacher pay (with a focus on struggling schools, partially funded with a legalization and taxation of marijuana), subsidization of rural broadband, and the reinstitution of a more progressive income tax.

In conversation with Republican Tyler Ruzich, seventeen, I couldn't help but compare him to the outgoing Republican governor Sam Brownback, whose signature achievement—a dramatic reduc-tion in state income taxes—had stalled the economy and decimated popular government services, before it was repealed by the Kansas legislature. Brownback had gambled with the welfare of his con-stituents and lost: 66 percent of Kansans now disapproved of his leadership. By contrast, Tyler seemed to have no interest in blow-up-the-system gambits. His approach seemed measured and practi-cal. He was informed about the issues, charismatic, and genuine. He wasn't devoid of relevant experience; he was just young. He bal-anced school, family responsibilities, and service, with a job at the local supermarket. And he'd seen things the adult slate of candidates had not, like what Brownback's "Kansas Experiment" budget cuts did to his public school.

In line with the psychological research suggesting that young people tend to be less doctrinaire than their older counterparts, Tyler appeared to draw from his conscience and his experiences, without caring much about party orthodoxy. As Tyler put it, "My loyalty lies in the common good." And that characteristic openness and independence of adolescence may, ironically, make teenage politicians less vulnerable to manipulation than those who have been stewing in the political pot for decades. Tyler admitted that his youth made it easier to break party ranks: "I don't really have any other interests to serve other than my own views and those of my supporters." When Tyler appeared on the news show *Matter of Fact with Soledad O'Brien* shortly after the Parkland school shooting, he told O'Brien that he favored gun control measures. When she pressed him, noting that that was not the standard Republican position, he replied: "If I'm making an enemy of the NRA, that's something I'm kind of proud of, to be honest. I've seen what gun violence does. It's time that we change the rhetoric and the discussion. Because clearly we are too far gone to say it's a mental illness problem." What would possibly lead him to say that? Simple: it's what he believed; he was being honest.

We need to stop pretending that no young people possess the disposition or talents to lead us. And we need to expose the hypocrisy of those who decry "ageism" when someone suggests that Joe Biden is too old to run for president but are utterly silent as every American under the age of thirty-five is formally barred from seeking the presidency. Perhaps then we might accept that there isn't an "optimal age" for a politician and that our focus should instead be on ensuring age diversity. In this light, it's not that there shouldn't be any eighty-year-old representatives; it's that there should also be some teenage ones. John Adams had it right: our representative assembly "should be in miniature, an exact portrait of the people at large. It should think, feel, reason, and act like them." The problem is that the minimum age rules he and the founders wrote into the Constitution made that empty rhetoric.

In the push for inclusion, the judicial branch should not be overlooked. Here, too, children often struggle to have a say, even when establishing their own beliefs, preferences, and experiences is the order of the day. In child custody disputes, judges routinely bypass listening to kids in favor of hearing from their parents: "Tell me how Bobby appears to you when he comes home from being with his father"; "How has Laura reacted to the divorce?"; "Why is it best for Lucas to spend more time with his mom?" In one multistate survey, family court judges reported asking children about their wishes related to custody only about half the time. In another study, only 6 percent of judges thought the custody preferences of a child aged eleven to thirteen ought to be the presumptive arrangement—and less than half thought that about a child aged fourteen to seventeen. As we touched on in chapter 3, in most states, there is no need for an eleven-year-old to consent to her own adoption—and in Vermont, Louisiana, and Wisconsin, it's not required for anyone under eighteen.

The justifications—that kids aren't capable of reflection or foresight, and that participation harms them—are confounded by the psychological evidence. Even young children have valuable insights about their family relationships and legitimate preferences about who takes care of them. And they want to have a voice in what happens. It is painful and frustrating to be excluded and silenced from a critical decision in your life. Allowing children to participate enhances their ability to cope with adversity, boosts their self-esteem, and, with the help of their observations and perspectives, leads to better decisions about care and custody.

This is largely what drove Article 12 of the United Nations Convention on the Rights of the Child, which states that a child shall "be provided the opportunity to be heard in any judicial . . . proceedings affecting the child." That ought to be the norm in the United States—not simply in family law, but in all matters. And we would do well to heed the guidance of the Committee on the Rights of the Child that the child's capacity to express her views and to participate should be presumed.

In part, that means removing impediments that block young people who attempt to use the law to pursue their interests and secure their rights. A minor—standing on their own two feet—should be able to write a valid will, file an antidiscrimination suit, or get a protective order against someone who threatens them. But, as seventeen-year-old M.D. learned when she tried to get a restraining order against her cousin, that isn't the case in many jurisdictions today. It wasn't that the New Jersey judges didn't believe that her cousin had brutally beaten her up—after all, she'd been taken to the hospital in an ambulance and criminal charges had been filed against him—or that he had then stalked her and made terroristic threats to get her to drop the case. M.D. simply did not have any standing to gain relief: she was under eighteen and none of the limited exceptions—like being married—applied. In New Jersey, that fundamental lack of status means that even your mom can't go to court on your behalf to get the order.

We must also make it easier for young people to sue the government for inaction on issues that affect them collectively. The legal system is designed to keep minors out and deny them relief—and, even when judges agree that kids' interests are being harmed, they will rarely intervene to address that injury if it requires any sort of novel approach.

When eleven-year-old Sahara and twenty other young people sued the U.S. government alleging that the failure to combat climate change was a violation of their fundamental rights under the Constitution, a federal appeals court explained that they did not have the necessary legal standing. Sure, they'd "made a compelling case that action is needed." Sahara herself had described how the smoke from forest fires near her home in Eugene, Oregon, triggers severe asthma attacks, causing her throat to close up, how her family's water supply is likely to be impacted by reduced snow melt, and how she fears that her own children and grandchildren won't be able to enjoy the best things in her life: camping, mushroom foraging, trips to the Mohawk River. The efforts Sahara makes to reduce carbon dioxide emissions—biking rather than driving, gardening and recycling, practicing vegetarianism—will not make any difference if the government does not chart a new course. But, according to the court, Sahara and her cohort's "case must be made to the political branches," not the courts. In other words, Sahara, you just need to vote!

A few recent victories by youth climate activists in other countries suggest that the tide could turn. In 2021, for example, an Australian federal court declared, for the first time, that the government had a duty of care to protect young people from future harm from climate change. But that ruling was reversed less than a year later on appeal. And ensuring the full and effective voice of children as litigants will always be limited if we do not also commit ourselves to including young people as legal decision makers. Just like the rest of us, judges view the law through lenses tinted by their backgrounds and experiences. And if the people reading the legal tea leaves are all old, the fundamental rights of children will rarely be recognized.

The last ten justices to leave the Supreme Court served until age eighty, on average, and more than half of all U.S. circuit court judges are sixty-five or older. Even staunch liberals—focused on bringing long-neglected perspectives to the judiciary—have a blind spot here. In a recent speech at the Brookings Institution, former attorney general Eric Holder declared that "a diverse bench is a better bench" and that "there is no reason that in 2021 we should have a federal judiciary that does not reflect the diversity of the American people," just seconds after he'd proposed "adding a minimum age requirement of fifty" for federal courts.

Instead of dismissing, out of hand, the idea of a seventeen-year-old judge, we should consider how we might remake the judiciary to involve young people. Could we rely more on panels, with younger judges called upon for their moral intuitions and older judges handling issues of procedure and legal nuance? Might we bring younger judges in on matters where young people's interests were particularly implicated?

At the very least, we ought to commit today to allowing those under eighteen to serve as jurors. In 1975, the Supreme Court explained that "[r]estricting jury service to only special groups or excluding identifiable segments playing major roles in the community cannot be squared with the constitutional concept of jury trial." To apply the court's language: children and adults "are not fungible; a community made up exclusively of one is different from a community composed of both." Even among adults, age matters: in mock juror studies, younger people are more likely than older people to convict a defendant in an acquittance rape scenario, regardless of how the law of sexual assault is written, and more likely to view a police chase as worth the risk it imposed on the public. Any exclusion based on age biases our legal outcomes. But the benefits of inclusion are much broader than that.

The cops had gone easy on Mary. Her headlights had been off when she'd passed them—and she was speeding. When they walked up alongside, they could see the text messages glowing in her lap. Still, they only wrote her up for the two young passengers: at sixteen, her license didn't allow for that. In court, though, the advocates Rio and Greg were pushing hard for a more significant sentence: "We must not turn a blind eye to the danger Mary put the community in." Mary's advocate, Claire, elected not to fight the facts—"Mary is here today because she understands her error and wishes to make it right"—but asked for just a third of the recommended community service hours. It was now left to the citizens of King County, Washington, seated in a circle. What if Mary had killed someone, or herself? Her errors seemed benign, but they carried unrealized menace. Was a fine a better means of deterrence? Was her remorse genuine? In the end, they dismissed the ticket, conditional on Mary completing thirty hours of community service and writing a "250-word essay on what she learned about the importance of restrictions on teen driver's licenses." What was astonishing was not that Mary calmly accepted the terms as just—acknowledging that they would make her "more aware of the harm [she] can cause while driving, and [encourage her] to be more careful"—but that the entire process was managed by teens.

Today, the Redmond Youth Court is one of over fourteen hundred youth courts, many of which employ teenagers as judges, jurors, and advocates on juvenile cases diverted from the criminal justice system. The most ingenious aspect of the model is that it marshals one of the key influences on youth law breaking—peers—to promote positive outcomes. As we have discussed, adolescents are particularly attuned to the judgments of other teens and so having young people as the legal decision makers can yield great benefits both in terms of increasing the apparent legitimacy of the legal process and reducing reoffending.

The other notable innovation is that youth courts commonly require those who appear first as defendants to return as jurors, lawyers, or judges. Part of Mary's sentence was to serve on another teen's case. And that experience is linked to improved attitude, behavior, and achievement. Indeed, those who go through the D.C. Youth Court have a higher graduation rate and college enrollment rate than the general youth population in the city.

Exercising real authority may inspire young people to dream of a different future for themselves. At the Newark Youth Court, sixteen-year-old Amanda has realized that she'd like to become a detective; eighteen-year-old Omar now plans to become an immigration lawyer; and sixteen-year-old Mary wants to go into family law. As Tyree, a former member, explains, "I would definitely credit Newark Youth Court for being part of my decision to get into the public service." Power is empowering.

Recognizing the value of youth leadership in government raises the prospect of similar reform in business, academia, and other fields. When important decisions are being made, young people should have a seat at the table. Medical ethics boards deciding whether terminally ill teenagers should be permitted to choose assisted suicide should have teenagers as fully participating and voting members. The rotating group charged with rating films for the Motion Picture Association of America should not be made up solely of parents; it should include children as well. And so should the boards of the country's major newspapers, our significant cultural institutions, and our Fortune 500 companies.

In 2021, the average age of an S&P 500 director was 63.1—and only 6 percent of directors were under 51. That ought to concern shareholders—and all the rest of us. Research shows that among top-level business executives, the most risk averse tend to be the oldest firm members—and that cautiousness can be crippling not just to businesses but to the overall economy. Indeed, economists have theorized that the hoarding of cash and securities by companies during and following the Great Recession—rather than investing in innovation and production capacity—was partially driven by the aging of corporate leadership. That ended up significantly reducing financial gains, harming job creation, and delaying recovery.

Young people can help us to make better decisions, better businesses, and better products. They can help us be fairer and more just. But they need our help—not simply in allowing them to have a voice but in readying them to use it.

When students in Rhode Island sued the state for failing to provide "an education that is adequate to prepare them to function productively as civic participants capable of voting [and] serving on a jury," U.S. District Court Judge William Smith called it "a cry for help from a generation of young people who are destined to inherit a country which we—the generation currently in charge—are not stewarding well." But he denied them relief: while American democracy may be "in peril," there is no constitutional right to a civics education, he explained.

Yet, there is nothing stopping states and municipalities from taking the initiative. It's time to make civics a core part of the curriculum: while nine states and D.C. require a full year of course work, eleven states have no requirement and the remainder require just half a year. Prompted by the lawsuit, Rhode Island passed a law in 2021 requiring students to be taught civics. But it's a single course between eighth and twelfth grade. As Precious Lopez, codirector of the Providence Student Union, questioned, "We have to take math and English for twelve years . . . Why not civics education?"

Elementary students should be learning about how our courts work. They should be having discussions about how much we should help people living in other countries, whether there should be universal healthcare, and how to balance values of privacy and security. Social studies should not entail memorizing state capitals and getting marked down for misspelling Montpelier.

In certain districts, there are already promising initiatives under way to promote civic engagement. New York's Mamaroneck High School, for example, recently began offering Organic Civic Research and Action, a four-year program that gets students involved on meaningful reform in their town of Mamaroneck. And at Palo Alto High School in California, a cohort of students are now enrolled in the "Social Justice Pathway," a three-year program centered on self-directed, community-based projects engaging important societal issues.

In 2017, I was invited to talk to the group about bias in our criminal justice system. At first, I considered watering down the critique I offered to judges, lawyers, and other adults. But the more I thought about it, the more I realized that I owed these students the full map of our legal landscape. It was high schoolers, not the existing legal establishment, who had the best chance of charting a new course. When I finally spoke to the students that Tuesday morning, the only thing to distinguish the audience from any other were the backpacks: they were just as engaged, they asked just as smart questions. We should not underestimate what our kids—even young kids—are capable of understanding and caring about, or how soon they will be the ones in charge.

At my public elementary school, we had a special unit on the Holocaust in fourth grade. It affected me greatly. We'd already learned about the Revolutionary War and I'd even been to Bull Run on a field trip. I knew about the Nazis and World War II. But I'd never allowed the past to penetrate to my present. I stopped at Hitler's mustache, the goosesteps, the salute. I did not link the dead of history with my own mortality. And, then, I was suddenly thinking about that very connection and appreciating, for the first time, the true destructive capacity of humans. I was upset by it, no doubt. But I don't regret being exposed to that material. Indeed, what strikes me as a wrong now is to give children that knowledge without giving them the training and power to ensure that it does not happen again.

We often think we are protecting young people by steering them away from our adult conversations. But it's worth asking who we are actually protecting: them or us? Adults regularly disparage young people as "snowflakes," writing them off as the "trigger warning" generation, but, often, it's school administrators and parents who better fit the description.

A few weeks after graduation, Christina told me about two stories that had been quashed while she was editor in chief of her Ohio public school newspaper. In the first instance, Christina was working on a piece on hate crimes and decided to investigate the local white supremacist movement. She contacted the Ku Klux Klan and ended up interviewing a member of the group. It was what a "real" journalist would do, but her adviser was horrified and the interview was cut.

In the second instance, Christina's team decided to put together a visual story—in the form of a comic—depicting how easy it is for underage people to buy guns. They focused on the local firearm convention in their town. As Christina explains, "We went to the convention. . . . They just let us right in. One of the journalists I work with almost got a gun until he said, 'I'm actually sixteen.' They didn't ID us. One of us actually bought ammo, but he decided to return it." The student reporters had been cautious and professional about the whole investigation—getting parental consents, talking to their adviser and a lawyer, lining up an artist—but when the result turned out to be the kind of hard-hitting feature you'd see in a "real" newspaper, the adults suddenly got scared. On the day of Christina's graduation, the piece fell apart. Their adviser reached out "to another lawyer and he said it was too much of a story to be published for our demographic and town."

It's an understandable response. It's frightening to learn about young teens' easy access to firearms. It's upsetting to think about seventeen-year-old Christina, the daughter of Asian immigrants, reaching out to the KKK in her own Ohio town. The truth is that these young journalists were at risk. And the adults were probably right that the stories would prompt complaints and even threats.

But we do not protect Christina and her cohort by telling student journalists that some topics are too "adult"—that the paper should stick to movie reviews and coverage of the school sports teams. The white supremacist presence in Christina's community is real. Anti-Asian hate crimes are real and on the rise. Underage guns sales are real and endanger us all. Christina had her eyes wide open: "It is my job as a journalist to be the messenger to society and talk about what people don't talk about because it's uncomfortable." Like Wylie, like the Parkland kids and Black Lives Matter protesters, and like Mary

Beth Tinker, Christina knew that standing up for something important is never costless.

Rather than silencing young journalists, schools need to use their resources to amplify the voices of young people who have the courage to tell us the difficult truth. The proper role of administrators and advisers and all of us adults is to push back against those who attack young people for delving into controversial topics and speaking their minds.

Christina's experience is not an anomaly. If anything, there has been a recent increase in school censorship, not only of student journalists but also of drama clubs performing plays with "adult themes" and valedictorians using their graduation speeches to talk about suicide, coming out, and sexual assault. The legal ground has shifted, allowing more and more student expression to be swallowed up along our cultural rifts.

In the middle of the twentieth century—thanks to children like Mary Beth—there was a set of major judicial decisions affirming that students have important constitutional rights that do not end, in the words of the Supreme Court in *Tinker v. Des Moines,* "at the schoolhouse gate." But in recent years, the majority has changed its mind, eroding the autonomy of students and allowing school administrators to muzzle young people in a whole range of contexts. Neo-Nazi men may freely display swastika flags as they march down our streets in front of Jewish children, but a high school student who unfurls a nonsensical banner reading "Bong Hits 4 Jesus" on a public sidewalk, during a school-sanctioned event, can be suspended. The president may not prevent adult editors from publishing top-secret documents related to our nation's war efforts, but a principal can delete articles on student pregnancy and the impact of divorce from the school paper. In 2021, when the Supreme Court declared that a Pennsylvania high school had overstepped in suspending a cheerleader for posting "Fuck school fuck softball fuck cheer fuck everything" on Snapchat, it was the first student free speech victory in the Supreme Court since 1969. But the opinion was tightly constrained, and it shows just how bold schools have become: the ninth grader was in a convenience store parking lot on a weekend. According to the court, that meant she fell "within the zone of parental, rather than school-related, responsibility."

Censors have gotten the permissive message on in-school muzzling and—cutting and pasting the Supreme Court's neutral catchalls—commonly bar student journalism, school plays, and speeches that are "poorly written, inadequately researched, biased or prejudiced, vulgar or profane, or unsuitable for immature audiences." Who gets to decide what is "inconsistent with the shared values of a civilized social order"? Adults, of course.

But why should that be? Young people should get a say in what is profane and uncivilized. They should get a say on whether a school continues to administer corporal punishment. And they should get a say on the curriculum they are taught.

When I asked Maria, a sophomore at Palo Alto High School, what she'd change if she were suddenly granted more of a voice in the direction of the school, she said she wouldn't amend any rules. She would focus on what is taught: "A lot of what we learn about is very white-washed and a lot of it is about straight white men. So, if I had more control over that, I would include more stories of women making a change, and people of color."

If "America's public schools are the nurseries of democracy," as Justice Stephen Breyer put it, truly democratic schools ought to be our aspiration. Giving students power over their education might seem like a hugely risky proposition. But it's shown great promise in the schools that have tried it. At the Sudbury Valley School in Massachusetts, all matters—from staffing to school rules—are resolved through the participation and equal vote of the members of the school community, regardless of age. At the Brooklyn Free School, students enjoy a similar "one person, one vote" right, and even the youngest students are put in charge of their own education.

Extending age-appropriate power makes sense for our schools and it also makes sense for our families. The psychological research is clear that listening to children's perspectives and allowing them to participate in decision-making aids in their development, in terms of their self-esteem, social skills, and cognitive abilities. And that fits with the many studies on the benefits of authoritative parenting, focused on extending more and more autonomy to young people as they get older. Authoritative parents respect their kids' voices, ideas, and beliefs and understand that the right to be wrong is part of what all humans deserve.

It was telling how many of the amazing young people I spoke to in writing this book referenced parents who listened to them and trusted their decisions. As Mary Beth Tinker explained, "My story is really a family story because our actions had so much to do with the way we were raised." Her parents involved their children in conversations about what was going on in their neighborhood and the world. They didn't hide the evils of racism—"like the swimming pool in our small town in Iowa that wouldn't let Black kids swim." They pointed it out, they spoke against it. Mary Beth's father, a Methodist preacher, lost his church because of that. As she remembers, both of her parents emphasized the importance of being aware of "what was going on" and taking action—not fiddling while "Rome burned." Her father "always said if you don't follow your conscience, we could have the Nazis." As Mary Beth recalls, she and her brother used that later: "That's how we won our dad over to support us during the arm band action because, at first, he wasn't in favor of what we were doing because he said the school board and the principal have a job to do, but we said, 'Dad, you always told us to follow our conscience!'" And there's a lesson there, too: you should have your kids' back when they speak, even when you don't agree with what they say. That doesn't mean silencing your own opinion or not challenging ideas you think are misguided. It means respecting their right to be their own person.

In my own life, I try hard to give my kids power in our family, but I'm a work in progress. I may be good at asking about their preferences, considering their arguments, and sharing authority, but, then, there I am pointing out, too strongly, when something turns out poorly, that I'd advised against it. I find myself offering too much explanation, too much lobbying, and failing to appreciate how that may, in itself, disrespect their autonomy. But I know I don't have to be perfect, just committed and diligent. And I also know, already, that this will never be a one-way street.

When you listen to your kids, you change, too. Wylie made that point to me, near the end of our conversation, when he considered his own dad. Wylie's protest had affected his father: "Before the whole Parkland thing he was much more pro-gun than he was afterwards." Every day, Wylie said, "I'm slowly pushing him left and left."

CHAPTER 6

ON THE CUSP OF ADULTHOOD

The Right to Start Fresh

"I was an emancipated juvenile when I was sixteen," Chris explains. He'd found his way to freedom. No longer under the thumb of his parents, he could make his own decisions—about his body, his health, his education, his future. "So, ten days after my seventeenth birthday, I walked into a recruiter's office—I was a senior in high school—and I said, 'I want to join the army.'"

As Chris explains, "I always knew I was gonna do it. I was just going to prove I was as tough as the rest of the guys in the family who came before me." "I'm ninth generation that have served. I'm part of the warrior class and I firmly believe there's a warrior class. You don't have to recruit those kids. They all want to be in the military at some point."

Chris's friend Tyler nods along, "There's a degree to which we"—combat arms guys—"are sort of programmed this way." There's a certain personality—the "sort of macho, athlete, tough guy" looking to measure himself up—that's drawn to the flame. But family history is "its own recruiting tool": "If you grow up in that lifestyle, and you're constantly moving around, and everybody that you know is connected to it, and prestige in life is very much tied up into that hierarchy, I mean, you're on the track already."

"I was, you know, sixteen, seventeen, eighteen years old; it was like I knew that I wanted to be a soldier of some kind." There was no sleight of hand necessary: "I was joining up in 2007. It's the height of the Iraq War . . . I was fully expecting to go to combat." Tyler wanted infantry and got armor, his second choice—tanks, reconnaissance. It didn't matter that combat arms takes most of the casualties. It didn't matter that he didn't believe in the mission. "Truth be told, I didn't think we should go into Iraq at the time it was happening. Even as I'm enlisting, I'm like, I think it's a mistake that we're there, the way we are there."

He wanted to fight in spite of all of that and now he wonders if he really had a choice. "As uncomfortable as it may be to our notions of free will," the military knows who it is "going to draw from for those combat arms slots." It knows the soldiers bred to run into the bullets, who will volunteer the moment you say they can.

And the military knows the other recruits that need a push or pull. To get someone who didn't grow up dreaming of being "a sergeant major," Chris points out, recruiters have to offer a pitch: "They tell them we're going to train you to do something. We're going to give you a job or going to give you money for college." They don't show up in the gym parking lot with mock M-16 rifles for those kids to check out. "They come in with, like, tech shit for them. They come in and say, 'Hey, we'll teach you to work on jet engines, and when you get out, you can go work for Boeing.'" As Tyler puts it, "They're selling anything *but* combat."

Whatever the tactic or grift, long game or short, the primary target is unambiguous: high schoolers. Recruiters go into schools to set up their tables, to coach teams, to chaperone events. The Pentagon partners with movie studios and the NFL, Black Hawks land on baseball fields, ninth graders are let out of math class to try their hand targeting enemy positions with Abrams tank simulators. Marketing campaigns appeal to youth by design.

In 2021, the army launched an animated film series showing cartoon children discovering their "calling" to the military. "This is the story of the soldier who operates this nation's Patriot Defense Systems. It begins in California with a little girl raised by two moms." Emma, with a blue ribboned ponytail to match her eyes, stands on a pier at sunset, chest-high against her beaming parents. "Although I had a fairly typical childhood, took ballet, played violin, I also marched for equality. I like to think I've been defending freedom from an early age."

In 2020, the navy partnered with social media influencers to embed "directly into trending YouTube content," challenging star chefs, DIYers, and others to go head-to-head with real sailors. As the marketing team explained, "By not taking over the channels, we became a part of them."

Banner ads with sign-up forms bull's-eye thirteen-year-olds playing video games on Twitch. "What is really getting us a ton of leads," Major General Frank Muth admits, "is we have a lot of recruiters doing what we call reverse cycle, so they are recruiting at night from 2200 to 0200. . . . [T]hey are going in and joining these different eSports tournaments—whether it's Call of Duty, League of Legends, Apex Legends, Fortnite, Overwatch—and you meet people and you go in there and you just start talking."

What they leave out is, in Tyler's words, "just how pervasive or suffocating the level of control" is going to be: once you sign on, "every decision about your body and your health and your life is now subject to the military." "You're in high school and you're like, oh, I'm going to get an adult job someday. Oh, it might be kind of cool to be in the army: like, I'd be like an adult, I'd get paid, but I'd go home at the end of the day and have my weekends. Well, you join up to be a cook or something and you get deployed, fucking twelve months." And you're not even cooking; they've moved you to a job you didn't sign on for: "Now you're sitting on top of a vehicle in a machine gun turret on a convoy moving fuel and food and water from one patrol base to another." "You come back for like twelve months. You get deployed again for twelve months. You come back for twelve months. You get deployed for fifteen months." Tyler shakes his head. "Oh, you have a positive PPD test"—to check for tuberculosis—"you have to take this medicine that might destroy your liver and not be able to drink for the rest of your life. And that's an order. You have no choice." "You really lose all freedom. You very much become property. That's why they call us G.I.s—government issue."

We are so inured to the idea that the young should fight and the old should lead that it can be hard to grasp the unfairness of our system. Young people, on the threshold of adulthood, sign away their future freedoms before we've let them be free. And even that decision is subject to our influence. The cost is immense. Too many young soldiers never recover from the sacrifices we demand of them; they bear the scars of war, without ever receiving the promised benefits of service.

Growing research suggests that young people may be more psychologically vulnerable to traumatic experiences than older people. In one study, men who fought in Vietnam before they turned twenty-five were almost seven times as likely to suffer from post-traumatic stress as men who were twenty-five or over. Similarly, a study of those who served in Iraq found that the younger veterans, those eighteen to twenty-four, were at a significantly greater risk for PTSD and other mental health problems than those forty and older. Although it can be challenging to separate out the effects of combat exposure—the young may be involved in more intense fighting—this data pattern fits with current theories about the negative effects of stress on the developing brain. A twenty-year-old's prefrontal cortex is more vulnerable than a forty-year-old's for the simple reason that it is still maturing. And alterations brought on by stress appear to have long-term negative consequences for learning, motivation, and cognition, and may also increase the risk of self-harm. The youngest cohort of veterans returning from combat—those aged eighteen to twenty-four—have a frighteningly high suicide rate of 124 per 100,000, more than four times the rate of soldiers in their forties.

The repercussions of combat trauma extend well beyond the young soldier himself. More than twenty-two hundred minor children lost a parent in Iraq or Afghanistan, and thousands more had a parent who returned badly wounded. One study of American children whose parent served during the height of the Iraq War found a significantly increased risk of abuse in the six months after a veteran returned home—a risk that doubled during the second deployment. And even for children who do not experience abuse or neglect, having a parent leave for weeks or months at a time can be traumatic, resulting in academic problems, depression, and lashing out. In another study, one third of kids who had a parent deployed were deemed at "high risk" for psychosocial issues.

The military's ads suggest that the experience in combat will leave young recruits better positioned to handle the challenges of adulthood, but the advantage can be illusory. The unemployment rate for male veterans aged twenty-two to twenty-four was 15 percent between 2008 and 2015. The median income in the first year after separation for a veteran with fewer than six years of service was $30,000.

Even when you land a good job, it can be hard to leave the war behind. As Tyler points out, the landscape may be entirely different when you return, but it can feel the same: join the police force and "you got all the gear that you had in Iraq and Afghanistan—all that stuff came home with you." You may be on patrol in Newark now, but you never stop feeling "like it's us against them," just like you did on surveillance in Kirkuk. "You're back in this military mentality, which is really dangerous"—particularly as one fifth of our police officers are veterans. In one recent study of Dallas police officers, those who were deployed were 2.9 times more likely to have discharged their gun while in uniform. A separate study of cops in Boston and Miami found that officers who had served in the military were disproportionately likely to have complaints about use of force filed against them. In the long term, we all are made to endure the cost of our exploitation.

This is not solely a military phenomenon.

Chris told me the story of what pushed him out of the army— "the moment where I said I will never reenlist"—and it stands as a broader metaphor: "My unit, to commemorate a battle that was fought in 1898, walked a hundred miles in a forced march over a little more than three days, carrying full rucks . . . 105 pounds on my back and I only weighed 145 pounds at the time. I got a blister on the inside of my heel at mile four and then walked the next 96 miles." When he finally took off his boot, it "ripped the skin off the side of my foot and needed thirteen stitches." "I remember this major looking down saying, 'Oh, my God . . . why did you keep walking?' " "Because it ain't a fucking democracy," Chris responded.

We deny children a voice and control over their lives, promising them that their time for freedom and independence will come. But reaching the verge of adulthood, they find themselves marching to our beat, pointed in the direction we set for them, encumbered with our baggage. When they are hobbled by the weight we place on their shoulders to lighten our own load, we act shocked. We blame them for failing to reach the major markers of adulthood—a college degree, a house, a good job, a spouse and kids, financial autonomy—when their long, lumbering adolescence is our making.

Today, the choices we make as parents and society to maximize our own liberty, wealth, and well-being in the present end up constraining the opportunities our children have as they prepare to enter adulthood. In twenty-first-century America, a country whose national identity is synonymous with the right of self-determination, many of the major life decisions a young person will make—what they will do, where and how they will live—are still largely determined by others. By placing such limits on the next generation, we place a cap on what we can achieve as a society.

Children have a right to begin their adult lives free of our burdens, liabilities, and restrictions. They have a right to start fresh. And that means eliminating practices, beliefs, and norms that inhibit our children's choices and interactions.

We can start by addressing one of the most significant ways that we constrain young people at the beginning of their adult lives: debt. Part of that is realizing that it is unethical to finance our current lifestyle and chosen pursuits with our children's dollars. In contrast to previous conflicts, which were funded through raising taxes, war bonds, and cutting nonmilitary spending, the forever wars in Afghanistan and Iraq were not paid for up front by the adults who chose to wage them. Instead, they gave themselves huge tax cuts and borrowed money, passing the debt—measured in trillions—to the generations to come. That imperils the future livelihoods of young people and our long-term health as a nation.

But combating the yoke of debt also entails rethinking a model premised on young people starting their adult life in the red. It's a catch-22: to secure future opportunities you need a college education, but to get a college education you must agree to restrict your future opportunities by joining the military, taking on debt, or both. We could have built a system that proclaimed to those embarking on adulthood, "We invest in you and benefit from your success." Instead, we offer a quid pro quo. As the navy's recruitment website puts it: "When you invest in your country, we invest in you." "The Navy can help you pay off your student loans. By enlisting in one of the following jobs, we can help pay off up to $65,000 of your Stafford, Perkins, PLUS and other Title 4 loans."

Roughly two out of three students must take on debt to go to college and, at graduation, the average student owes around $30,000. In 2022, 43.4 million people had federal student loan debt, and more than two million owed more than $100,000.

A self-finance system of education does not simply restrict young people at the back end but also at the front. Most colleges take into consideration the ability of a person to pay in the admissions process, which has the effect of making it harder for poor students to get in. When they do land a spot, students often end up choosing the institution that will leave them less in debt, even when that means giving up their dream school.

That was the situation for Christina: as she admits, "money did play a big role" in her decision-making. She wanted to go to San Diego, but the cost made it impossible. With in-state tuition, scholarships, and some grants from local organizations, Ohio State, close to mom and dad, was the realistic choice. In Christina's case, she was lucky that the affordable option was a great university, but sometimes the choice is between an expensive elite institution and a full ride at a mediocre regional school and that can present a terrible bind. Students who go to the most selective colleges end up with similar salaries, regardless of their parents' wealth, but for poor students to secure that major long-term benefit, they've got to take on a frightening (and perhaps impossible) financial burden in the short term.

Worse still, a significant number of qualified students who would ultimately come out ahead by taking on debt to go to college forgo higher education altogether. When these talented low- and middle-income students don't apply or enroll, it limits their career prospects and endangers our future as a country. By 2025, it is estimated that two thirds of positions will require credentialing beyond a high school diploma, but we won't have the graduates—a shortfall of some eleven million workers.

It's not that these students are irrational. The risk is real and the costs of trying and failing are immense. Almost a third of Americans who take out loans to pay for college don't get a degree. Five years into repayment, nearly one third of students in the United States are in default, severely delinquent, or facing other major problems paying back their loans. For-profit colleges present a particularly significant danger to young people: a whopping 44 percent of students at these schools who borrowed money were in serious loan distress. And unlike other kinds of debt, it is very hard to discharge educational loans with bankruptcy—college debt is there to drag you down for life. Even when a lender agrees to allow a person to defer payments when they fall behind, the interest keeps adding up. What are the implications for our future economy? To provide some perspective, in 2018, the percentage of student loans more than ninety days past due was higher than the percentage of delinquent mortgages during the last financial collapse.

The negative repercussions of forcing young people to take on debt prior to beginning their careers go beyond limiting their professional and financial futures. Emerging research suggests that the millstone of early indebtedness—what we require for adult success—inhibits growing up. People put off getting married. They delay purchasing a house. They wait to have kids. They live with their parents. Here is your key to adult freedom, we say, and then lock them in their childhood bedrooms.

In July 2020, 52 percent of eighteen- to twenty-nine-year-olds were living with their parents (the number was 47 percent just before the pandemic). That's greater than the percentage of young adults living with family during the Great Depression.

That hurts all of us because marriage and home ownership have long been core bulwarks of societal stability. These dynamics can also endanger the financial health of our country by reducing spending in an economy heavily driven by consumption and by overleveraging entire families. What happens when students reach their borrowing limits under the federal loan program? Parents often dip into retirement or mortgage their house. That can prove to be catastrophic when illness, a lost job, or a recession hits. Good luck moving back in with mom and dad when they're being evicted—that critical safety net is gone.

Even for young people who make enough money after college to cover their loan payments, educational debt may still derail their dreams. With interest accruing, many graduates settle for *a* job rather than the *right* job. In one recent survey, 44 percent of those who borrowed to earn a bachelor's degree reported taking an undesirable position or one outside their field of interest because of the debt they had accrued, compared with just 28 percent who graduated without owing any money.

Being in major debt certainly influenced the way I considered my options after graduation. I felt an incredible pull to work at a large law firm not because it was the job I wanted—and not because I thought it would be great training—but because it would allow me to pay off my loans faster. And I saw the same pattern with many of my friends, who came to law school planning to work for the public interest and ended up, three years later, at corporate law firms working off their debt—unhappy, but moving toward the light of financial freedom. You thought staying in school was opening doors, but in fact it was closing them. The people who designed the system fashioned it that way.

We need to work harder to ensure that all young people start off their professional lives without financial baggage, prioritizing those who are most imperiled by the current system. It is awful to think that the best means for rising out of poverty—higher education—is often the path to sinking deeper into it.

At the 2019 Morehouse College graduation, with a blue May Atlanta sky above and the four hundred seniors seated in neat lines in front of Harkness Hall, the crimson-robed commencement speaker,

Robert Smith, spoke to the need for youth economic justice: "The opportunity you access should be determined by the fierceness of your intellect, the courage in your creativity, and the grit that allows you to overcome expectations that weren't set high enough." From a man with a $7 billion fortune, it was lofty stuff—and perhaps a bit daydreamingly abstract to the graduates who would be stepping out moments later into the real world with, on average, $35,000 to $40,000 of student loan debt. But then Smith delivered his Oprah moment: "On behalf of the eight generations of my family that have been in this country, we're going to put a little fuel in your bus. This is my class, 2019. And my family is making a grant to eliminate their student loans."

As Kamal Medlock told NPR, "When he said those words . . . all of my classmates' mouths dropped. We were speechless." The faculty and administrators behind Smith rose to their feet. Chants of "MVP" broke out. The president of Morehouse, David A. Thomas, described it as a "liberation gift."

For Kamal, Smith's message to "pay this forward"—to "make sure every class has the same opportunity"—resonated deeply: "I think that's an amazing thing, because it really shows Black men taking care of other Black men."

The feel-good story went viral, as Smith must have anticipated. Big reveal billionaire pledges to address student debt have become a trend. A year earlier, former New York City mayor Michael Bloomberg gave $1.8 billion to Johns Hopkins to ensure that admissions to his alma mater would be "need blind" and Home Depot founder Ken Langone pledged $100 million to pay medical school tuition at NYU.

This giving can be life-changing for students like Kamal, who said he and his mom had about $80,000 of debt. But Daniel Edwards, in the class below, had a different take: while he was pleased for his "brothers who got economic freedom," "[i]t's a Band-Aid fix." And he has a point: "liberation gifts" to the lucky few aren't sufficient to address the magnitude of the student loan crisis. We must stop depriving so many young people of financial liberty in the first place.

The coda to the Smith donation echoes the theme. A year later, in 2020, Smith admitted to an illegal fifteen-year scheme to evade taxes using offshore accounts and paid the government $139 million to settle the case against him. That is just over four times the amount he gave to relieve the educational debt of the class of 2019.

Instead of relying on the charitable whims of a handful of billionaires, we should ensure that every wealthy American lives up to Smith's words and pays it forward in the form of taxes. In the near term, funding more modest proposals—like extending grants to low-income applicants or tuition-free community college—may be all that is politically feasible. But our ultimate goal should be free higher education for every young person. That means forgiving existing student loan debt and making a degree a cost-free entitlement, including covering living expenses that tend to hold poor students back.

In fact, there is a strong argument for also freeing young people from other debts—like medical debt, rent debt, and even consumer debt. Part of that is on moral grounds: many of the purported "victims" of financial amnesty—insurance providers, credit card companies, and the like—have a business model that is consciously built around capitalizing on the vulnerabilities of the young.

Tyler describes the exploitation of young soldiers in stark terms: "There's a whole economy that is designed to milk these young kids." "You drive around any military installation, it is like, man, the rubes are in town, let's take them for all they got. Like, you know, car dealerships, strip clubs, pawn shops, gun stores—any kind of business that would be attractive to a young, uneducated, impressionable risk-willing person. . . . They just prey upon these kids." Young enlisted servicemembers are between two and ten times more likely to be delinquent on a debt payment or have a derogatory mark appear in their credit record in the six months after they end their service as compared with the six months prior to their separation. "A lot of these kids take out big loans. . . . They can use the fact that they're in the military to get the security to get the loan for the car, but then they leave the military and they weren't saving money and now they don't have that steady income and you see it a lot: people overextend themselves." A third of all soldiers who leave the military with auto debt after having served for seven to thirty-five months become ninety days delinquent or default on their car loan within one year.

It can be hard for some of us to accept debt forgiveness because it seems to allow people to get something for nothing. But glaring in the rearview misses what is in front of us: making young people pay into adulthood for their past mistakes leaves society poorer in the future. Yes, that young soldier got to drive a pickup truck for a couple of years that he only partially paid for. But if we allow crippling interest and ruined credit to imperil his ability to secure housing, land a job, and achieve the other hallmarks of productive citizenship in the decades ahead, it can cost us hundreds of thousands of dollars in terms of lost tax revenue and additional government expenditure.

Even where our desire for financial accountability may be strongest—as with fines in the justice system—we need to be conscious of how distortional debt can be. New Jersey has shown us that meaningful reform is possible when you are guided by the data. Before the state eliminated fines for children in 2020, some people who had been given fines when they were fourteen or fifteen years old were still paying them off into their thirties. But the research was clear that these fines and fees didn't cut down on reoffending; they made things worse by imperiling the transition to a law-abiding adult life.

If we fear that leniency will promote recklessness, we need to realize how often debt problems are a result of bad luck and bad situations—not bad dispositions. For example, although millennials' higher debt load is often blamed on their poor consumer choices, researchers have shown that their preferences don't differ significantly from earlier generations'. What's different is that millennials are just in a far more precarious financial position than boomers were when they were young. They make less money. They have less wealth. They own fewer assets. And when they draw a short straw, they've got no way to recover.

Courtney's name is written in white chalk bubble letters above her bottom bunk. She has a small flat-screen television, a twin bed, and a night-light. A red towel hangs on a hook. At PodShare in Los Angeles, you can choose to pay for the day, the week, or the month. There's not much privacy, but it's clean and modern and there's a way podders spin it that doesn't feel boardinghouse bleak: communal living is an anti-loneliness antidote to modern city life. "I'm not going to be here for the rest of my life," she explains. "A year and a half ago, I was diagnosed with stage 2B colon cancer." Her health insurance didn't cover the chemo. "I was about ready to be homeless because my credit score went from like a 780 to like a 350 overnight because I just kept taking out money to"—she pauses and looks away—"keep me alive." It doesn't matter that she now has a job and a solid salary; the credit score means she still "can't get approved for an apartment."

We need to confront the fact that the reason that so many young people today are struggling economically—and can't seem to get a foothold to climb into full adulthood—is because we've chosen to advantage older Americans. We've pursued policies—like lower tax rates for stock earnings than wages—that privilege those who already have wealth over those who are setting off in search of it. We are covering the Social Security, hospital bills, and nursing home payments of boomers knowing that that means we won't be able to do the same for millennials and Gen Z. During the pandemic, the youngest adults were the most likely of any age group to have their compensation cut or lose their job. That's not a fluke; that's by design.

We restrict the professional futures of our young people for the benefit of existing workers.

In many industries, there have always been seniority rules, like last-in first-out during downsizing, that severely limit the prospects for workers who are just starting their careers. And rather than standing up for new entrants in the labor market, unions, with their strict hierarchies and older memberships, have long tended to discriminate against them. When the pandemic forced major layoffs in the hospitality sector, organized labor pushed hard for "recall and retention" ordinances in cities like Los Angeles, San Diego, and Philadelphia that forced hotels to give preference in rehiring to the most senior workers. As San Diego councilman Chris Ward explained, "This helps to ensure we're putting some of the most experienced people back on the job first."

In recent years, senior employees across a number of fields have sought to maximize their returns at the expense of new hires. Law firms, for example, have raised billable hours requirements for new associates, lengthened the years it takes to go up for partner, and greatly increased the ratio of associates to partners, all of which have led to record profits per partner. In business, interns, short-term workers, and independent contractors have replaced new full-time employees.

The privileging of seniority has been particularly devastating for young people hoping to enter academia. Universities are pumping out far more PhDs than ever before—and taking full advantage of that talent to advance research and teaching priorities—without increasing the number of tenure-track jobs. A recent study showed that half of budding academic scientists end up dropping out of the field within five years. In 1960, it took a full thirty-five years for half of the initial cohort to leave academia. It is sobering to think of the dire career prospects that face the best and brightest young people in our country. Drawn by the prospects of life as a professor, most end up stuck in temporary worker limbo—lab techs, RAs, postdocs—until they finally move on. While just a quarter of scientists in 1960 spent their whole career without a first-author publication to their name, now it is over 60 percent.

Part of the issue is that people just aren't retiring like they used to. More than ten million Americans over the age of sixty-five are still working, many for reasons other than economic necessity. That limits opportunities for entry-level employees, not simply because it reduces turnover but also because older workers generally have the highest salaries, benefit costs, and retirement plan contributions. In legal academia, for instance, a sixty-eight-year-old professor with the same teaching load and research output might cost a law school twice as much as a new hire. The entrenchment of the workforce—who are disproportionately white men—also acts as a significant damper on efforts to improve diversity. When I occasionally hear a junior white male professor or postdoc whisper his frustration at being passed over in favor of a young woman or person of color, I like to point out that his lack of employment options isn't caused by these youthful peers; it's old white male professors who are holding on to the good thing they have going for as long as they can. Between 2000 and 2010, the percentage of full-time professors older than sixty-five almost doubled.

Far from counteracting these dynamics, our legal rules reinforce them. Under federal law, it is illegal to harass or discriminate against someone based on that person's age, but only if the person is forty or older. There is no such protection for a teenager or recent college graduate: they can be called names, given inferior work to an older colleague despite being equally qualified, and denied a job or fired for the simple reason that they are young. Quips by co-workers about not yet being able to get a driver's license are okay; jokes about losing your driver's license on account of senility are out.

You might assume that this is simply a reflection of the fact that only older workers face age discrimination, but recent findings suggest that's false: it is young workers who may have the highest levels of discriminatory experiences of any age group. They are the target of damaging stereotypes related to disloyalty, immaturity, selfishness, and irresponsibility. In comparison to older workers, they are viewed as less conscientious, more emotionally unstable, and poorer performers when it comes to showing initiative and demonstrating strong organizational citizenship. And these negative perceptions of the young appear to drive poor treatment, including reduced training opportunities, lower pay, restricted autonomy, less job security, and fewer opportunities for advancement.

Far from putting those on the cusp of adulthood first—aiming to maximize their opportunities as they begin their careers—we have chosen to elevate and maintain the positions of existing adults.

Consider where people decide to settle down at the end of childhood.

Young Americans once set out for new opportunities when prospects dried up in the places they were born. But no more: geographic mobility is at the lowest level since we started tracking it in the mid-

1940s. It's not that half as many people want to move as did in 1985; it's that they can't.

Tightly regulated land use in our cities has driven up housing prices, making a move to New York, San Francisco, or Boston all but impossible for most Americans. The average rent for an apartment in Los Angeles is nearly $2,500 a month, but you'll probably need three times that when you sign the lease. The spartan pod where Courtney sleeps doesn't require a security deposit or credit check and costs her and her bunkmates $1,000 each per month—a comparative bargain. But that's still beyond what's realistic for most people starting out.

Moreover, since public benefits often don't transfer between states, a change of venue can require jumping without a safety net— too risky a proposition for many lower-income Americans, particularly those who rely on government assistance to get by. Even for those with promising job prospects, a big rise in state licensing requirements for occupations ranging from barbers to psychologists to cosmetologists has compounded the challenge of moving between states. A quarter of Americans now need a license to do their job. And jumping through the necessary hoops to get qualified in a new city can be so time-consuming and costly that people may elect to stay put, even when the long-term career opportunities favor a move.

Why these legal barriers to entry and exit have developed is hard to nail down, but they appear to reflect a systematic bias in local and state public policy that prioritizes ensuring population stability at the expense of mobility. And that may itself have a lot to do with privileging older constituents' concerns over those of the young.

Contrast the preferences of a sixty-one-year-old professional to those of a recent college graduate. The older professional already has a job, so he favors occupational licensing that keeps many younger competitors from settling in the state or, at least, delays their entry. That makes his position more secure and drives up his wages. He also likes the existing defined-benefit pension policy that requires a worker to remain in a job for years before he can access his benefits. After all, the sixty-one-year-old's rights have already vested and the policy prevents new people from coming in who would threaten the long-term funding of the program. As he already owns his own house, he supports homeowner subsidies and zoning restrictions that increase his property value, including the ban on lower-income housing. And, like many of his fellow baby boomers, he's embraced the ideal of aging in place—further reducing supply and driving up housing prices where he lives. Politically, he is more likely than his young counterpart to favor policies that maintain strong borders and that prop up dying industries and the decaying cities that host them—policies that further restrict population mobility.

Whatever the cause, in nearly every corner of the United States, state and local governments have elected to privilege the stability preferences of the older citizen over the mobility preferences of the recent graduate, limiting entry into the areas of the country with the most promise and reducing exit from the areas whose best days are long behind them.

The problem of being geographically locked in is greatly compounded for young people of color. A hundred years ago, we struck down zoning ordinances that mandated segregated housing, and fifty years ago, with the Fair Housing Act, we made racial discrimination in private real estate transactions illegal. But on the ground, how much has changed in the decades since the 1968 Kerner Commission warned that America was "moving toward two societies, one black, one white—separate and unequal"? How much more choice does a young Black man, considering where he wants to settle down, have than his father had or his grandfather had?

In 2010, the average white American lived in a neighborhood that was more than 75 percent white and the average Black American lived in a neighborhood that was 35 percent white—almost identical figures to the 1950 census. When my parents bought their 1,200-square-foot house, in a postwar middle-class cookie-cutter suburb outside Washington, D.C., in 1984, the deed contained the crossed-out words "no negroes." But there were no Black families living on the street and, thirty-nine years later, there are still none.

The conventional story—ingrained in current Supreme Court jurisprudence—is that the lingering existence of Black and white neighborhoods today reflects the private preferences of individuals, not discrimination. In such a light, attempts at further integration today amount to—in the words of Ben Carson, the secretary of Housing and Urban Development under Donald Trump—"social engineering."

But that perspective fails to acknowledge how our segregated landscape itself was engineered to be segregated—and how little we've done to remove the bulwarks we built to keep Black people from living where they want.

Over the course of the twentieth century, those intent on maintaining racialized spaces learned that they no longer needed to articulate their racism to get what they wanted. Because public housing and schools had once been segregated, the surrounding neighborhoods remained so even when the laws changed. And it turned out that localities didn't need racially reconstructive covenants if they could just ban low-income apartment buildings in a white neighborhood or rezone the outskirts of an expanding Black neighborhood from residential to commercial to halt further encroachment. The federal government repeatedly helped to subsidize such restrictions on the movement of people, through funding urban renewal projects that used new highways to blockade Black boroughs and by refusing to offer guarantees for private mortgages in integrated neighborhoods.

So what does this mean today? If you are a young Black person on the cusp of adulthood, the law may say "live anywhere," but the physical space does not. And the neighborhood where you are "most welcome," where your parents lived, where the real estate agent takes you is also the neighborhood with the poorest-performing schools, the least services, the longest commutes to the good jobs, the least property appreciation, and the most toxic waste sites. It is likely to be both the most over-policed (when it comes to being stopped and frisked) and the most under-policed (when it comes to being the victim of crime). In American cities, the wealthiest, whitest neighborhoods are, on average, five degrees cooler in the summer than the poorest, Blackest neighborhoods. Why? For decades, trees and parks have gone to the white areas of the city; Black areas have been allotted the freeways, industrial zones, and endless asphalt and concrete.

When positive change comes—when the derelict lot is turned

into a community garden, the houses get rehabbed, the local elementary lands an ambitious young principal, and hip eateries sprout in long-dead storefronts—it doesn't tend to benefit young Black residents. It pushes them out.

In a recent empirical study of Philadelphia, sociologists found that poor people moving from historically Black neighborhoods experiencing gentrification tended to move to more disadvantaged areas than where they'd been living. But residents moving from poor neighborhoods that were not historically Black tended to depart for wealthier tracts in the city and suburbs. In other words, while gentrification benefits many Philly residents, it restricts the options for poor Black people, forcing them over time to the least desirable locations in the urban environment where there is little or no gentrification. That's, in part, because Black people may have less access to credit or savings that can allow them to hold out on the gentrifying block in spite of rent or property tax increases—or afford comparable spots in a hot market. They may also get worse offers from landlords, buyers, and sellers.

For people of color, the negative consequences of our failure to heal the scars of racism in the landscape are readily apparent: by limiting where young Black people live, we inhibit their health, their economic prospects, and their educational opportunities—and those of their children. But we also constrain broader society—the ability of our cities to thrive, our nation to realize a true post-racial reality, our businesses to profit.

Many of our restrictions on youth mobility hold down our economic output and growth. Economies thrive when labor and capital share a common locus. Prevent people from going where the jobs are and you stagnate: in depressed areas of the country, employable people remain unemployed or receive lower wages; in thriving areas, employers can't hire the workers they need so they aren't as productive as they might be. In recent times, places with deep labor markets like New York, Silicon Valley, and San Francisco have been incredibly fertile for wage growth, innovation, and investment in human capital, but the gains might have been far greater if more young people had been able to move there. One study estimated that if just these three areas had reduced their land-use restrictions to spur mobility, the entirety of U.S. growth during the period of 1964 to 2009 might have been 8.9 percent higher.

Moreover, stymying the ability of young people to move around badly undermines the effective operation of the social safety net. Not only are more people likely to be unemployed when mobility is restricted, exhausting antipoverty resources, but those people also end up stuck in depressed areas that lack the tax base to fund the social programs they desperately need.

Even if there weren't great economic benefits for our country to ensuring the geographic mobility of young people starting out their lives, removing the barriers that allow people to live where they want would be the right path forward. It is immoral for older Americans who benefited greatly from mobility in their youth to now champion policies that tether the next generation to the counties of their birth. It is immoral to do nothing when the color of a person's skin still determines where they settle down, and neighborhoods remain astoundingly unequal on every measure a person might care about.

One place to start is shifting away from local control of land use, public benefits, and job licensing. Our legal forebears knew that allowing cities and states to directly restrict the movement of people could be detrimental to our union: that was a motivating force behind the so-called right-to-travel doctrine. But indirect bars on mobility can be just as damaging and it is past time for us to take national action. Lawyers, psychologists, pediatrists, hairdressers, auctioneers, interior designers, and numerous other professionals could be licensed at the national level without endangering the public. Core benefits—like healthcare—should attach to the person, not the job or jurisdiction. And localities ought to be encouraged—through federal incentives and more robust enforcement of the Fair Housing Act—to address exclusionary zoning that prevents young people from being able to move to booming job markets and that preserves segregated neighborhoods. Again, zoning laws that bar multifamily buildings, mandate minimum lot sizes, and require off-street parking hurt both young people and people of color—and especially young people of color.

One of the reasons for optimism is that "upzoning" efforts—to address racial and economic immobility—have recently begun to break through in a few states and cities. In 2018, Minneapolis got rid of its single-family home zoning and San Francisco eliminated its minimum parking requirement for new homes. In 2019, Oregon ended single-family housing zones and, in 2021, it banned cities and counties from requiring driveways and parking spaces in building applications.

We might also consider investing directly in helping those starting out to move where they want, with tax breaks or direct grants. Settling in the community where you grew up can be a great choice—to remain connected to family and friends, to inhabit a place rich with memories, to build upon a solid and known foundation—but it ought to be a choice. Embarking on adulthood, every American should have the option of pursuing dreams near or far—not just those born to parents able to cover relocation expenses. But helping people to climb over the fences we've built is never going to be as effective a strategy as tearing down the barriers we've erected.

In this chapter, I've focused on three of the most critical aspects of personal autonomy—financial independence, job choice, and mobility. By failing to ensure that young people are able to start life without debt, do what they want, and live where they desire, we imperil their transition to adulthood, our collective prospects, and our national identity. But these aren't the only axes of freedom that matter. And we also ought to consider the many other areas in which we impose our preferences upon our children and grandchildren as they cross the threshold into adulthood. We must stop ourselves from expecting our young people to follow precisely in our footsteps, to be carefully crafted reproductions, dutifully adhering to our values and traditions. Even as we work to intervene earlier and more effectively to set children on track for happier, healthier, more successful lives—a major theme of this book—we must let our future generations grow up to be their own people.

One way we can meet that larger challenge is to dedicate ourselves to giving up control on a personal and societal level as we age and eventually pass away. That can feel counterintuitive: indeed, for many people, their instinct as they approach their later years is to ensure their legacy by locking things down, casting their beliefs and desires in bronze, and cladding what they have built in stone so that it may withstand the test of time. The law reflects our thoughts as we consider our own mortality: there are numerous structures that provide for so-called dead-hand control, from "fee simple" ownership—the norm in the United States—that allows dominion over property for all time, to irrevocable trusts and wills that permit a person to specify exactly how assets will or will not be used long after she is dead.

A few blocks down the street from my house in downtown Philadelphia is one of the greatest collections of impressionist, post-impressionist, and modern art in the world. Worth more than $25 billion, it includes some 181 Renoirs, 69 Cézannes, 59 Matisses, and 46 Picassos. The art is housed in a beautiful, light-filled space that is frequently opened up to the public for educational activities and performances. On a recent Sunday, my daughter and I participated in an open modern dance class led by a French choreographer, watched a breakdancing troupe spin and slide and bend, and then made our way through the galleries on a homemade treasure hunt, finding a monkey in a Rousseau, a dog in a Gauguin, a bird in a de Chirico. I walk by the Barnes Foundation every day, but it still feels a bit like magic to have this strange, wonderful jewel in my city.

And, in fact, it was never meant to be. Albert C. Barnes made his fortune on an antiseptic silver compound used to treat gonorrhea and used his millions to create a museum for his art in Lower Merion, Pennsylvania. Barnes had a particular vision for his collection, obsessively arranging it—a Chardin washerwoman by an El Greco annunciation, Amish wrought-iron hinges interspersed with paintings—and a set plan for how the public would engage with it for the rest of eternity. As he set down in the charter and bylaws of his foundation, the works would remain in the museum in Merion on the walls exactly as he had placed them, there would be public admission just two days a week, the paintings and sculptures could not be loaned to other museums, and no colored reproductions could be made of the art. Only twelve hundred people were allowed to visit each week.

Had Barnes left sufficient funds to maintain the museum under his stipulations, our laws would have kept the collection in its strait-jacket in perpetuity. No matter that thousands more children like my daughter can now enjoy the art, no matter that the collection is now illuminated with cutting-edge lights that allow viewers to see details that were once shrouded in shadow, no matter that Barnes's desire to use art for egalitarian education is now far closer to realization. It was only pending bankruptcy that allowed the foundation to go to court to facilitate the move to downtown Philadelphia. And, though, I can say without reservation—having schlepped out to visit the old Barnes more than a decade ago—that the new home for the collection is a vast improvement, I share the concerns of critics like *The New York Times'* Roberta Smith, who wished for even more freedom from Barnes's control from the grave: that "every so often the pieces of even his most revelatory ensembles should be freed from his matrix, just as his amazing achievement has been liberated from Merion."

As we prepare to leave this world, we need to trust our trustees—the next generation. We need to give them flexibility. We need to be more modest. We need to understand that the things that seem so critical and settled—that lead grandparents to insert testamentary conditions barring their grandchildren from marrying a non-Jewish person or someone of the same sex; that lead authors to prohibit the publication of their work in any other medium decades into the future; that lead collectors to stipulate that their museum shall be closed every Sunday of the year—might not seem that way if we were able to keep on living as the world changed and changed again.

Are there circumstances where locking things down for perpetuity can actually protect the interests of young people and those yet to be born? Of course. Conservation efforts come to mind. In the Pacific Northwest, for example, the Blue Mountain Land Trust works with landowners to permanently protect fish and wildlife habitat for future generations from development and harmful natural resource extraction.

But too often our efforts to preserve our status quo create less liberty for our children and grandchildren, not more. In fact, in many ways, the law has got things exactly backward: rather than ruling out "any general authority to question the wisdom, fairness, or reasonableness of the donor's decisions about how to allocate his or her property," in the words of the influential Restatement (Third) of Property, that ought to be the starting point. We ought to care more about the interests of the living than the interests of the dead. We ought to privilege the autonomy of the generations to come over the autonomy of those departed.

PART II

A CHILD-FIRST MINDSET

CHAPTER 7

THE INVISIBLE KID

What Holds Us Back

On a summer morning a few years ago, my wife, daughter, and I were walking home through the center of Philadelphia. With the added weight of a generous breakfast burrito, I was pushing the stroller at an uncharacteristically leisurely pace—a true and appropriate stroll. There was no rush. It was a Sunday; it was warm; there were no bouncy house birthdays awaiting or music classes beckoning. But just as I came to turn north, a bike came shooting around the corner, dodging my daughter, in one of those horrible near-miss moments that leave you feeling fingernails across the chalkboard of your spine.

The rider had to take a steadying couple of hopped steps and I said, "Come on, man. No bikes on the sidewalk." I didn't swear—in large part, I'll admit, because I expected him to be contrite. He'd almost wiped out a three-year-old and was clearly in the wrong: it's against the law to ride on the sidewalk in the city and particularly reckless to do so at speed around tight corners. But, instead, regaining his balance, he turned to give me (and my daughter) the middle finger. "No strollers on the sidewalk," he yelled.

The rest of the day, I wondered: Who would do that? Was he a sociopath? Had something terrible just happened to leave him angry and distracted? Maybe, but the most reasonable explanation is that he was just an average guy on urban autopilot, rushing to get to the gym or to brunch or to meet his girlfriend. He got into one of the inevitable city tussles with strangers and did the normal thing. My daughter was invisible to him.

I look for the blindness to children now and I see it all around. I take my daughter to school, holding her scooter and her hand as we step out into the crosswalk, and watch the cars accelerate around the curve to try to make it across in front of us. Perhaps they'll shave off a few seconds from their commute, perhaps they'll arrive just a bit earlier at work, an extra minute, perhaps, to look at NFL draft projections or hear their colleague's story about her sick dog. As I walk by a loft rehab, a construction worker sands old paint off a window frame; as we pass below, he blows the dust to admire his progress. The particles are caught in the light as they drift down over my infant son. I see it at the park: one hand behind the swing pushing, one hand with the iPhone, scrolling, head buried. I catch myself reading the words of a bedtime book, in character, with my mind entirely elsewhere, rehearsing an argument I may have with the guys who installed the fence in the backyard.

So often, children are at the back of our minds, not the front. They are afterthoughts or never noticed at all. They are invisible when they are right before us. What's particularly worrying is that even those charged directly with protecting kids are often infected with this heedlessness, a careless apathy. At critical moments, even they are just going through the motions.

Before my family moved into our 1860 row house, I called up the Philadelphia Water Department to get the drinking water tested. As I explained to the technician who came out, I was concerned about the lead service line in the basement. I had a two-year-old daughter and I really wanted to protect her. He assured me that the water was very unlikely to be contaminated because "unlike Flint," Philadelphia adequately treats its water so the pipes maintain a protective coating that prevents leaching. The test results showed as much. As the technician wrote to me, "the water appeared to be normal city water and there [was] no cause for concern regarding lead in it."

My wife, daughter, and I moved in and began drinking, cooking, and bathing with the water.

That ought to be the end of the story, but several months later we did something that virtually no one does after receiving a clean bill of health on their water—we had it retested by a third party.

We'd heard about a nonprofit collecting data for a research study on residential lead in the city and we volunteered to help, fully expecting that we'd receive the same results. Indeed, my initial response on opening the letter from Dr. Marc Edwards at Virginia Tech's Department of Civil and Environmental Engineering, who was part of the team that exposed the Flint crisis, was that he must have sent the analysis to the wrong address.

The first sample from our house had more than seventy times the amount of lead as Philadelphia Water had detected; the second had more than ten times the amount. We had, what was described in the materials as a "*serious* lead contamination problem."

How could that be?

As I discovered, unlike Dr. Edwards, the city didn't actually sample the water that had been sitting in that lead service line—the one I'd repeatedly emphasized was the reason for getting my water tested in the first place. Instead, they tested the water sitting in the new non-lead pipes directly next to the kitchen sink and—after letting the water flush for ten minutes—the water from the non-lead main.

My wife and I were shocked. People, like us, who contact Philadelphia Water are not interested in the minimum lead exposure level—if our kids let the tap run for ten minutes every time they get a glass of water or brush their teeth. We want to know what the water contains when they act like normal children, who turn on the faucet when they are thirsty, drink down the cup as soon as it is filled, and head back to what they were doing.

Why, then, would Philadelphia Water conduct the test this way?

There's no trick to figuring out if the lead plumbing you see in someone's basement is poisoning their water. Measure the pipes, fill your bottles at set intervals, and you can get a profile of contamination across the entire system. That's exactly what Philadelphia Water did after I contacted them about the conflicting results. And, in the sectors they'd neglected on the first visit—corresponding to the suspect piping—they found lead, just like Dr. Edwards. They know how to assess the danger.

But testing the water left stagnant in the suspect pipes carries a huge downside for municipalities like Philadelphia—precisely because it is a far more accurate means of capturing the risk to kids.

The EPA's Lead and Copper Rule states that if more than 10 percent of sampled sites exceed the "action level" of fifteen parts per billion, a utility must address the contamination, including replacing lead pipes. By instructing its technicians to avoid sampling water left sitting in the lead service lines and instead to take water from the main, Philadelphia Water can avoid costly regulation.

In fact, Philadelphia has a long history of testing in ways that hide lead problems. Before being forced to change their methods in 2016, Philadelphia Water would ask residents to do a "pre-flush"—running the tap for several minutes—before the federally mandated six-hour period when water must sit in the pipe. Often, technicians would remove the aerator at the end of the faucet during testing, which would ensure that no bits of lead had collected in the filter (a possible reason our first sample with Dr. Edwards was so dangerously high). Both actions were flagged by the EPA as distorting results and counter to the intent of the regulations, but neither was formally banned—a fact that those at Philadelphia Water appear to see as critical and vindicating.

The department mails out beautiful iris blue postcards to trumpet its compliance: "We tested your water tens of thousands of times last year." Download the department's "Drinking Water Quality Report" and you'll find more to put your mind at ease: "We continue to deliver safe, reliable, high-quality drinking water from source to tap. Our drinking water quality is better than standards set by the EPA." The people in the photographs are shown with their goggles on, their lab coat pockets filled with pens, smiling over microscopes and beakers. It all looks so convincing, exactly as it should: rigorous, scientific, objective.

But it's a façade. Philadelphia Water is telling people the water their children drink is safe without knowing if it is or not. You don't need a PhD and lab coat to know you can't find out the temperature in the refrigerator by checking the thermometer in the oven. And it doesn't matter if you test it "tens of thousands of times a year." It doesn't matter if you use the most accurate equipment.

And what of the underlying EPA standards—the ones Philadelphia purportedly exceeds? It would be quite reasonable to assume—as I did—that the fifteen parts per billion action level for lead is the threshold between safe and unsafe drinking water. But that's not what it is.

Under the 1974 Safe Drinking Water Act, the EPA was required to determine the level at which various contaminants in water produced no adverse health effects. For lead, the maximum exposure level was identified as *zero* parts per billion: there is no amount of lead in water that is safe.

When fetuses and children are exposed to even very low levels, the consequences can be devastating. Lead has been linked to lower IQs, learning disabilities, nervous system damage, and social and emotional dysfunction. Indeed, there is a particularly troubling correlation between early childhood lead exposure and later violent criminal behavior.

The problem for the EPA was that, for decades, we built houses with lead pipes and lead solder joints. Setting a maximum contaminant level at zero would mean replacing all that plumbing. At fifteen parts per billion, though, most of it could be left in place (particularly as the regulations allowed water utilities to get away with up to 10 percent of their samples exceeding that figure). While logic would suggest that the action level is set so high because lead is not a major threat to children, ironically, the level is so high because the threat to children is so pervasive.

So, what we have, then, is children's health ignored at the moment of building core infrastructure, ignored at the moment of crafting regulations to address harms from that infrastructure, and ignored at the moment of complying with those regulations.

This is not a story about people setting out to harm children. This is a story about not focusing on them. And it is a common story: in many ways, the biggest threat to kids comes not from our deliberate actions to disadvantage children, but from our lack of awareness. Far too often, we either don't know that children are being affected by our actions or fail to ensure that the processes we've created to protect kids have their intended purpose. Most of the time, even those of us specifically tasked with guarding children's welfare are just going down our lists, walking through the protocol, cursory cogs turning, turning, turning.

We assume that our existing structures and processes adequately protect children's welfare, but our trust is often misplaced. I learned that lesson at the very beginning of my career. The first case I got to argue in court was a family law case. The client was an amazing woman who'd figured out how to make ends meet for her two girls on a poverty-level income. She'd sought out help from social workers and she'd found my firm to offer her free counsel in her custody and support dispute. Her ex-husband had been released from prison and was eager to spend more time with his girls, but he was having trouble with the payments given his very limited income. He was seeking an adjustment so that he could meet his responsibilities.

Talking with my client, she made it clear that she wanted to take a hard-line position. She wanted no reduction in support and visitation only to occur in her presence in her house. So, I took my marching orders and prepared for battle. In the great adversarial model I'd been taught, the two sides made their cases with partisan vigor, and through that clash, the truth was revealed. It was not my role to consider or pursue what was best for the kids—that was for the court. I served the system by being a zealous advocate.

When I found out who would be sitting across from me, I prepared more. I was going up against the sister of my criminal law professor at Harvard, who also happened to be Michelle Obama's close friend and roommate at Princeton. I knew that family court was sometimes formal—with strict adherence to the rules of evidence—and sometimes loose—with the judge casually asking the parties questions. I was ready for whatever the morning held. Out of the gate, I pushed hard. And I expected the attorney on the other side to come right back. But this wasn't *her* first case in court. Indeed, as a public defender, she was swamped with cases, many more pressing than this one. She hadn't been up memorizing the relevant precedent. We won on everything. And I felt a sickness in my stomach.

I don't know what happened to my client or her children. And I hope my gut was wrong. But I know I did not put those two little girls first. I never asked how they felt about matters or what they wanted. I never spoke to them at all. I did what I was taught. I stuck to the protocol that was given to me and did what was expected. I put my faith in the adversarial system, just as those at Philadelphia Water trust in the testing protocols and EPA oversight.

In numerous contexts, rather than ask people to protect children, we ask them to follow procedures that purport to protect children but often come up short. We don't tell officers to protect young suspects from harm. We demand that they adhere strictly to use-of-force and Miranda protocols, heedless of the fact that these protocols fail many children, who may struggle to control their behavior after receiving an order from police, whose bodies are particularly vulnerable to the restraints that were developed for adults, who do not understand their rights, and who are particularly susceptible to interrogation techniques that lead to false confessions.

In immigration court, we playact through farcical proceedings in which the process appears to be perfectly in order: case numbers and dockets, a defendant seated at a table, a government prosecutor, and a robed judge, asking the questions you'd expect to hear when assessing whether asylum is warranted: "Why did you come to America?" "What would happen to you if you were returned to Guatemala?" The only thing that's out of place—that renders the whole scene ridiculous—is that the defendant, the one being asked, through an interpreter, whether he understands the proceedings, is a one-year-old.

Migrant children, even toddlers, are regularly called to court without their parents to recount things they don't know and weigh options they don't fully understand. Yet, rather than confront the obvious injustice and chart a new course, we soldier on. We make the best of the procedure we have rather than pausing to ensure that the procedure actually ensures children's welfare. As Jack H. Weil, an immigration judge in charge of training other judges for the Department of Justice, put it, "I've taught immigration law literally to 3-year-olds and 4-year-olds. It takes a lot of time. It takes a lot of patience. They get it. It's not the most efficient, but it can be done."

A consequence of procedure dominating over substance is that we have come to devote much of our attention to avoiding liability for harm to children rather than addressing the harm. That's a theme in the municipal response to lead exposure. Rather than act to remove lead paint, we have people sign "disclosures" acknowledging that the risk has been divulged before they move in. Instead of paying to replace lead service lines, we hand out pamphlets with recommendations about flushing the pipes before you have a glass of water, knowing full well that most people will not read them or heed the advice.

Across the board, the most prominent and authoritative entities in society—churches, universities, businesses, and governments—that could do a huge amount to curb danger to kids, instead put their efforts into protecting themselves from lawsuits and bad press. Rather than giving up button batteries, which we've known for decades can be fatal if swallowed, we attach a label: WARNING—KEEP OUT OF REACH OF CHILDREN. Rather than hiring scientists to make safer pesticides, we hire lobbyists to ensure that the ones that cause cancer are legal. With a waiver at your water park, you can cut back on monitoring, put off updating equipment, and avoid paying for kids who get hurt. With a nondisclosure agreement after a sexual assault, you can minimize scandal, additional claims, and "disruptive" reforms.

When all that matters is whether the proper procedures are followed, people end up feeling less responsible when harm does befall children and more at liberty to pursue other ends—like profit, efficiency, or higher conviction rates—even at the expense of children's welfare. Exploiting loopholes and pushing the envelope to win become fair play. Detectives have figured out how to deliver the Miranda warning—slipping it into a stream of conversation, playing it down as a "mere formality," and implying that a waiver will result in better treatment—so that it is least likely to be effective. The multimillionaire Jeffrey Epstein's lawyers saw the damning evidence against him: the shockingly consistent accounts of abuse from dozens of underage girls, detailing everything from his methods of recruiting his victims to the appearance of his penis, the phone records, the flight logs. And they set to work, smearing the girls' reputations—accusing them of lying and suggesting they couldn't be trusted because of drug use—suing their lawyers to try to frighten them from pursuing a civil suit, investigating individual prosecutors on the case in search of damaging personal facts they could leverage, pressuring the lead federal prosecutor to hide the plea deal from the victims so they wouldn't object, and securing a thirteen-month sentence in a private wing of the Palm Beach County jail, which Epstein was allowed to leave six days a week for twelve hours to work in his office. So, did the lawyers feel regret or guilt? Epstein's attorney and Harvard Law School Professor Alan Dershowitz offered a flippant summation: "We outlawyered him"—meaning the head prosecutor.

A system focused on blind adherence to procedure rather than the substantive welfare of children will never adequately ensure children's welfare. If you work at the water department, your goal should be to provide safe water to children. With that proper outlook, you *want* to know the amount of lead in pipes and so you design the most sensitive tests possible. You don't cross your fingers and *hope* that parents will protect their kids by routinely cleaning out aerators, replacing old pipes, and running the tap for five minutes before filling a glass of water; you check if they do and, if they don't, you act. You don't wait for children in your city to become poisoned or wait to be sanctioned by the EPA before you change course. You don't wait for public outrage. When you tell someone that the unsafe water out of their tap is safe—that it is "normal city water and that there is no cause for concern regarding lead in it"—you face up to your mistake and ensure it does not happen again on your watch. When I wrote to the head of Philadelphia Water about the experience of my family, I didn't hear back from her. Instead, I got a letter from the City Solicitor's Office informing me that "the Water Department never instructed or advised you not to remove the potential lead sources in your plumbing." You don't ensure the safety of kids with double negatives from lawyers.

In the end, my family was incredibly lucky. We caught the lead problem very early. We had the money to pay the $6,700 to have the service line and basement pipes replaced. And my daughter, being a milk-aholic, drank very little water from the house during the critical period, so the lead levels in her blood were normal. But many children are not so fortunate—and the harm from our inattention is profound and lasting. They drink contaminated water, sleep in apartments with peeling lead paint, and play in toxic dirt lots for their entire childhoods. They live in cities—like Newark and Flint—which have far worse records on lead safety than Philadelphia. In 2019, as Philadelphia became the biggest U.S. municipality to require landlords to test for lead paint, widespread problems with Newark's drinking water forced the city to distribute bottled water and filters to tens of thousands of people and shut off water fountains in more than thirty schools. In the five years after thirty thousand Flint schoolchildren were exposed to toxic drinking water, the percentage of students qualifying for special ed nearly doubled.

We all need to wake up. We must stop being passive when it comes to children's welfare. The previous chapters have set us on that path: while each of the six rights we've discussed is worthy of our attention on its own merits, the ultimate aim has not been to create a definitive inventory of what children deserve but rather to instill a broad child-first mindset. We're now ready to consider that charge directly.

But before we address how we might reorient ourselves as individuals, groups, and institutions to prioritize kids—the focus of the final chapter—we need to look more closely at what's holding us back. There is an active resistance to child-first change—a guarding of the status quo in which children are invisible, ignored, and secondary. It is embodied in both the wayward bicyclist yelling, "No strollers on the sidewalk" and the carefully crafted language of the Parental Rights Amendment to the Constitution, introduced in Congress as a bulwark against the possibility that the United States might actually sign the UN's Convention on the Rights of the Child one day.

As soon as there is any movement to better protect children, to vindicate their interests, someone pops up to argue that it harms an adult's rights. Of course, the "what about me?" response is common whenever there are efforts to advance the lot of a deprivileged group. Black Lives Matter was met with claims that Blue Lives Matter, White Lives Matter, and All Lives Matter. Gay marriage was derided as a threat to straight marriage. But, then, the knee-jerk reaction to children's rights claims seems particularly noteworthy because it's felt across the ideological spectrum. If we sanction lawyers who engage in delay tactics to put off the trials of people accused of sexually assaulting children, think of how much harder it will be for all defendants to gain representation! Red flag laws that prohibit those convicted of domestic violence from possessing firearms threaten the Second Amendment rights of responsible gun owners! Barring those who are pregnant from working in conditions where they are exposed to high levels of lead is unlawful employment discrimination against women! Limiting advertising for high-calorie foods during Saturday morning cartoons infringes the free speech rights of corporations! Allowing kids to get vaccinated without their parents' approval is an attack on parents' fundamental liberty interests! Start a conversation about protecting kids and just watch it morph into a conversation about the rights of adults: taxpayer rights, teachers' rights, elder rights.

Part of this can be written off as simple reactance—an irrational fear that any change to existing conditions will unfairly threaten the freedoms various individuals now enjoy—but there is an aspect of the concern that warrants more attention. To say that children also face mistreatment and are also deserving of autonomy and protection is not to minimize the mistreatment of other groups who have faced subjugation and silencing or to give credence to the bigots who once likened the capacities of women and people of color to children in order to deny them rights. The zero-sum frame—the idea that making children better off means making everyone else worse off—is false. Their second-class citizenship harms us all.

To adopt a child-first mindset is not to choose protecting children over combating racism or fighting climate change. It is to strive for racial justice by prioritizing the interests of Black and Brown children. It is to work for sustainability by prioritizing the interests of the world's young people.

For some, there is a separate fear that to focus on the welfare of children is to open ourselves to the bias of sentimentality. It is to lose proper perspective and be swayed into unfair decisions. We see that reticence in statutes and court opinions that direct our attention away from children, away from the realities of their mistreatment.

Early on, law students are taught to free themselves of their moral misgivings, to not be distracted by the plight of child victims. The first-year casebook I use in Criminal Law has several cases where judges assume the role of Abraham, demonstrating their devotion to the rule of law, their fealty to the underlying legal principle or procedure, by denying a young child substantive justice. In *Oxendine v. State,* for example, the Supreme Court of Delaware laments that "it is extremely difficult to be objective about the death of a child." While a lay person might find a father responsible for his six-year-old son's death when he knowingly fails to protect his son from his girlfriend's violent abuse, severely beats the boy himself, and, later, callously refuses to take his critically injured son to the hospital, an objective judicial mind considers the death with detachment and unyielding formalism. The anger a non-lawyer might experience lingering over the details—the neighbors who could hear the boy crying through the wall, "Please stop, Daddy, it hurts" as Oxendine hit him repeatedly for ten minutes before delivering "a great blow"—are a distraction. What's most important, you see, is that the proper legal process was followed: the prosecutor submitted the wrong theory of causation to the jury, so Oxendine cannot be held to account for his son's death; sure, there was evidence to support a different theory of causation and, actually, there was evidence to support the theory that was submitted, but it wasn't entered into the record at the right time.

The notion that prudent decision-making requires ignoring children is also evident in how people often complain that bringing up kids in a policy debate is a "cheap trick"—a distraction tactic that encourages looking at an issue with irrational emotion rather than reason and objectivity. Using Sandy Hook or Parkland to argue for gun control is underhanded and distortionary. Highlighting birth defects in babies exposed to phthalates—plasticizers found in numerous consumer products—is to engage in "scare mongering" and badly bias the conversation. To be objective is to disregard the impact on children. As one woman put it, commenting on a Facebook video of a militia group rounding up asylum-seeking families at gunpoint: "Got to stop being sympathetic because of the kids. Got to consider them as collateral damage now. We are DONE." As a conservative friend wrote to me concerning coverage of the so-called migrant caravan just before the 2018 midterm elections: "My fear is that the media will wave a couple of terrified mothers and crying kids at us on CNN and our government will open the gates." A couple of weeks later, when news outlets did run pictures of children being teargassed along the border, that seemed to prove his point.

But feeling emotion for children is clarifying: it doesn't cloud the truth, it wakes up our moral sense, reminds us of our values, and allows us to focus on the real costs and benefits of our actions.

Consider the most impactful photographs of the last century: the ones that changed the way people thought about unfolding events. It is not a coincidence that so many have been images of children: Mary Anne Vecchio, fourteen, kneeling over the body of Jeffrey Miller, a student shot dead by national guardsmen at Kent State University; Kim Phuc, nine, running naked from the napalm attack on her home near Trang Bang, South Vietnam; Aylan Kurdi, three, lying dead on the sand of a Turkish beach. The widely circulated picture of Maria Meza, a mother from Honduras, scrambling with her twin five-year-old daughters, Saira and Cheili, as a gas canister spews white smoke behind them is a case in point.

Every parent has held their child like that, in a moment of fear, maybe just caught in the street as the light changes or after a wave knocks you both down, gripping arm or wrist, not willing to risk the uncertainty of a child's hold, moving forward, hurrying, away from danger. And there is Saira, barefooted, hair in her face. And there is Cheili stumbling, right before the spill, her pink flip-flop pulling off, her legs crumpling. You notice the diaper. And, suddenly, the stakes are starkly revealed. We cannot be both moral people and people who do this. Saira and Cheili are not a threat to us. Migrant mothers like Maria have not brought their children to garner sympathy; they have not brought them because they are bad parents but because they are good parents. They have brought their children because they are desperate to save them from dire conditions in Central America and offer them lives that we, as Americans, take for granted. Policing the border, defending the wall, suddenly seems an utterly inapt solution to a migration crisis. When you see Saira and Cheili, you realize our resources ought best be used for securing opportunity—back in Guatemala and here in the United States for those fleeing gangs, corruption, and poverty—not in making bigger and better barriers.

New psychological research supports the benefits to everyone of focusing on children. In a series of experiments, participants whose attention was drawn to kids were more motivated to address social problems and help others, and expressed more empathy for the challenges other adults faced. In fact, when researchers looked at real-world behavior, they found that adults were roughly twice as likely to donate to charity when children were present on a public street than when only adults were present. The "child salience effect" seemed to influence everyone: it didn't matter how old people were, or if they were men or women, of if they were parents or not. Focusing on children had a pro-social impact even on those who reported negative general attitudes toward kids. And it didn't matter that the charity wasn't dedicated to children: the salience of youth produced a broad pro-social impulse. As the psychologists concluded, having children at the forefront of our minds and present in our public forums—not hidden from view and excluded from participation—can be a key means of ensuring that we live up to our values.

Yet there is more to why focusing on children leads to good policy. Kids are canaries in our coal mines. The things that harm kids also tend to harm adults, but kids are more sensitive to the bad effects.

Take tear gas and pepper spray. Children are especially vulnerable to these types of agents because they have considerably faster respiration than adults, so they may inhale a proportionately far larger dose of toxin. An infant might take upward of fifty breaths a minute, while an adult is averaging just twelve to sixteen. And infants' and preschoolers' lungs and trachea are particularly sensitive to chemicals and can quickly become dangerously inflamed, when a comparable adult might suffer only minor distress. If children are your focus—the population you consider first in deciding what the policy of the United States should be—it becomes hard to justify using noxious agents, like tear gas, on migrants trying to cross the border illegally.

If, instead, you use an average adult man to decide the danger posed by riot-control agents, car crashes, psychotropic medications, pesticides, particulate matter from truck exhaust, adulterated food, and the like, everyone ends up exposed to far more harm than they otherwise would be. And anyone who is more vulnerable than the average adult man ends up being put, quite unfairly, at greater risk. The asthma rates in Honduras and El Salvador are roughly twice as high as those in the United States, and when asthmatics breathe in toxins, the result can be fatal. Ban spraying tear gas on migrants and all those individuals benefit.

But we haven't taken a child-centric approach with assessing riot control agents—or many other risks. How did we decide that o-chlorobenzylidene malononitrile tear gas—the most commonly used agent—was safe? Arguably the most influential study on the subject involved a controlled exposure with a set of thirty-five healthy, male, adult volunteers. Now, though, police and military officials around the world spray it indiscriminately into crowds filled with people who are not healthy, male, or adult. A ten-pound preemie drinks the same water, mixed into her formula, as the 154-pound healthy male used to develop many national drinking water standards. The eight-year-old takes the same antidepressant "off-label" as the thirty-year-old for whom the drug was designed, tested, and FDA-approved. Focusing on the response of the most robust and resilient human beings is a terrible strategy for protecting a diverse population. By contrast, make kids your primary focus, and you will intervene earlier and more completely, with major health benefits for everyone. Our beauty products will generate fewer cancers across all age groups. Medicines will have less serious side effects. The air in our cities and the water out of our taps will be far cleaner. Our airplanes will cruise more smoothly through turbulence.

She was writing fiction, but Alice Walker, the Pulitzer and National Book Award winner, could not have given us a more profound truth: "What is the fundamental question one must ask of the world? . . . *Why is the child crying?*"

CHAPTER 8

STOP AND GIVE A THOUGHT

What Change Looks Like

We ought to assess everything we do from the position of trying to ensure the welfare of children. That's it—the elevator pitch to save the world. The plot is simple. Take your field, your institution, your system, and stop and give a thought.

You are an architect. You own an orchard. You're in pharmaceuticals. You are a soldier. You are an elementary school principal. You are a truck driver, a priest, a big tech CEO. Start by noticing children's "absent presence" in your familiar realm—how their substantive interests are both ignored and profoundly affected by the rules, processes, and norms you know so well. And then imagine what it would look like if your field were rebuilt to prioritize children's well-being.

To show what I mean, I'm going to choose criminal law—something I teach about nearly every year and the topic of my last book.

As we enacted new mandatory minimums and three-strikes laws, as prosecutors used their discretion to bring maximum charges, as we invested billions in new prisons, no one really considered how that might hurt kids. Since we were not deliberately acting to harm children, it didn't seem like we could. But the result of these criminal justice initiatives is that today five million kids have, or have had, a parent locked up. A majority of people in our prisons have minor children and most of those parents were living with their kids before they were taken away. Our "justice" casts a terrible shadow, darkening the lives of kids from the moment their mom or dad is arrested and lingering across generations. But we either don't notice the harm or treat it as natural and inevitable. Kirstjen Nielsen, President Trump's Homeland Security secretary, perfectly captured that indifference, as she batted away criticism of the migrant child separation policy on the grounds that it is no different from what we routinely do in the criminal justice system to American families: "In the United States, we call that law enforcement."

In the United States today, police officers kick down doors in the deep of night with guns drawn to drag away fathers as their terrified children watch. They wrestle mothers to the ground. They yank children away from their parents' arms, threatening those who stand in the way or hold on too long.

And what happens subsequently when a single mother can't make bail or ends up in prison? Do the police or courts check in on the kids? The shocking answer is that, in many jurisdictions around the country, no one in the criminal justice system is charged with following up to make sure the kids are okay. It's left to child welfare services, who may be completely unaware that mom is now gone.

In 2012, a mail carrier was making her rounds along the narrow back roads of Splendora, Texas, when she found two kids, eleven and five, who seemed to be unsupervised. "The little girl's hair was just matted, like a stray dog's," she recalled later. The kids were living in an abandoned school bus. Their clothes were dirty and they weren't wearing shoes. Toys and trash were scattered around the property. When authorities checked, neither of the siblings was on the local school rolls. Months earlier, their parents had been convicted of embezzling money from victims of Hurricane Ike and were sent to prison. An aunt was supposed to care for the kids, but no one checked to see if she actually was. Meticulous attention and resources were devoted to ensuring that the children's parents were brought to justice, that they were tried in federal court, that they were locked in their cells each night. But, as so often happens, once the ties of parent to child were cut, no one looked where the kids fell.

Even when children end up in an orphanage or foster care, the same general dynamics of neglect are evident, frequently with tragic consequences. Sarah and Jen were four and seven when the police took them away from their mom, Tina. She would eventually be given twenty years for acting as a middleman in a meth sale.

Early childhood for the girls was being shifted in the shadows: as Sarah recalls, "We jumped around, we went to a few foster homes, and then bad things were happening. I don't remember them, my sister, [Jen], does. She would take a lot of the bad stuff that people would do; she was trying to protect me because I was so little." Sarah does have one specific memory from that time: "I remember one place we went to had cockroaches all over the bathroom and [our foster mom] would grab a wooden spoon and threaten to hit us. She would ask her boyfriend if she should do it. It was like a little game that they played." No one intervened. Those aren't the rules. And then, improbably, a ray of light seemed to appear: there was a rich family who'd "adopted children before," who were "a big part of the foster system," who, "from the outside looking in," seemed "like the great all-American Christian family." They welcomed Sarah and Jen into their home.

But it was a darker abyss. Now there really was no oversight. As Sarah explains, if the foster norm is "do the bare minimum about checking up or listening to the kids"—literally, "shove them over there and then forget about it"—that's doubly true when you have a wealthy, religious family that appears to have "been through everything." For years, Sarah and Jen were molested by their foster father, Jim. No one noticed. No one came to their rescue. The only reason it stopped was that the wives of Jim and Ellen's biological kids found out that their own children were being abused; they took pictures, called Child Protective Services, and got Jim arrested.

Sarah and Jen's experience is not an anomaly: it is standard American law enforcement. When people commit crimes, we respond by harming their children. It's staring us in the face and we don't see it. Why were Sarah and Jen abused? Because we locked up their mom. Why did Sarah end up later using heroin? Because we locked up her mom. Why did Jen end up in prison? Because we locked up her mom. And, as we saw back in chapter 1, the harm does not stop at one generation. With Jen incarcerated, her four kids are now in the foster system—just like Sarah and Jen two decades before. Tina's youngest grandchild is ten years old. He's in a group home, barred from seeing his mom or his three older sisters. He's on Prozac.

When I teach Business Organizations and we get to talking about criminal corporate liability, I like to ask my students whether they think it's a good idea. Invariably, the students are quick to point out that it would be unfair to hold a corporation itself criminally responsible because that would punish innocent shareholders who were not themselves involved in the wrongdoing. But what about the kids of human criminals that we lock up? Aren't they just as innocent— indeed, far more innocent? When I bring these points up, the students scratch their heads: they hadn't thought of that. The unfortunate truth is that it's easier for them to recognize the *hypothetical* injustice to shareholders than the *real* harm inflicted upon the children of the incarcerated.

And that's true of the legislatures that have given us our sentencing guidelines, and the prosecutors and judges who execute their will. The children of the defendant are usually invisible in the formal criminal justice process. Think back to Adam and Ariel, from chapter 1, whose parents were arrested for drug crimes when they were three and six. They "were kept very far out of the trial," and Adam wonders now, "What if we had been there? Like, 'Oh my God, they have three kids?'" "The jury had no idea." How can you rightfully convict a woman without knowing if, in doing so, you are sending her young children to an orphanage? And, if you are a judge, how can you figure out the appropriate punishment for a defendant when, in Adam's words, "the effect on their kids' lives is not considered whatsoever"?

But this blindness to kids is by design. The *United States Sentencing Commission Guidelines Manual* makes clear that judges should pay no heed to the existence of children when determining an appropriate sentence. And so, the prosecutor appealed Adam and Ariel's mother Jackie's sentence of seventy-eight months for conspiracy to distribute cocaine and marijuana, arguing that the judge erred by taking into consideration that she "had three minor children" and that she should have been sentenced to 188 to 235 months. Three judges on the Fourth Circuit agreed about the total irrelevance of the children—and children in general: "Because there is nothing extraordinary about the fact that [the defendant] had three minor children, a departure on that basis was improper." So what that a fifteen-to-twenty-year sentence would mean that these three kids would have both of their parents taken away from them for their entire childhoods? While the guidelines are now advisory rather than required, judges continue to toe the line. In 2015, a downward departure from the sentencing guidelines on account of family ties was granted in just 9 percent of federal cases.

Even when there has been a push to address the effects of incarceration on the parent-child relationship, the conversation has generally focused on adults—and that's consistently derailed reform. If you look at the history of the guidelines, the motivation for disregarding children in sentencing parents was a concern that taking into account a person's dependents would mean gross sentencing disparities between those with young children and those without. But what of the far more damaging and unfair disparity to children under the current sentencing regime: completely innocent three-year-olds have their parents erased from their lives for decades, while other three-year-olds get to enjoy all of the financial, psychological, and developmental benefits of having an intact family?

Similarly, when the First Circuit was presented with a case concerning the impact of incarceration on babies, the court reasoned that "to allow a departure downward for pregnancy could set a precedent that would have dangerous consequences in the future, sending an obvious message to all female defendants that pregnancy is 'a way out.'" They glossed over the far more dangerous—and empirically documented, not hypothetical—consequences to children of the precedent they were setting. We know the lifetime harm to kids born to incarcerated mothers, and we know the long-term costs to society. But that's never how the discussion is framed, and that lets those with the power to change the system off the hook. With the focus solidly on the rights of guilty prisoners—and not innocent children—it becomes easy for lawmakers to say, "You should have thought about how getting locked up would harm your ability to raise your child before you committed the crime." It becomes easy for the Supreme Court to say, the prisoner's "freedom of association is among the rights least compatible with incarceration," and move on. The cruelty becomes routine, part of the established order: as the First Circuit wrote, yes, "a child will bear a stigma from being born in prison. But it has been recognized since time memorial that the sins of parents are visited upon their children."

As we explored in chapter 1, redesigning our criminal justice system with children's interests in mind means opening our eyes to how our approach to corrections imperils children's attachment to their parents. With a child-first mentality, you build spaces of incarceration that are crafted to make it easy for kids to stay closely connected with their parents—but better yet, most of the time, you don't lock parents up at all. Indeed, if we really adopted a child-first mentality, we wouldn't focus much on punishment. We'd stop looking to hurt parents for their bad decisions and instead help them avoid messing up in the first place. We'd listen to Tina: "I got addicted to methamphetamine. . . . I didn't need sixteen years in prison and two kids' lives destroyed. . . . I needed help." Putting children first, our criminal justice system would be largely dedicated to rehabilitation and prevention. And that would be good for everyone.

What if Tina hadn't been taken away from Sarah and Jen for two decades? Tina is smart and diligent—in prison, she went to college and then worked her way up to the top position in Federal Prison Industries, the labor program for inmates, at the facility where she was housed. She loved her daughters: in fact, the whole reason she started acting as a middleman in a drug scheme was because she was told she was going to lose Sarah and Jen permanently if she didn't immediately secure housing. She'd completed rehab—all her tests were clean, she'd done all the classes—but her house had been foreclosed on. "They gave me a timeline, you know; they said, time is running out and you got to get a place or we're not going to give them back to you. So, I thought, how can I make money fast? And the only way I knew how, in my mind, was to sell drugs." It was a foolish choice, but it was us—not Tina—who turned it into a devastating one for her children and grandchildren. It was us—not Tina—who callously turned our back on them. And it is all of us who pay the cost.

The broad benefits to a child-first reimagining of the criminal justice system extend to every facet of our process. When you focus on the experience of children, you are able to recognize the failure of casting the police as warriors, trained in violence and justified in doing whatever it takes to defeat the bad guys. You can no longer ignore—as "collateral damage"—the Rochester, New York, toddler whose mother was pepper-sprayed and knocked to the ground after being accused of shoplifting or the pregnant Arizona woman whose car was intentionally rammed and flipped upside down because she didn't pull over fast enough or the sixteen-year-old autistic boy who suffocated under violent restraint in a strip mall parking lot after getting upset playing laser tag. You must face the fact that one third of the people bitten by police dogs in Baton Rouge are under eighteen and the fact that innocent young people are more susceptible to pleading guilty. These are not the safely disregarded exceptions to just rules. They are red flags of general injustice. Children's vulnerability can guide us to the right approaches for all of us.

Where we have paused to consider the impact of the criminal justice system on children and made changes, it has pointed us in the right direction for everyone. We have begun to limit solitary confinement for minors and the next step is to ban it for all prisoners. We have begun to prohibit police officers from lying when interrogating juveniles and the next step is to bar lying to any suspects. We abolished the death penalty and mandatory life without the possibility of parole for those under eighteen and the next step is to end them for all people.

While today, we approach crime at the back end—with police officers, prosecutors, investigations, trials, prisons, parole officers, and halfway houses—focusing on children allows us to realize the value of prevention. In the future, we will keep our communities safe by investing in preschools, top-quality healthcare, excellent public housing, mentoring, and other social services for young people.

Across domains we can reorient ourselves to prioritize children's rights. The hardest thing is simply admitting that we've been doing it wrong and questioning practices, laws, theories, and norms that we've long treated as settled.

Imagine that the dominant approach to interpreting the Constitution was not originalism—asking what reasonable people living in the eighteenth century would have thought the text meant—but what the words ought to mean in light of the best interests of children. Why is originalism any more legitimate than a child-first perspective when, say, deciding whether the Second Amendment ensures an individual the right to possess a firearm? Does it really make more sense to construe "the right of the people to keep and bear Arms" in light of the meaning attached by folks who lived in a time of muskets and cartouche boxes and who died two centuries ago than to read it in light of the experiences of children exposed to the threat of gun violence today and in the years to come?

There is nothing stopping us from changing our method of interpreting statutes and regulations or changing what those laws tell people and institutions to maximize. States, for example, could recast the shareholder primacy norm in corporate governance, whereby shareholders' interests are held above all other stakeholders, to one that prioritized the welfare of children—call it a kid primacy norm. That might seem very strange, but corporations are legal fictions, chartered by the state, and it is entirely up to us what we want them to do. We've seen what happens to the fate of children when you encourage many of the wealthiest and most powerful entities in the world to pursue profit alone.

At the birth of our daughter, we received a few gifts from friends and family, including not one but two Fisher-Price Rock 'n Play Sleepers. To the uninitiated, that might seem an odd coincidence. But we'd heard about the Rock 'n Play—described in terms usually reserved for religious miracles—well before. And, in those early weeks, this simple inclined rocker—that you could pull right up next to the bed, that could be set in gentle motion with a half-awake hand, that seemed to beckon sleep, as if by magic—seemed to live up to its reputation. Unlike in her crib, when she was in the Rock 'n Play, our daughter slept, long and deep—the kind of nights that are so good you dare to think that maybe this parenting thing will be easier than you thought.

So, it was jarring to have our pediatrician tell us—unequivocally—to stop using the Rock 'n Play. Babies slept too well in it, she said—it wasn't safe; indeed, it tended to flatten out the back of a baby's head because infants in the Rock 'n Play didn't move like they did tossing around in the crib. Although I'd been excelling in my role as the hypervigilant first-time parent—ensuring that relatives washed their hands before handling the baby, double-checking the car seat installation instructions, and rinsing off each dropped pacifier—the sleeper had never registered as a threat. I assumed that it had been subject to numerous safety tests and clinical trials. After all, sleep-related deaths are among the top mortality risks for children under the age of one. And this was a product made by Fisher-Price, sold and used by millions of people.

Just how wrong I'd been was only revealed, five years later, when the Rock 'n Play was recalled, after being implicated in the deaths of dozens of infants. Not only had the sleeper been built without any safety tests, but the company had only consulted with a single doctor—who would later lose his medical license—before launching it into the market. No one had apparently checked whether inclined sleeping aligned with the latest medical consensus on what was best for babies.

A two-minute search of the relevant literature would have shown it was not. Inclined sleep is dangerous because infants can shift into positions that can result in suffocation, and the deep all-through-the-night slumber that parents crave is not actually how babies are meant to sleep. In fact, it appears correlated with sudden infant death syndrome. But when profit is your goal, you build the sleeper that parents want—not the one that's best for babies—and then you work to fight anything that might harm sales.

When the Consumer Product Safety Commission moved to limit the incline of bassinets in 2010—potentially barring the sale of the Rock 'n Play—Fisher-Price managed to convince regulators to create a new standard specifically for inclined sleepers with the assistance of the American Society for Testing and Materials. More than half of the ASTM committee was made up of industry members, and the voluntary standard they created—five years later—was opposed by the American Academy of Pediatrics. When there was an initial lawsuit, Fisher-Price vigorously defended the Rock 'n Play. And, even with the millions of dollars in losses entailed in the recall, the company is still likely to come out way ahead.

That's the story for many businesses. Even when you are making food for babies, it is easy to lose focus on protecting children's lives without it being articulated as your primary goal. For decades, rather than market formula only to those mothers who truly needed a breastmilk alternative, Nestlé and other companies created broad demand for a product linked to lower IQ, obesity, diabetes, and infant mortality. In a single year—1981—some sixty-six thousand babies in poorer countries died as a result of the availability of breastmilk substitutes. If you don't have clean water, breastmilk is almost certainly a better option. But each mother who breastfeeds is a lost customer.

It would be nice to think that the corporate world has changed, but you only need to look at the scathing 2021 congressional report showing "dangerously high levels of toxic metals" in baby foods to understand that it hasn't. And why would it? Just like the attorneys in our adversarial system, we continue to tell Nestlé's fiduciaries to zealously pursue the narrow interests of those they represent—the shareholders—and leave it to others—the government—to ensure the health and safety of children.

The notion that such an approach could ever adequately protect the welfare of kids is absurd in the abstract and devastating in practice. Those meant to defend societal values are inevitably playing catch-up. With a new product, it often takes kids actually getting sick and dying for the dangers to even get noticed by regulators. And any company, seeking to maximize its profit, has already been working hard with lobbyists to reduce existing government oversight, cut the budgets of regulators like the FDA and EPA, and install industry insiders as political appointees to manage the risk that the product will be removed from the market.

In 2018, when the World Health Assembly took up a resolution by Ecuador to limit the inaccurate marketing of formula, lobbyists and sympathetic American officials were there working to delete language that called upon states to "protect, promote and support breast-feeding" and threatening Ecuador with trade sanctions if they didn't pull it. Consumers may believe, as the congressional report on heavy metals explains, that baby food manufacturers "would not sell products that are unsafe" and that the "federal government would not knowingly permit the sale of unsafe baby food," but that's a fairy tale. When the Trump administration was given a secret industry presentation in 2019 showing that the final products going to market—which were known to have much higher levels of toxic metals than the initial ingredients—weren't even being tested, they took no action. For most baby foods, there is still no requirement to test for heavy metals and no duty to provide a label or warning to parents.

With their eye trained on profit, companies view harm to children in purely monetary terms—and keep that cost down by relying on liability waivers and fighting tooth and nail in court. If, against the odds, a case gets past summary judgment, you quickly settle to dodge a bad court precedent and have the harmed individuals sign a nondisclosure agreement to avoid publicity. If journalists or public officials do start to investigate, you hire public relations firms to control the narrative, you ensure that "independent" panels looking into the issue are "balanced" with plenty of industry folks, and you sponsor academic research to call the dangerousness of the product into question. You understand that you don't have to prove that cigarettes or sugar-sweetened beverages are safe; you just have to make it look like a debate and shift the conversation to one emphasizing government overreach, reduced consumer choice, and higher prices. In the unlikely event that state or federal regulators back you into a corner—as happened to cigarette companies—you negotiate superficial changes (disclosure of the risk of harm in bigger font), focus on repackaging the good (think e-cigarettes and vapes), and shift to selling the product in other jurisdictions with less stringent oversight (think China). You trade off higher onetime monetary penalties for the ability to keep peddling. Big tobacco didn't die; it just put on a new cloak: Altria owns Philip Morris and has a 35 percent stake in Juul. When anti-cigarette efforts pushed down teen smoking rates, tobacco companies got two million middle-schoolers and high-schoolers hooked on vaping, erasing those gains. Kids are always going to be imperiled in such a system.

Time and time again, stymied in our efforts to rein in corporate actions that harm children through direct regulation, we've settled on voluntary industry-led efforts, like the "standards" for inclined sleepers. But self-regulation has not been effective at protecting children from harms created by commercial interests. Voluntary guidelines in Spain, Canada, Australia, Mexico, and the United States, for example, have all failed, in any meaningful way, to reduce advertisements of unhealthy foods and beverages to children. Today, many companies trumpet their corporate social responsibility activities—including those aimed at children's welfare—but too often it has amounted to an "insincere eloquence," in the words of Jaap Doek, the former chair of the UN Committee on the Rights of the Child. It is public relations management—social-justice washing.

There was much fanfare when the Business Roundtable, which had long championed shareholder primacy, released a new Statement on the Purpose of a Corporation in 2019 expressing "a fundamental commitment to all of our stakeholders," including shareholders, customers, employees, suppliers, and "the communities in which we work." But when researchers looked at the impact on the 181 publicly traded companies that signed on, they found none at all: profit maximization continued to rule the roost. As a WHO-UNICEF-Lancet Commission concluded, "many enterprises" continue to believe that "considering child well-being in their decisions and actions" is "irrelevant or inimical to their activities."

But the empty social responsibility rhetoric does point to something positive: the public thinks corporations should operate differently—that's why companies have changed how they speak. Roughly two out of three Americans believe that a company's "primary purpose" ought to include "making the world better"—about the same proportion as believe it ought to include "making money for shareholders."

In early 2018, Jana Partners and the California State Teachers' Retirement System, two of the largest investors in Apple, who hold some $2 billion of stock, publicly called on the company to better protect children from the impact of digital technology. The investors emphasized that "paying special attention to the health and development of the next generation" was not simply "the right thing to do" but also "good business": "We believe that addressing this issue now will enhance long-term value for all shareholders, by creating more choices and options for your customers today and helping to protect the next generation of leaders, innovators, and customers tomorrow." Most notably, they emphasized that companies themselves had to take on a proactive role and not simply react when regulators or researchers raised concerns: "There is a developing consensus around the world including Silicon Valley that the potential long-term consequences of new technologies need to be factored in at the outset, and no company can outsource that responsibility." Apple's reply—that they were "committed to meeting and exceeding our customers' expectations, especially when it comes to protecting kids"—showed they were listening. But whether this positive rhetoric translates into concrete action when the next major innovation appears on the horizon is entirely in the hands of Apple and other tech companies. That's not good enough: it's time to ensure that companies do the right thing and the only way we can do that is changing a mere suggestion into a duty.

We need to use that public sentiment to make prioritizing children's welfare binding law. In making a decision—to create an Instagram for kids, develop a Peloton treadmill, or train the Saudi navy in its blockage of Yemen—corporate actors should first consider the impact on children. A child primacy norm should be based in the precautionary principle: when a potential activity presents a significant risk to children, the default shouldn't be to proceed in the face of uncertainty; it should be to gather more information, consider alternative approaches, and act to address the threat. And the burden of proof ought to be on those creating the risk to provide evidence of safety, not on those subject to the risk to provide evidence of harm. When corporate executives are tasked with proactively putting children first, a product like the Rock 'n Play does not appear on the market without careful vetting and parents don't have to worry that the carrot puree baby food they are feeding their toddler might have high levels of cadmium. When child primacy leads companies to rigorously test the safety of their products, protect the privacy of their customers, ensure their supply chains are child-labor free, scrutinize their advertisements for gender stereotypes, and forgo tax avoidance strategies, that leaves us all better off. The annual drain on the global economy from companies marketing breastmilk substitutes to mothers for whom it is a poor choice is estimated to come in at $302 billion.

Child primacy isn't a ban on making products from which some adults derive great pleasure—think cigarettes. It's a prompt to make better products that provide pleasure and also don't give millions of people around the world cancer. It's a prompt to develop screening tools that prevent child rape scenes from being uploaded on your pornography site and algorithms that distinguish a child's swiping of the screen from an adult's. A business that cannot innovate and that can only remain profitable if it harms children isn't a business that should stay open. But that is not most businesses. Indeed, there is tremendous new profit in a landscape where children's interests are prioritized.

Perhaps, then, child primacy isn't radical at all. We've already agreed that we don't want ten-year-olds losing fingers in our factories, dying after eating adulterated food, or getting sick from drinking water contaminated by a power plant. This is just a better way to get to where we already want and expect to be. Requiring companies to act in ways that maximize children's interests on the front end is always going to be better than trying to punish them for harming children on the back end. Once established, it means we don't need to devote so much effort to regulatory enforcement and companies don't have to spend so much money on regulatory evasions.

There is no reason that government couldn't be similarly reimagined to ensure a child-first approach in setting policy. What if we required a child-impact assessment each time we considered a proposed regulation, law, or zoning change? In line with how we might reframe business decision-making, we could mandate that any new government action be subject to an audit of the likely effects on children. The aim would be to get lawmakers to consider and prioritize children's interests, both in areas where children are front and center—like a bill cutting infant healthcare coverage—and areas where the benefit or harm to children is significant but hidden—like a proposal to increase the cost of energy.

Consider a new state law, meant to create uniform labor conditions, that prevents localities from raising the minimum wage on their own. Nothing to do with children, right? Well, when researchers actually assessed the impact, they estimated that 605 infant deaths could be attributed to such laws in a single year. Sometimes the driest, most-adult-sounding things—preemption rules, tax code provisions, intellectual property guidelines—can have visceral implications for our youngest citizens. But we don't know because we don't check.

The great news is that there is solid precedent for such impact assessments. Faced with America's worst disparity between Black and white incarceration rates, New Jersey passed a 2018 law requiring any proposed criminal justice regulation to be assessed for its likely effects on racial and ethnic minorities. The law acknowledges that sometimes a bill looks neutral on its face but can harm distinct groups of citizens. And it explicitly endorses the value of anticipating and avoiding adverse consequences: the inertia of bureaucracy means that reversing course after action has already been taken can be impossible even when the negative effects become clear to everyone.

While racial impact statements are a recent development, fiscal and environmental impact statements have a long history. The 1970 National Environmental Policy Act, requiring federal agencies to prepare a statement for actions "significantly affecting the quality of the human environment," was prompted by public outrage at the government's failure to protect our precious natural resources—much as it has failed to protect our children today. And there are many aspects of the environmental framework that can serve as a valuable model in building a child impact process: it, too, should have a proactive focus, emphasize transparency, rely on experts, and require the analysis of alternatives to the proposed action, including taking no action at all. But we can also do better. In contrast to the National Environmental Policy Act, child impact assessments ought to be a formal constraint, not merely informational. And we should require follow-up auditing to see whether the proposed law has measured up as anticipated.

As we consider specifics—whether the process should be cast as a new auditing requirement or framed as a tweak on existing cost-benefit mandates, whether the focus should be on children as a unified group or on subgroups based on age, gender, race, and other factors—we can learn from the experiences of other countries. Spurred by the UN's Convention on the Rights of the Child, Austria, Belgium, Italy, Finland, Sweden, and the United Kingdom have all adopted provisions mandating child impact assessments. We don't have to invent new criteria; we don't have to blaze new trails.

In fact, we can take inspiration from what has already been done in our own backyard. In 2008, Memphis and Shelby County, Tennessee, launched their own child impact statement initiative to get local government decision makers to better understand the consequences of their actions on children. For decades, kids living along the Mississippi River delta had been an afterthought. When manufacturing plants were built, no one considered how industrial contamination might affect their development. When funding cuts were proposed for a hospital, no one thought about how that might increase infant mortality. Reformers aimed to change that by getting officials collecting and assessing data about child safety, early development, education, child health, and other factors as part of their proposal process. The effort was limited by tight budgets and practical constraints, but over the next five years, roughly 150 impact statements were drafted by policy makers.

We can build on these experiences to make child impact assessment a reality across the United States. Legislatures—at all levels—ought to act to make consideration of the effect of government action on children a required part of lawmaking and administrative governance. Child impact assessments could be handled entirely within the existing institutional frameworks, with individual agencies conducting their own reviews as part of a standardized protocol. That's likely to be the least disruptive and most politically feasible approach.

But, in the interests of consistency, accuracy, and efficiency, we should also consider empowering a single independent agency to conduct the impact assessments across the government. More broadly, such an agency could promote children's interests and coordinate children's welfare issues across agencies. We need to do a better job of connecting juvenile delinquency issues handled by the Department of Justice with educational performance issues handled by the Department of Education with environmental hazard issues handled by the Environmental Protection Agency with family eviction issues handled by Health and Human Services. You can't adequately tackle a problem like lead paint exposure if you use a siloed approach.

Much as we did with the creation of the Environmental Protection Agency in 1970, when various environmental responsibilities delegated across agencies were consolidated into a single, new independent agency, we could centralize the bulk of child-centered government activity within this stand-alone entity. Rather than create an agency from scratch, we might reinvigorate and recast the Children's Bureau, that first federal agency in the world designed to focus exclusively on children's welfare.

Today, the bureau is fixed within a complex patchwork of twenty-one offices comprising the Administration for Children and Families, one of eleven operating divisions in the Department of Health and Human Services. Its mission has been significantly trimmed back and the broad vision it embodied has been superseded by one that might be best likened to a haphazard group quilting project, with overlapping pieces, gaping holes, and clashing patterns— indeed, with squares sewn onto trousers, curtains, and coats, all pulling in different directions. If, as this book has argued, children have unique capacities and vulnerabilities that are being ignored to their— and our—great detriment, if we have a bad habit of shifting to talking about parents' rights or shareholders' rights or defendants' rights every time children's rights are brought up, if we frequently get into trouble by focusing on one facet of the child or one period of development without appreciating the whole child over the course of their life, it makes sense to have a separate, independent agency specifically and solely tasked with ensuring the well-being of children.

There are plenty of people who will tell you that a Children's Bureau to stand alongside the Department of Defense, the Department of Commerce, and the Department of Agriculture is a pipe dream. But those people ignore the long history of Americans confronting injustice and major threats with bold actions—actions far more sweeping and disruptive than would be entailed with the establishment of a new Children's Bureau. We are people who fought World War II, implemented the New Deal, oversaw Reconstruction, and formed an entirely new country. Are the circumstances really less grave than those that led to the creation of a Department of Homeland Security in 2002 or a Consumer Financial Protection Bureau in 2011? Are we really more cautious and cynical than previous generations? It was no progressive who led the creation of the EPA; it was Richard Nixon calling Americans to "a common cause of all the people of this country," "a cause beyond party and beyond factions." That cause today is children's rights. There could be a federal Children's Bureau and a Children's Bureau in every state.

What limits us is not our capacity to accomplish big things—extending the vote to kids, a child primacy norm for corporations, child impact assessment in government, Children's Bureaus across the country—it is our capacity for humility. Progress, then, depends just as much on changing how we see *ourselves* as on changing how we see *children*.

What is our role—adults of the present—in our families, in our neighborhoods, as a nation, at work and on Saturday mornings, when we are together and when we are alone? One of the greatest benefits of adopting a child-first mindset is to help us remove ourselves from the center of the narrative. Why is the seat at the head of the table ours to claim, night after night? Do we deserve what we take? What right do we have to discount the interests of generations to come? Do we inherit the world from our ancestors or borrow it from our children?

Prioritizing young people can help us give up the idea that everything is ours to decide, to use as we see fit, to the exclusion of everyone else. It can put us on track to understand the impact of our choices, not simply on children but on future generations, on people living in other countries, on other species. Giving a thought to children can allow us to live sustainably, aware of and respectful of the lives of others.

ACKNOWLEDGMENTS

I wrote this book during a period when I often felt like turning away from humanity—taking my family from the sick heart of the city, from an America aflame with foolishness, enmity, and injustice, to an island populated only by pine trees. But the project survived a pandemic, an insurrection, civil unrest, a biblical flood, and all the other upheaval of this anxious era because people did not turn away from me.

I thank my wife, Brooke, most of all, for being my steadfast partner, always there to offer comfort, strength, wisdom, and joy. You show me every day how good people can be.

This book is dedicated to all children, but I could not have written it without the two who are most special to me. The love I have for them made it almost unbearable to conduct research on topics like climate change and gun violence, but my kids are also what gives me the greatest hope for the future. Thank you, too, to my wonderful parents who forged my belief, through their example, that it is possible to both protect and empower children.

I am greatly indebted to the talent of two amazing editors. Emma Berry nurtured this book from its infancy with great care and intelligence and never stopped believing in its potential, even in its awkward adolescence: when it arrived one day, twice as long as it was meant to be, inconsistent, and moody. Aubrey Martinson matched Emma's enthusiasm, and brought her own sharp insights, thoughtful edits, and passion to the project, ensuring that the manuscript blossomed into adulthood. I feel so lucky to have worked with both of them and to get to continue my relationship with the amazing team at Crown, who did such a fantastic job with my first book, *Unfair*. For helping to secure that ongoing partnership and for his astute stewardship of the book as it launches into the world, I thank my inimitable agent, Rafe Sagalyn.

Along the way, I benefited from an incredible group of research assistants: Dejah Adams, Marisabel Alonso, Erin Brill, Stephanie Burke, Samantha DiGiuseppe, Matthew Foster, Annelise Gress, Amanda Lewis, Danielle Paterno, Erin Rein, Madelena Rizzo, Lindsay Romeo, Kayla Rubin, Lewis Sorokin, Christa Tomasulo, Kerry Weiner, Mary Whaley, and Allison Wickman. I am also grateful to the Drexel Legal Research Center staff, including Eric Berg, Margaret DeFelice, and David Haendler, and especially Lindsay Steussy, for tracking down sources with great ingenuity and efficiency. And I extend my appreciation to Tyra Mwai and Justin Andreani-Fabroni for excellent administrative assistance.

Thank you to my tremendous colleagues at Drexel for lending their expertise and keen observations to this project and to Dean Dan Filler for his unwavering and enthusiastic support. Thank you, as well, to my many students over the years—particularly in the Rights of Children—who, in sharing their experiences and insights, indelibly shaped my own views about how to better the lives of young people. And thank you to the numerous scholars and activists whose work on children's rights inspires me every day. I am particularly grateful for the feedback from participants at the "Children's Rights at 30" AALS International Human Rights Panel and the Duke Law School Criminal Justice Books Conference, and for the valuable guidance from the Juvenile Justice Center, Families Against Mandatory Minimums, Beat the Streets, and Upstream USA.

I also wish to extend my gratitude to my brilliant co-authors Geoff Goodwin and Jon Hanson, my brother and extended family, and friends who offered encouragement and advice, especially Dom Tierney, Peter Leckman, Catherine Price, and the intrepid writers of Team Onagadori.

Finally, I want to thank all of the people I interviewed for this project. You shared your lives with great honesty, perception, and courage. For some of you, you revisited your most painful moments in the hope that other children might be spared similar fates. I am in awe of your resilience and commitment and I hope I can amplify your voice to spur progress. Together, we can remake this world.

NOTES

Introduction

ix *"When your children"* "Little Boy and Girl Toilers Grow Pallid at Work Benches," *Spokane Press*, June 19, 1906, 4.

ix *On a summer evening* "Toilers," 4.

ix *The story* "Toilers," 4.

ix *Give a thought* "Toilers," 4.

ix *Five inches short* "Toilers," 4.

ix *They dangle like* "Nicotine—Alcohol and Drug Foundation," Alcohol and Drug Foundation, accessed June 1, 2021, https://adf.org.au/drug-facts/nicotine/.

ix *His body smells* "Toilers," 4; "Odor Descriptor Listing for Tobacco," The Good Scents Company, accessed June 2, 2021, http://www.thegoodscents company.com/odor/tobacco.html.

ix *His widowed mother* "Toilers," 4.

ix *For this boy* "Toilers," 4.

ix *Sunday is but* "Toilers," 4.

ix *Stop and give* "Toilers," 4.

ix *Her eyes cast* "Toilers," 4.

ix *She arrives* "Toilers," 4.

ix *"Her hands are thin"* "Toilers," 4.

ix *All day, she stands* "Toilers," 4.

ix *But she does not eat* "Toilers," 4.

x *At the turn* "Toilers," 4; Mary Ann Mason, "The U.S. and the International Children's Rights Crusade: Leader or Laggard?" *Journal of Social History* 38, no. 4 (Summer 2005): 959, 1175.

x *They considered* "Toilers," 4; Mason, "Children's Rights Crusade," 959, 1175; Kasey L. Wassenaar, "Defenseless Children: Achieving Competent Representation for Children in Abuse and Neglect Proceedings Through Statutory Reform in South Dakota," *South Dakota Law Review* 56, no. 1 (2011): 182.

x *Sitting in the heat* "Spokane Agriculture: Inland Northwest Agribusiness," Advantage Spokane, accessed June 2, 2021, https://advantagespokane.com/agribusiness/; "Starving in London; A Story Written by One of Starving," *Spokane Press*, June 19, 1906, 3.

x   *It was their scrape* "Starving in London," 3.

x   *Chairs weren't included* "Starving in London," 3.

x   *The outside light* "Starving in London," 3.

x   *If they came up* "Starving in London," 3.

x   *For the Twopenny Coffin* "Starving in London," 3.

x   *It stuck* "Starving in London," 3.

x   *As the mother explained* "Starving in London," 3.

x   *They keep* "Starving in London," 3.

x   *The day her daughter* "Starving in London," 3.

x   *That left the ashes* "Starving in London," 3.

x   *The people of Spokane* "Starving in London," 3.

x   *Above the fold* "Child-Savers Hold Meeting," *Spokane Press,* June 19, 1906, 4.

xi   *Their aim was* Wayne Carp, "The Sealed Adoption Records Controversy in Historical Perspective: The Case of the Children's Home Society of Washington, 1895–1988," *Journal of Sociology and Social Welfare* 19, no. 2 (May 1992): 27–33; April Anderson-Zorn, "Double Duty: Processing and Exhibiting the Children's Home Society of Florida Collection as an Archivist and Historian," *Electronic Theses and Dissertations* (May 2007): 47.

xi   *And every week* See, e.g., "National Congress of Mothers Meet," *Spokane Press,* May 5, 1903, 3.

xi   *In 1906* Melissa Moon et al., "Is Child Saving Dead? Public Support for Juvenile Rehabilitation," *Crime & Delinquency* 46, no. 1 (Jan. 2000): 38; Calli M. Cain, "Child Savers," in *The Encyclopedia of Juvenile Delinquency and Justice,* ed. Christopher J. Schreck (Hoboken, N.J.: John Wiley & Sons, 2018), 93–95.

xi   *The child savers* Cain, "Child Savers"; Mason, "Children's Rights Crusade." Some critics are skeptical that the ultimate purposes of these reformers was the betterment of children and not simply the control of poor, urban immigrants and the threat they posed to the existing social and economic order. See, e.g., Cain, "Child Savers"; Barry Krisberg, *Juvenile Justice: Redeeming Our Children* (Thousand Oaks, Calif.: Sage, 2005), 37; Anthony M. Platt, *The Child Savers: The Invention of Delinquency* (Chicago: University of Chicago Press, 1977).

xi   *They gave us* Cain, "Child Savers."

xi   *They helped marshal* Stuart N. Hart, "From Property to Person Status: Historical Perspective on Children's Rights," *American Psychologist* 46, no. 1 (1991): 53–59; Wassenaar, "Defenseless Children," 182; Geraldine Steinmets, "The Clean Milk Campaign in Hamilton," *American Journal of Public Hygiene* 20, no. 1 (1910): 98; "A Clean Milk Campaign," *Lancet* 176, no. 4555 (Dec. 17, 1910): 1780.

xi   *As supper beckoned* "Beef Bill Is Passed," *Spokane Press,* June 19, 1906, 1.

xi   *By the end of 1906* "Mrs. Winslow's Soothing Syrup," *Spokane Press,* June 19, 1906, 4.

xi   *Mrs. Winslow's had long been* Arthur Joseph Cramp, *Nostrums and Quackery* (Chicago: American Medical Association Press, 1912), 432; "Poison in the Sleeping Potion," *Seattle Daily Times,* Apr. 5, 1907, 1.

xi   *For thousands of kids* "A Note from the Collections: Dangerous 'Soothing Syrups': Patent Medicines," International Museum of Surgical Science, last modified Feb. 10, 2020, https://imss.org/2020/02/10/a-note-from -the-collections-dangerous-soothing-syrups-patent-medicines/; "Mrs. Winslow's Soothing Syrup—Another Baby Sacrificed," *Journal of the American Medical Association* 54, no. 17 (Apr. 23, 1910): 1390.

xi *Regulation came* Cramp, *Nostrums and Quackery,* 435; "Another Baby Sacrificed," 1390; Troy R. Bennet, "This 'Baby Killer' Drug Was Invented in Maine and Made a Bangor Pharmacist a Millionaire," WGME, Nov. 11, 2019; Samuel Hopkins Adams, *The Great American Fraud,* 4th ed. (New York: P. F. Collier & Son, 1907), 40–42; "Illegal Drugs. Druggists of Idaho Are Warned by State Drug Inspector," *Twin Falls (Idaho) Times,* Feb. 27, 1912, 1.

xii *They pressed on* Bennet, "'Baby Killer' Drug"; "A Note from the Collections"; "Use of Narcotics Means Child Murder," *Seattle Daily Times,* Apr. 7, 1907, 10.

xii *Reformers were following* Richard Lawrence and Mario Hesse, *Juvenile Justice* (Los Angeles: Sage, 2010), 17; Theodore Ferdinand, "History Overtakes the Juvenile Justice System," *Crime & Delinquency* 37, no. 2 (Apr. 1991): 204–24; Moon et al., "Is Child Saving Dead?" 38–60; Martin Guggenheim, *What's Wrong with Children's Rights* (Cambridge, Mass.: Harvard University Press, 2005), 4–5.

xii *On page one* "Boys Robbed Flower Beds," *Spokane Press,* June 19, 1906, 1.

xii *The previous night* "Boys Robbed Flower Beds," 1.

xii *The young teens* "Boys Robbed Flower Beds," 1.

xii *As a Spokane prosecutor* "New Court for Bad Boys," *Spokane Press,* June 10, 1904, 2.

xii *But in 1905* "First Juvenile Court Held in Spokane County," *Spokane Press,* July 29, 1905, 1.

xii *They'd remodeled rooms* "Poindexter Is Now Arbiter of Marital Woes," *Spokane Press,* July 15, 1905, 1.

xii *In his words* "Court of Correction, Not of Punishment," *Spokane Press,* July 31, 1905, 1.

xii *The transformation* "Juvenile Court," *Spokane Press,* Jan. 16, 1905, 3; "Governor Opposes Lobbying," *Spokane Press,* Jan. 11, 1905, 1.

xii *The legal system* "Juvenile Court," 3; "Governor Opposes Lobbying," 1.

xii *Newspapers amplified* "Juvenile Court Idea," *Seattle Star,* Aug. 12, 1903, 4.

xii The Spokane Press *published* "Justice to a Boy," *Spokane Press,* Sept. 27, 1904, 2; "Boys' Friend Runs for Governor of Colorado," *Spokane Press,* Oct. 11, 1906, 2; "Judge 'Ben' B. Lindsey of Denver, Father of Juvenile Court System," *Spokane Press,* July 3, 1905, 4.

xii *The standout in the series* "Justice to a Boy," 2.

xii *The boy had been* "Judge 'Ben,'" 4.

xiii *But "a new cop"* "Justice to a Boy," 2.

xiii *Lindsey listened* "Judge 'Ben,'" 4.

xiii *"A live boy"* "Judge 'Ben,'" 4.

xiii *It was, to the paper* "Justice to a Boy," 2.

xiii *The other forces* "Boys Robbed," 1.

xiii *Rather than being sent* "Boys Robbed," 1.

xiii *A separate juvenile justice system* Mason, "Children's Rights Crusade," 959.

xiii *As the editors* "Widen the School Idea," *Spokane Press,* Feb. 20, 1903, 2.

xiii *On the same page* "Great Increase Noted in School Attendance" and "First Ward Wants Another School," *Spokane Press,* June 19, 1906, 1.

xiii *The paper had warned* "Widen the School Idea," 2.

xiii *Across fields* See, e.g., Joseph M. Hawes, *The Children's Rights Movement: A History of Advocacy and Protection* (Boston: Twayne, 1991), xi; Robin Walker Sterling, "Fundamental Unfairness: *In Re Gault* and the Road Not Taken," *Maryland Law Review* 72, no. 3 (2013): 617–18.

xiv *Saving children* Cain, "Child Savers," 95.

xiv *By 1912, President William Taft* Kriste Lindenmeyer, "The U.S. Children's Bureau and Infant Mortality in the Progressive Era," *Journal of Education* 177, no. 3 (1995): 57; "History," Children's Bureau: An Office of the Administration for Children and Families, last reviewed July 1, 2021, https://www .acf.hhs.gov/cb/about/history. Four years earlier, in 1909, President Teddy Roosevelt created the White House Conference on Children—the first of seven such meetings held by presidents in the succeeding decades—to address education, health, and other issues affecting American children. 1909 White House Conference on the Care of Dependent Children (Jan. 25–26, 1909); Maria Grahn-Farley, "The U.N. Convention on the Rights of the Child and the Forgotten History of the White House Children's Conferences, 1909–1971," *Transnational Law & Contemporary Problems* 20, no. 2 (June 2011): 309–74.

xiv *As the bureau's* U.S. Department of Labor, *First Annual Report of the Chief, Children's Bureau to the Secretary of Labor for the Fiscal Year Ended June 30 1913* (Washington, D.C.: Government Printing Office, 1914), 6.

xiv *True advancement* Paula S. Fass, "A Historical Context for the United Nations Convention on the Rights of the Child," *ANNALS of the American Academy of Political and Social Science* 633, no. 1 (Jan. 1, 2011): 21.

xiv *In America today* Emily A. Shrider et al., U.S. Census Bureau, Current Population Reports, *Income and Poverty in the United States: 2020* (Washington, D.C.: U.S. Government Publishing Office, Sept. 2021): 13, https://www .census.gov/content/dam/Census/library/publications/2021/demo/p60 -273.pdf.

xiv *In our largest cities* Ian Lundberg and Louis Donnelly, "A Research Note on the Prevalence of Housing Eviction Among Children Born in U.S. Cities," *Demography* 56, no. 1 (Feb. 2019): 391.

xiv *And, on any given night* Meghan Henry et al., U.S. Department of Housing and Urban Development, Office of Community Planning and Development, *The 2020 Annual Homeless Assessment Report (AHAR) to Congress* (Jan. 2021): 8.

xv *The agonizing decision* Annie Nova, "Millions of Americans May Not Be Able to Pay Their Rent in October. What to Do If You're One of Them," CNBC, Oct. 2, 2020, https://www.cnbc.com/2020/10/02/millions-of -americans-may-not-be-able-to-pay-rent-in-october.html.

xv *One in eight households* "Food Security Status of U.S. Households with Children in 2019," U.S. Department of Agriculture Economic Research Service, updated Sept. 9, 2020, https://www.ers.usda.gov/topics/food -nutrition-assistance/food-security-in-the-us/key-statistics-graphics.aspx

#children; Tim Arango, "Just Because I Have a Car Doesn't Mean I Have Enough Money to Buy Food," *New York Times*, Sept. 3, 2020.

xv *Without adequate care leave* "Starving in London," 3; "Parental Leave: Is There a Case for Government Action?" CATO Institute, Oct. 2, 2018, https://www.cato.org/policy-analysis/parental-leave-there-case-government-action#side-effects-of-mandated-or-subsidized-leave; "Failing Its Families: Lack of Paid Leave and Work-Family Supports in the US," Human Rights Watch, Feb. 23, 2011, https://www.hrw.org/report/2011/02/23/failing-its-families/lack-paid-leave-and-work-family-supports-us.

xv *Nearly a million children* Santadarshan Sadhu et al., *Assessing Progress in Reducing Child Labor in Cocoa Production in Cocoa Growing Areas of Côte d'Ivoire and Ghana*, NORC at the University of Chicago (Oct. 2020): 9–11, https://www.norc.org/PDFs/Cocoa%20Report/NORC%202020%20Cocoa%20Report_English.pdf.

xv *Tens of thousands* Peter Whoriskey and Rachel Siegel, "Cocoa's Child Laborers," *Washington Post*, June 5, 2019; Peter Whoriskey, "Supreme Court Weighs Child-Slavery Case Against Nestlé USA, Cargill," *Washington Post*, Dec. 1, 2020.

xv *They drink polluted water* Whoriskey and Siegel, "Cocoa's Child Laborers"; Whoriskey, "Supreme Court Weighs."

xv *They are locked up* Whoriskey and Siegel, "Cocoa's Child Laborers"; Whoriskey, "Supreme Court Weighs."

xv *We may have barred* Jeffrey Gettleman and Suhasini Raj, "As Covid-19 Closes Schools, the World's Children Go to Work," *New York Times*, Sept. 27, 2020; Samantha Raphelson, "It Is Legal for Kids to Work on Tobacco Farms, but It Can Make Them Sick," NPR, July 13, 2018, https://www.npr.org/2018/07/13/628585912/it-is-legal-for-kids-to-work-on-tobacco-farms-but-it-can-make-them-sick.

xv *And they work* Raphelson, "It Is Legal for Kids."

xv *It is legal* Raphelson, "It Is Legal for Kids"; Fair Labor Standards Act, U.S. Code 29 (1938), § 213(c)(1)(A–B).

xv *Not the toil* Margaret Wurth, "Teens of the Tobacco Fields," Human Rights Watch, Dec. 9, 2015, https://www.hrw.org/report/2015/12/09/teens-tobacco-fields/child-labor-united-states-tobacco-farming.

xv *Not the reasons* Wurth, "Teens."

xv *And not the cost* Wurth, "Teens."

xv *At night* Wurth, "Teens."

xv *More than a hundred years* Robert H. McKnight and Henry A. Spiller, "Green Tobacco Sickness in Children and Adolescents," *Public Health Reports* 120, no. 6 (Nov.–Dec. 2005): 604.

xv *They are still breathing* Raphelson, "It Is Legal for Kids"; Wurth, "Teens"; Natalia A. Goriounova and Huibert D. Mansvelder, "Short- and Long-Term Consequences of Nicotine Exposure During Adolescence for Prefrontal Cortex Neuronal Network Function," *Cold Spring Harbor Perspectives in Medicine* 2, no. 12 (Dec. 2012): 1–14; Jennifer B. Dwyer, Susan C. McQuown, and Frances M. Leslie, "The Dynamic Effects of Nicotine on the Developing Brain," *Pharmacology & Therapeutics* 122, no. 2 (May 2009): 125–39; Catherine Karr, "Children's Environmental Health in Agricultural Settings," *Journal of Agromedicine* 17, no. 2 (Apr. 10, 2012): 127–39; James R. Roberts and J. Routt Reigart, "Chronic Effects," in *Recognition and Management of Pesticide Poisonings,* 6th ed. (Washington, D.C.: Office of Pesticide Programs, 2013), 212–38; Karen Coates and Valeria Fernández, "The Young Hands That Feed Us," *Pacific Standard,* July 9, 2019; Paul K. Mills and Purvi Shah, "Cancer Incidence in California Farm Workers, 1988–2010," *American Journal of Industrial Medicine* 57, no. 7 (July 2014): 737–47.

xv *They—thirty-three each day* Coates and Fernández, "The Young Hands That Feed Us."

xv *In 2018, the Department* Ben Penn, "Trump Administration Wants to Train Teens in 'Hazardous' Jobs," *Bloomberg Law,* May 8, 2018.

xv *In 2020, the Environmental Protection Agency* Nadja Popovich, Livia Albeck-Ripka, and Kendra Pierre-Louis, "The Trump Administration Rolled Back More Than 100 Environmental Rules. Here's the Full List," *New York Times,* Oct. 16, 2020.

xvi *A child born today* Bonnie Berkowitz et al., "How Many Years Do We Lose to the Air We Breathe?" *Washington Post,* Nov. 19, 2018.

xvi *This year, roughly half a million* Nicholas Kristof, "Our Children Deserve Better," *New York Times,* Sept. 11, 2019.

xvi *Mrs. Winslow's Syrup* Alysha Strongman, "Mrs. Winslow's Soothing Syrup: The Baby Killer," Museum of Health Care Blog, July 28, 2017, https://museumofhealthcare.blog/mrs-winslows-soothing-syrup-the-baby-killer/.

xvi *As Mallinckrodt* Sari Horwitz et al., "'SELL BABY SELL!': Inside the Opioid Industry's Marketing Machine," *Washington Post,* Dec. 6, 2019.

xvi *So, today, every fifteen minutes* Blake Farmer, "In the Fight for Money for the Opioid Crisis, Will the Youngest Victims Be Left Out?" Maine Public, Nov. 22, 2019, https://www.mainepublic.org/2019-11-22/in-the-fight-for-money-for-the-opioid-crisis-will-the-youngest-victims-be-left-out.

xvi *How is it possible* Jacqueline Howard, "Childhood Obesity Is Getting Worse, Study Says," CNN, Mar. 13, 2018, https://www.cnn.com/2018/02/26/health/childhood-obesity-in-the-us-study/index.html; Centers for Disease Control and Prevention, "Obesity," last revised Sept. 18, 2018, https://www.cdc.gov/healthyschools/obesity/index.htm; Asheley Cockrell Skinner et al., "Prevalence of Obesity and Severe Obesity in US Children, 1999–2016," *Pediatrics* 141, no. 3 (Mar. 1, 2018): 6.

xvi *Count the number of spots* Walter Gantz et al., "Food for Thought: Television Food Advertising to Children in the United States," KFF, Mar. 2007, https://www.kff.org/other/food-for-thought-television-food-advertising-to/; Rob Moodie et al., "Profits and Pandemics: Prevention of Harmful Effects of Tobacco, Alcohol, and Ultra-Processed Food and Drink Industries," *Lancet* 381, no. 9867 (Feb. 23, 2013): 670–79; Boyd A. Swinburn et al., "The Global Obesity Pandemic: Shaped by Global Drivers and Local Environments," *Lancet* 378, no. 9793 (Aug. 27, 2011): 804–14.

xvi *The average American* Helen Clark et al., "A Future for the World's Children? A WHO–UNICEF–Lancet Commission," *Lancet* 395, no. 10224 (Feb. 2020): 605–58; Gantz et al., "Food for Thought."

xvi *Among the twenty richest* Ashish P. Thakar, "Child Mortality in the U.S. and

19 OECD Comparator Nations: A 50-Year Time-Trend Analysis," *Health Affairs* 37, no. 1 (2018): 140–49.

xvi *An American kid* Thakar, "Child Mortality in the U.S. and 19 OECD Comparator Nations," 140–49; Sarah Kliff, "American Kids Are 70 Percent More Likely to Die Before Adulthood Than Kids in Other Rich Countries," *Vox*, Jan. 8, 2018, https://www.vox.com/health-care/2018/1/8/16863656/childhood-mortality-united-states.

xvi *That wasn't true* Gopal K. Singh et al., "Infant Mortality in the United States: Trends, Differentials, and Projections, 1950 Through 2010," *American Journal of Public Health* 85, no. 7 (July 1995): 957–64; David Leonhardt, "Letting American Kids Die," *New York Times*, Feb. 17, 2018.

xvi *But while our peers* Joan Alker and Olivia Pham, "Nation's Progress on Children's Health Coverage Reverses Course," Georgetown University Health Policy Institute, Nov. 2018; Leonhardt, "Letting American Kids Die."

xvi *Even today* Alker and Pham, "Nation's Progress."

xvi *Car crashes* Rebecca M. Cunningham et al., "The Major Causes of Death in Children and Adolescents in the United States," *New England Journal of Medicine* 379, no. 25 (Dec. 20, 2018): 2468–75; David Hemenway and Matthew Miller, "Firearm Availability and Homicide Rates Across 26 High-Income Countries," *Journal of Trauma* 49, no. 6 (Dec. 2000): 985–88; Leonhardt, "Letting American Kids Die."

xvii *We've somehow ended up with a child* U.S. Department of Health & Human Services, Children's Bureau, *Child Maltreatment 2020* (2022), xi–xii, https://www.acf.hhs.gov/sites/default/files/documents/cb/cm2020.pdf; U.S. Department of Health & Human Services, Children's Bureau, *Foster Care Statistics 2019* (March 2021), 3, https://www.childwelfare.gov/pubpdfs/foster.pdf.

xvii *We've somehow ended up with a justice* Justice Abe Fortas noted the confounding situation in his 1966 opinion in *Kent v. United States:* "There is evidence, in fact, that there may be grounds for concern that the child receives the worst of both worlds: that he gets neither the protections accorded to adults nor the solicitous care and regenerative treatment postulated for children." Kent v. United States, 383 U.S. 541 (1966). And in subsequent decades the situation for children has only deteriorated.

xvii *Since 2002* John MacDonald et al., "The Effects of Local Police Surges on Crime and Arrests in New York City," *PLOS ONE* 11, no. 6 (June 16, 2016): 1–13. The majority of those kids were Black or Hispanic. Ailsa Chang, "For City's Teens, Stop-and-Frisk Is Black and White," WNYC News, May 29, 2012, https://www.wnyc.org/story/212460-city-teenagers-say-stop-and-frisk-all-about-race-and-class/; "Stop and Frisk 2011," New York Civil Liberties Union, NYCLU Briefing, 2012. While these stops were no more likely than chance to turn up a gun—and roughly nine out of ten resulted in no citation or arrest at all—the costs on children was immense. Ashley Southall and Michael Gold, "Why 'Stop-and-Frisk' Inflamed Black and Hispanic Neighborhoods," *New York Times*, Nov. 17, 2019; Rod K. Brunson, "'Police Don't Like Black People': African-American Young Men's Accumulated Police Experiences," *Criminology & Public Policy* 6, no. 1 (2007): 71–101. It is traumatic to be pushed up against a wall and frisked by men with guns simply because you were looking over your shoulder—a "furtive" movement—while walking home from school. Southall and Gold, "Inflamed"; Andrew Bacher-Hicks and Elijah de la Campa, "Social Costs of Proactive Policing" (working paper, Harvard University, Kennedy School of Government, Cambridge, Mass., Feb. 26, 2020), https://drive.google.com/file/d/1sSxhfmDY3N1VAN5XwyRObE65tm AZzhTj/view. Recent research shows that such aggressive policing reduces Black students' school attendance, decreases test scores, increases high school dropout rates, and depresses later college enrollment. Joscha Legewie and Jeffrey Fagan, "Aggressive Policing and the Educational Performance of Minority Youth," *American Sociological Review* 84, no. 2 (2019): 220–47; Bacher-Hicks and de la Campa, "Proactive Policing."

xvii *And two out of three* Civilian Complaint Review Board, "CCRB Report on Youth and Police," NYC Civilian Complaint Review Board, June 2020, 1–55.

xvii *The youngest are not spared* Bill Hutchinson, "More Than 30,000 Children Under Age 10 Have Been Arrested in the US Since 2013: FBI," ABC News, Oct. 1, 2019, https://abcnews.go.com/US/30000-children-age-10 -arrested-us-2013-fbi/story?id=65798787.

xvii *And, overall, roughly* Charles Puzzanchera, Melissa Sickmund, and Anthony Sladky, "Youth Younger Than 18 Prosecuted in Criminal Court: National Estimate, 2015 Cases," National Center for Juvenile Justice, Pittsburgh, Pa., 2018, 2; Richard A. Mendel, *No Place for Kids* (Baltimore: The Annie E. Casey Foundation, 2011), 6–7.

xvii *In the later part* Hart, "From Property to Person Status," 54–55; Tinker v. Des Moines Independent Community School District, 393 U.S. 503 (1969).

xvii *But, in recent decades* Justin Driver, "Do Public School Students Have Constitutional Rights?" *New York Times*, Aug. 31, 2018; Justin Driver, *The Schoolhouse Gate* (New York: Pantheon Books, 2018); New Jersey v. T.L.O, 468 U.S. 325 (1985); Ingraham v. Wright, 430 U.S. 651 (1977); Morse v. Frederick, 551 U.S. 393 (2007).

xvii *When minors have sought* Guggenheim, *What's Wrong with Children's Rights*, 11.

xvii *Today,* The Spokane Press's "Justice to a Boy," 2.

xviii *So, too, is their vision* "Widen the School Idea," *Spokane Press*, Feb. 20, 1903, 2.

xviii *Against their expectations* "Widen the School Idea," 2.

xviii *In my well-off neighborhood* "Widen the School Idea," 2.

xviii *Overall, where once* Stephen S. Lim, "Measuring Human Capital: A Systematic Analysis of 195 Countries and Territories, 1990–2016," *Lancet* 392, no. 10154 (Oct. 6, 2018): 1217–34.

xviii *That matters in the present* Maria Gutiérrez-Domènech, "School Dropouts in Europe: Trends and Drivers," La Caixa Working Papers Series (Apr. 2011).

xviii *And that matters in the future* Lauren Leatherby, "Five Charts Show Why Millennials Are Worse Off Than Their Parents," *Financial Times*, Aug. 29, 2017.

xviii *Because of our actions* "Millennial Generation: Information on the Economic Status of Millennial Households Compared to Previous Generations," U.S. Government Accountability Office, Dec. 2019.

xviii *In the coming years* David Wallace-Wells, *The Uninhabitable Earth*, (New York: Tim Duggan Books, 2019); Coral Davenport, "Major Climate Report Describes a Strong Risk of Crisis as Early as 2040," *New York Times*, Oct. 7, 2018; Clark et al., "A Future for the World's Children?" 607.

xix *They had to figure* "The Wright Brothers | Fundamental Flight Problems," Smithsonian National Air Space Museum, accessed June 3, 2021, https:// airandspace.si.edu/exhibitions/wright-brothers/online/fly/1899 /fundamentals.cfm; "The Road to the First Flight," Wright Brothers National Memorial, U.S. National Park Service, accessed June 3, 2021, https:// www.nps.gov/wrbr/learn/historyculture/theroadtothefirstflight.htm.

xix *It was flawed* "The Road to the First Flight."

xix *Even as they professed* Geoff K. Ward, *The Black Child Savers: Racial Democracy and Juvenile Justice* (Chicago: University of Chicago Press, 2012); Krisberg, *Juvenile Justice*.

xix *Even as they spoke broadly* Guggenheim, *What's Wrong with Children's Rights*, 6; Manfred Liebel, "Schools of Thought in Children's Rights," in *Children's Rights from Below: Cross-Cultural Perspectives*, ed. Manfred Liebel (Basingstoke, Eng.: Palgrave Macmillan, 2012), 64.

xix *Viewing children more* Hart, "From Property to Person Status," 54; Wassenaar, "Defenseless Children," 185; Merril Sobie, "The Child Client: Representing Children in Child Protective Proceedings," *Touro Law Review* 22 (2006): 748–50; In Re Gault, 387 U.S. 1 (1967); Walker Sterling, "Fundamental Unfairness," 621.

xix *The early juvenile* Hart, "From Property to Person Status," 54; Wassenaar, "Defenseless Children," 185.

xix *The breath of social activism Walker* Sterling, "Fundamental Unfairness," 617–18; Ward, *The Black Child Savers*, 73–86; Guggenheim, *What's Wrong with Children's Rights*, 6; Liebel, "Schools of Thought in Children's Rights," 64.

xix *But the new generation* Guggenheim, *What's Wrong with Children's Rights*, 5–9; Manfred Liebel, "Introduction," in *Children's Rights from Below*, 37–39; Barry Feld, *Bad Kids: Race and the Transformation of the Juvenile Court* (New York: Oxford University Press, 1999), 79. For some of the books advocating for the liberation of children, see, e.g., Richard Farson, *Birthrights* (New York: Penguin, 1978); John Holt, *Escape from Childhood* (New York: Dutton, 1974); Beatrice Gross and Ronald Gross, eds., *The Children's Rights Movement: Overcoming the Oppression of Young People* (Garden City, N.Y.: Anchor Books, 1977).

xx *The new blueprints* Liebel, "Introduction."

xx *Faced with the challenge* Guggenheim, *What's Wrong with Children's Rights*, 12–13.

xx *Under the auspices* Feld, *Bad Kids*, 80.

xx *The animating idea* Kriste Lindenmeyer, "The U.S. Children's Bureau and Infant Mortality in the Progressive Era," *Journal of Education* 177, no. 3

(1995): 65. The idea of focusing on the "whole child" did not win the day in the international sphere, either, with a sectoral approach emphasizing particular aspects of children's experience—education, health, employment—coming to dominate. Clark et al., "A Future for the World's Children?" 629.

xx *And, more important* Lindenmeyer, "Children's Bureau," 64.

xx *Those were the result* Lindenmeyer, "Children's Bureau," 65.

xx *By the end of the century* Lindenmeyer, "Children's Bureau," 65; Ann Cammett, "Deadbeat Dads & Welfare Queens: How Metaphor Shapes Poverty Law," *Boston College Journal of Law & Social Justice* 34, no. 2 (2014): 233–65; Catherine Wimberly, "Deadbeat Dads, Welfare Moms, and Uncle Sam: How the Child Support Recovery Act Punishes Single-Mother Families," *Stanford Law Review* 53, no. 3 (2000): 729–66.

xxi *And they are reflected* United Nations Convention on the Rights of the Child, Nov. 20, 1989, 1577 U.N.T.S. 3; Hart, "From Property to Person Status," 53–59; Howard Davidson, "Does the U.N. Convention on the Rights of the Child Make a Difference?" *Michigan State International Law Review* 22, no. 2 (2014): 497–530; UNICEF, *The State of the World's Children: Celebrating 20 Years of the Convention on the Rights of the Child* (New York: United Nations Children's Fund, 2009), https://www.unicef.org/reports/state-worlds-children-2010.

xxi *By the 1970s* Fass, "A Historical Context," 26–27; Geneva Declaration of the Rights of the Child, Sept. 26, 1924, League of Nations O.J. Spec. Supp. 21; Declaration of the Rights of the Child, Nov. 20, 1959, G.A. Res. 1386, U.N. GAOR, 14th Sess., Supp. No. 16, U.N. Doc. A/4354.

xxi *With distance* Declaration of the Rights of Child; Fass, "A Historical Context," 26–27.

xxi *With the UN designating* Fass, "A Historical Context," 27.

xxi *Adopted by the General Assembly* Convention on the Rights of the Child.

xxi *It combines* Convention on the Rights of the Child.

xxi *It is as close* Barbara Bennett Woodhouse, *Hidden in Plain Sight: The Tragedy of Children's Rights from Ben Franklin to Lionel Tate* (Princeton, N.J.: Princeton University Press, 2008), 10–11.

xxi *And the United States* Sarah Mehta, "There's Only One Country That Hasn't Ratified the Convention on Children's Rights: US," American Civil Liberties Union, last modified Nov. 20, 2015, https://www.aclu.org/blog/human-rights/treaty-ratification/theres-only-one-country-hasnt-ratified-convention-childrens; Rachel Hagues, "The U.S. and the Convention on the Rights of the Child: What's the Hold-up?" *Journal of Social Work* 13, no. 3 (Apr. 24, 2013): 319–24; Lainie Rutkow and Joshua T. Lozman, "Suffer the Children: A Call for United States Ratification of the United Nations Convention on the Rights of the Child," *Harvard Human Rights Journal* 19 (2006): 161–90.

xxi *We are the sole holdout* Mehta, "There's Only One Country"; Rutkow and Lozman, "Suffer the Children," 164.

xxi *Although the convention had* Woodhouse, *Hidden in Plain Sight,* 2; Karen Attiah, "Why Won't the U.S. Ratify the U.N.'s Child Rights Treaty?" *Washington Post,* Nov. 21, 2014; So Jee Lee, "A Child's Voice vs. a Parent's Control: Resolving a Tension Between the Convention on the Rights of the Child and

U.S. Law," *Columbia Law Review* 117, no. 3 (2017): 70–71; Susan Kilbourne, "The Wayward Americans—Why the USA Has Not Ratified the UN Convention on the Rights of the Child," *Child and Family Law Quarterly* 10, no. 3 (1998): 244–45, 252.

xxi   *Champions of the fundamental sovereignty* Davidson, "Does the U.N. Convention," 497–530; Hart, "From Property to Person Status," 55–56; Cris R. Revaz, "An Introduction to the U.N. Convention on the Rights of the Child," in *The U.N. Convention on the Rights of the Child: An Analysis of Treaty Provisions and Implications of U.S. Ratification*, ed. Jonathan Todres, Mark E. Wojcik, and Cris R. Revaz (New York: Brill Nijhoff, 2006): 9, 13–14; Lee, "A Child's Voice." Pushback against a perceived threat to parental autonomy has also been evident in state and local efforts to enact children's rights legislation. For example, in the face of unrelenting attacks, the sponsors of a California children's bill of rights were forced to recast their provisions in terms of ensuring parents' rights to have access to government services. Amy Rothschild, "Is America Holding Out on Protecting Children's Rights?" *The Atlantic*, May 2, 2017; California Legislative Information, "Bill of Rights for the Children and Youth of California: Joint Legislative Committee," last amended Apr. 3, 2017, https://leginfo.legislature.ca.gov/faces/billTextClient.xhtml?bill_id=201720180SB18.

xxii   *Their fear* Convention on the Rights of the Child; Lee, "A Child's Voice"; Luisa Blanchfield, *The United Nations Convention on the Rights of the Child*, Congressional Research Service, Apr. 1, 2013, 3, 9–12.

xxii   *Moreover, an unwillingness* Tom O'Neill and Dawn Zinga, "Introduction," in *Children's Rights: Multidisciplinary Approaches to Participation and Protection* (Toronto: University of Toronto Press, 2008), 5; Blanchfield, *The United Nations Convention*, 15–16.

xxii   *Iran, for instance* O'Neill and Zinga, "Introduction," 5.

xxii   *Indeed, even as the convention* Liebel, "Introduction," 14; United Nations Committee on the Rights of the Child, *General Comment No. 12 (2009) The Right of the Child to Be Heard* (Geneva: July 1, 2009).

xxii   *So, while the convention* Charlotte S. Alexander and Jonathan Todres, "Evaluating the Implementation of Human Rights Law: A Data Analytics Research Agenda," *University of Pennsylvania International Law Journal* 43, no. 1 (2021): 9; Davidson, "Does the U.N. Convention," 515–16; Curtis Bradley and Jack Goldsmith, "Treaties, Human Rights and Conditional Consent," *University of Pennsylvania Law Review* 149, no. 2 (Dec. 2000): 399–468; Laura Lundy, Ursula Kilkelly, and Bronagh Byrne, "Incorporation of the United Nations Convention on the Rights of the Child in Law: A Comparative Review," *International Journal of Children's Rights* 21, no. 3 (2013): 442–63. There is hope that the convention may continue to gain force. In 2021, the Scottish parliament, for example, voted to make public authorities subject to the convention and to give children the power to go to court to enforce their rights. Scottish Government, "Landmark for Children's Rights," last modified Mar. 16, 2021, https://www.gov.scot/news/landmark-for-childrens-rights/.

xxii   *Rights violations remain* UNICEF, *For Every Child, Every Right: The Convention on the Rights of the Child at a Crossroads* (New York: United Nations

Children's Fund, 2019), 2, 11–13, https://www.unicef.org/reports/con
vention-rights-child-crossroads-2019; Jonathan Todres, "Making Children's Rights Widely Known," *Minnesota Journal of International Law* 29,
no. 1 (2020): 112.

xxii   *And the treaty* UNICEF, *For Every Child*, 2.

xxii   *For most children* Clark et al., "A Future for the World's Children?" 615, 629.
For example, the births of around one fourth of the global population of
children under five have never been registered. UNICEF, "Despite Significant Increase in Birth Registration, a Quarter of the World's Children Remain 'Invisible,'" Dec. 10, 2019, https://www.unicef.org/press-releases
/despite-significant-increase-birth-registration-quarter-worlds-children
-remain.

xxii   *The puzzle of incorporating* Some scholars have concluded that these different conceptions of rights are "totally incompatible." Guggenheim, *What's
Wrong with Children's Rights*, 13.

xxii   *Empirical research* Guggenheim, *What's Wrong with Children's Rights*, 12–13.

xxiii   *The research provides* Clark et al., "A Future for the World's Children?" 607.

xxiii   *The first years of life* "Brain Architecture," Center on the Developing Child,
accessed June 10, 2021, https://developingchild.harvard.edu/science/key
-concepts/brain-architecture/; Peter R. Huttenlocher, *Neural Plasticity:
The Effects of Environment on the Development of the Cerebral Cortex* (Cambridge, Mass.: Harvard University Press, 2002); Jack P. Shonkoff and Deborah A. Phillips, eds., *From Neurons to Neighborhoods: The Science of Early
Childhood Development* (Washington, D.C.: National Academy Press, 2000).

xxiii   *Moreover, the capabilities* Clark et al., "A Future for the World's Children?"
612; James J. Heckman, "The Economics of Inequality: The Value of Early
Childhood Education," *American Educator* 35, no. 1 (2011): 31–35; Maureen M. Black et al., "Early Childhood Development Coming of Age: Science Through the Life Course," *Lancet* 389, no. 10064 (2017): 77–90.

xxiii   *Strengthening infant health* Clark et al., "A Future for the World's Children?"
612.

xxiii   *Providing a safe and stable home* Clark et al., "A Future for the World's Children?" 607–8, 612.

xxiii   *And every year* Elsevier, "Childhood Neglect Leaves Generational Imprint:
Distinct Neural Connectivity Found in the Babies of Mothers Who Experienced Neglect as Children," *ScienceDaily*, Jan. 19, 2021, https://www
.sciencedaily.com/releases/2021/01/210119085222.htm; Cassandra L. Hen-
drix et al., "Maternal Childhood Adversity Associates with Front Amygdala
Connectivity in Neonates," *Biological Psychiatry: Cognitive Neuroscience
and Neuroimaging* 6, no. 4 (2021): 470–78; Louise Dixon et al., "Attributions
and Behaviours of Parents Abused as Children," *Journal of Child Psychology
and Psychiatry* 46, no. 1 (2005): 58–68; Lisa J. Berlin, Karen Appleyard, and
Kenneth A. Dodge, "Intergenerational Continuity in Child Maltreatment:
Mediating Mechanisms and Implications for Prevention," *Child Development* 82, no. 1 (2011): 162–76.

xxiii   *Childhood is the window* Clark et al., "A Future for the World's Children?"
610.

xxiv   *They accrue* Clark et al., "A Future for the World's Children?" 605, 608.

xxiv *Focusing on the broad benefits* In human rights circles, there is often an understandable reluctance to argue in favor of extending rights from a utilitarian perspective. Hart, "From Property to Person Status," 55. But the intrinsic or natural rights position has not been sufficient to ensure the welfare of children, and it is beneficial to make a broader case. Clark et al., "A Future for the World's Children?" 608.

xxiv *But the standard model* Guggenheim, *What's Wrong with Children's Rights,* 8–9.

xxiv *To many* Guggenheim, *What's Wrong with Children's Rights,* 9; Onora O'Neill, "Children's Rights and Children's Lives," *Ethics* 98, no. 3 (Apr. 1988): 446–48, 460–61.

xxiv *Another frame is needed* Others have noted the problematic nature of a theory of children's rights premised on capacity. See, e.g., Katherine Hunt Federle, "Children, Curfews, and the Constitution," *Washington University Law Quarterly* 73, no. 3 (1995): 1315–16, 1319; Katherine Hunt Federle, "On the Road to Reconceiving Rights for Children: A Postfeminist Analysis of the Capacity Principle," *DePaul Law Review* 42, no. 3 (1993): 983–1028. Indeed, there is a long history of theorists—Rousseau, Locke, Bentham, and Mill among them—excluding children from being holders of full (or in some cases even partial) rights on account of their lack of various predicate capacities. See, e.g., Jean-Jacques Rousseau, *Jean Jacques Rousseau: His Educational Theories Selected from Émile, Julie and Other Writings,* ed. R. L. Archer and S. E. Frost, Jr. (Woodbury, N.Y.: Barron's Educational Series, 1964), 92; Thomas Hobbes, *Leviathan,* ed. Richard Tuck (Cambridge: Cambridge University Press, 1991), 187; John Locke, *The Second Treatise of Government,* ed. Thomas P. Peardon (New York: The Library of Liberal Arts, 1952), 31–33, 42; Jeremy Bentham, *The Collected Works of Jeremy Bentham: An Introduction to the Principles of Morals and Legislation,* ed. J. H. Burns and H.L.A. Hart (Oxford: Oxford University Press, 1996), 244–45; John Stuart Mill, *On Liberty; with the Subjection of Women; and Chapters on Socialism,* ed. Stefan Collini (Cambridge: Cambridge University Press, 1989), 13–14. In addition, as we will see, our judgments of capacity are often biased in the self-interested favor of adults, wildly inaccurate (e.g., children are both capable of a lot more than we give them credit for and a lot more vulnerable than we often recognize), and unevenly applied (e.g., we deny children rights on the grounds of incapacity when the elderly are equally lacking in capacity). Perhaps most importantly, capacity isn't set in stone: we can increase many capacities through education and empowerment, and we can provide accommodations that render incapacity irrelevant.

xxiv *When I asked Sidney* Sidney, interview by author, July 1, 2018. I have generally used only first names or employed pseudonyms in the book to protect the privacy of the people involved.

xxiv *That, in a nutshell* It is the "at least, we can agree on this" compromise of a pluralist world told not to ask for too much by the free market evangelists. Amy Kapczynski, "What Comes After Not Enough?" LPE Project, June 11, 2018, https://lpeproject.org/blog/what-comes-after-not-enough/; Samuel Moyn, *Not Enough: Human Rights in an Unequal World* (Cambridge, Mass.: Harvard University Press, 2018).

xxiv *It is a claim* Kapczynski, "What Comes After Not Enough?"; Moyn, *Not Enough;* Clark et al., "A Future for the World's Children?" 628; Anthony Costello and Sarah Dalglish, *Towards a Grand Convergence for Child Survival and Health: A Strategic Review of Options for the Future Building on Lessons Learnt from IMNCI* (Geneva: WHO, 2016), https://apps.who.int /iris/bitstream/handle/10665/251855/WHO-MCA-16.04-eng.pdf.

xxv *We must ensure* Agnel Philip et al. "63 Million Americans Exposed to Unsafe Drinking Water," *USA Today,* Aug. 14, 2017; Samantha M. Shapiro, "The Children in the Shadows: New York City's Homeless Students," *New York Times,* Sept. 9, 2020; Miranda Martin, "The School Year Is Over, but Food Insecurity Continues for Children and Families," Child Trends, June 22, 2016, https://www.childtrends.org/blog/the-school-year-is-over-but-food -insecurity-continues-for-children-and-families; Alison Gopnik, *The Gardener and the Carpenter* (New York: Farrar, Straus and Giroux, 2016), 242.

xxv *But we must also* Clark et al., "A Future for the World's Children?" 628; Kapczynski, "What Comes After Not Enough?"; Moyn, *Not Enough,* xii, 3–11.

xxv *It asks us all* This vision is a return, in some respects, to the broader coalition that advocated for children at the turn of the twentieth century and presents a stark departure from the narrowness of the post-1960s children's rights movement, which has been dominated by lawyers seeking relief in court. See, e.g., Guggenheim, *What's Wrong with Children's Rights,* 8.

xxv *To advance* While the maturation periods I've chosen are inevitably rough, this life course approach aligns with much of the existing research organized around developmental periods and is useful in drawing our attention to particular life circumstances and developmental realities that affect many young people at these points in their lives. Clark et al., "A Future for the World's Children?" 644.

xxvi *I've chosen to focus* See, e.g., Clark et al., "A Future for the World's Children?" 628; Didier Reynaert, Maria Bouverne-De Bie, and Stijn Vandevelde, "Between 'Believers' and 'Opponents': Critical Discussions on Children's Rights," *International Journal of Children's Rights* 20, no. 1 (2012): 155–68; E. Kay and M. Tisdall, "Children's Rights and Children's Wellbeing: Equivalent Policy Concepts?" *Journal of Social Policy* 44, no. 4 (2015): 807–23; Amartya Sen, *Development as Freedom* (Oxford: Oxford University Press, 2001); Martha C. Nussbaum, *Creating Capabilities: The Human Development Approach* (Boston: Belknap Press, 2013); Tyler J. VanderWeele, "On the Promotion of Human Flourishing," *Proceedings of the National Academy of Sciences* 114, no. 31 (2017): 8148–56; Elizabeth L. Pollard and Patrice D. Lee, "Child Well-being: A Systematic Review of the Literature," *Social Indicators Research* 61 (2003): 59–78; Laura H. Lippman, Kristin Anderson Moore, and Hugh McIntosh, "Positive Indicators of Child Well-being: A Conceptual Framework, Measures, and Methodological Issues," *Applied Research in Quality of Life* 6, no. 4 (2011): 425–49.

xxvi *In the conclusion* Even if the publisher granted me the ability to enumerate all the rights I could think of, I would resist doing so because I don't believe I'm capable of a truly complete list and certainly not one capable of remaining fixed over time or across all cultures. Amartya Sen, "Human Rights and Capabilities," *Journal of Human Development* 6, no. 2 (2005): 157–60. I am confident, though, in the fundamental principle of prioritizing children.

xxvii   *There's no question* Emily Oster, *Cribsheet: A Data-Driven Guide to Better, More Relaxed Parenting, from Birth to Preschool* (New York: Penguin Press, 2019), xv.

xxvii   *We invest far more* Claire Cain Miller, "The Relentlessness of Modern Parenting," *New York Times,* Dec. 25, 2018.

xxvii   *We spend billions* Gopnik, *The Gardener and the Carpenter,* 34.

xxviii   *Amazon has* Search for "Parenting Books," Amazon, accessed Mar. 13, 2022, https://www.amazon.com/s?k=parenting+books&i=stripbooks&rh =n%3A283155&lo=list&page=5&crid=Y1TWW8Y1LUGB&qid= 1564328372&sprefix=PARENTING%2Caps%2C128&ref=sr_pg_4; Gopnik, *The Gardener and the Carpenter,* 4.

xxviii   *But that's misguided* Miller, "The Relentlessness of Modern Parenting."

xxviii   *In general, when it comes* Emily Oster, "There's Evidence on How to Raise Children, but Are Parents Listening?" *New York Times,* May 23, 2019.

xxviii   *Meanwhile, some two million* Danilo Trisi and Matt Saenz, *Deep Poverty Among Children Rose in TANF's First Decade, Then Fell as Other Programs Strengthened,* Center on Budget and Policy Priorities, Feb. 27, 2020, 1, https://www.cbpp.org/sites/default/files/atoms/files/2-27-20pov.pdf; Nicholas Kristof, "America Is Guilty of Neglecting Kids: Our Own," *New York Times,* June 27, 2018; "Juvenile Population Characteristics," Office of Juvenile Justice and Delinquency Statistical Briefing Book (U.S. Department of Justice, Oct. 13, 2020), https://www.ojjdp.gov/ojstatbb /population/qa01104.asp?qaDate=2020; Nazgol Ghandnoosh, Emma Stammen, and Kevin Muhitch, "Parents in Prison," The Sentencing Project (Feb. 2021), 1, https://www.sentencingproject.org/wp-content /uploads/2021/11/Parents-in-Prison.pdf.

xxviii   *It was "self-evident"* Thomas Jefferson, The Declaration of Independence, 1776.

xxviii   *The Universal Declaration* UN General Assembly, Universal Declaration of Human Rights, 217 A (III), Dec. 10, 1948.

xxix   *We even still have* Children's Bureau, "What We Do," The Administration for Children and Families, 2021, https://www.acf.hhs.gov/cb/about/what -we-do.

xxix   *But kids aren't the same* There are prominent thinkers, after all, who assert that young children cannot have rights because they are without moral agency. See, e.g., Carl Wellman, *Real Rights* (Oxford: Oxford University Press, 1995), 107, 113–25; James Griffin, *On Human Rights* (Oxford: Oxford University Press, 2008), 94–95.

1. The First Years: The Right to Attachment

5   *The boy was put out* This account of Sujit Kumar's life is drawn from a number of sources. Catherine Masters, "Flying Above a Life with the Chickens," *NZ Herald,* Sept. 5, 2008; Audrey Young, "NZ Pitching In for 'Chicken Boy,'"

NZ Herald, Feb. 13, 2006; Catherine Masters, "A Lost 'Boy' Learns Life from the Start," *NZ Herald,* July 2, 2004; Mary Vallis and Scott Stinson, "'Chicken Man' Learning to Love: Raised in Coop, Fijian 'Making Up for Lost Time,'" *National Post,* July 15, 2004; Jenny Forsyth, "Four Years Locked in a Poultry Coop, the Next 20 Tied to a Bed," *Guardian,* July 10, 2004; Adam Gilders, "The Wilderness Within," *The Walrus,* May 26, 2020; "Sujit Kumar," *The Sujit Kumar Happy Home Trust,* accessed Mar. 19, 2022, https://web.archive .org/web/20140111064007/http://www.thehappyhometrust.com/sujit -kumar/.

5 *He wasn't* Masters, "Flying Above."

5 *Sujit's mother* Forsyth, "Four Years."

5 *His father* Happy Home Trust, "Sujit Kumar."

5 *There is not anyone* Masters, "Flying Above."

5 *In the rural village* Masters, "Flying Above"; *Raised Wild* (Animal Planet, 2012).

5 *But, for years* Masters, "Flying Above."

5 *When social workers* Masters, "Flying Above."

5 *He could not* Masters, "Flying Above."

5 *And he didn't move* Masters, "Flying Above."

5 *He would hop* Masters, "Flying Above."

5 *When food* Masters, "Flying Above."

5 *The sounds* Masters, "Flying Above."

5 *He didn't want* Masters, "Flying Above"; Forsyth, "Four Years."

5 *He set down* Masters, "Flying Above."

5 *There are animals* Walter E. Boles, "A Brief History of the Megapodes (*Megapodiidae*)," National Malleefowl Recovery Team, Sept. 2014, 95, http://www.nationalmalleefowl.com.au/uploads/pdfs/17_W%20Boles _History%20of%20Megapodes.pdf.

5 *The stocky* Cagan Sekercioglu, "Megapodes: A Fascinating Incubation Strategy," *Harvard Journal of Undergraduate Sciences* 5, no. 2 (1999): 78; Laura Howard, "Megapodiidae Megapodes," Animal Diversity Web, accessed Mar. 21, 2022, http://animaldiversity.org/accounts/Megapodiidae/.

5 *They spend* Howard, "Megapodiidae Megapodes."

5 *While most birds* Sekercioglu, "Megapodes," 77, 79–81; Howard, "Megapodiidae Megapodes."

5 *Their offspring* Sekercioglu, "Megapodes," 82; Howard, "Megapodiidae Megapodes."

5 *The youngsters* Howard, "Megapodiidae Megapodes."

5 *Within an hour* Sekercioglu, "Megapodes," 83; Howard, "Megapodiidae Megapodes."

5 *They aren't taught* Sekercioglu, "Megapodes," 78, 82–83; Howard, "Megapodiidae Megapodes."

5 *Even in their first day* Howard, "Megapodiidae Megapodes."

6 *One chick* Sekercioglu, "Megapodes," 83.

6 *As the Children's Bureau's* Max West, *Infant Care* (Washington, D.C.: Government Printing Office, 1914), 59; Virginia M. Shiller, *The Attachment Bond: Affectional Ties Across the Lifespan* (Lanham, Md.: Lexington Books, 2017), 1.

6 *The influential psychologist* John B. Watson, *Psychological Care of Infant and Child* (New York: W. W. Norton, 1928), 84–85; Shiller, *The Attachment Bond*, 4.

6 *It was not until* Amanda M. Dettmer et al., "Intergenerational Effects of Early-Life Advantage: Lessons from a Primate Study," Working Paper No. 27737, National Bureau of Economic Research, Cambridge, Mass. (Aug. 2020): 4–5, https://www.nber.org/system/files/working_papers/w27737/w27737.pdf.

6 *While rhesus monkeys* Dettmer, "Intergenerational Effects," 1; Richard A. Gibbs et al., "Evolutionary and Biomedical Insights from the Rhesus Macaque Genome," *Science* 316, no. 5822 (Apr. 13, 2007): 1.

6 *They can also be randomly* Brita Belli, "Studies with Monkeys Find Early Attachment Brings Generations of Benefits," *Yale News*, Sept. 25, 2020; Dettmer, "Intergenerational Effects," 1–3.

6 *When, in the 1950s* Shiller, *The Attachment Bond*, 13; Lane DeGregory, "The Girl in the Window," *St. Petersburg Times*, Aug. 3, 2008; Harry F. Harlow and Robert R. Zimmermann, "The Development of Affectional Responses in Infant Monkeys," *Proceedings of the American Philosophical Society* 102, no. 5 (Oct. 20, 1958): 502–3.

6 *In one recent study* Dettmer, "Intergenerational Effects," 6, 8.

6 *When they were born* Dettmer, "Intergenerational Effects," 1–2; Belli, "Studies with Monkeys."

6 *The nursery conditions* Belli, "Studies with Monkeys."

7 *At eight months* Dettmer, "Intergenerational Effects," 1–2; Belli, "Studies with Monkeys."

7 *Each generation* Dettmer, "Intergenerational Effects," 1–2; Belli, "Studies with Monkeys."

7 *What researchers found* Dettmer, "Intergenerational Effects," 19–20.

7 *Monkeys allowed* Dettmer, "Intergenerational Effects," 19–20; Belli, "Studies with Monkeys."

7 *They had the strongest chance* Dettmer, "Intergenerational Effects," 1–2; Belli, "Studies with Monkeys."

7 *The intergenerational benefit* Dettmer, "Intergenerational Effects," 20; Belli, "Studies with Monkeys."

7 *As the authors concluded* Dettmer, "Intergenerational Effects," 4.

7 *And if you're denied* Gabriella Conti et al., "Primate Evidence on the Late Health Effects of Early-Life Adversity," *Proceedings of the National Academy of Sciences* 109, no. 23 (2012): 8866–71.

7 *After just eight months* Belli, "Studies with Monkeys."

7 *Young people* "Young Children Develop in an Environment of Relationships," National Scientific Council on the Developing Child Working Paper 1 (Oct. 2009): 1, http://developingchild.harvard.edu/wp-content/uploads/2004/04/Young-Children-Develop-in-an-Environment-of-Relationships.pdf; Shiller, *The Attachment Bond*.

7 *Secure bonds* "Young Children Develop," 1; Perri Klass, "Why a Baby's Connection with a Parent Matters," *New York Times*, June 26, 2017.

7 *It is within these vital* "Young Children Develop," 1–2; Naoki Kanaboshi,

James F. Anderson, and Natalia Sira, "Constitutional Rights of Infants and Toddlers to Have Opportunities to Form Secure Attachment with Incarcerated Mothers: Importance of Prison Nurseries," *International Journal of Social Science Studies* 5, no. 2 (Feb. 2017): 58.

7   *The costs of isolation* Matthew Liao, *The Right to Be Loved* (New York: Oxford University Press, 2015), 88–89.

7   *Seventy-six years ago* Benjamin Spock, *The Common Sense Book of Baby and Child Care* (New York: Duell, Sloan and Pearce, 1957).

7   *Though it is often* Spock, *The Common Sense Book;* "Dr. Spock's Children," *New York Times,* Mar. 17, 1998.

8   *I was a Spock baby* Jeff Wallenfeldt, "Benjamin Spock," Britannica, last modified Mar. 11, 2022, https://www.britannica.com/biography/Benjamin-Spock.

8   *For him the equation* Spock, *The Common Sense Book,* 570.

8   *Indeed, in Spock's view* Spock, *The Common Sense Book,* 569–70.

8   *While Spock couldn't rise* Spock, *The Common Sense Book,* 570.

8   *As he reasoned* Spock, *The Common Sense Book,* 569–70.

8   *Especially in the early years* Darby Saxbe and Sofia Cardenas, "What Paternity Leave Does for a Father's Brain," *New York Times,* Nov. 8, 2021.

8   *Paid childcare leave* AEI-Brookings Working Group on Paid Family Leave, *Paid Family and Medical Leave: An Issue Whose Time Has Come,* 6, 19, http://www.aei.org/wp-content/uploads/2017/06/Paid-Family-and-Medical-Leave-An-Issue-Whose-Time-Has-Come.pdf; Sakiko Tanaka, "Parental Leave and Child Health Across OECD Countries," *Economic Journal* 115, no. 501 (Feb. 2005): F19, F23, F26; Jenna Stearns, "The Effects of Paid Maternity Leave: Evidence from Temporary Disability Insurance," *Journal of Health Economics* 43 (Sept. 2015): 91–92, 99; C. R. Winegarden and Paula M. Bracy, "Demographic Consequences of Maternal-Leave Programs in Industrial Countries: Evidence from Fixed-Effects Models," *Southern Economic Journal* 61, no. 4 (Apr. 1995): 1026–27, 1034; Christopher J. Ruhm, "Parental Leave and Child Health," *Journal of Health Economics* 19, no. 6 (Nov. 2000): 946–48, 955; Barbara Gault et al., "Paid Parental Leave in the United States: What the Data Tell Us About Access, Usage, and Economic and Health Benefits," *Institute for Women's Policy Research* (Jan. 23, 2014): 14–15.

8   *With time off* "Paid Family and Medical Leave," 6; Michael Baker and Kevin Milligan, "Maternal Employment, Breastfeeding, and Health: Evidence from Maternity Leave Mandates," *Journal of Health Economics* 27, no. 4 (July 2008): 880–82, 884; Brian Roe et al., "Is There Competition Between Breast-Feeding and Maternal Employment?" *Demography* 36, no. 2 (May 1999): 164–67; Alison Earle, Zitha Mokomane, and Jody Heymann, "International Perspectives on Work-Family Policies: Lessons from the World's Most Competitive Economies," *The Future of Children* 21, no. 2 (Fall 2011): 192; Lawrence M. Berger, Jennifer Hill, and Jane Waldfogel, "Maternity Leave, Early Maternal Employment and Child Health and Development in the US," *Economic Journal* 115, no. 501 (Feb. 2005): F29–F47; Sheila B. Kamerman, "Maternity, Paternity, and Parental Leave Policies: The Potential Impacts on Children and Their Families," *Encyclopedia on Early Child-*

hood Development, 3rd rev. ed. (Mar. 2007), https://www.child-encyclopedia
.com/parental-leave/according-experts/maternity-paternity-and-parental
-leave-policies-potential-impacts.

8   *Paid leave also supports* "Paid Family and Medical Leave," 19; Earle, Mokomane, and Heymann, "International Perspectives on Work-Family Policies," 192–95.

8   *When researchers looked* Pedro Carneiro, Katrine V. Løken, and Kjell G. Salvanes, "A Flying Start? Maternity Leave Benefits and Long-Run Outcomes
of Children," *Journal of Political Economy* 123, no. 2 (Apr. 2015): 365, 383–
88, 405.

9   *The effects* Carneiro, Løken, and Salvanes, "A Flying Start?" 397–400, 408–9.

9   *Part of the reason* "Paid Family and Medical Leave," 6–7; María del Carmen
Huerta et al., "Fathers' Leave, Fathers' Involvement and Child Development: Are They Related? Evidence from Four OECD Countries," OECD
Social, Employment and Migration Working Papers, no. 140 (Jan. 14, 2013):
29–33; Linda Haas and C. Philip Hwang, "The Impact of Taking Parental
Leave on Fathers' Participation in Childcare and Relationships with Children: Lessons from Sweden," *Community, Work & Family* 11, no. 1 (Feb. 12,
2008): 85–104.

9   *In one study* Richard J. Petts, Chris Knoester, and Jane Waldfogel, "Fathers'
Paternity Leave-Taking and Children's Perceptions of Father-Child Relationships in the United States," *Sex Roles* 82 (May 4, 2019): 180, 182, 184.

9   *And the children* "Paid Family and Medical Leave," 6–7; Catherine S. Tamis-
LeMonda et al., "Fathers and Mothers at Play with Their 2- and 3-Year-Olds:
Contributions to Language and Cognitive Development," *Child Development* 75, no. 6 (Nov./Dec. 2004): 1813–16; Huerta et al., "Fathers' Leave,
Fathers' Involvement and Child Development," 34–37; Earle, Mokomane,
and Heymann, "International Perspectives on Work-Family Policies,"
193.

9   *Scientists have begun* Alison Gopnik, *The Gardener and the Carpenter* (New
York: Farrar, Straus and Giroux, 2016), 84.

9   *And it seems that* Gopnik, *The Gardener and the Carpenter*, 87.

9   *Spending time touching* Gopnik, *The Gardener and the Carpenter*, 84; Saxbe
and Cardenas, "What Paternity Leave Does"; Robin S. Edelstein et al.,
"Prospective and Dyadic Associations Between Expectant Parents' Prenatal
Hormone Changes and Postpartum Parenting Outcomes," *Developmental
Psychobiology* 59, no. 1 (Jan. 2017): 82–84.

9   *In fact, caregiving appears* Saxbe and Cardenas, "What Paternity Leave
Does"; María Paternina-Die, "The Paternal Transition Entails Neuroana-
tomic Adaptations That Are Associated with the Father's Brain Response to
His Infant Cues," *Cerebral Cortex Communications* 1, no. 1 (2020): 7–9;
Elseline Hoekzema et al., "Pregnancy Leads to Long-lasting Changes in
Human Brain Structure," *Nature Neuroscience* 20, no. 2 (2017): 293–95;
Françoise Diaz-Rojas et al., "Development of the Paternal Brain in Expect-
ant Fathers During Early Pregnancy," *NeuroImage* 225 (2021); Madelon M.
E. Riem et al., "A Soft Baby Carrier Intervention Enhances Amygdala Re-
sponses to Infant Crying in Fathers: A Randomized Controlled Trial," *Psy-
choneuroendocrinology* 132 (2021): 7–8; Eyal Abraham, "Father's Brain Is

Sensitive to Childcare Experiences," *Proceedings of the National Academy of Sciences* 111, no. 27 (2014): 9794–96.

9 *In a recent study* Saxbe and Cardenas, "What Paternity Leave Does"; Riem et al., "A Soft Baby Carrier Intervention," 3.

9 *After three weeks* Saxbe and Cardenas, "What Paternity Leave Does"; Riem et al.; "A Soft Baby Carrier Intervention," 4.

9 *The men who'd carried* Saxbe and Cardenas, "What Paternity Leave Does"; Riem et al., "A Soft Baby Carrier Intervention," 7.

9 *Moreover, the effect* Saxbe and Cardenas, "What Paternity Leave Does"; Riem et al., "A Soft Baby Carrier Intervention," 7.

9 *Against this overwhelming evidence* Amanda Lenhart, Haley Swenson, and Brigid Schulte, *Lifting the Barriers to Paid Family and Medical Leave for Men in the United States* (Washington, D.C.: Better Life Lab of New America, 2019), 7, https://www.newamerica.org/better-life-lab/reports/lifting-barriers-paid-family-and-medical-leave-men-united-states/.

9 *If your two-year-old* Steven Findlay, "Biden and Democrats Propose National Paid Leave," Health Affairs Forefront, June 24, 2021, https://www.healthaffairs.org/do/10.1377/forefront.20210617.789833/full/.

9 *There are no federal laws* Earle, Mokomane, and Heymann, "International Perspectives on Work-Family Policies," 191.

9 *In other advanced nations* Earle, Mokomane, and Heymann, "International Perspectives on Work-Family Policies," 191.

10 *Indeed, America* Claire Cain Miller, "The World 'Has Found a Way to Do This': The U.S. Lags on Paid Leave," *New York Times*, Oct. 25, 2021.

10 *In November 2014* Jennifer Liu, "Read Joe Biden's 2014 Memo to Staff About Making Time for Family: 'This Is Very Important to Me,'" CNBC, Nov. 9, 2020, https://www.cnbc.com/2020/11/09/read-joe-bidens-2014-memo-to-staff-about-making-time-for-family.html.

10 *He wanted* Liu, "Read Joe Biden's 2014 Memo."

10 *It concerned* Liu, "Read Joe Biden's 2014 Memo."

10 *The memo* Liu, "Read Joe Biden's 2014 Memo."

10 *If you're a member* Earle, Mokomane, and Heymann, "International Perspectives on Work-Family Policies," 195.

10 *In a recent survey* Promundo and Dove Men+Care, *Helping Dads Care* (2018), https://promundoglobal.org/wp-content/uploads/2018/06/Promundo-DMC-Helping-Men-Care-Report_FINAL.pdf.

11 *Every important thing* Ryan D'Agostino, "Things My Father Taught Me: An Interview with Joe and Hunter Biden," *Popular Mechanics*, Nov. 9, 2020.

11 *By generous* Kali Grant et al., *The Paid Family and Medical Leave Opportunity: What Research Tells Us About Designing a Paid Leave Program That Works for All*, Georgetown Center on Poverty and Inequality, July 2019, 7–8.

11 *By inclusive* Grant et al., *The Paid Family and Medical Leave Opportunity*, 7–8.

11 *Roughly three quarters* Amy Raub et al., *Paid Parental Leave: A Detailed Look at Approaches Across OECD Countries*, WORLD Policy Analysis Center, 2018, 7.

11 *Many of our close peers* Earle, Mokomane, and Heymann, "International Perspectives on Work-Family Policies," 201.

11 *Roughly three quarters* Raub et al., *Paid Parental Leave*, 10.

11 *When researchers looked* Earle, Mokomane, and Heymann, "International Perspectives on Work-Family Policies," 202.

11 *Of the thirteen* Earle, Mokomane, and Heymann, "International Perspectives on Work-Family Policies," 201.

11 *Full cover* Jessica Grose, "Why Dads Don't Take Parental Leave," *New York Times*, Feb. 19, 2020; Lenhart, Swenson, and Schulte, *Lifting the Barriers*, 7.

11 *And the data suggests* Seema Jayachandran, "Universal Paternity Leave Needs More Than New Laws for a Push," *New York Times*, June 25, 2021; Magnus Bygren and Ann-Zofie Duvander, "Parents' Workplace Situation and Fathers' Parental Leave Use," *Journal of Marriage and Family* 68, no. 2 (May 2006): 363.

11 *Like three quarters* Sarah Jane Glynn, "Administering Paid Family and Medical Leave," Center for American Progress, Nov. 2015, 8; Grant et al., *The Paid Family and Medical Leave Opportunity*, 7–8; AEI-Brookings Working Group on Paid Family Leave, *Paid Family and Medical Leave*, 24; Bryce Covert, "Biden's Paid Leave Plan Is Years Out of Date," *New York Times*, June 22, 2021.

12 *In December 1972* D'Agostino, "Things My Father Taught Me."

12 *A tractor-trailer plowed* D'Agostino, "Things My Father Taught Me."

12 *Neilia and one-year-old Naomi* D'Agostino, "Things My Father Taught Me."

12 *Hunter and Beau* D'Agostino, "Things My Father Taught Me."

12 *Biden had just been* D'Agostino, "Things My Father Taught Me."

12 *As his son Hunter describes* D'Agostino, "Things My Father Taught Me."

12 *"Anywhere"* D'Agostino, "Things My Father Taught Me."

12 *"They could pick"* D'Agostino, "Things My Father Taught Me."

13 *For Ariel and Adam* Ariel, interview by author, Aug. 20, 2018; "Success on the Inside: Kenny Kubinski," Stories, FAMM, accessed Mar. 26, 2022, https://famm.org/stories/success-on-the-inside-kenny-kubinski/#.W7TNlQumLyw.twitter.

13 *In that bright before* Ariel, interview.

13 *There was a pond* Ariel, interview.

13 *Ariel liked* Ariel, interview.

13 *When I spoke to Adam* Adam, interview by author, Aug. 20, 2018.

13 *They loved their parents* Adam, interview.

13 *Everything was gone* Adam, interview.

13 *Kenny and Jackie* Ariel, interview; "Success on the Inside," FAMM.

13 *Awoken to darkness* Adam, interview.

13 *Jackie had thought* Ariel, interview.

13 *She had thought* Ariel, interview.

13 *Entering first grade* Adam, interview.

13 *Ariel's memories* Ariel, interview.

13 *One day* Ariel, interview.

13 *As Ariel recounts* Ariel, interview.

13 *The orphanage* Ariel, interview.

13 *Their parents were both given* Ariel, interview; U.S. v. Kubinski, 91 F.3d 135 (1996); Criminal Docket for Jacquelyn M. Kubinski, U.S. District Court, No. 00028, 8.

14 *None of their relatives* Adam, interview.

14 *One in five kids* Amy B. Cyphert, "Prisoners of Fate: The Challenges of Creating Change for Children of Incarcerated Parents," *Maryland Law Review* 77, no. 2 (2018): 393; Roy L. Austin, Jr., and Karol Mason, "Empowering Our Young People, and Stemming the Collateral Damage of Incarceration," The White House: President Barack Obama, Oct. 8, 2014, https://obama whitehouse.archives.gov/blog/2014/10/08/empowering-our-young -people-and-stemming-collateral-damage-incarceration.

14 *And incarcerated parents* Eli Hager and Anna Flagg, "How Incarcerated Parents Are Losing Their Children Forever," Marshall Project, Dec. 2, 2018, https://www.themarshallproject.org/2018/12/03/how-incarcerated -parents-are-losing-their-children-forever.

14 *That's largely down* Cyphert, "Prisoners of Fate," 394; Caitlin Mitchell, "Family Integrity and Incarcerated Parents: Bridging the Divide," *Yale Journal of Law and Feminism* 24, no. 1 (2012): 176; Pub. L. No. 105–189, §103, 111 Stat. 2118-20 (codified as amended at 42 U.S.C. §675[5]).

14 *The problem, of course* Hager and Flagg, "How Incarcerated Parents."

14 *While terminations* Adjoa D. Robinson et al., "Preserving Family Bonds: Examining Parent Perspectives in the Light of Practice Standards for Out-of-Home Treatment," *American Journal of Orthopsychiatry* 57, no. 4 (2005): 632–43; New York's Family Defense Organizations, Letter to the Governor Regarding 2021 Legislative Priorities, Feb. 11, 2021, https://www .bronxdefenders.org/wp-content/uploads/2021/02/Joint-Family -Defense-Providers-2021-Legislative-Priorities.pdf; LaDoris Hazzard Cordell, *Her Honor* (New York: Celadon Books, 2021), 90–93.

14 *Adam does not mince words* Adam, interview.

14 *The couple* Adam, interview.

14 *But they could not* Adam, interview.

14 *The U.S. Department* Kristin Turney "Adverse Childhood Experiences Among Children of Incarcerated Parents," *Children and Youth Services Review* 89, no. 1 (2018): 218–25.

14 *These experiences* Child Welfare Information Gateway, *Child Welfare Practice with Families Affected by Parental Incarceration,* U.S. Department of Health and Human Services, Administration for Children and Families, Children's Bureau, Jan. 2021, https://www.childwelfare.gov/pubPDFs/parental _incarceration.pdf; Kristin Turney, "Stress Proliferation Across Generations? Examining the Relationship Between Parental Incarceration and Childhood Health," *Journal of Health and Social Behavior* 55, no. 3 (2014): 302–19.

14 *Indeed, the children* Ann & Robert H. Lurie Children's Hospital of Chicago, "Lifetime Sentence: Incarcerated Parents Impact Youth Behavior: Unhealthy Behaviors Such as Smoking, Sex and Alcohol Abuse," *ScienceDaily,* July 9, 2018, www.sciencedaily.com/releases/2018/07/180709101203.htm; Nia Heard-Garris et al., "Health Care Use and Health Behaviors Among Young Adults with History of Parental Incarceration," *Pediatrics* 142, no. 3 (Sept. 2018): e20174314; Rosalyn D. Lee, Xiangming Fang, and Feijun Luo, "The Impact of Parental Incarceration on the Physical and Mental Health of Young Adults," *Pediatrics* 131, no. 4 (Apr. 2013): e1188–95; Sarah Still-

man, "America's Other Family-Separation Crisis," *New Yorker,* Nov. 5, 2018; Ann & Robert H. Lurie Children's Hospital of Chicago, "Young Adults Exposed to Incarceration as Children Prone to Depression: Anxiety High Among This Population," *ScienceDaily,* Sept. 4, 2019, www .sciencedaily.com/releases/2019/09/190904113208.htm.

15 *In one recent study* Ann & Robert H. Lurie Children's Hospital of Chicago, "Lifetime Sentence."

15 *In another study* Duke University, "Children of Incarcerated Parents Have More Substance Abuse, Anxiety," *ScienceDaily,* Aug. 23, 2019, https://www .sciencedaily.com/releases/2019/08/190823140734.htm; Elizabeth J. Gifford et al., "Association of Parental Incarceration with Psychiatric and Functional Outcomes of Young Adults," *JAMA Network Open,* Aug. 23, 2019, https://jamanetwork.com/journals/jamanetworkopen/fullarticle/2748665.

15 *One of the reasons* Cyphert, "Prisoners of Fate," 392; Ofira Schwartz-Soicher, Amanda Geller, and Irwin Garfinkel, "The Effect of Paternal Incarceration on Material Hardship," *Social Service Review* 85, no. 3 (2011): 447–73; Kathryn Edin, Timothy J. Nelson, and Rechelle Paranal, "Fatherhood and Incarceration as Potential Turning Points in the Criminal Careers of Unskilled Men," in *Imprisoning America: The Social Effects of Mass Incarceration,* ed. Mary Patillo, David Weiman, and Bruce Western (New York: Russell Sage, 2004), 46–75; Joyce A. Arditti, "Families and Incarceration: An Ecological Approach," *Families in Society* 86, no. 2 (2005): 251–60.

15 *As Ariel explains* Ariel, interview.

15 *As Adam points out* Adam, interview.

15 *When you take a father* Nancy Gertner and Chiraag Bains, "Mandatory Minimum Sentences Are Cruel and Ineffective. Sessions Wants Them Back," *Washington Post,* May 15, 2017; Executive Office of the President of the United States, *Economic Perspectives on Incarceration and the Criminal Justice System,* Apr. 2016, https://obamawhitehouse.archives.gov/sites /whitehouse.gov/files/documents/CEA%2BCriminal%2BJustice %2BReport.pdf.

15 *The loss of family income* Cyphert, "Prisoners of Fate," 392; Annie E. Casey Foundation, *A Shared Sentence: The Devastating Toll of Parental Incarceration on Kids, Families and Communities* (Baltimore: Kids Count, 2016), 1–7; Rucker C. Johnson, "Ever Increasing Levels of Parental Incarceration and the Consequences for Children," in *Do Prisons Make Us Safer? The Benefits and Costs of the Prison Boom,* ed. Steven Raphael and Michael Stoll (New York: Russell Sage Foundation, 2009); The Pew Charitable Trusts, *Collateral Costs: Incarceration's Effects on Economic Mobility* (Washington, D.C.: The Pew Charitable Trust, 2010), 5; Kim Eckart, "Dads in Prison Can Bring Poverty, Instability for Families on the Outside," Phys .org, Nov. 27, 2019, https://phys.org/news/2019-11-dads-prison-poverty -instability-families.html; Christine Leibbrand et al., "Barring Progress: The Influence of Paternal Incarceration on Families' Neighborhood Attainment," *Social Science Research* 84, no. 1 (Nov. 2019): 102321; "Fragile Families & Child Wellbeing Study," Princeton University, accessed Mar. 27, 2022, https://fragilefamilies.princeton.edu.

15 *You might expect* Elisa Minoff, "Entangled Roots: The Role of Race in Poli-

cies That Separate Families," Center for the Study of Social Policy, Oct. 2018, https://cssp.org/resource/entangled-roots; Elizabeth Davies et al., *Understanding the Experiences and Needs of Children of Incarcerated Parents: Views from Mentors* (Washington, D.C.: Urban Institute, Justice Policy Center, Feb. 2008), https://www.urban.org/sites/default/files/publication /31481/411615-Understanding-the-Needs-and-Experiences-of-Children -of-Incarcerated-Parents.pdf.

15 *Adam and Ariel* Adam, interview; Ariel, interview.

15 *They'd spent years* Adam, interview.

15 *But, as Adam recounts* Adam, interview.

16 *She was simmering* Adam, interview; Ariel, interview.

16 *Adam remembers thinking* Adam, interview.

16 *Ariel felt* Ariel, interview.

16 *Ariel highlighted that question* Ariel, interview.

16 *"But it's hard"* Ariel, interview.

16 *Paroled parents* Annie E. Casey Foundation, *A Shared Sentence*, 4.

16 *Those who find work* Gertner and Bains, "Mandatory Minimum Sentences"; Executive Office of the President of the United States, *Economic Perspectives on Incarceration*.

16 *Almost half of U.S. kids* Rebecca Vallas et al., "Removing Barriers to Opportunity for Parents with Criminal Records and Their Children: A Two-Generation Approach," Center for American Progress, Dec. 2015, 1, https://americanprogress.org/wp-content/uploads/2015/12 /CriminalRecords-report2.pdf?_ga=2.173783588.643376288.1648396440 -1709471034.1648396439.

16 *If you've been incarcerated* Vallas et al., "Removing Barriers to Opportunity," 1–2.

16 *An adolescent boy* Stillman, "America's Other Family-Separation Crisis"; Albert M. Kopak and Dorothy Smith-Ruiz, "Criminal Justice Involvement, Drug Use, and Depression Among African American Children of Incarcerated Parents," *Race and Justice* 6, no. 2 (Apr. 1, 2016): 89–116; Gifford et al., "Association of Parental Incarceration."

17 *In America* Minoff, "Entangled Roots," 3.

17 *On any given day The Adoption and Foster Care Analysis and Reporting System (AFCARS) Report No. 28*, U.S. Department of Health and Human Services, Children's Bureau: 2021, https://www.acf.hhs.gov/sites/default /files/documents/cb/afcarsreport28.pdf.

17 *The vast majority* Kendra Hurley, "How the Pandemic Became an Unplanned Experiment in Abolishing the Child Welfare System," *New Republic*, Aug. 18, 2021; Chris Gottlieb, "Black Families Are Outraged About Family Separation Within the U.S.," *Time*, Mar. 17, 2021.

17 *Most investigations* Dorothy Roberts, "Abolishing Policing Also Means Abolishing Family Regulation," *The Imprint*, June 16, 2020, https://im printnews.org/child-welfare-2/abolishing-policing-also-means-abolishing -family-regulation/44480.

17 *As law professor* Dorothy E. Roberts, "Poverty, Race, and New Directions in Child Welfare Policy," *Washington University Journal of Law & Policy* 1, no. 1 (Jan. 1, 1999): 63–76.

17 *One in ten Black children* Christopher Wildeman and Natalia Emanuel, "Cumulative Risks of Foster Care Placement by Age 18 for U.S. Children, 2000–2011," *PLOS ONE* 9, no. 3 (Mar. 26, 2014); Nicholas Kristof, "America Is Guilty of Neglecting Kids: Our Own," *New York Times*, June 27, 2018; Minoff, "Entangled Roots," 15; Hurley, "How the Pandemic Became."

17 *Even short periods* Mical Raz and Vivek Sankaran, "Opposing Family Separation Policies for the Welfare of Children," *American Journal of Public Health* 109, no. 11 (Nov. 2019): 1529–30; Eli Hager, "The Hidden Trauma of 'Short Stays' in Foster Care," Marshall Project, Feb. 11, 2020, https://www.themarshallproject.org/2020/02/11/the-hidden-trauma-of-short-stays-in-foster-care; Minoff, "Entangled Roots," 15–16.

17 *Young children* Minoff, "Entangled Roots," 15–16; Joseph J. Doyle, "Child Protection and Child Outcomes: Measuring the Effects of Foster Care," *American Economic Review* 97, no. 5 (2007): 1583–610; Vivek S. Sankaran and Christopher Church, "Easy Come, Easy Go: The Plight of Children Who Spend Less Than Thirty Days in Foster Care," *University of Pennsylvania Journal of Law and Social Change* 19, no. 3 (2016): 211.

17 *They are suddenly* Minoff, "Entangled Roots," 15–16; Doyle, "Child Protection"; Sankaran and Church, "Easy Come, Easy Go," 211.

17 *Longer removals* Minoff, "Entangled Roots," 15–16; Doyle, "Child Protection"; Matthew H. Morton, Amy Dworsky, and Gina Miranda Samuels, *Missed Opportunities: Youth Homelessness in America* (Chicago: Chapin Hall at the University of Chicago, Nov. 2017); Amy Dworsky, "Midwest Evaluation of the Adult Functioning of Former Foster Youth," Chapin Hall at the University of Chicago, 2011, https://www.chapinhall.org/research/midwest-evaluation-of-the-adult-functioning-of-former-foster-youth/.

17 *One in five people* Matthew Liao, *The Right to Be Loved* (New York: Oxford University Press, 2015), 180; Dworsky, "Midwest Evaluation"; Thom Reilly, "Transition from Care: Status and Outcomes of Youth Who Age Out of Foster Care," *Child Welfare* 82, no. 6 (Dec. 2003): 727–46.

17 *By age twenty-five* "Issues: Education," Juvenile Law Center, 2022, https://jlc.org/issues/education.

17 *In 2018* William A. Kandel, *The Trump Administration's 'Zero Tolerance' Immigration Enforcement Policy*, Congressional Research Service, Feb. 2, 2021, https://sgp.fas.org/crs/homesec/R45266.pdf; Maggie Jo Buchanan, Philip E. Wolgin, and Claudia Flores, *The Trump Administration's Family Separation Policy Is Over: What Comes Next?* Center for American Progress, Apr. 12, 2021, https://www.americanprogress.org/article/trump-administrations-family-separation-policy/.

17 *But breaking* Minoff, "Entangled Roots," 5–6; Randy Capps et al., "Implications of Immigration Enforcement Activities for the Well-being of Children in Immigrant Families: A Review of the Literature," Migration Policy Institute, Sept. 17, 2015, https://www.migrationpolicy.org/research/implications-immigration-enforcement-activities-well-being-children-immigrant-families; Marc R. Rosenblum, "Understanding the Potential Impact of Executive Action on Immigration Enforcement," Migration Policy Institute, July 2015, https://www.migrationpolicy.org/sites/default/files/publications/ExecAction-Removals-SCOMM.pdf.

18 *Since 2009* Minoff, "Entangled Roots," 5–6; Cecilia Menjívar and Andrea Gómez Cervantes, "The Effects of Parental Undocumented Status on Families and Children," American Psychological Association, Nov. 2016, https://www.apa.org/pi/families/resources/newsletter/2016/11/undocumented-status; Capps et al., "Implications of Immigration."

18 *And the experience* Minoff, "Entangled Roots," 6.

18 *It was okay* Laura Briggs, *Taking Children: A History of American Terror* (Berkeley: University of California Press, 2020); Anne C. Bailey, "They Sold Human Beings Here," *New York Times*, Feb. 12, 2020.

18 *It was right* Rukmini Callimachi and Sharon Chischilly, "Lost Lives, Lost Culture: The Forgotten History of Indigenous Boarding Schools," *New York Times*, July 19, 2021; Minoff, "Entangled Roots," 17–18; Julie Davis, "American Indian Boarding School Experiences: Recent Studies from Native Perspectives," *OAH Magazine of History* 15, no. 2 (Winter 2001): 20-22.

18 *To remove poor city children* Minoff, "Entangled Roots," 17.

18 *As American businessman* Michael B. Katz, *In the Shadow of the Poorhouse: A Social History of Welfare in America* (New York: Basic Books, 1986), 111.

18 *Stable, quality relationships* The National Scientific Council on the Developing Child, "Young Children Develop in an Environment of Relationships," Center on the Developing Child, Harvard University, Working Paper 1 (2004), http://developingchild.harvard.edu/wp-content/uploads/2004/04/Young-Children-Develop-in-an-Environment-of-Relationships.pdf.

18 *Recognizing a right to attachment* United Nations Convention on the Rights of the Child, Nov. 20, 1989, 1577 U.N.T.S. 3.

18 *That promising language* Likewise, the convention recognizes that "[a] child temporarily or permanently deprived of his or her family environment . . . shall be entitled to special protection and assistance provided by the State," but then states that "[s]uch care could include . . . foster placement . . . [or] placement in suitable institutions for the care of children." Convention on the Rights of the Child, art. 20.

19 *Respecting a right to attachment* New Hampshire Department of Corrections Policy and Procedure Directive 7.09.IV.I.3 (2017); Tennessee Department of Corrections Administrative Policies and Procedures 507.01.VI.M.2.g (2020).

19 *We would never prohibit* Associated Press, "Judge: New Mexico Prison Breast-Feeding Ban Unconstitutional," *U.S. News*, July 1, 2017; Maya Schenwar, "A Virtual Visit to a Relative in Jail," *New York Times*, Sept. 29, 2016.

19 *We would not charge kids* Katrina vanden Heuvel, "The Staggeringly High Price of a Prison Phone Call," *Washington Post*, Nov. 30, 2021.

19 *The research on the value* Cyphert, "Prisoners of Fate," 395; Ross D. Parke and K. Alison Clarke-Stewart, "Effects of Parental Incarceration on Young Children," U.S. Department of Justice, Jan. 2002, https://www.ojp.gov/ncjrs/virtual-library/abstracts/effects-parental-incarceration-young-children; Nancy G. La Vigne, Elizabeth Davies, and Diana Brazzell, *Broken Bonds: Understanding and Addressing the Needs of Children with Incarcerated Parents*, Urban Institute Justice Policy Center, Feb. 2008, https://www.urban.org/sites/default/files/publication/31486/411616-Broken

-Bonds-Understanding-and-Addressing-the-Needs-of-Children-with
-Incarcerated-Parents.pdf.

19   *Yet, shockingly* Cyphert, "Prisoners of Fate," 396; Keva M. Miller, "The
     Impact of Parental Incarceration on Children: An Emerging Need for Ef-
     fective Interventions," *Child and Adolescent Social Work Journal* 23, no. 4
     (Oct. 17, 2006): 472–86.

19   *That's often because* Jeremy Travis, Elizabeth Cincotta McBride, and Amy L.
     Solomon, "Families Left Behind: The Hidden Costs of Incarceration and
     Reentry," Urban Institute Justice Policy Center, 2006; *"You Miss So Much
     When You're Gone": The Lasting Harm of Jailing Mothers Before Trial in
     Oklahoma,* Human Rights Watch, Sept. 26, 2018, https://www.hrw.org
     /report/2018/09/26/you-miss-so-much-when-youre-gone/lasting-harm
     -jailing-mothers-trial-oklahoma.

19   *As Ariel recalls* Ariel, interview.

19   *Kenny was then transferred* Ariel, interview.

19   *We would increase* Lucius Couloute, "Comment Letter: Florida's Depart-
     ment of Corrections Should Not Reduce Visitation," Prison Policy Initia-
     tive, May 31, 2018, https://www.prisonpolicy.org/blog/2018/05/31/fl
     _comment_letter/.

19   *When Ariel recalled her saddest moment* Ariel, interview.

20   *Does physical affection* Virginia Casper, "In-Person Visits with Jailed Parents
     Are a Child's Right," *HuffPost,* Feb. 9, 2018, https://www.huffpost.com
     /entry/opinion-casper-video-prison_n_5a7caff5e4b08dfc9301a139.

20   *The truth* Cyphert, "Prisoners of Fate," 424.

20   *Both Adam and Ariel* Ariel, interview.

20   *At seven, Ariel remembers* Ariel, interview.

20   *Ariel emphasized* Ariel, interview.

20   *When other children* Ariel, interview.

20   *So why does Pennsylvania* Mia Armstrong, "Prisons Are Increasingly Ban-
     ning Physical Mail," *Slate,* Aug. 9, 2021, https://slate.com/technology
     /2021/08/prisons-banning-physical-mail.html; Samantha Melamed, " 'I
     Feel Hopeless': Families Call New Pa. Prison Mail Policy Devastating,"
     Philadelphia Inquirer, Oct. 15, 2018; FAMM Foundation (@FAMMfounda
     tion), "Every letter sent to a PA prisoner first has to go to #Florida to be
     scanned," Twitter, Nov. 26, 2018, https://twitter.com/FAMMFoundation
     /status/1067156101379096576.

20   *In 2019* Zoe Greenberg, "Phone Calls from New York City Jails Will Soon
     Be Free," *New York Times,* Aug. 6, 2018; Thomas Tracy and John Annese,
     "De Blasio: Inmates in NYC Jails Can Now Make Free Phone Calls," *Daily
     News,* May 1, 2019.

20   *Overnight, call volume* Julia Marsh and Aaron Feis, "NYC Inmates Made
     30 Percent More Calls After They Were Made Free," *New York Post,*
     Dec. 25, 2019.

20   *In Norway* Helen Crewe, " 'No Babies in Prison?'—Norway's Exception
     Explained," *Cambridge Quarterly,* Oct. 26, 2020; Doran Larson, "Why
     Scandinavian Prisons Are Superior," *The Atlantic,* Sept. 24, 2013.

20   *For correctional officials* Cyphert, "Prisoners of Fate," 395–96; La Vigne,
     Davies, and Brazzell, *Broken Bonds;* Grant Duwe and Valerie Clark,

"Blessed Be the Social Tie That Binds: The Effects of Prison Visitation on Offender Recidivism," *Criminal Justice Policy Review* 24, no. 3 (May 1, 2013): 271–96.

21 *Adam is right* Adam, interview.

21 *Allowing women* Kanaboshi, Anderson, and Sira, "Constitutional Rights of Infants and Toddlers," 55.

21 *Since the 1970s* Chris Gottlieb, "Black Families Are Outraged About Family Separation Within the U.S.," *Time,* Mar. 17, 2021.

21 *But it would be much better* Joint Family Defense Providers, "Legislative Priorities," Feb. 11, 2021, https://www.bronxdefenders.org/wp-content/uploads/2021/02/Joint-Family-Defense-Providers-2021-Legislative-Priorities.pdf; Roberts, "Abolishing Policing Also Means."

21 *Instead of pouring billions* Hurley, "How the Pandemic Became."

21 *For private entities* Ed Harris, "Family Equality Council Welcomes Senate Introduction of Every Child Deserves a Family Act," Family Equality, June 13, 2019, https://www.familyequality.org/press-releases/family-equality-welcomes-senate-every-child-deserves-a-family-act/.

21 *When Congress passed* Aída Chávez and Ryan Grim, "While Everybody Slept, Congress Did Something Extraordinary for Vulnerable Children," The Intercept, Feb. 11, 2018, https://theintercept.com/2018/02/11/foster-care-congress-did-something-extraordinary-for-vulnerable-children/.

21 *But for-profit group homes* Chávez and Grim, "While Everybody Slept."

21 *Indeed, private agencies' power* Adoption and Foster Care Analysis and Reporting System, "Preliminary 2019 Estimates as of June 23, 2020," Children's Bureau, 2020, https://www.acf.hhs.gov/sites/default/files/documents/cb/afcarsreport27.pdf.

22 *Children raised in institutions* Mark Wade et al., "Long-Term Effects of Institutional Rearing, Foster Care, and Brain Activity on Memory and Executive Functioning," *Proceedings of the National Academy of Sciences* 116, no. 5 (Jan. 29, 2019): 1808–13.

22 *This, in turn* Wade et al., "Long-Term Effects"; David M. Fergusson, Joseph M. Boden, and L. John Horwood, "Childhood Self-Control and Adult Outcomes: Results from a 30-Year Longitudinal Study," *Journal of the American Academy of Child and Adolescent Psychiatry* 52, no. 7 (July 2013): 709–17.e1; Terrie E. Moffitt et al., "A Gradient of Childhood Self-control Predicts Health, Wealth, and Public Safety," *Proceedings of the National Academy of Sciences* 108, no. 7 (Feb. 15, 2011): 2693–98.

22 *If you are raised* Brian Joseph, "The Brief Life and Private Death of Alexandria Hill," *Mother Jones,* Feb. 26, 2015; Aram Roston and Jeremy Singer-Vine, "Fostering Profits: Abuse and Neglect at America's Biggest For-Profit Foster Care Company," *BuzzFeed News,* Feb. 20, 2015, https://www.buzzfeednews.com/article/aramroston/fostering-profits; The National Scientific Council on the Developing Child, "Young Children Develop," 1.

22 *For a young human to thrive* The National Scientific Council on the Developing Child, "Young Children Develop," 1.

22 *Nearly half* Lawrence B. Finer and Mia R. Zolna, "Declines in Unintended Pregnancy in the United States, 2008–2011," *New England Journal of Medicine* 374, no. 9 (Mar. 3, 2016): 843–52.

23 *When Colorado launched* Taking the Unintended Out of Pregnancy: Colorado's Success with Long-Acting Reversible Contraception, Colorado Department of Public Health and Environment (Jan. 2017), x, 25; Sabrina Tavernise, "Colorado's Effort Against Teenage Pregnancies Is a Startling Success," *New York Times*, July 5, 2015.

23 *Over the next five years* Taking the Unintended Out of Pregnancy, viii.

23 *With the highest rate* Kathryn Kost, Isaac Maddow-Zimet, and Shivani Kochhar, *Pregnancy Desires and Pregnancies at the State Level: Estimates for 2014*, Guttmacher Institute, Dec. 11, 2018; Mark Edwards, "All Women Deserve Access to the Birth Control Method of Their Choice," Upstream USA (blog), Jan. 17, 2019, https://upstream.org/blog/2019/01/17/all-women-deserve-access-to-the-birth-control-method-of-their-choice/.

23 *As a result* Marc Edwards, "Delaware Unintended Pregnancy Rate Declines More Than 2x Compared to Other States," Upstream USA (blog), Oct. 6, 2021, https://upstream.org/blog/2021/10/06/delaware-unintended-pregnancy-rate-declines-more-than-2x-compared-to-other-states/.

23 *Those who count themselves* See, e.g., Jill Filipovic, "The Anti-Abortion Movement Could Reduce Abortions If It Wanted To," *New York Times*, Dec. 14, 2021.

23 *Expanding contraception* Filipovic, "The Anti-Abortion Movement."

23 *In the first five years* Taking the Unintended Out of Pregnancy, x, 25. That is in line with the evidence that about 40 percent of unplanned pregnancies end in abortion. Isabel V. Sawhill and Katherine Guyot, *Preventing Unplanned Pregnancy: Lessons from the States* (Brookings, June 2019), 1, https://www.brookings.edu/wp-content/uploads/2019/06/Preventing-Unplanned-Pregnancy-2.pdf.

23 *Many of the top factors* Claire Cain Miller, "Americans Are Having Fewer Babies. They Told Us Why," *New York Times*, July 5, 2018.

23 *Parents today* Claire Cain Miller, "The Relentlessness of Modern Parenting," *New York Times*, Dec. 25, 2018; Susan M. Shaw, "Family Leisure and Changing Ideologies of Parenthood," *Sociology Compass* 2, no. 2 (Jan. 2008): 688–703.

23 *Research consistently shows* Joe Pinsker, "It Isn't the Kids. It's the Cost of Raising Them," *The Atlantic*, Feb. 27, 2019.

23 *And it is a myth* Glynnis MacNicol, "I'm in My 40s, Child-Free and Happy. Why Won't Anyone Believe Me?" *New York Times*, July 5, 2018; Claire Cain Miller, "They Didn't Have Children and, Most Said, They Don't Have Regrets," *New York Times*, July 23, 2018.

23 *The singer Adele* Lisa Robinson, "Adele, Queen of Hearts," *Vanity Fair*, Oct. 31, 2016.

24 *Anne and her husband* Anne, interview by author, July 15, 2019, email.

24 *At the point* Anne, interview.

24 *"Women who have children"* Anne, interview.

24 *"I love children"* Anne, interview.

24 *For her, the solution* Anne, interview; Mary Kate Skehan, "The Unexpected Joys of Aunting," Institute for Family Studies, Aug. 16, 2021, https://ifstudies.org/blog/the-unexpected-joys-of-aunting; Anne Roderique-Jones, "Aunting: The New Childfree and Why I Love It," *SELF*, Nov. 4, 2018.

24 *As Anne puts it* Anne, interview.
24 *"My niece and nephew"* Anne, interview.
24 *So, she has cultivated* Anne, interview.
24 *She and her husband* Anne, interview.
24 *One of the great aspects* Anne, interview.
24 *The research is clear* The National Scientific Council on the Developing Child, "Young Children Develop," 3.
24 *They don't sap* The National Scientific Council on the Developing Child, "Young Children Develop," 3.
25 *Derek, like Anne* Derek, interview by author, Aug. 6, 2019.
25 *"I grew up"* Derek, interview.
25 *But, as he admits* Derek, interview.
25 *By 2014* Derek, interview.
25 *As Derek recalls* Derek, interview.
25 *Derek's boldness* Derek, interview.
25 *"We did things"* Derek, interview.
25 *The first step* Derek, interview.
25 *As Derek and Jonathan* Derek, interview.
25 *Indeed, 83 percent of people 2017 US Adoption Attitudes Survey,* Harris Poll on Behalf of the Dave Thomas Foundation for Adoption, Feb. 2018, 77, https://www.davethomasfoundation.org/wp-content/uploads/2018/02/2017-adoption-attitudes-survey-us.pdf.
25 *Yet foster care adoptions* Child Welfare Information Gateway, *Planning for Adoption: Knowing the Costs and Resources* (Washington, D.C.: U.S. Department of Health and Human Services, Children's Bureau, Nov. 2016), 3–4, https://www.childwelfare.gov/pubPDFs/s_costs.pdf; Derek, interview.
25 *Just the price* Child Welfare Information Gateway, *The Adoption Home Study Process* (Washington, D.C.: U.S. Department of Health and Human Services, Children's Bureau: Oct. 2020), https://www.childwelfare.gov/pubs/f-homstu/; Child Welfare Information Gateway, *Planning for Adoption*, 3.
25 *"As gay men"* Derek, interview.
25 *As Derek explains* Derek, interview.
26 *That made surrogacy* Derek, interview.
26 *But they* Derek, interview.
26 *In an amazing act* Derek, interview.
26 *The fact that she was British* Derek, interview.
26 *Although Jonathan's mother* Sarah Mervosh, "Gay U.S. Couple Sues State Dept. for Denying Their Baby Citizenship," *New York Times,* July 23, 2019.
26 *So, they began* Derek, interview.
26 *As required* Derek, interview.
26 *They had the mandated blood tests* Derek, interview.
26 *Derek recalls* Derek, interview.
26 *They received eleven eggs* Derek, interview.
26 *On the second try* Derek, interview.
26 *Derek went* Derek, interview.
26 *"Jonny and I"* Derek, interview.
26 *They were there* Derek, interview.
26 *They watched Simone* Derek, interview.

26 *But then* Derek, interview.

27 *In England, six weeks* Derek, interview.

27 *They were at the court* Derek, interview.

27 *The additional process* Derek, interview.

27 *As Derek explains* Derek, interview.

27 *Eight months* Derek, interview.

27 *Yet when they went* Mervosh, "Gay U.S. Couple Sues."

27 *According to State Department policy* Scott Bixby, "Trump Administration to LGBT Couples: Your 'Out of Wedlock' Kids Aren't Citizens," *Daily Beast,* May 17, 2019, https://www.thedailybeast.com/state-department-to-lgbt -married-couples-your-out-of-wedlock-kids-arent-citizens?ref=scroll.

27 *And if you were born* Bixby, "Trump Administration to LGBT Couples."

27 *Jonathan hadn't been* Derek, interview.

27 *If they stayed* Derek, interview; Sarah Mervosh, "Both Parents Are American. The U.S. Says Their Baby Isn't," *New York Times,* May 21, 2019; Mervosh, "Gay U.S. Couple Sues."

27 *When I asked Derek* Derek, interview.

27 *"If there is a child"* Derek, interview.

27 *"So, when Simone"* Derek, interview.

28 *In 2020* Mize v. Pompeo, 482 F. Supp. 3d 1317 (N.D. Ga. 2020); Lara Jakes and Sarah Mervosh, "The State Department Reverses a Policy That Denied Citizenship to Some Babies Born Abroad to Same-Sex Parents," *New York Times,* May 18, 2021.

28 *In a 2017 survey* 2017 US Adoption Attitudes Survey, 59.

28 *Eleven states currently permit* Stephen Vider and David S. Byers, "A Supreme Court Case Poses a Threat to L.G.B.T.Q. Foster Kids," *New York Times,* June 5, 2021.

28 *And, in 2021* Fulton v. City of Philadelphia, 593 U.S. (2021); Vider and Byers, "A Supreme Court Case."

28 *Should the political winds* Aris Folley, "Pence Lauds Proposed Rule to Allow Faith-Based Adoption Groups Bar LGBTQ Parents," *The Hill,* Nov. 11, 2019, https://thehill.com/homenews/administration/470534-pence-lauds -proposed-rule-to-allow-faith-based-adoption-groups-bar?sfns=mo&rl=1; Sam Baker and Swan Jonathan, "Trump's Plan to Let Adoption Agencies Turn Away Same-Sex Parents," *Axios,* May 24, 2019, https://www.axios .com/trump-lgbtq-adoption-rules-religious-exemption-85f5fb22-d76d -4536-b275-0b279e904933.html; Jennifer Finney Boylan, "The Latest Victims of Trump's Cruelty? Foster Children," *New York Times,* Aug. 7, 2019.

28 *That's particularly damaging* Laura Baams, Bianca D. M. Wilson, and Stephen T. Russell, "LGBTQ Youth in Unstable Housing and Foster Care," *Pediatrics* 143, no. 3 (Mar. 1, 2019): e20174211; Vider and Byers, "A Supreme Court Case."

28 *Many of those kids* Boylan, "The Latest Victims."

28 *And there is growing evidence* Vider and Byers, "A Supreme Court Case"; Michael Waters, "The Untold Story of Queer Foster Families," *New Yorker,* Feb. 28, 2021.

29 *As Derek points out* Derek, interview.

29 *There are kids* See, e.g., Cordell, *Her Honor,* 97–99.

29 *There are siblings* Jill Elaine Hasday, *Family Law Reimagined* (Cambridge, Mass.: Harvard University Press, 2014), 13, 161–93.
29 *There are godparents* Sixto Cancel, "Our Foster Care System Is Fundamentally Broken," *New York Times,* Sept. 16, 2021.
29 *As Sixto Cancel* Cancel, "Our Foster Care System."
29 *For the rest* Cancel, "Our Foster Care System."
29 *At the age of twenty-seven* Cancel, "Our Foster Care System."
29 *One of those aunts* Cancel, "Our Foster Care System."
29 *"That's how close I'd been"* Cancel, "Our Foster Care System."
29 *Sixto has founded a nonprofit* Cancel, "Our Foster Care System."
29 *Derek echoes the point* Derek, interview.
29 *He draws an analogy* Derek, interview.

2. Early Childhood: The Right to Investment

31 *For Harold* Harold, interview by author, Sept. 19, 2019.
31 *"This is right after"* Harold, interview.
31 *Everything to that point* Harold, interview.
31 *But then* Harold, interview.
31 *Harold's mom loses* Harold, interview.
31 *In the two years* Harold, interview.
31 *There will be fights* Harold, interview.
31 *There will be substance* Harold, interview.
31 *There will be depression* Harold, interview.
31 *But in this moment* Harold, interview.
31 *"I vividly remember"* Harold, interview.
31 *As Harold recalls* Harold, interview.
32 *Reflecting back now* Harold, interview.
32 *In the country* Sarah Jackson, "These 20 Countries and Territories Are Home to Most of the World's 2,755 Billionaires," *Business Insider,* Oct. 7, 2021, https://www.businessinsider.com/these-20-countries-are-home-to -the-most-billionaires-forbes-2021-10; Alyson Sulaski Wyckoff, "Census Report: Child Poverty Rate Increases to 16.1% in 2020," *American Academy of Pediatrics News,* Sept. 14, 2021, https://publications.aap.org/aapnews /news/15633/Census-report-Child-poverty-rate-increases-to-16-1.
32 *Based on the 2020 census* Wyckoff, "Census Report."
32 *If you are born* Alana Semuels, "Why It's So Hard to Get Ahead in the South," *The Atlantic,* Apr. 4, 2017.
32 *In Atlanta* Semuels, "Why It's So Hard to Get Ahead in the South."
32 *A son born* Raj Chetty et al., "The Fading American Dream: Trends in Absolute Income Mobility Since 1940," *Science* 356, no. 6336 (Apr. 28, 2017): 6.
32 *The travesty* Alla Katsnelson, "A Novel Effort to See How Poverty Affects Young Brains," *New York Times,* Apr. 7, 2021; Selcuk R. Sirin, "Socioeconomic Status and Academic Achievement: A Meta-analytic Review of Research," *Review of Educational Research* 75, no. 3 (Fall 2005): 438.
32 *And there is an abundance* James E. Bennett et al., "Contributions of Diseases and Injuries to Widening Life Expectancy Inequalities in England

from 2001 to 2016: A Population-Based Analysis of Vital Registration Data," *Lancet Public Health* 3, no. 12 (Nov. 22, 2018): e586–e597.

32 *A recent study* Imperial College London, "Poorest Dying Nearly 10 Years Younger Than the Rich in 'Deeply Worrying' Trend for UK," *ScienceDaily*, Nov. 23, 2018, https://www.sciencedaily.com/releases/2018/11/181123135003.htm.

32 *And the threat* Imperial College London, "Poorest Dying."

32 *When researchers analyzed* Raquel E. Gur et al., "Burden of Environmental Adversity Associated with Psychopathology, Maturation, and Brain Behavior Parameters in Youths," *JAMA Psychiatry* 76, no. 9 (2019): 973.

33 *The brains of children* Gur, "Burden of Environmental Adversity," 966.

33 *Other studies have identified* Alla Katsnelson, "A Novel Effort to See How Poverty Affects Young Brains," *New York Times*, Apr. 7, 2021; Daniel A. Hackman and Martha J. Farah, "Socioeconomic Status and the Developing Brain," *Trends in Cognitive Science* 13, no. 2 (Feb. 2009): 66; Daniel A. Hackman, Martha J. Farah, and Michael J. Meaney, "Socioeconomic Status and the Brain: Mechanistic Insights from Human and Animal Research," *Nature Reviews Neuroscience* 11, no. 9 (Sept. 2010): 652–53; Kimberly G. Noble et al., "Neural Correlates of Socioeconomic Status in the Developing Human Brain," *Developmental Science* 15, no. 4 (2012): 522–23; Gwendolyn M. Lawson, Cayce J. Hook, and Martha J. Farah, "A Meta-analysis of the Relationship Between Socioeconomic Status and Executive Function Performance Among Children," *Developmental Science* 21, no. 2 (2018): 16.

33 *Scientists have now begun* Deanna M. Barch et al., "Early Childhood Socioeconomic Status and Cognitive and Adaptive Outcomes at the Transition to Adulthood: The Mediating Role of Gray Matter Development Across Five Scan Waves," *Biological Psychiatry: Cognitive Neuroscience and Neuroimaging* 7, no. 1 (Jan. 2022): 37.

33 *In one example* Barch et al., "Early Childhood Socioeconomic Status," 35.

33 *Controlling for factors* Barch et al., "Early Childhood Socioeconomic Status," 37, 39.

33 *And the pathway* Barch et al., "Early Childhood Socioeconomic Status," 37.

33 *Those experiencing poverty* Barch et al., "Early Childhood Socioeconomic Status," 37–39.

33 *That, in turn* Barch et al., "Early Childhood Socioeconomic Status," 39.

33 *Yet, we need* Katsnelson, "Novel Effort"; Baby's First Years, accessed Mar. 15, 2022, https://www.babysfirstyears.com/; Barch et al., "Early Childhood Socioeconomic Status," 39–41.

33 *Poor kids are less* Jeff Guo, "In the U.S., Rich Kids See the Doctor More. In the Netherlands, Poor Kids Do," *Washington Post*, Dec. 29, 2015.

33 *In 2020* Wyckoff, "Census Report."

33 *Affluent parents* Heather Long, "By Age 3, Inequality Is Clear: Rich Kids Attend School. Poor Kids Stay with a Grandparent," *Washington Post*, Sept. 26, 2017; Claire Cain Miller, "Class Differences in Child-Rearing Are on the Rise," *New York Times*, Dec. 17, 2015; *Parenting in America*, Pew Research Center, Dec. 17, 2015, https://www.pewresearch.org/social-trends/2015/12/17/parenting-in-america/.

33 *Poor children* Nalini Ranjit et al., "Socioeconomic Inequalities in Children's Diet: The Role of the Home Environment," *International Journal of Behavioral Nutrition and Physical Activity* 12 (Suppl 1), no. S4 (2015): 1–2, 5.

33 *And they are exposed* Lindsey Konkel, "Pollution, Poverty and People of Color: Children at Risk," *Scientific American*, June 6, 2012.

34 *Parents in families* Parenting in America.

34 *"I kept switching schools"* Harold, interview.

34 *"In sixth grade"* Harold, interview.

34 *At this point* Harold, interview.

34 *He begged his mom* Harold, interview.

34 *But it wasn't* Harold, interview.

34 *It was only when* Harold, interview.

34 *He was big* Harold, interview.

34 *The next year* Harold, interview; "About Us," Beat the Streets Philadelphia, accessed Mar. 16, 2022, https://btsphilly.org/about-us.

34 *He began traveling* Harold, interview.

34 *We'd "get absolutely smacked"* Harold, interview.

34 *But it was "wonderful"* Harold, interview.

34 *And it led to a scholarship* "Vision, Mission & Philosophy," William Penn Charter School, accessed Mar. 16, 2022, https://www.penncharter.com/about-us/vision-mission-philosophy.

34 *Harold's initial visit* Harold, interview.

34 *The prompt* Harold, interview.

35 *"They had grass"* Harold, interview.

35 *And as he looked around* Harold, interview; "Our Campus," William Penn Charter School, accessed Mar. 16, 2022, https://www.penncharter.com/about-us/our-campus.

35 *Everything was scaled up* Harold, interview.

35 *It's forty-seven acres* Harold, interview; "Our Campus."

35 *"There's a building across"* Harold, interview.

35 *"It was obvious"* Harold, interview.

35 *The kids here* Harold, interview.

35 *It was not simply* Harold, interview.

35 *"People who have been"* Harold, interview.

35 *Growing up destitute* Harold, interview.

36 *"You are able"* Harold, interview.

36 *Bussing or redrawing* Eliza Shapiro, "How White Progressives Undermine School Integration," *New York Times*, Aug. 21, 2020.

36 *When poor inner-city students* Avi Wolfman-Arent, " 'The Money Shot': How School Districts Find and Prove Residency Fraud," WHYY, May 2, 2018, https://whyy.org/segments/the-money-shot-how-school-districts-find-and-prove-residency-fraud/; Avi Wolfman-Arent, "Suburban Schools' Residency Enforcement Mostly Affects Kids of Color," WHYY, May 1, 2018, https://whyy.org/segments/suburban-schools-residency-enforcement-disproportionately-affects-kids-of-color/.

36 *Fork over $10,000* Dana Goldstein and Jugal K. Patel, "Need Extra Time on Tests? It Helps to Have Cash," *New York Times*, July 30, 2019; Stephen G. Sireci, Stanley E. Scarpati, and Shuhong Li, "Test Accommodations for

Students with Disabilities: An Analysis of the Interaction Hypothesis," *Review of Educational Research* 75, no. 4 (Winter 2005): 481.

36 *Roughly one* Goldstein, "Extra Time on Tests."

37 *Experts recently calculated* Sophie Alexander and Ben Steverman, "For an Edge in Ivy League Admissions, Grab an Oar and Row," *Chicago Tribune,* Mar. 31, 2019.

37 *How can it be* Gregor Aisch et al., "Some Colleges Have More Students from the Top 1 Percent Than the Bottom 60. Find Yours," *New York Times,* Jan. 18, 2017.

37 *At three years old* Editorial Board, "Donald Trump and the Self-Made Sham," *New York Times,* Oct. 2, 2018; David Barstow, Susanne Craig, and Russ Buettner, "Trump Engaged in Suspect Tax Schemes as He Reaped Riches from His Father," *New York Times,* Oct. 2, 2018.

37 *"I built"* Editorial Board, "Donald Trump."

37 *In this version* Editorial Board, "Donald Trump."

37 *As numerous experiments* Lee Ross and Richard E. Nisbett, *The Person and the Situation: Perspectives of Social Psychology* (New York: McGraw-Hill, 1991).

38 *Overestimating the ability people* Roland Benabou and Jean Tirole, "Belief in a Just World and Redistributive Politics," *Quarterly Journal of Economics* 121, no. 2 (May 2006): 705; E. J. Langer, "The Illusion of Control," *Journal of Personality and Social Psychology* 32, no. 2 (1975): 311–28.

38 *Sixty percent of Americans* Benabou and Tirole, "Belief in a Just World," 701; Everett Carll Ladd and Karlyn H. Bowman, *Attitudes Toward Economic Inequality* (Washington, D.C.: AEI Press, 1998).

38 *And, just 29 percent* Benabou and Tirole, "Belief in a Just World," 701; Alberto Alesina, Edward Glaeser, and Bruce Sacerdote, "Why Doesn't the US Have a European-Style Welfare System?" National Bureau of Economic Research, Oct. 2001.

38 *In addition* Melvin J. Lerner, *The Belief in a Just World: A Fundamental Delusion* (New York: Plenum Press, 1982).

38 *In the laboratory* Benabou and Tirole, "Belief in a Just World," 705.

38 *It makes sense* John Jost and Orsolya Hunyady, "The Psychology of System Justification and the Palliative Function of Ideology," *European Review of Social Psychology* 13, no. 1 (Aug. 2002); Emmeline S. Chen and Tom R. Tyler, "Cloaking Power: Legitimizing Myths and the Psychology of the Advantaged," in *The Use and Abuse of Power: Multiple Perspectives on the Causes of Corruption,* ed. Annette Y. Lee-Chai and John A. Bargh (Philadelphia: Psychology Press, 2001), 241–61; John Jost et al., "Social Inequality and the Reduction of Ideological Dissonance on Behalf of the System: Evidence of Enhanced System Justification Among the Disadvantaged," *European Journal of Social Psychology* 33, no. 1 (July 2002): 24.

38 *But the motivation* Jost and Hunyady, "The Psychology of System Justification," 145–47; Adam Benforado, Jon Hanson, and David Yosifon, "Broken Scales: Obesity and Justice in America," *Emory Law Journal* 53, no. 1645 (2004): 1664–68.

38 *In essence* Jost and Hunyady, "The Psychology of System Justification," 145–47; Benforado, Hanson, and Yosifon, "Broken Scales," 1664–68;

James R. Kluegel et al., *Beliefs About Inequality* (New York: Routledge, 1986).

38   *These findings* Patricia Cohen, "Southerners, Facing Big Odds, Believe in a Path Out of Poverty," *New York Times*, July 4, 2019.

38   *Alabamans estimate* Cohen, "Southerners, Facing Big Odds."

38   *Faith that a good disposition* Alberto Alesina, Stefanie Stantcheva, and Edoardo Teso, "Intergenerational Mobility and Preferences for Redistribution," *American Economic Review* 108, no. 2 (Feb. 2018): 521–54.

39   *Indeed, recent research* Simone M. Schneider and Juan C. Castillo, "Poverty Attributions and the Perceived Justice of Income Inequality: A Comparison of East and West Germany," *Social Psychology Quarterly* 78, no. 3 (2015): 278.

39   *What's more, in experiments* Cohen, "Southerners, Facing Big Odds"; Alesina, Stantcheva, and Teso, "Intergenerational Mobility."

39   *"Growing up"* Harold, interview.

39   *It felt* Harold, interview.

39   *He always had* Harold, interview.

39   *They seemed* Harold, interview.

39   *When he was* Harold, interview.

39   *As Harold points out* Harold, interview.

39   *Harold was homeless* Harold, interview.

39   *Harold's public schools* Harold, interview.

39   *There was a shooting* Aaron Carter, "Penn-Bound Harold Anderson Is Blazing a Trail at Penn Charter and Helping Others to Follow," *Philadelphia Inquirer*, May 12, 2017.

39   *That's behind the conflict* Harold, interview.

40   *No one ever seemed* Harold, interview.

40   *Even as he was being celebrated* "Overbrook High School," GreatSchools, https://www.greatschools.org/pennsylvania/philadelphia/2107-Overbrook-High-School/.

40   *"It became"* Harold, interview.

40   *His answer* Harold, interview.

40   *"It puts people"* Harold, interview.

41   *It "tells people"* Harold, interview.

41   *It tells a poor child* Harold, interview.

41   *But, as Harold points out* Harold, interview.

41   *With the entire landscape* Harold, interview.

41   *And over time* Harold, interview.

41   *A recent study of 195 countries* Neelam Iqbal et al., "Girls' Hidden Penalty: Analysis of Gender Inequality in Child Mortality with Data from 195 Countries," *BMJ Global Health* (2018): 2; Queen Mary University of London, "Gender Inequality Could Be Driving the Deaths of Girls Under Five," *ScienceDaily*, Oct. 30, 2018, https://www.sciencedaily.com/releases/2018/10/181030184504.htm.

41   *The higher the gender inequality* Iqbal et al., "Girls' Hidden Penalty," 1.

41   *Likewise, troubling new data* "Parents Of Only Boys Place Greater Priority On College Than Parents of Only Girls," T. Rowe Price, Sept. 21, 2017,

https://www.troweprice.com/corporate/us/en/press/t--rowe-price
--parents-of-only-boys-place-greater-priority-on-co.html.

41 *Give all children access* Iqbal et al., "Girls' Hidden Penalty," 1.

42 *If you are Black* Raj Chetty et al., "Race and Economic Opportunity in the United States," Opportunity Insights (Apr. 2018), 2, https://oppor tunityinsights.org/wp-content/uploads/2018/04/race_summary.pdf; Raj Chetty et al., "Race and Economic Opportunity in the United States: An Intergenerational Perspective," *Quarterly Journal of Economics* 135, no. 2 (May 1, 2020): 711–83.

42 *A Black child* Chetty et al., "An Intergenerational Perspective," 733.

42 *While a rich white boy* Emily Badger et al., "Extensive Data Shows Punishing Reach of Racism for Black Boys," *New York Times,* Mar. 19, 2018.

42 *In 99 percent of neighborhoods* Chetty et al., "An Intergenerational Perspective," 711.

42 *The same is not true* Chetty et al., "Race and Economic Opportunity," 3.

42 *When researchers looked* Chetty et al., "Race and Economic Opportunity," 3; Chetty et al., "An Intergenerational Perspective," 747–52.

42 *A Black boy* Chetty et al., "Race and Economic Opportunity," 3; Badger et al., "Extensive Data."

42 *The few neighborhoods* Chetty et al., "Race and Economic Opportunity," 4.

42 *Having a large proportion* Badger et al., "Extensive Data"; Chetty et al., "Race and Economic Opportunity," 4.

42 *They live in places* Badger et al., "Extensive Data"; Chetty et al., "An Intergenerational Perspective," 744–46.

43 *While 63 percent* Chetty et al., "An Intergenerational Perspective," 718.

43 *He describes his father* Harold, interview.

43 *With his mother's struggles* Harold, interview.

43 *As he reflects now* Harold, interview.

43 *"We have to look"* Harold, interview.

43 *"You are a product"* Harold, interview.

43 *"I would look around"* Harold, interview.

43 *As he recalls* Harold, interview.

44 *He supposed* Harold, interview.

44 *"I would feel bad"* Harold, interview.

44 *"We think we have found"* David Nasaw, *Andrew Carnegie* (New York: Penguin Books, 2006), 350 (quoting letter from Louise Carnegie to William Gladstone, June 19, 1889).

44 *She enclosed* Nasaw, *Andrew Carnegie,* 350.

44 *And much to their delight* Nasaw, *Andrew Carnegie,* 351; William E. Gladstone, "Mr. Carnegie's 'Gospel of Wealth': A Review and a Recommendation," *Nineteenth Century* 28, no. 165 (Nov. 1890): 677–93.

44 *It seemed* Nasaw, *Andrew Carnegie,* 351 (quoting letter from Andrew Carnegie to William Gladstone, Nov. 24, 1890); *American Experience,* "Biography: Andrew Carnegie," PBS, accessed Mar. 29, 2022, https://www.pbs.org/wgbh/americanexperience/features/carnegie-biography/.

44 *With grand ambition* In contrast to his philanthropic bent, Carnegie was a ruthless businessman who worked tirelessly to keep costs down, often at the

expense of the health, safety, and well-being of his workers. In 1901, Carnegie sold his steel company to J. P. Morgan for $480 million and became the richest man in the world. *American Experience,* "Biography."

44 *"Why should men"* Andrew Carnegie, "Wealth," *North American Review* 148, no. 391 (June 1889): 658.

44 *Carnegie saw* Carnegie, "Wealth," 658.

45 *Provocative as it was* Nasaw, *Andrew Carnegie,* 351; Gladstone, "Mr. Carnegie's," 683.

45 *And although Carnegie American Experience,* "Biography."

45 *On average* Lily Batchelder, "Tax the Rich," *New York Times,* June 24, 2020.

45 *That's just an average* "Changes in U.S. Family Finances from 2016 to 2019," *Federal Reserve Bulletin* 106, no. 5 (Sept. 2020).

45 *If you are* Batchelder, "Tax the Rich."

45 *Over time* Thomas Piketty, Emmanuel Saez, and Gabriel Zucman, "Distributional National Accounts: Methods and Estimates for the United States," *Quarterly Journal of Economics* 133, no. 2 (May 2018): 553–609.

45 *It is one of the reasons* Batchelder, "Tax the Rich"; Jeffrey P. Thompson and Gustavo A. Suarez, "Exploring the Racial Wealth Gap Using the Survey of Consumer Finances," *Finance and Economics Discussion Series,* Aug. 22, 2015.

45 *Today, 41 percent* Tatjana Meschede et al., "'Family Achievement?': How a College Degree Accumulates Wealth for Whites and Not for Blacks," *Federal Reserve Bank of St. Louis Review* 99, no. 1 (2017): 127–37; Bethany Romano, "Racial Wealth Gap Continues to Grow Between Black and White Families, Regardless of College Attainment," Brandeis Heller School for Social Policy and Management, July 16, 2018, https://heller.brandeis.edu/news/items/releases/2018/meschede-taylor-college-attainment-racial-wealth-gap.html.

45 *By contrast* Meschede et al., "Family Achievement?"; Romano, "Racial Wealth Gap."

45 *As he exhorted* Carnegie, "Wealth," 658.

46 *In the words* David Cay Johnston, "Dozens of Rich Americans Join in Fight to Retain the Estate Tax," *New York Times,* Feb. 14, 2021.

46 *It's akin* Johnston, "Dozens of Rich Americans."

46 *By combining tax returns* David Leonhardt, "Lost Einsteins: The Innovations We're Missing," *New York Times,* Dec. 4, 2017.

46 *If your parents* Alex Bell et al., "Who Becomes an Inventor in America? The Importance of Exposure to Innovation," The Equality of Opportunity Project, 1, https://opportunityinsights.org/wp-content/uploads/2018/03/inventors_summary.pdf.

46 *Race, gender* Leonhardt, "Lost Einsteins."

46 *As the researchers concluded* Bell et al., "Who Becomes an Inventor," 5.

46 *Indeed, in a separate recent study* Andrew Van Dam, "It's Better to Be Born Rich Than Gifted," *Washington Post,* Oct. 9, 2018; Nicholas W. Papageorge and Kevin Thom, "Genes, Education, and Labor Market Outcomes: Evidence from the Health and Retirement Study," Working Paper No. 25114, National Bureau of Economic Research, Cambridge, Mass. (Sept. 2018).

46 *Wealthy children* Van Dam, "It's Better"; Papageorge and Thom, "Genes, Education, and Labor," 21–22.

46 *Our nation was founded* Editorial Board, "The Smartest Way to Make the Rich Pay Is Not a Wealth Tax," *Washington Post,* July 21, 2021.

46 *In the late eighteenth century* Mary Ann Mason, *From Father's Property to Children's Rights: The History of Child Custody in the United States* (New York: Columbia University Press, 1994), 69; C. Ray Keim, "Primogeniture and Entail in Colonial Virginia," *William and Mary Quarterly* 25, no. 4 (Oct. 1968): 545–86.

47 *Thomas Jefferson* Thomas Jefferson, Letter to John Adams, Oct. 28, 1813, https://founders.archives.gov/documents/Jefferson/03-06-02-0446; Daniel J. Kornstein, "Inheritance: A Constitutional Right," *Rutgers Law Review* 36, no. 4 (Summer 1984): 759–60; Keim, "Primogeniture," 548–50.

47 *"These laws"* Jefferson, Letter to Adams; Kornstein, "Inheritance," 760.

47 *As he wrote* Jefferson, Letter to James Madison, Sept. 6, 1789, https://founders.archives.gov/documents/Madison/01-12-02-0248.

47 *More than one hundred* Paul Krugman, "Tax the Rich, Help America's Children," *New York Times,* Oct. 25, 2021; Thomas Piketty, "Piketty on the U.S.: The Birthplace of Freedom and Progressive Taxation," *PBS NewsHour,* May 14, 2014, https://www.pbs.org/newshour/nation/piketty-u-s-birthplace-freedom-progressive-taxation; IRS, "Income Tax History, Tax Code and Definitions. United States," eFile, Sept. 2, 2021, https://www.efile.com/tax-history-and-the-tax-code/; Darien B. Jacobson, Brian G. Raub, and Barry W. Johnson, "The Estate Tax: Ninety Years and Counting," *Statistics of Income* 27, no. 1 (Summer 2007): 118–28, https://www.irs.gov/pub/irs-soi/ninetyestate.pdf; Carnegie, "Wealth," 659.

47 *And it was Teddy Roosevelt* Krugman, "Tax the Rich"; Tax Analysts, "The Income Tax Arrives," Tax History Project (2022), http://www.taxhistory.org/www/website.nsf/Web/THM1901.

47 *The total tax* Piketty, Saez, and Zucman, "Distributional National Accounts."

47 *We've hacked away* Batchelder, "Tax the Rich."

47 *And we've riddled* David Kamin, "Taxing Capital: Paths to a Fairer and Broader U.S. Tax System," Washington Center for Equitable Growth, 2016, https://equitablegrowth.org/wp-content/uploads/2016/08/081016-kamin-taxing-capital.pdf.

47 *But the good news* Batchelder, "Tax the Rich"; Raymond Fisman et al., "Do Americans Want to Tax Wealth? Evidence from Online Surveys," *Journal of Public Economics* 188 (Aug. 2020): 12–13.

47 *Historically, the U.S. economy* Krugman, "Tax the Rich"; Jane G. Gravelle and Donald J. Marples, *Tax Rates and Economic Growth,* Congressional Research Service, Jan. 2, 2014, https://sgp.fas.org/crs/misc/R42111.pdf.

47 *And research shows* Batchelder, "Tax the Rich"; Lily L. Batchelder, "What Should Society Expect from Heirs? A Proposal for a Comprehensive Inheritance Tax," *Tax Law Review* 63, no. 1 (Feb. 23, 2010): 1–112; Wojciech Kopczuk, "Taxation of Intergenerational Transfers and Wealth," in *Hand-*

book of Public Economics, vol. 5, ed. Alan J. Auerbach et al. (Amsterdam: North Holland, 2013), 329–90.

47 *In fact, inheritance* Batchelder, "Tax the Rich"; Douglas Holtz-Eakin, David Joulfaian, and Harvey S. Rosen, "The Carnegie Conjecture: Some Empirical Evidence," *The Quarterly Journal of Economics* 108, no. 2 (May 1, 1993): 413–35.

47 *To move forward* Carnegie advocated for philanthropy: "Surplus wealth . . . administered during their lives by its possessors." Carnegie, "Wealth," 657. And that model has been embraced by a number of billionaires today. Bill Gates, the founder of Microsoft, has echoed Carnegie's concern with passing all his assets to his children: "I knew I didn't think it was a good idea to give the money to my kids. That wouldn't be good either for my kids or society." Megan Willett, "15 Tycoons Who Won't Leave Their Fortunes to Their Kids," Yahoo! Finance, Aug. 20, 2013, http://finance.yahoo.com/news/15-tycoons-who-won-t-leave-their-fortunes-to-their-kids-195610442.html. In 2010, he and Warren Buffett created the Giving Pledge, asking billionaires to "publicly commit to give the majority of their wealth to philanthropy." "About the Giving Pledge," The Giving Pledge, accessed Mar. 29, 2022, https://givingpledge.org/About.aspx. Today, more than two hundred of the world's wealthiest people have signed up. Those commitments will have a greatly positive effect on the world and are a clear step in the right direction when it comes to ending dynastic wealth. But relying on the charitable intentions of the superrich is insufficient. For one thing, when we turn to philanthropy, we have no guarantees that the money will flow where we as a society believe it is most needed and will make the biggest difference. You may get investment in kids and you may not.

47 *We ought to* Nelson D. Schwartz and Guilbert Gates, "Democrats Want to Tax the Rich. Here's How Those Plans Would Work (or Not)," *New York Times,* Sept. 24, 2019; Editorial Board, "The Smartest Way to Make the Rich Pay"; OECD, *The Role and Design of Net Wealth Taxes in the OECD* (OECD Publishing, 2018), 12.

47 *We might consider* Neil Irwin, "Elizabeth Warren Wants a Wealth Tax. How Would That Even Work?" *New York Times,* Feb. 18, 2019; Thomas Kaplan, "Bernie Sanders Proposes a Wealth Tax: 'I Don't Think That Billionaires Should Exist,'" *New York Times,* Sept. 24, 2019; Batchelder, "Tax the Rich"; Batchelder, "What Should Society Expect"; Thomas Piketty and Emmanuel Saez, "A Theory of Optimal Inheritance Taxation," *Econometrica* 81, no. 5 (2013): 1851–86.

48 *A related idea* Henry Aaron, "Rich Kids Can Spare Some of Their Inheritance," *New York Times,* Oct. 15, 2019; Batchelder, "Tax the Rich"; Lily L. Batchelder, "Leveling the Playing Field Between Inherited Income and Income from Work Through an Inheritance Tax," in *Tackling the Tax Code: Efficient and Equitable Ways to Raise Revenue,* ed. Jay Shambaugh and Ryan Nunn (Brookings, Jan. 2020), 43–88.

48 *A tax of 40 percent* Aaron, "Rich Kids Can Spare"; Batchelder, "Tax the Rich"; Batchelder, "Leveling the Playing Field."

48 *Right now, baby boomers* Batchelder, "Tax the Rich"; Board of Governors of the Federal Reserve System, "Distribution of Household Wealth in the

U.S. Since 1989," Federal Reserve, 2022, https://www.federalreserve.gov /releases/z1/dataviz/dfa/distribute/table/.

48 *We are ranked* Hilary W. Hoynes and Diane Schanzenbach, "Safety Net Investments in Children," *Brookings Papers on Economic Activity* (Spring 2018): 89–150, https://www.brookings.edu/bpea-articles/safety-net-investments -in-children/; Jeff Stein, "The U.S. Spends Less on Children Than Almost Any Other Developed Nation," *Washington Post,* May 16, 2018.

48 *On average* Louis Jacobson, "Federal Spending on Old and Young, by the Numbers," PolitiFact, Jan. 28, 2013, https://www.politifact.com/article /2013/jan/28/federal-spending-old-young-numbers/.

48 *As we touched on* Helen Clark et al., "A Future for the World's Children? A WHO–UNICEF–Lancet Commission," *Lancet* 395, no. 10224 (Feb. 2020): 614, 616; National Research Council and Institute of Medicine Committee on Integrating the Science of Early Childhood Development, *From Neurons to Neighborhoods: The Science of Early Childhood Development,* ed. Jack P. Shonkoff and Deborah A. Phillips (Washington, D.C.: National Academies Press, 2000); James J. Heckman, "The Economics of Inequality," *American Education* 35 (2011): 31–35.

48 *If you wait* Nicholas Kristof, "Our Children Deserve Better," *New York Times,* Sept. 12, 2019.

49 *If you want* Josephine Sedgwick, "25-Year-Old Textbooks and Holes in the Ceiling: Inside America's Public Schools," *New York Times,* Apr. 16, 2018.

49 *The pages* Sedgwick, "25-Year-Old Textbooks."

49 *There are lead water pipes* Sedgwick, "25-Year-Old Textbooks."

49 *Mold constellates* Debbie Truong, " 'Borderline Criminal': Many Public Schools Teeter on the Edge of Decrepitude," *Washington Post,* May 25, 2019.

49 *The heat fails in winter* Truong, " 'Borderline Criminal' "; Sarah Larimer, " 'Kids Are Freezing': Amid Bitter Cold, Baltimore Schools, Students Struggle," *Washington Post,* Jan. 5, 2018; Christopher Flavelle, "Hotter Days Widen Racial Gap in U.S. Schools, Data Shows," *New York Times,* Oct. 5, 2020.

49 *According to the American Society* American Society of Civil Engineers, "Schools," *ASCE's 2021 Infrastructure Report Card,* Jan. 17, 2017, https:// infrastructurereportcard.org/cat-item/schools/.

49 *In a recent survey* Guardian Teacher Takeover, " 'We Shouldn't Be on Food Stamps': Teachers on How to Fix America's Education System," *Guardian,* Sept. 5, 2018.

49 *These are people* Alvin Chang, "Your State's Teachers Are Underpaid. Find Out by How Much," *Vox,* Mar. 9, 2018, https://www.vox.com/policy-and -politics/2018/3/9/17100404/teacher-pay-salary-underpaid-database.

49 *One in five* Madeline Will, "To Make Ends Meet, 1 in 5 Teachers Have Second Jobs," *Education Week,* June 19, 2018.

49 *The picture for pre-K* Claire Zillman, "Childcare Costs More Than College Tuition in More Than Half of U.S. States," *Fortune,* Oct. 22, 2018.

49 *As a percentage of GDP* Zillman, "Childcare Costs More."

49 *In the United States* Jonathan Cohn, "The Hell of American Day Care," *New Republic,* Apr. 15, 2013; U.S. Department of Health and Human Ser-

vices, "The NICHD Study of Early Childcare and Youth Development," National Institutes of Health (2006), https://www.nichd.nih.gov/sites /default/files/publications/pubs/documents/seccyd_06.pdf.

49 *And only about a third* Nicholas Kristof, "Turning Child Care into a New Cold War," *New York Times,* June 5, 2021; Claire Cain Miller, "How Other Nations Pay for Child Care. The U.S. Is an Outlier," *New York Times,* Oct. 6, 2021.

49 *With a median salary* Claire Cain Miller, "How Public Preschool Can Help, and How to Make Sure It Doesn't Hurt," *New York Times,* Nov. 8, 2021; Jeneen Interlandi, "Why Are Our Most Important Teachers Paid the Least?" *New York Times,* Jan. 9, 2018; Emma Garcia and Elaine Weiss, *Low Relative Pay and High Incidence of Moonlighting Play a Role in the Teacher Shortage, Particularly in High-Poverty Schools,* Economic Policy Institute, May 9, 2019.

49 *Improving school outcomes* C. Kirabo Jackson, Rucker C. Johnson, and Claudia Persico, "The Effects of School Spending on Educational and Economic Outcomes: Evidence from School Finance Reforms," *Quarterly Journal of Economics* 131, no. 1 (Feb. 1, 2016): 157–218.

50 *We now have* Jorge Luis García et al., "The Long-Term Benefits of Quality Early Childcare for Disadvantaged Mothers and Their Children," *Vox EU,* Aug. 25, 2017, https://voxeu.org/article/long-term-benefits-quality-early -childcare; Miller, "How Public Preschool Can Help"; James Heckman, Rodrigo Pinto, and Peter Savelyev, "Understanding the Mechanisms Through Which an Influential Early Childhood Program Boosted Adult Outcomes," *American Economic Review* 103, no. 6 (Oct. 2013): 2052–86; Kai Hong, Kacie Dragan, and Sherry Glied, "Seeing and Hearing: The Impacts of New York City's Universal Prekindergarten Program on the Health of Low-Income Children," Working Paper No. 23297, National Bureau of Economic Research, Cambridge, Mass. (Mar. 2017), https://doi.org/10 .3386/w23297.

50 *In 1962* Jorge Luis García, James J. Heckman, and Victor Ronda, "Boosting Intergenerational Mobility: The Lasting Effects of Early Childhood Education on Skills and Social Mobility," The Heckman Equation (2021), https://heckmanequation.org/www/assets/2021/11/F_Heckman_Perry -2021_OnePager_092321.pdf; James J. Heckman and Ganesh Karapakula, "The Perry Preschoolers at Late Midlife: A Study in Design-Specific Inference," Human Capital and Economic Opportunity Global Working Paper 2019-034 (May 2019): 5–6, http://humcap.uchicago.edu/RePEc/hka /wpaper/Heckman_Karapakula_2019_perry-late-midlife-design-specific -r2.pdf.

50 *Each school day* Heckman and Karapakula, "The Perry Preschoolers at Late Midlife," 5–6; Shankar Vedantam, "Since the 1960s, Researchers Track Perry Preschool Project Participants," NPR, May 23, 2019, https://www .npr.org/2019/05/23/726035330/since-the-1960s-researchers-track -perry-preschool-project-participants.

50 *The researchers supposed* James J. Heckman, "Early Childhood Education Strengthens Families and Can Break the Cycle of Poverty," The Heckman Equation (2019), https://heckmanequation.org/www/assets/2019/05/F

_Heckman_PerryMidlife_OnePager_050819.pdf; Heckman and Karapakula, "The Perry Preschoolers at Late Midlife."

50 *And, at that point* Heckman, "Early Childhood Education"; Heckman and Karapakula, "The Perry Preschoolers at Late Midlife"; James J. Heckman and Ganesh Karapakula, "Intergenerational and Intragenerational Externalities of the Perry Preschool Project," Working Paper No. 25889, National Bureau of Economic Research, Cambridge, Mass. (May 2019).

50 *They were, on average,* Heckman, "Early Childhood Education"; Heckman and Karapakula, "The Perry Preschoolers at Late Midlife"; Heckman and Karapakula, "Intergenerational and Intragenerational Externalities."

50 *Moreover, they had* Heckman, "Early Childhood Education"; Heckman and Karapakula, "The Perry Preschoolers at Late Midlife"; Heckman and Karapakula, "Intergenerational and Intragenerational Externalities."

50 *The more stable* García, Heckman, and Ronda, "Boosting Intergenerational Mobility"; Heckman and Karapakula, "Intergenerational and Intragenerational Externalities," 19–22.

50 *Just as we saw* Amanda M. Dettmer et al., "Intergenerational Effects of Early-Life Advantage: Lessons from a Primate Study," Working Paper No. 27737, National Bureau of Economic Research, Cambridge, Mass. (Aug. 2020): 20, https://doi.org/10.3386/w27737.

50 *All of this means* James J. Heckman, "Invest in Early Childhood Development: Reduce Deficits, Strengthen the Economy," The Heckman Equation, (2012), https://heckmanequation.org/www/assets/2013/07/F_Heckman DeficitPieceCUSTOM-Generic_052714-3-1.pdf; Jorge Luis García et al., "The Life-Cycle Benefits of an Influential Early Childhood Program," Institute of Labor Economics (Dec. 2016), https://ftp.iza.org/dp10456.pdf.

51 *When economists ran* García et al., "The Life-Cycle Benefits."

51 *Every child should enjoy* Kimberly Jenkins Robinson, ed., *A Federal Right to Education: Fundamental Questions for Our Democracy* (New York: New York University Press, 2019); Miller, "How Public Preschool Can Help"; Marta Tienda, "Thirteenth Annual Brown Lecture in Education Research: Public Education and the Social Contract: Restoring the Promise in an Age of Diversity and Division," *Educational Researcher* 46, no. 6 (Aug. 1, 2017): 271–83.

51 *The same pattern* Clark et al., "A Future for the World's Children?" 612; Drew Bailey et al., "Persistence and Fadeout in the Impacts of Child and Adolescent Interventions," *Journal of Research on Educational Effectiveness* 10, no. 1 (2017): 7–39; Heckman, "The Economics of Inequality," 31–35.

51 *Heart disease* Center for Medicare and Medicaid Services, "Background: The Affordable Care Act's New Rules on Preventive Care," CMS, July 14, 2010, https://www.cms.gov/CCIIO/Resources/Fact-Sheets-and-FAQs /preventive-care-background#_ftn9.

51 *Experts estimate* C. K. Mishra, "Invest in Children's Health to Secure India's Future Well-Being," *Hindustan Times*, Apr. 24, 2017.

51 *And we should think* Mary Ellen O'Connell, Thomas Boat, and Kenneth E. Warner, "Benefits and Costs of Prevention," in *Preventing Mental, Emotional, and Behavioral Disorders Among Young People: Progress and Possibilities* (Washington, D.C.: National Academies Press, 2009), https://www.ncbi

.nlm.nih.gov/books/NBK32767/; Clark et al., "A Future for the World's Children?" 605.

51 *When researchers* Elise Gould, "Childhood Lead Poisoning: Conservative Estimates of the Social and Economic Benefits of Lead Hazard Control," *Environmental Health Perspectives* 117, no. 7 (July 2009): 1162–67.

51 *The upside* Gould, "Childhood Lead Poisoning."

51 *One of the great things* Clark et al., "A Future for the World's Children?" 612.

51 *Poor children* Paul Krugman, "The Republican War on Children," *New York Times,* Dec. 7, 2017; Paul Krugman, "Biden and the Future of the Family," *New York Times,* May 3, 2021; Martha Bailey et al., "New Working Paper Shows Long-Term U.S. Economic and Health Benefits of the Supplemental Nutrition Assistance Program," Washington Center for Equitable Growth, May 11, 2020, http://www.equitablegrowth.org/new -working-paper-shows-long-term-u-s-economic-and-health-benefits-of -the-supplemental-nutrition-assistance-program/.

51 *Nearly half* Berhanu Alemayehu and Kenneth E. Warner, "The Lifetime Distribution of Health Care Costs," *Health Services Research* 39, no. 3 (June 2004): 627–42.

52 *Homeless children* Nikita Stewart and Gabriella Angotti-Jones, "Baby Antonio: 5 Pounds, 12 Ounces and Homeless from Birth," *New York Times,* Oct. 30, 2018.

52 *The Big Apple* Samantha M. Shapiro, "The Children in the Shadows: New York City's Homeless Students," *New York Times,* Sept. 9, 2020.

52 *And, although* Jonathan Todres and Lauren Meeler, "Confronting Housing Insecurity—A Key to Getting Kids Back to School," *JAMA Pediatrics* 175, no. 9 (Sept. 1, 2021): 889–90.

52 *In New York City* Shapiro, "The Children in the Shadows"; Todres and Meeler, "Confronting Housing Insecurity," 889–90.

52 *What happens* Shapiro, "The Children in the Shadows"; Todres and Meeler, "Confronting Housing Insecurity," 889–90.

52 *They fall behind* Shapiro, "The Children in the Shadows."

52 *Just 62 percent* Shapiro, "The Children in the Shadows."

52 *Without a diploma* Shapiro, "The Children in the Shadows."

52 *It is estimated* United States Interagency Council on Homelessness, "Ending Chronic Homelessness in 2017," https://www.usich.gov/resources /uploads/asset_library/Ending_Chronic_Homelessness_in_2017.pdf.

53 *And there is plenty* See, e.g., Davarian L. Baldwin, "Higher Education Has a Tax Problem and It Hurts Local Communities," *Time,* Apr. 7, 2021; Kristen A. Graham, "Philly Schools Lose More Money to Tax Breaks Than Any District in the Country, a New Report Says," *Philadelphia Inquirer,* Apr. 13, 2021.

53 *When economists* Raj Chetty et al., "The Opportunity Atlas: Mapping the Childhood Roots of Social Mobility, Executive Summary," Opportunity Insights (Jan. 2020): 2–3, https://opportunityinsights.org/wp-content /uploads/2018/10/atlas_summary.pdf; Raj Chetty et al., *The Opportunity Atlas: Mapping the Childhood Roots of Social Mobility* (Cambridge, Mass.: National Bureau of Economic Research, Oct. 2018), 3, https://opportuni tyinsights.org/wp-content/uploads/2018/10/atlas_paper.pdf.

53 *There are poor* Emily Badger and Quoctrung Bui, "Detailed Maps Show How Neighborhoods Shape Children for Life," *New York Times*, Oct. 1, 2018.

53 *And every year* "Neighborhoods Matter," Opportunity Insights, Apr. 2, 2018, https://opportunityinsights.org/neighborhoods/.

53 *You can try* David Brooks, "Who Is Driving Inequality? You Are," *New York Times*, Apr. 23, 2020; Chetty et al., "The Opportunity Atlas" (executive summary), 4; Gareth Cook, "The Economist Who Would Fix the American Dream," *The Atlantic*, July 17, 2019.

53 *Within the same metropolitan area* Chetty et al., "The Opportunity Atlas" (executive summary), 3; Chetty et al., *The Opportunity Atlas*, 6.

53 *Researchers have already begun* Chetty et al., "The Opportunity Atlas" (executive summary), 5; Chetty et al., *The Opportunity Atlas*, 4.

53 *And there is work under way* Peter Bergman et al., "Creating Moves to Opportunity: Experimental Evidence on Barriers to Neighborhood Choice," Opportunity Insights, https://opportunityinsights.org/wp-content/uploads/2019/08/cmto_summary.pdf.

54 *As part of the federal response* Rosa DeLauro, "The Fight Against Child Poverty in America Finally Takes a Big Step Forward," *Time*, Mar. 11, 2021.

54 *The money* DeLauro, "The Fight Against Child Poverty"; Claire Cain Miller, "Why the New Monthly Child Tax Credit Is More Likely to Be Spent on Children," *New York Times*, July 16, 2021.

54 *The program* "Economist Letter to Majority Leader Schumer, Speaker Pelosi, and Minority Leader McCarthy," Sept. 15, 2021, https://static1.squarespace.com/static/5ecd75a3c406d1318b20454d/t/6148f183c62fb147d0d25138/1632170373799/Economist+CTC+Letter+9-14-21+430pm.pdf; Zachary Parolin et al., "The Initial Effects of the Expanded Child Tax Credit on Material Hardship," Working Paper No. 29285, National Bureau of Economic Research, Cambridge, Mass. (Sept. 2021), https://www.nber.org/papers/w29285.

54 *Economists estimated* Gregory Acs and Kevin Werner, "How a Permanent Expansion of the Child Tax Credit Could Affect Poverty," Urban Institute, Aug. 2021, https://www.urban.org/sites/default/files/publication/104626/how-a-permanent-expansion-of-the-child-tax-credit-could-affect-poverty_1.pdf.

54 *And looking at returns* Irwin Garfinkel et al., "The Costs and Benefits of a Child Allowance," *Poverty & Social Policy Brief* 5, no. 1 (Aug. 2, 2021), https://static1.squarespace.com/static/5743308460b5e922a25a6dc7/t/61081baa32c9d257a80438b2/1627921323005/Child-Allowance-CBA-Brief-CPSP-August-2021.pdf.

54 *A growing body of research* AliceAnn Crandall et al., "ACEs and Counter-ACEs: How Positive and Negative Childhood Experiences Influence Adult Health," *Child Abuse & Neglect* 96 (Oct. 2019): 104089; Margaret S. Kelley and Meggan J. Lee, "When Natural Mentors Matter: Unraveling the Relationship with Delinquency," *Children and Youth Services Review* 91 (Aug. 2018): 319–28.

54 *Indeed, it appears* Brigham Young University, "For Kids Who Face Trauma, Good Neighbors or Teachers Can Save Their Longterm Health," *Science-*

Daily, Sept. 16, 2019, https://www.sciencedaily.com/releases/2019/09/190916144004.htm; Kelley and Lee, "When Natural Mentors Matter," 319–28.

54 *And the benefits of strong bonds* Crandall et al., "ACEs and Counter-ACEs"; Peter A. Wyman et al., "Peer-Adult Network Structure and Suicide Attempts in 38 High Schools: Implications for Network-Informed Suicide Prevention," *Journal of Child Psychology and Psychiatry* 60, no. 10 (Oct. 2019): 1065–75.

55 *In one study* Kelley and Lee, "When Natural Mentors Matter," 326.

55 *A basketball coach* Kelley and Lee, "When Natural Mentors Matter," 326.

55 *Other research shows* Bell et al., "Who Becomes an Inventor in America?"

55 *A girl's likelihood* Bell et al., "Who Becomes an Inventor in America?" 4.

55 *And the type of innovation* Bell et al., "Who Becomes an Inventor in America?"; Leonhardt, "Lost Einsteins."

55 *Rather than using* Bell et al., "Who Becomes an Inventor in America?" 4.

55 *Researchers have estimated* Bell et al., "Who Becomes an Inventor in America?" 4.

55 *When he began wrestling* Harold, interview.

55 *As he explains* Harold, interview.

56 *"There's no one"* Harold, interview.

56 *But to be successful* Harold, interview.

56 *That changed Harold's life* Harold, interview.

56 *And it instilled in him* Harold, interview.

56 *There was a point* Harold, interview.

56 *"I started to think"* Harold, interview.

56 *The doubts* Harold, interview.

3. Late Childhood: The Right to Community

57 *Daniel Stoltzfus told the police* Amelia McDonell-Parry, "Why Did Ex-Amish Family Sell Their 14-Year-Old Daughter?" *Rolling Stone,* June 22, 2016.

57 *He wanted to make sure* McDonell-Parry, "Why Did Ex-Amish Family."

57 *Lee Kaplan had been* McDonell-Parry, "Why Did Ex-Amish Family."

57 *Blacklisted by the Amish* "Testimony Begins in Bucks County Child Rape Case Involving Destitute Amish Family," *Delco Times,* June 2, 2017.

57 *They were being evicted* "Testimony Begins."

57 *At the darkest moment* Associated Press, "Lancaster County Couple Told Police They Thought 'Gift' of Daughter Was Legal," PennLive, June 18, 2016, https://www.pennlive.com/news/2016/06/lancaster_county_couple_told_p.html.

57 *They gave him* "Testimomy Begins"; Christian Alexandersen, "'He Told Me Not to Tell Anybody': Children Ages 9 to 15 Testify About Sexual Abuse by 'Husband,'" PennLive, June 1, 2017, http://www.pennlive.com/news/2017/06/he_told_me_not_to_tell_anybody.html; Adam Lusher, "Paedophile 'Prophet' Took Brainwashed Couple's Six Children as Wives, Court Told," *Independent,* June 3, 2017.

57   *The idea that children* Stuart N. Hart, "From Property to Person Status: Historical Perspective on Children's Rights," *American Psychologist* 46, no.1 (Jan. 1991): 53.

57   *More than two thousand* Aristotle, *The Nicomachean Ethics*, 1134b, in *The Complete Works of Aristotle*, vol. 2, ed. Jonathan Barnes, trans. Harold H. Joachim (Princeton, N.J.: Princeton University Press, 1984), 1790.

57   *A father* Mary Ann Mason, *From Father's Property to Children's Rights* (New York: Columbia University Press, 1994), 7; William Forsyth, *A Treatise on the Law Relating to the Custody of Infants, in Cases of Difference Between Parents or Guardians* (London: William Benning, 1850), 2–3.

57   *For centuries* Mason, *From Father's Property to Children's Rights*, 6; Doris Foster and Henry Freed, "Life with Father: 1978," *Family Law Quarterly* 11, no. 4 (Winter 1978): 322; Henry H. Foster, Jr., "Relational Interests of the Family," *University of Illinois Law Forum*, no. 4 (Winter 1962): 493, 497–505; Michael Grossberg, *Governing the Hearth: Law and Family in Nineteenth-Century America* (Chapel Hill: University of North Carolina Press, 1985), 235; Andre P. Derdeyn, "Child Custody Contests in Historical Perspective," *American Journal of Psychiatry* 133, no. 12 (Dec. 1976): 1369; Roscoe Pound, "Individual Interests in the Domestic Relations," *Michigan Law Review* 14, no. 3 (Jan. 1916): 177–96.

57   *The currents* Mary Ann Mason, "The U.S. and the International Children's Rights Crusade: Leader or Laggard?" *Journal of Social History* 38, no. 4 (Summer 2005): 961.

57   *Across the colonies* Mason, *From Father's Property to Children's Rights*, 6.

57   *It could be used* Mason, *From Father's Property to Children's Rights*, 6; Barbara Bennett Woodhouse, *Hidden in Plain Sight: The Tragedy of Children's Rights from Ben Franklin to Lionel Tate* (Princeton, N.J.: Princeton University Press, 2008), 63–64.

57   *By the age of ten* Mason, *From Father's Property to Children's Rights*, 2.

58   *At age twelve* "The New England Courant," The Electric Ben Franklin, Independence Hall Association, accessed Mar. 14, 2022, http://www .ushistory.org/franklin/courant/story.htm; Susan E. Klepp, "Benjamin Franklin and Apprenticeship in the 18th Century," *Pennsylvania Legacies* (May 2006): 8.

58   *Children who ran away* Woodhouse, *Hidden in Plain Sight*, 67–68, 112.

58   *Assailants who assaulted* Woodhouse, *Hidden in Plain Sight*, 67–68.

58   *Their body was his* Woodhouse, *Hidden in Plain Sight*, 52.

58   *Even at death* Woodhouse, *Hidden in Plain Sight*, 63; Barbara Bennett Woodhouse, "Who Owns the Child? Meyer and Pierce and the Child as Property," *William & Mary Law Review* 33, no. 4 (Summer 1992): 1046.

58   *When women* Mason, *From Father's Property to Children's Rights*, 77.

58   *In 1924* "Says Amendment Would Invade Home," *New York Times*, Dec. 7, 1924; Martin Guggenheim, *What's Wrong with Children's Rights* (Cambridge, Mass.: Harvard University Press, 2005), 2–3.

58   *When the Texas GOP* Republican Party of Texas, *Report of the Permanent Committee on Platform and Resolutions as Amended and Adopted by the 2016 State Convention of the Republic Party of Texas* (2016): 12, https://www .texasgop.org/wp-content/uploads/2016/01/PERM-PLATFORM.pdf.

58 *Today, you can find* Stephanie Nolasco, "Rapper T.I. Says He Accompanies His Daughter to the Gynecologist Every Year to Ensure She's a Virgin," Fox News, Nov. 6, 2019, https://www.foxnews.com/entertainment/rapper-t-i-deyjah-harris-virgin-test.

58 *"So I say"* Nolasco, "Rapper T.I."

59 *In this country* Mason, "The U.S. and the International Children's Rights Crusade," 961.

59 *We may tweet* Brooke Migdon, "Movement to Ban—or Even Burn—School Library Books Gains Momentum," *The Hill*, Nov. 11, 2021, https://thehill.com/changing-america/enrichment/education/581134-movement-to-ban-or-even-burn-school-library-books-gains.

59 *You can flip open* Robert Nozick, *The Examined Life* (New York: Simon & Schuster, 1989), 28.

59 *But it's also there* Kathryn Edin and Maria Kefalas, *Promises I Can Keep: Why Poor Women Put Motherhood Before Marriage* (Berkeley: University of California Press, 2007), 207.

59 *Sonia, a young Philadelphia mother* Edin and Kefalas, *Promises I Can Keep*, 211.

60 *But "you are mine"* See, e.g., David Archard and Colin M. Macleod, "Introduction," in *The Moral and Political Status of Children* (New York: Oxford University Press, 2002), 1.

60 *As Janusz Korczak* Janusz Korczak, *The Child's Right to Respect* (Strasbourg, France: Council of Europe, 2009), 25.

60 *You can watch videos* Rachel Bertsche, "'Psychopath' or 'Best Parent in the World'? Dad's Unusual Punishment for Son Stirs Debate," Yahoo! News, May 15, 2015, https://www.yahoo.com/news/psychopath-or-best-parent-in-the-world-dads-119043392822.html.

60 *But if you are disciplining* Denver Nicks, "Hitting Your Kids Is Legal in All 50 States," *Time*, Sept. 17, 2014.

60 *In Oklahoma* Nicks, "Hitting Your Kids."

60 *In Texas* Nicks, "Hitting Your Kids."

61 *That's baffling* Aristotle, *The Nicomachean Ethics*, 1134b, trans. K.A. Thomson (London: Penguin Books, 1953), 130.

61 *When Daniel met Lee* Christine Vendel, "Was Lancaster County Couple 'Brainwashed' into Giving Away 14-Year-Old Daughter?" PennLive, June 19, 2016, https://www.pennlive.com/news/2016/06/lancaster_county_couple_gave_a.html.

61 *He was losing faith* Vendel, "Was Lancaster County Couple 'Brainwashed.'"

61 *Lee offered redemption* Vendel, "Was Lancaster County Couple 'Brainwashed.'"

61 *Whatever they needed* Christine Vendel, "How Lee Kaplan Allegedly Brainwashed a Former Amish Family," PennLive, May 31, 2017, https://www.pennlive.com/news/2017/05/lee_kaplan_gifting_case_amish.html.

61 *Savilla, too* Justine McDaniel, "Girls' Future in Hands of Court," *Philadelphia Inquirer*, June 11, 2017.

61 *They were desperate* Christine Vendel, "Mother Accused of 'Gifting' Teen Daughter Testifies About Jealousy as One of Seven 'Wives,'" Penn-

Live, May 31, 2017, https://www.pennlive.com/news/2017/05/mother _accused_of_gifting_teen.html.

61 *Eventually, they gifted* Claire Sasko, "Additional Charges for Bucks County Man Who Was 'Gifted' Teen Girls," *Philadelphia: City Life*, Oct. 31, 2016.

61 *When the authorities arrived* Jean Casarez, Ann Roche, and Mallory Simon, "Inside the Pennsylvania Home Where 12 Girls Were Kept for Years," CNN, June 22, 2016, https://www.cnn.com/2016/06/22/us/pennsylvania -girls-found-arrests/index.html.

61 *The daughters were* Vendel, "Mother Accused of 'Gifting' Teen Daughter"; Justine McDaniel, "'Gifted Girls' Trial to Begin This Week," *Philadelphia Inquirer*, May 28, 2017.

61 *Not one of them* Vendel, "Mother Accused of 'Gifting' Teen Daughter."

61 *None had ever gone* Vendel, "Mother Accused of 'Gifting' Teen Daughter."

61 *A detective testified* Vendel, "Mother Accused of 'Gifting' Teen Daughter"; Casarez, Roche, and Simon, "Inside the Pennsylvania Home."

61 *The children slept* Casarez, Roche, and Simon, "Inside the Pennsylvania Home."

61 *Only Lee* Vendel, "Mother Accused of 'Gifting' Teen Daughter."

61 *They did not know* Christine Vendel, "'Prophet' Convicted of Sexually Assaulting Girls He Took as 'Wives,'" PennLive, June 6, 2017, https://www .pennlive.com/news/2017/06/lee_kaplan_gifting_case_bucks.html.

61 *Daniel and Savilla* See, e.g., Pierce v. Society of Sisters, 268 U.S. 510 (1925).

62 *From that perspective* Stanley v. Illinois, 405 U.S. 645 (1972).

62 *Lee may have been* Justine McDaniel, "Mother, Father, Accused of 'Gifting' Teen Daughter to Lee Kaplan Enter Guilty, No-Contest Pleas," *Philadelphia Inquirer*, Apr. 6, 2017; McDaniel, "'Gifted Girls' Trial."

62 *When he chatted in town* Casarez, Roche, and Simon, "Inside the Pennsylvania Home."

62 *A neighbor had thought* Evan Simko-Bednarski, "Pennsylvania Parents Get Jail Time in 'Gifted' Girls Case," CNN, July 19, 2017, https://www.cnn .com/2017/07/19/us/pennsylvania-parents-gifted-girls-case/index.html.

62 *They were "never outside"* Simko-Bednarski, "Pennsylvania Parents Get Jail Time."

62 *She thought* Simko-Bednarski, "Pennsylvania Parents Get Jail Time."

62 *And, as the authorities acknowledged* McDaniel, "Girls' Future in Hands of Court."

62 *He told them* McDaniel, "Girls' Future in Hands of Court."

63 *As we'll see* Casarez, Roche, and Simon, "Inside the Pennsylvania Home."

63 *Before the accident* Vendel, "Was Lancaster County Couple 'Brainwashed.'"

63 *They lived next door* Vendel, "Was Lancaster County Couple 'Brainwashed.'"

63 *"They shared the children"* Vendel, "Was Lancaster County Couple 'Brainwashed.'"

63 *Whenever a new baby* Vendel, "Was Lancaster County Couple 'Brainwashed.'"

63 *She felt bound* Vendel, "Was Lancaster County Couple 'Brainwashed.'"

63 *One day* Vendel, "Was Lancaster County Couple 'Brainwashed.'"

63 *"He asked to be"* Vendel, "Was Lancaster County Couple 'Brainwashed.'"

63 *Breaking with the church* Vendel, "Was Lancaster County Couple 'Brainwashed.'"

63 *"It was the hardest"* Vendel, "Was Lancaster County Couple 'Brainwashed.'"

63 *She kept trying* Vendel, "Was Lancaster County Couple 'Brainwashed.'"

63 *When the Amish* McDonell-Parry, "Why Did an Ex-Amish Family Sell."

63 *In America* Kevin Noble Maillard, "Rethinking Children as Property: The Transitive Family," *Cardozo Law Review* 32 (2010): 117; Troxel v. Granville, 530 U.S. 57, 65–67 (2000).

63 *As the Supreme Court Troxel,* 530 U.S. at 65.

63 *It does not matter Troxel,* 530 U.S. at 68.

64 *As we will discuss* Mason, *From Father's Property to Children's Rights,* 122.

64 *In every state* The general parental consent requirement may be overridden in certain circumstances. Child Welfare Information Gateway, *Consent to Adoption,* U.S. Department of Health and Human Services, Administration for Children and Families, Children's Bureau (2021), 2, https://www.childwelfare.gov/pubpdfs/consent.pdf.

64 *But, in forty-five states* Child Welfare Information Gateway, *Consent to Adoption,* 2.

64 *Each year* Rachel Aviv, "The Shadow Penal System for Struggling Kids," *New Yorker,* Oct. 11, 2021.

64 *As Paris Hilton explains* Paris Hilton, "America's 'Troubled Teen Industry' Needs Reform So Kids Can Avoid the Abuse I Endured," *Washington Post,* Oct. 18, 2021.

64 *Mom and dad sign* Hilton, "America's 'Troubled Teen'"; Aviv, "The Shadow Penal System."

65 *It's widely accepted* Woodhouse, *Hidden in Plain Sight,* 119.

65 *As we've already seen* See, e.g., Jessica Fritz et al., "A Systematic Review of Amenable Resilience Factors That Moderate and/or Mediate the Relationship Between Childhood Adversity and Mental Health in Young People," *Frontiers in Psychiatry* 9, no. 230 (2018): 1–17; Ann S. Masten, "Resilience Theory and Research on Children and Families: Past, Present, and Promise," *Journal of Family Theory & Review* 10, no. 1 (2018): 18.

65 *We are beginning* Helen Clark et al., "A Future for the World's Children? A WHO–UNICEF–Lancet Commission," *Lancet* 395, no. 10224 (Feb. 2020): 619; Lu Gram et al., "Promoting Women's and Children's Health Through Community Groups in Low-Income and Middle-Income Countries: A Mixed-Methods Systematic Review of Mechanisms, Enablers and Barriers," *BMJ Global Health* 4, no. 6 (Dec. 1, 2019): e001972; Seye Abimbola, "Beyond Positive a Priori Bias: Reframing Community Engagement in LMICs," *Health Promotion International* 35, no. 3 (June 1, 2020): 598–609.

65 *Community ties* Clark et al., "A Future for the World's Children?" 619.

65 *And they can also be* Aviv, "The Shadow Penal System."

65 *The routine interactions* Aviv, "The Shadow Penal System."

65 *Take children away suddenly* Aviv, "The Shadow Penal System."

65 *On every front* Justine McDaniel, "With Verdict, Girls Freed from Lee Kaplan's 'World,'" *Philadelphia Inquirer,* June 11, 2017.

65 *Even if they had been* Matt Mirro, "Feasterville Man Lee Kaplan Guilty in 'Gifted' Amish Children Case," WBCB News, June 7, 2017.

65 *We touched on that* Rukmini Callimachi, "Lost Lives, Lost Culture: The Forgotten History of Indigenous Boarding Schools," *New York Times,* July 19, 2021.

66 *We have failed* Callimachi, "Lost Lives."

66 *Yet we can take* Steve Inskeep, "For 50 Years, I Was Denied the Story of My Birth," *New York Times,* Mar. 26, 2021.

66 *For decades* Inskeep, "For 50 Years."

66 *Pam Hasegewa* "Shift in Law Will Allow Adopted Children in New Jersey to Learn Names of Birth Parents," CBS New York, Dec. 28, 2016, https://www.cbsnews.com/newyork/news/new-jersey-adoption/; Gabrielle Glaser, "Don't Keep Adopted People in the Dark," *New York Times,* June 17, 2018.

66 *Yet, today, only ten* Inskeep, "For 50 Years"; "The United States of OBC | Adoptee Rights Law," Adoptee Rights Law Center, accessed Mar. 9, 2022, https://adopteerightslaw.com/united-states-obc/.

66 *While a changing culture* "Open vs. Closed Adoptions: A Post Adoption Mental Health Perspective," Boston Post Adoption Resources, Oct. 23, 2019, https://bpar.org/open-vs-closed-adoptions-a-post-adoption-mental -health-perspective/; Harold D. Grotevant, "Open Adoption," in *The Routledge Handbook of Adoption,* ed., Gretchen Miller Wrobel, Emily Helder, and Elisha Marr (New York: Routledge, 2020).

66 *We ought to heed* "Outcomes for Adopted Children and Adolescents," Rudd Adoption Research Program, University of Massachusetts Amherst, accessed Mar. 10, 2022, https://www.umass.edu/ruddchair/research/mtarp /key-findings/outcomes-adopted-children-and-adolescents; Harold D. Grotevant et al., "Adaptive Behavior in Adopted Children: Predictors from Early Risk, Collaboration in Relationships Within the Adoptive Kinship Network, and Openness Arrangements," *Journal of Adolescent Research* 14, no. 2 (1999): 231–47.

67 *In 2009, the River of Life* Robert T. Pennock, "Should Students Be Able to Opt Out of Evolution? Some Philosophical Considerations," *Evolution: Education and Outreach* 3, no. 2 (June 2010): 163–69.

67 *If you checked* Pennock, "Opt Out."

67 *Just like that* Pennock, "Opt Out."

67 *As the Wisconsin Assembly committee* Mitchell Schmidt, "Republicans Advance Bill Banning Critical Race Theory in Schools," *Wisconsin State Journal,* Sept. 23, 2021.

67 *The bill passed* Mike Ivey, "No State Worse Than Wisconsin for Black Children, Says New National Study," *Capital Times,* Apr. 1, 2014; "Race for Results," Annie E. Casey Foundation, Mar. 30, 2014, https://www.aecf.org /resources/race-for-results.

67 *As they explained in 1925 Pierce,* 268 U.S. at 534–35.

67 *If it is your child Pierce,* 268 U.S. at 535.

68 *Yes, the court has affirmed* Wisconsin v. Yoder, 406 U.S. 205, 213 (1972).

68 *When Beatrice Weber* Beatrice Weber and Chaim Levin, "My Son's Yeshiva Is Breaking the Law," *New York Times*, Apr. 7, 2021.

68 *Her son is now eight* Weber and Levin, "Yeshiva."

68 *"He tells me he wants"* Weber and Levin, "Yeshiva."

68 *In New York* New York State Education Department, *Manual for New Administrators of Nonpublic Schools: State Requirements and Programs*, 2018, http://www.p12.nysed.gov/nonpub/manualfornewadministratorsofnps /statereqs.html.

68 *But, for years* Shulem Deen, "Why Is New York Condoning Illiteracy?" *New York Times*, Apr. 4, 2018; Young Advocates for Fair Education (YAFFED), "Uneducated: Substantial Equivalency and Hasidic Yeshivas," Apr. 2021, https://yaffed.org/report/.

68 *English is considered profane* Deen, "Condoning Illiteracy."

68 *As the Satmar Rebbe* Yossi Newfield, "NYC Is Cracking Down on Yeshivas— and the Satmar Rebbe Has Declared War," *Forward*, Dec. 4, 2018, https:// forward.com/scribe/415395/nyc-is-cracking-down-on-yeshivas-and-the -satmar-rebbe-has-declared-war/.

68 *Despite a 2019* Weber and Levin, "Yeshiva"; Eliza Shapiro and Jeffery C. Mays, "Why New York's Inquiry into Yeshivas Mysteriously Stalled," *New York Times*, Dec. 18, 2019.

68 *In part, they've been wary* Weber and Levin, "Yeshiva"; Jesse McKinley and Vivian Wang, "Brooklyn Senator's Request Is Blamed for Budget Stall, but Deal Could Be Near," *New York Times*, Mar. 30, 2018; Zoe Greenberg, "A Law Tailored for Orthodox Jewish Schools Is Unconstitutional, Lawsuit Says," *New York Times*, July 23, 2018.

68 *Quite simply* Deen, "Condoning Illiteracy."

68 *If, at eighteen* Deen, "Condoning Illiteracy"; YAFFED, "Uneducated"; Valerie Strauss, "The Problem with New York's Ultra-Orthodox Jewish Schools During the Pandemic," *Washington Post*, Oct. 16, 2020.

68 *Most lack the basic requirements* Sam Roberts, "A Village with the Numbers, Not the Image, of the Poorest Place," *New York Times*, Apr. 21, 2011; Deen, "Condoning Illiteracy"; YAFFED, "Uneducated."

68 *It can be a struggle* Deen, "Condoning Illiteracy"; YAFFED, "Uneducated."

69 *Kiryas Joel* Roberts, "Poorest Place."

69 *Half of the twenty-one thousand* Roberts, "Poorest Place."

69 *Many others are on Medicaid* Roberts, "Poorest Place."

69 *It is not simply* Deen, "Condoning Illiteracy"; YAFFED, "Uneducated."

69 *What Beatrice is asking* Weber and Levin, "Yeshiva."

69 *And she is eager* Weber and Levin, "Yeshiva."

69 *"Many yeshivas offer"* Weber and Levin, "Yeshiva."

69 *Whether New York is able* Shapiro and Mays, "Inquiry into Yeshivas"; Yoav Gonen and Reuven Blau, "Some Yeshivas Defying City Push to Boost Secular Studies," *Brooklyn Eagle*, Jan. 29, 2020.

69 *In thirty-one states* Jessica Huseman, "Homeschooling Regulations by State," ProPublica, Aug. 27, 2015, http://projects.propublica.org/graphics /homeschool; Coalition for Responsible Home Education (CRHE), "Home-

school Notification," Feb. 20, 2014, https://responsiblehomeschooling.org
/research/current-policy/notification/.

69 *In the other nineteen* Huseman, "Homeschooling Regulations."

69 *Critically, in every jurisdiction* Huseman, "Homeschooling Regulations";
CRHE, "Homeschool Notification."

70 *In forty-one states* Huseman, "Homeschooling Regulations"; CRHE,
"Homeschool Notification."

70 *For the most part* Huseman, "Homeschooling Regulations"; CRHE, "Homeschool Notification."

70 *In one recent study* University of Missouri-Columbia, "Students Taught by
Highly Qualified Teachers More Likely to Obtain Bachelor's Degree:
Schools with More Teachers Who Majored in Their Teaching Subject Are
More Likely to Have Students Succeed Both Short and Long Term," *ScienceDaily*, May 22, 2018, https://www.sciencedaily.com/releases/2018/05
/180522114820.htm; Se Woong Lee, "Pulling Back the Curtain: Revealing
the Cumulative Importance of High-Performing, Highly Qualified Teachers on Students' Educational Outcome," *Educational Evaluation and Policy
Analysis* 40, no. 3 (Sept. 1, 2018): 359–81.

70 *Before Lee took over* Christopher Mele, "Parents Who 'Gifted' a Daughter
to Man Are Sentenced," *New York Times*, July 20, 2017.

70 *She readily acknowledged* Mele, "Parents Who 'Gifted.'"

70 *There are no assessment requirements* Huseman, "Homeschooling Regulations."

70 *There are no curricula* Huseman, "Homeschooling Regulations"; CRHE,
"Homeschool Notification."

70 *About a year before Lee* Casarez, Roche, and Simon, "Inside the Pennsylvania Home."

70 *When the police arrived* Casarez, Roche, and Simon, "Inside the Pennsylvania Home."

70 *None of this is to suggest* See, e.g., Paul Elie, "The Homeschool Diaries," *The
Atlantic*, Sept. 20, 2012.

71 *And we cannot ignore* John Taylor Gatto, "Against School," *Harper's Magazine*, Sept. 2003.

71 *As he told* Gatto, "Against School," 37; Woodrow Wilson, "The Meaning of
Liberal Education," in *High School Teachers Association of New York*, vol. 3
(1908–1909), 19–31.

71 *The critic H. L. Mencken* H. L. Mencken, "The Little Red Schoolhouse,"
American Mercury, Apr. 1924, 504.

71 *When psychologists looked* Gopnik, *The Gardener and the Carpenter*, 130;
Cristine H. Legare et al., "The Coexistence of Natural and Supernatural
Explanations Across Cultures and Development," *Child Development* 83,
no. 3 (2012): 779–93; Cristine H. Legare, Susan A. Gelman, and Henry M.
Wellman, "Inconsistency with Prior Knowledge Triggers Children's
Causal Explanatory Reasoning," *Child Development* 81, no. 3 (2010):
929–44.

71 *But as both urban and rural* Gopnik, *The Gardener and the Carpenter*, 130;
Legare, "Coexistence"; Legare, Gelman, and Wellman, "Inconsistency."

71 *Think about the implications* Suzuka Satoh and Elisa Boyer, "HIV in South Africa," *Lancet* 394, no. 10197 (Aug. 2019): 467.

72 *Nearly one in five South Africans* Satoh and Boyer, "HIV in South Africa."

72 *In 2018, a mother* Andrew Marra, "Spanish River High Principal Refused to Call the Holocaust a Fact," *Palm Beach Post*, July 5, 2019.

72 *Principal Latson wrote back* Marra, "Spanish River High."

72 *She shot off a follow-up* Marra, "Spanish River High"; William Latson, Email, Apr. 18, 2018, https://www.documentcloud.org/documents/6181956 -Spanish-River-principal-email-2.html#document/p1/a510623.

72 *As he explained* Latson, Email.

72 *His role* Latson, Email.

72 *He pointed out* Latson, Email.

72 *In a recent survey* Harriet Sherwood, "Nearly Two-Thirds of US Young Adults Unaware 6m Jews Killed in the Holocaust," *Guardian*, Sept. 16, 2020.

72 *One in two reported* Sherwood, "Young Adults Unaware."

72 *In 2021, one in four Jews* Paul Caine, "Report Finds Antisemitism on the Rise in America," WTTW News, Oct. 26, 2021, https://news.wttw.com /2021/10/26/report-finds-antisemitism-rise-america.

72 *Our laws and practices* Gopnik, *The Gardener and the Carpenter*, 231.

73 *In most of the United States* Alex Horton, "Unvaccinated Teens Are Fact-Checking Their Parents—and Trying to Get Shots on Their Own," *Washington Post*, Feb. 11, 2019. While a complex set of exceptions exists, parental consent is the general default when it comes to medical decision-making. Lois A. Weithorn, "When Does a Minor's Legal Competence to Make Health Care Decisions Matter?" *Pediatrics* 146 (Suppl 1) (Aug. 1, 2020): S25–32.

73 *In June 2021* Jan Hoffman, "As Parents Forbid Covid Shots, Defiant Teenagers Seek Ways to Get Them," *New York Times*, June 26, 2021.

73 *After an early summer dip* "Tracking Coronavirus in Florida: Latest Map and Case Count," *New York Times*, last updated Mar. 25, 2022.

73 *But Charisse had heard* Hoffman, "Defiant Teenagers."

73 *Public health officials* Hoffman, "Defiant Teenagers."

73 *Isabella, Charisse's daughter* Hoffman, "Defiant Teenagers."

73 *She didn't agree* Hoffman, "Defiant Teenagers."

73 *As Charisse explained* Hoffman, "Defiant Teenagers."

73 *Charisse was listening* Hoffman, "Defiant Teenagers"; Susanna McGrew and Holly A. Taylor, "Adolescents, Parents, and Covid-19 Vaccination—Who Should Decide?" *New England Journal of Medicine*, Dec. 29, 2021.

73 *As Charisse explained* Hoffman, "Defiant Teenagers."

73 *Arrian was a typical teenager* "A Few of the Children," IdahoChildren.org, accessed Mar. 10, 2022, http://idahochildren.org/articles/a-few-of-the -children/.

73 *She ran track* Dan Tilkin and Dusty Lane, "Fallen Followers: Investigation Finds 10 More Dead Children of Faith Healers," KATU, Nov. 7, 2013, https://katu.com/news/local/fallen-followers-investigation-finds-10 -more-dead-children-of-faith-healers-11-23-2015; "A Few of the Children."

73 *She loved snowboarding* Tilkin and Lane, "Fallen Followers"; "A Few of the Children."

73 *One day, she got sick* Tilkin and Lane, "Fallen Followers."

73 *It was bad* "A Few of the Children."

73 *For three days* Tilkin and Lane, "Fallen Followers."

73 *But her family* "A Few of the Children."

73 *Even as she fell* "A Few of the Children."

73 *They were members* Cameron Rasmusson, "Idaho's 'Faith' Healing Dilemma," *Idaho Press*, July 16, 2020.

73 *So, instead* "A Few of the Children."

73 *When the coroner arrived* Steve Rhodes, "Case Summary," Canyon County Coroner's Record, Case No. 0298/N/B/12, Decedent: Granden, Arrian Jade, http://idahochildren.org/wp-content/uploads/2014/12/Granden -autopsy.pdf.

74 *In the largest* Rasmusson, "Healing Dilemma."

74 *Many of these children* Tilkin and Lane, "Fallen Followers"; "A Few of the Children."

74 *But no charges* Jerry A. Coyne, "Faith-Healer Parents Who Let Their Child Die Should Go to Jail," *New Republic*, Mar. 2, 2015.

74 *Although Idaho takes* Aleksandra Sandstrom, "Most States Allow Religious Exemptions from Child Abuse and Neglect Law," Pew Research Center, Aug. 12, 2016, http://www.pewresearch.org/fact-tank/2016/08/12/most -states-allow-religious-exemptions-from-child-abuse-and-neglect-laws/.

74 *As Idaho state representative* Coyne, "Faith-Healer Parents."

74 *As Senator Rand Paul* Elise Viebeck, "Rand Paul: Parents 'Own' Children, Not the State," *The Hill*, Feb. 2, 2015, https://thehill.com/policy /healthcare/231501-rand-paul-the-state-doesnt-own-your-children.

74 *He's a doctor* Viebeck, "Rand Paul."

75 *As investigators walked* Justine McDaniel, "With Verdict, Girls Freed from Lee Kaplan's 'World,'" *Philadelphia Inquirer*, June 11, 2017.

75 *When they spoke* Vendel, "'Prophet' Convicted."

75 *They did not know* Vendel, "'Prophet' Convicted."

75 *Two of the girls* Vendel, "'Prophet' Convicted."

75 *Nearly every child needed* Vendel, "'Prophet' Convicted."

75 *Rights—to healthcare* Hallie Ludsin, "Relational Rights Masquerading as Individual Rights," *Duke Journal of Gender and Law Policy* 15, no. 2 (2008): 195–97.

75 *Our major infectious disease victories* Aaron E. Carroll, "Vaccine Mandates Are Needed in the U.S.," *New York Times*, June 28, 2021; "Vaccination Laws," Public Health Professionals Gateway, Centers for Disease Control and Prevention, Feb. 22, 2022, https://www.cdc.gov/phlp/publications /topic/vaccinationlaws.html.

76 *It's about understanding* This is directly counter to what some scholars believe. See, e.g., Guggenheim, *What's Wrong with Children's Rights*, 13.

76 *Yet a lot depends* Pamela Druckerman, "The Bad News About Helicopter Parenting: It Works," *New York Times*, Feb. 7, 2019; Matthias Doepke and Fabrizio Zilibotti, *Love, Money, and Parenting: How Economics Explains the Way We Raise Our Kids* (Princeton, N.J.: Princeton University Press, 2019), 24–27.

76 *To conservative commentators* Druckerman, "Helicopter Parenting"; Doepke and Zilibotti, *Love, Money, and Parenting*.

76 *However, researchers have found* Druckerman, "Helicopter Parenting"; Doepke and Zilibotti, *Love, Money, and Parenting*, 30–34; Tak Wing Chan and Anita Koo, "Parenting Style and Youth Outcomes in the UK," *European Sociological Review* 27, no. 3 (Mar. 7, 2010): 396.

76 *When your mom and dad* Druckerman, "Helicopter Parenting"; Doepke and Zilibotti, *Love, Money, and Parenting*, 30–34; Chan and Koo, "Parenting Style," 396.

76 *Many facets of authoritative parenting* Druckerman, "Helicopter Parenting"; Doepke and Zilibotti, *Love, Money, and Parenting*, 30–31.

77 *The payoff* Chan and Koo, "Parenting Style," 396.

77 *Across cultures* Druckerman, "Helicopter Parenting"; Doepke and Zilibotti, *Love, Money, and Parenting*, 31–34; Chan and Koo, "Parenting Style," 391–96.

77 *The damaging version* Druckerman, "Helicopter Parenting"; Doepke and Zilibotti, *Love, Money, and Parenting*, 31–34; Chan and Koo, "Parenting Style," 386, 391–96.

77 *Authoritarian parents* Doepke and Zilibotti, *Love, Money, and Parenting*, 24–27.

77 *But even those of us* Gopnik, *The Gardener and the Carpenter*, 88; Druckerman, "Helicopter Parenting."

77 *Despite the research* Gopnik, *The Gardener and the Carpenter*, 22, 88, 90.

77 *We're not proper parents* Gopnik, *The Gardener and the Carpenter*, 88–90.

77 *We feel obliged* Gopnik, *The Gardener and the Carpenter*, 201.

77 *We shuttle them* Gopnik, *The Gardener and the Carpenter*, 201.

78 *As researchers have* Druckerman, "Helicopter Parenting."

78 *In some cases* Annette Lareau, Elliot B. Weininger, and Amanda Barrett Cox, "How Entitled Parents Hurt Schools," *New York Times*, June 24, 2018; Richard V. Reeves, "The Glass-Floor Problem," Opinionator (blog), *New York Times*, Sept. 29, 2013, https://opinionator.blogs.nytimes.com/2013/09/29/the-glass-floor-problem/.

78 *Other times* Jennifer Lighter, "We're Ignoring the Biggest Cause of the Measles Crisis," *New York Times*, Sept. 22, 2019.

78 *Parents end up* Emily Anthes, "The Hot New Back-to-School Accessory? An Air Quality Monitor," *New York Times*, Oct. 10, 2021.

78 *When scientists looked* Université Catholique de Louvain, "Parental Burnout Hits Individualist Western Countries Hardest," *ScienceDaily*, Mar. 18, 2021, https://www.sciencedaily.com/releases/2021/03/210318085604.htm; Isabelle Roskam et al., "Parental Burnout Around the Globe: A 42-Country Study," *Affective Science*, Mar. 18, 2021.

79 *"Our individualistic countries"* Université Catholique de Louvain, "Parental Burnout Hits Western Countries"; Roskam et al., "Parental Burnout."

79 *"Parenthood in these countries"* Université Catholique de Louvain, "Parental Burnout Hits Western Countries"; Roskam et al., "Parental Burnout."

79 *People there may have* Université Catholique de Louvain, "Parental Burnout Hits Western Countries"; Roskam et al., "Parental Burnout."

79 *And they are supported* Roskam et al., "Parental Burnout."

79 *Our stress and disillusionment* Université Catholique de Louvain, "Parental Burnout Hits Western Countries"; Roskam et al., "Parental Burnout."

79 *"The first [step]"* Université Catholique de Louvain, "Parental Burnout Hits Western Countries"; Roskam et al., "Parental Burnout."

79 *And, she adds* Université Catholique de Louvain, "Parental Burnout Hits Western Countries"; Roskam et al., "Parental Burnout."

79 *We evolved* Gopnik, *The Gardener and the Carpenter*, 76.

80 *In 2018, in a scene* Ernesto Londoño, "Argentine Police Officer Promoted After Breast-Feeding Neglected Baby," *New York Times*, Aug. 23, 2018.

80 *Taken to the hospital* Londoño, "Argentine Police Officer Promoted."

80 *"I noticed"* Haroon Siddique, "Police Officer Who Breastfed Baby on Duty in Argentina Promoted," *Guardian*, Aug. 22, 2018.

80 *She had a sixteen-month-old* Londoño, "Argentine Police Officer Promoted."

80 *"I asked to hug him"* Siddique, "Police Officer Who Breastfed Baby."

80 *The nurses warned* Jessica McKay, "Police Officer Praised for Breastfeeding 'Smelly and Dirty' Neglected Baby," *Metro*, Aug. 17, 2018.

80 *But "I didn't doubt"* Londoño, "Argentine Police Officer Promoted."

80 *In the photo* Londoño, "Argentine Police Officer Promoted."

80 *The boy's head* Londoño, "Argentine Police Officer Promoted."

80 *His face is pressed* Londoño, "Argentine Police Officer Promoted."

80 *"I want to make public"* Londoño, "Argentine Police Officer Promoted."

80 *The post was shared* Siddique, "Police Officer Who Breastfed Baby."

4. Early Adolescence: The Right to Be a Kid

81 *The policy was* Keith L. Alexander, "D.C. Defense Attorneys Want Juveniles Released from Shackles in Court," *Washington Post*, Aug. 24, 2014; Michael Zuckerman, "Andrew Manuel Crespo," *Harvard Magazine*, July–Aug. 2015; Andrew Crespo (@AndrewMCrespo), "My first client wore handcuffs, a waist chain, and shackles to his first court appearance per a similar policy. He was eight years old. 1/," Twitter, May 31, 2017, https://twitter.com/AndrewMCrespo/status/869986913502900224.

81 *It was Christmas Eve* Andrew Crespo (@AndrewMCrespo), "He was 3 feet 9 inches tall and weighed less than 50 pounds. It was Christmas Eve. 2/," Twitter, May 31, 2017, https://twitter.com/AndrewMCrespo/status/869987371214938114.

81 *So, when D.C. Public Defender* Crespo, "My first client."

81 *The fetters make it difficult* Andrew Crespo (@AndrewMCrespo), "But for the rest of my life I'll remember that scared, confused little eight-year-old boy, shuffling into court, shackled hand and foot. 5/5," Twitter, May 31, 2017, https://twitter.com/AndrewMCrespo/status/869987715105693696.

81 *He was eight* Crespo, "He was 3 feet."

81 *His feet didn't touch* Zuckerman, "Andrew Manuel Crespo."

81 *Prosecutors alleged* Alexander, "D.C. Defense Attorneys."

81 *Police had arrested him* Alexander, "D.C. Defense Attorneys."

81 *And now the scared* Alexander, "D.C. Defense Attorneys."

81 *Where we set* Rebecca Epstein, Jamilia J. Blake, and Thalia González, *Girlhood Interrupted: The Erasure of Black Girls' Childhood*, Georgetown Law Center on Poverty and Inequality, https://www.law.georgetown.edu

/poverty-inequality-center/wp-content/uploads/sites/14/2017/08
/girlhood-interrupted.pdf; Laurence Steinberg et al., "Are Adolescents
Less Mature Than Adults? Minors' Access to Abortion, the Juvenile Death
Penalty, and the Alleged APA 'Flip-Flop,'" *American Psychologist* 64, no. 7
(2009): 583–94; Thomas Grisso and Laurence Steinberg, "Between a Rock
and a Soft Place: Developmental Research and the Child Advocacy Process," *Journal of Clinical Child & Adolescent Psychology* 34, no. 4 (Nov.
2005): 619–27.

81 *Children are more* Epstein, Blake, and González, *Girlhood Interrupted;*
Steinberg et al., "Are Adolescents Less Mature."

81 *They are less developed* Epstein, Blake, and González, *Girlhood Interrupted;*
Steinberg et al., "Are Adolescents Less Mature."

81 *That's why* Chase Burton, "Child Savers and Unchildlike Youth: Class,
Race, and Juvenile Justice in the Early Twentieth Century," *Law & Social
Inquiry* 44, no. 4 (Nov. 2019): 1251–69.

81 *That made the existing criminal framework* Laurence Steinberg and Elizabeth Scott, "Less Guilty by Reason of Adolescence: Developmental Immaturity, Diminished Responsibility and the Juvenile Death Penalty,"
American Psychologist 58, no. 12 (Jan. 1, 2004): 1009–18; Elizabeth S. Scott
and Laurence Steinberg, "Blaming Youth Essay," *Texas Law Review* 81,
no. 3 (2003): 799–840.; Elizabeth Cauffman and Laurence Steinberg,
"(Im)Maturity of Judgment in Adolescence: Why Adolescents May Be
Less Culpable Than Adults," *Behavioral Sciences & the Law* 18, no. 6
(2000): 741–60.

81 *Decades later* Roper v. Simmons, 543 U.S. 551 (2005).

82 *Each year* Bill Hutchinson, "More Than 30,000 Children Under Age 10
Have Been Arrested in the US Since 2013: FBI," ABC News, Oct. 1, 2019,
https://abcnews.go.com/US/30000-children-age-10-arrested-us-2013
-fbi/story?id=65798787; Uniform Crime Reporting, "Crime in the United
States, Arrests by Age," 2013–2020, FBI, https://ucr.fbi.gov/crime-in-the
-u.s.

82 *Prosecuting minors* "Age Matrix," Interstate Commission for Juveniles, Jan.
20, 2022, https://www.juvenilecompact.org/age-matrix; "Thirteen States
Have No Minimum Age for Adult Prosecution of Children," Equal Justice
Initiative, accessed Sept. 6, 2021, https://eji.org/news/13-states-lack
-minimum-age-for-trying-kids-as-adults/.

82 *Each day, about ten thousand kids* "Children in Adult Prison," Equal Justice
Initiative, accessed Sept. 30, 2021, https://eji.org/issues/children-in
-prison/.

82 *On his sixteenth birthday* At the time of the alleged aggravated assault charge,
he was out on bond for an alleged armed robbery when he was thirteen, so
he was not entitled to bail. Lauren Gill, "Mississippi Teen Who Has Lan-
guished In Jail for 17 Months Without an Indictment Is Just 'One of Thousands,'" *The Appeal,* July 30, 2020, https://theappeal.org/mississippi-teen
-who-has-languished-in-jail-for-17-months-without-an-indictment-is-just
-one-of-thousands/.

82 *Though presumed innocent* Gill, "Mississippi Teen."

82 *The accuser no longer wanted* Gill, "Mississippi Teen."

82 *Asked to comment* Gill, "Mississippi Teen."

82 *Bryan Stevenson* Bryan Stevenson, "Changing the Criminal Justice System on Behalf of Children," interviewed by Kelly Corrigan, *PBS NewsHour*, Dec. 9, 2020, https://www.pbs.org/newshour/show/changing-the-criminal-justice-system-on-behalf-of-children.

82 *You cannot kill a boy* Jones v. Mississippi, 141 U.S. 1307, 1322 (2021).

82 *Roughly three thousand children* "Children in Adult Prison."

82 *That was the deal* Ghani, interview by author, Oct. 31, 2018.

82 *He ran away* Ghani, interview.

82 *They wanted to be men* Ghani, interview.

82 *Less than a year later* Ghani, interview.

82 *"We were in captivity"* Ghani, interview.

83 *His previous existence* Ghani, interview.

83 *Anjo Price* Ghani, interview.

83 *To look at Anjo* Ghani, interview.

83 *"He was an artist"* Ghani, interview.

83 *Ghani had noted* Ghani, interview.

83 *They were arguing* Ghani, interview.

83 *Ghani and Dameon were tried* Ghani, interview.

83 *In Texas, you can go hunting* "Hunter Education," Texas Parks and Wildlife, accessed Oct. 1, 2021, https://tpwd.texas.gov/regulations/outdoor-annual/hunting/hunter-education.

84 *In Mississippi, with parental consent* MS Code § 93-1-5 (2019); MS Code § 15-3-11 (2010).

84 *At your Passaic* "Spray Paint," City of Passaic, N.J., Ord. No. 873-85, Art. I § 195-5 (Sept. 12, 1985).

84 *We celebrate* ME Rev Stat § 22:1503 (2011).

84 *In one study* Phillip Atiba Goff et al., "The Essence of Innocence: Consequences of Dehumanizing Black Children," *Journal of Personality and Social Psychology* 106, no. 4 (2014): 530–32.

84 *On average* Goff et al., "The Essence of Innocence," 530–32.

84 *Participants also perceived* Goff et al., "The Essence of Innocence," 530–32.

84 *Other research suggests* Epstein, Blake, and González, *Girlhood Interrupted*, 1.

84 *Black kids, like Ghani* "Children in Adult Jails," *Economist*, Mar. 28, 2015. See, generally, Dorothy E. Roberts, "Criminal Justice and Black Families: The Collateral Damage of Over-Enforcement," *U.C. Davis Law Review* 34, no. 4 (2001): 1023–25.

84 *And prosecutors* Epstein, Blake, and González, *Girlhood Interrupted*, 12; Kim Taylor-Thompson, "Girl Talk—Examining Racial and Gender Lines in Juvenile Justice," *Nevada Law Journal* 6, no. 3 (2006): 1137–38; American Bar Association and National Bar Association, "Justice by Gender: The Lack of Appropriate Prevention, Diversion and Treatment Alternatives for Girls in the Justice System," *William & Mary Journal of Women and the Law* 9, no. 1 (2002): 85–86; Kristin N. Henning, "Criminalizing Normal Adolescent Behavior in Communities of Color: The Role of Prosecutors in Juvenile Justice Reform," *Cornell Law Review* 98, no. 2 (2012): 429–31.

84 *They are also more likely* Epstein, Blake, and González, *Girlhood Interrupted,* 12; Priscilla A. Ocen, "(E)racing Childhood: Examining the Racialized Construction of Childhood and Innocence in the Treatment of Sexually Exploited Minors," *UCLA Law Review* 62, no. 6 (2015): 1613, 1634; Center for Girls & Young Women, "Getting the Facts Straight About Girls in the Juvenile Justice System," National Council on Crime & Delinquency, Feb. 2009, 7, https://www.evidentchange.org/sites/default/files/publication_pdf/fact-sheet-girls-in-juvenile-justice.pdf; Lori D. Moore and Irene Padavic, "Racial and Ethnic Disparities in Girls' Sentencing in the Juvenile Justice System," *Feminist Criminology* 5, no. 3 (July 2010): 263.

84 *A Black girl* Epstein, Blake, and González, *Girlhood Interrupted,* 10; Edward W. Morris and Brea L. Perry, "Girls Behaving Badly? Race, Gender, and Subjective Evaluation in the Discipline of African American Girls," *Sociology of Education* 90, no. 2 (Apr. 2017): 143.

84 *And schools are roughly* Jamilia Blake et al., "Unmasking the Inequitable Discipline Experiences of Urban Black Girls: Implications for Urban Educational Stakeholders," *The Urban Review* 43 (Mar. 2011): 97–99. See, generally, Kimberlé Williams Crenshaw, Priscilla Ocen, and Jyoti Nanda, "Black Girls Matter: Pushed Out, Overpoliced and Underprotected," *African American Policy Forum,* Feb. 2015, 18, https://doi.org/10.1163/2210-7975_HRD-9978-2015002.

85 *In a recent study of North Carolina* Kate M. Wegmann and Brittanni Smith, "Examining Racial/Ethnic Disparities in School Discipline in the Context of Student-Reported Behavior Infractions," *Children and Youth Services Review* 103 (Aug. 2019): 22.

85 *With a Black boy* Wegmann and Smith, "Examining Racial/Ethnic Disparities," 18-19.

85 *When teachers* Robin Bernstein, "Let Black Kids Just Be Kids," *New York Times,* July 26, 2017.

85 *As twenty-eight-year-old* Bernstein, "Let Black Kids."

85 *Trayvon was still* Bernstein, "Let Black Kids."

85 *That has special relevance* Epstein, Blake, and González, *Girlhood Interrupted,* 13; Malika Saada Saar et al., *The Sexual Abuse to Prison Pipeline: The Girls' Story,* Human Rights Project for Girls (2015): 7–9, https://www.law.georgetown.edu/poverty-inequality-center/wp-content/uploads/sites/14/2019/02/The-Sexual-Abuse-To-Prison-Pipeline-The-Girls%E2%80%99-Story.pdf; Ocen, "(E)racing Childhood," 1591.

85 *When the protective label* Epstein, Blake, and González, *Girlhood Interrupted,* 1; Ocen, "(E)racing Childhood," 1591–92; Nesheba Kittling, "God Bless the Child: The United States' Response to Domestic Juvenile Prostitution," *Nevada Law Journal* 6, no. 3 (2006): 913.

85 *They suddenly reflect* Epstein, Blake, and González, *Girlhood Interrupted,* 1; Kittling, "God Bless the Child," 925–6.

85 *A Black girl is more likely* Epstein, Blake, and González, *Girlhood Interrupted,* 1; Kittling, "God Bless the Child," 920–21; Ocen, "(E)racing Childhood," 1594.

85 *A Black girl ends up dismissed* Epstein, Blake, and González, *Girlhood Inter-*

rupted, 1; Kittling, "God Bless the Child," 920; Ocen, "(E)racing Childhood," 1591.

85 *When my colleague* Adam Benforado, *Unfair: The New Science of Criminal Injustice* (New York: Crown, 2015), 193.

85 *In fact, on average,* Benforado, *Unfair,* 193.

86 *The default in place* Amy S. Rosenberg, "Teen Killers, Prison Lifers, Given a Ray of Hope," *Philadelphia Inquirer,* Feb. 7, 2016; Patrice Taddonio, "'Living with Murder': An Update on Kempis Songster's Case," PBS, Dec. 1, 2017, https://www.pbs.org/wgbh/frontline/article/living-with-murder-an-update-on-kempis-songsters-case/.

86 *When the Supreme Court* Miller v. Alabama, 567 U.S. 460, 474 (2012); Amy S. Rosenberg, "'Yes.' Juvenile Lifer Kempis Songster Released from Prison After 30 Years," *Philadelphia Inquirer,* Dec. 28, 2017.

86 *But Dameon's parole board* Amy S. Rosenberg, "Freed Juvenile Lifer Kempis Songster Attended the Super Bowl. So Why Was His Codefendant Denied Parole?" *Philadelphia Inquirer,* Feb. 28, 2018.

86 *Denials like this* Editorial Board, "New York Forgets Its Juvenile Lifers," *New York Times,* Mar. 24, 2018; Erica L. Ramstad, "Monster Under the Bed: The Nightmare of Leaving Juvenile Life Sentences Up to the Parole Board," *South Dakota Law Review* 64, no. 1 (2019): 126; Kate Hatheway, "Creating a Meaningful Opportunity for Review: Challenging the Politicization of Parole for Life-Sentenced Prisoners," *American Criminal Law Review* 54, no. 2 (2017): 622.

86 *And, around the country* Sharon Cohen and Adam Geller, "After 2016 Ruling, Battles over Juvenile Lifer Cases Persist," AP News, Jan. 21, 2019, https://apnews.com/article/us-news-ap-top-news-courts-supreme-courts-north-america-422236ad63c64636a2e9f3622abed55d; Megan R. Pollastro, "Where Are You, Congress? Silence Rings in Congress as Juvenile Offenders Remain in Prison for Life," *Brooklyn Law Review* 85, no. 1 (2019): 289–90.

86 *But when something really bad* Robert Johnson and Sonia Tabriz, "Sentencing Children to Death by Incarceration: A Deadly Denial of Social Responsibility," *Prison Journal* 91, no. 2 (June 1, 2011): 200; Steinberg and Scott, "Less Guilty," 1009–10; Stephen J. Morse, "Immaturity and Irresponsibility," *Journal of Criminal Law and Criminology* 88, no. 1 (1997): 15.

86 *This cognitive need* Steinberg and Scott, "Less Guilty," 1009–10; Scott and Steinberg, "Blaming Youth," 800, 806–11.

86 *Research suggests* Dylan B. Jackson et al., "Police Stops Among At-Risk Youth: Repercussions for Mental Health," *Journal of Adolescent Health* 65, no. 5 (Nov. 2019): 627–32.

86 *In one recent study* Jackson et al., "Police Stops."

87 *When officers use force* Char Adams and Randi Richardson, "'Beaten Like I Was an Adult': Police Violence Against Children Sparks Demand for Use-of-Force Laws," NBC News, Apr. 7, 2021, https://www.nbcnews.com/news/nbcblk/beaten-i-was-adult-police-violence-against-kids-spark-demand-n1265535; Leah Metzger, "Don't Shoot: Race-Based Trauma and Police Brutality," *Orphans and Vulnerable Children Student Scholarship* 7 (Spring 2019): 2, https://pillars.taylor.edu/ovc-student/7.

87 *So, we get* Sharon Coolidge and Cameron Knight, "Mom of Girl Stunned by Cop: If You Can't Restrain Little Kids, 'Find a Different Job,'" *Cincinnati Enquirer,* Aug. 9, 2018; Matthew Hendrickson, "New Video Shows Chicago Cops Dragging, Punching and Tasing CPS Student," *Chicago Sun-Times,* Apr. 11, 2019; Tom Jones, "Police Chief Defends Officer After Controversial Video of 12-Year-Old's Arrest," WSB-TV—Atlanta, Oct. 16, 2018, https://www.wsbtv.com/news/local/cobb-county/viral-video-of-cobb-cop-apprehending-young-black-boy-draws-outrage/854171706/.

87 *The one-size-fits-all approach* Allison Redlich et al., "The Police Interrogation of Children and Adolescents," in *Interrogations, Confessions, and Entrapment,* ed. G. D. Lassiter (New York: Kluwer Academic/Plenum, 2004), 107–25; Steven A. Drizin and Richard A. Leo, "The Problem of False Confessions in the Post-DNA World," *North Carolina Law Review* 82, no. 3 (2004): 963–64; Saul M. Kassin et al., "Police-Induced Confessions: Risk Factors and Recommendations," *Law and Human Behavior* 34, no. 1 (Feb. 2010): 19–21.

87 *In one study of DNA* Samuel R. Gross and Michael Shaffer, *Exonerations in the United States, 1989–2012: Report by the National Registry of Exonerations,* National Registry of Exonerations, June 2012, 60, https://www.law.umich.edu/special/exoneration/Documents/exonerations_us_1989_2012_full_report.pdf.

87 *Overall, minors appear* Samuel R. Gross et al., "Exonerations in the United States 1989 Through 2003," *Journal of Law and Criminology* 95, no. 2 (Winter 2005): 554; Lindsay C. Malloy, Elizabeth P. Shulman, and Elizabeth Cauffman, "Interrogations, Confessions, and Guilty Pleas Among Serious Adolescent Offenders," *Law and Human Behavior* 38, no. 2 (2014): 181–93.

87 *An initial problem* Naomi E. S. Goldstein, Heather Zelle, and Thomas Grisso, *Miranda Rights Comprehension Instruments: Manual for Juvenile and Adult Evaluations* (Sarasota, Fla.: Professional Resource Press, 2014), 93; Naomi Goldstein et al., "Juvenile Offenders' Miranda Rights Comprehension and Self-Reported Likelihood of Offering False Confessions," *Assessment* 10, no. 4 (Dec. 2004): 359–69.

87 *Those under fifteen* Kassin et al., "Police-Induced Confessions," 8.

87 *As a result* Kassin et al., "Police-Induced Confessions," 8–9; Marsha Levick and Neha Desai, "Still Waiting: The Elusive Quest to Ensure Juveniles a Constitutional Right to Counsel at All Stages of the Juvenile Court Process," *Rutgers Law Review* 60, no. 1 (2007): 175–77.

87 *Once an interrogation* Jason Mandelbaum and Angela Crossman, "No Illusions: Developmental Considerations in Adolescent False Confessions," American Psychological Association, Dec. 2014, https://www.apa.org/pi/families/resources/newsletter/2014/12/adolescent-false-confessions; Saul M. Kassin, "False Confessions: Causes, Consequences, and Implications for Reform," *Policy Insights from the Behavioral and Brain Sciences* 1, no. 1 (Oct. 1, 2014): 116; Gregory P. Scholand, "Re-Punishing the Innocent: False Confession as an Unjust Obstacle to Compensation for the Wrongfully Convicted," *Case Western Reserve Law Review* 63, no. 4 (2013): 1404–6.

87 *Combining the deceptive* Kassin et al., "Police-Induced Confessions," 19–20.

87 *The wrongful convictions* Kassin et al., "Police-Induced Confessions," 19; Drizin and Leo, "Post-DNA World," 900–901; Saul M. Kassin, "The Social Psychology of False Confessions: False Confessions," *Social Issues and Policy Review* 9, no. 1 (Jan. 2015): 25–28; Marco Luna, "Juvenile False Confessions: Juvenile Psychology, Police Interrogation Tactics, and Prosecutorial Discretion," *Nevada Law Journal* 18, no. 1 (Jan. 2018): 295–96.

88 *Ghani and Dameon* Ghani, interview.

88 *As Ghani recalls* Ghani, interview.

88 *"They say two minds"* Ghani, interview.

88 *So, they convinced themselves* Ghani, interview.

88 *"There was no sense"* Ghani, interview.

88 *"We were sixteen"* Ghani, interview.

88 *They "went back"* Ghani, interview.

88 *The knockout* Ghani, interview.

88 *As I teach* Ghani, interview.

88 *But Ghani and Dameon's lawyers* Ghani, interview.

88 *As Ghani reflects* Ghani, interview.

89 *Kids who end up suspended* Epstein, Blake, and González, *Girlhood Interrupted*, 9; Kathryn C. Monahan et al., "From the School Yard to the Squad Car: School Discipline, Truancy, and Arrest," *Journal of Youth and Adolescence* 43, no. 7 (July 2014): 1110–22; Daniel J. Losen and Tia E. Martinez, *Out of School and Off Track: The Overuse of Suspensions in American Middle and High Schools,* The Center for Civil Rights Remedies, Apr. 8, 2013, https://escholarship.org/uc/item/8pd0s08z; Joel Mittleman, "A Downward Spiral? Childhood Suspension and the Path to Juvenile Arrest," *Sociology of Education* 91, no. 3 (2018): 183–204; Abigail Novak, "The School-to-Prison Pipeline: An Examination of the Association Between Suspension and Justice System Involvement," *Criminal Justice and Behavior* 46, no. 8 (Aug. 1, 2019): 1165–80.

89 *In Philadelphia* Samantha Melamed, "Philly DA Larry Krasner Unveils Plan to Shrink Juvenile Justice System. Does It Go Far Enough?" *Philadelphia Inquirer,* Feb. 6, 2019; Mensah M. Dean, "DA Larry Krasner Aims to Keep Teen Offenders Out of Criminal Justice System with New Restorative Program," *Philadelphia Inquirer,* July 12, 2021.

89 *The charges* Dean, "New Restorative Program."

89 *As Krasner explains* Dean, "New Restorative Program."

89 *We all lose* Dean, "New Restorative Program."

89 *A child placed* Goff et al., "The Essence of Innocence," 526; Jennifer L. Woolard et al., "Juveniles Within Adult Correctional Settings: Legal Pathways and Developmental Considerations," *International Journal of Forensic Mental Health* 4, no. 1 (2005): 9; Daniel C. Murrie et al., "Psychiatric Symptoms Among Juveniles Incarcerated in Adult Prison," *Psychiatric Services* 60, no. 8 (Aug. 1, 2009): 1092–97; Jessica Lahey, "The Steep Costs of Imprisoning Juveniles with Adults," *The Atlantic,* Jan. 8, 2016.

89 *And young people* Jessica Feierman and Jenny Lutz, "Placing Juveniles in Solitary Confinement Doesn't Fix Them. In Fact, It Makes Them Worse," *USA Today,* Jan. 11, 2019; Jessica Lee, "Lonely Too Long: Redefining and Reforming Juvenile Solitary Confinement," *Fordham Law Review* 85, no. 2

(2016): 856–60; Laura Anne Gallagher, "More Than a Time Out: Juvenile Solitary Confinement," *UC Davis Journal of Juvenile Law & Policy* 18, no. 2 (Summer 2014): 248–50; American Civil Liberties Union, *Alone and Afraid: Children Held in Solitary Confinement and Isolation in Juvenile Detention and Correctional Facilities,* Nov. 2013, 6, https://www.aclu.org/sites/default/files/field_document/alone_and_afraid_complete_final.pdf.

89   *That's led to* Feierman and Lutz, "Placing Juveniles in Solitary"; Nathan James, *The First Step Act of 2018: An Overview,* Congressional Research Service, Mar. 4, 2019, 21, https://crsreports.congress.gov/product/pdf/R/R45558.

89   *However, at the state level* Feierman and Lutz, "Placing Juveniles in Solitary"; Amy Roe, "Solitary Confinement Is Especially Harmful to Juveniles and Should Not Be Used to Punish Them," ACLU of Washington, Nov. 17, 2017, https://www.aclu-wa.org/story/solitary-confinement-especially-harmful-juveniles-and-should-not-be-used-punish-them; Laura Anne Gallagher, "More Than a Time Out: Juvenile Solitary Confinement," *UC Davis Journal of Juvenile Law & Policy* 18, no. 2 (Summer 2014): 248–50; American Civil Liberties Union, *Alone and Afraid,* 6.

90   *Throughout history* Sarah-Jayne Blakemore, *Inventing Ourselves: The Secret Life of the Teenage Brain* (New York: PublicAffairs, 2018), 2–7.

90   *In a passage* William Shakespeare, *The Winter's Tale,* 3.3.65–69 (quoted in Blakemore, *Inventing Ourselves,* 6).

90   *But it has only been* Blakemore, *Inventing Ourselves,* 3–5; Laurence Steinberg et al., "Around the World, Adolescence Is a Time of Heightened Sensation Seeking and Immature Self-Regulation," *Developmental Science* 21, no. 2 (2018).

90   *That work has been complemented* Blakemore, *Inventing Ourselves,* 192.

90   *What we know* Blakemore, *Inventing Ourselves,* 7; Laurence Steinberg, "Adolescent Development and Juvenile Justice," *Annual Review of Clinical Psychology* 5, no. 1 (2009): 459–85.

90   *As Ghani explains* Ghani, interview.

90   *But it doesn't follow* Steinberg and Scott, "Less Guilty," 1010; Nathalie F. P. Gilfoyle et.al., "Miller v. Alabama," *Brief for the American Psychological Association, American Psychiatric Association & National Association of Social Workers as Amici Curiae in Support of Petitioners* (2012).

90   *We must* Ghani, interview.

90   *In searching* Ghani, interview.

90   *Modern statistics* Blakemore, *Inventing Ourselves,* 133, 192.

91   *First, adolescents appear* Alison Gopnik, *The Gardener and the Carpenter* (New York: Farrar, Straus and Giroux, 2016), 203; Blakemore, *Inventing Ourselves,* 141; Steinberg, "Adolescent Development," 469.

91   *So, they may overestimate* Gopnik, *The Gardener and the Carpenter,* 203.

91   *The area of the brain* Gopnik, *The Gardener and the Carpenter,* 203; Steinberg, "Adolescent Development," 465; Blakemore, *Inventing Ourselves,* 135.

91   *Second, it's not just that adolescents* Steinberg, "Adolescent Development," 469.

91   *The prefrontal cortex* Mariam Arain et al., "Maturation of the Adolescent Brain," *Neuropsychiatric Disease and Treatment* 9 (Apr. 2013): 451.

91   *That means* Blakemore, *Inventing Ourselves,* 135; Steinberg, "Adolescent Development," 466.

91   *In this light* Blakemore, *Inventing Ourselves,* 135.

91   *Third, adolescents are* Steinberg, "Adolescent Development," 469.

91   *Approaching the teen years* Blakemore, *Inventing Ourselves,* 31.

91   *The heightened desire* Blakemore, *Inventing Ourselves,* 39; Sarah-Jayne Blakemore and Kathryn L. Mills, "Is Adolescence a Sensitive Period for Sociocultural Processing?" *Annual Review of Psychology* 65 (2014): 187–207.

92   *In the latter case* Blakemore, *Inventing Ourselves,* 33; Laurence Steinberg, "A Social Neuroscience Perspective on Adolescent Risk-Taking," *Developmental Review* 28, no. 1 (Mar. 2008): 83.

92   *In one study* Blakemore, *Inventing Ourselves,* 33; Steinberg, "A Social Neuroscience Perspective," 91.

92   *Sometimes the drivers* Blakemore, *Inventing Ourselves,* 33; Steinberg, "A Social Neuroscience Perspective," 83.

92   *It was a significant risk* Blakemore, *Inventing Ourselves,* 33; Steinberg, "A Social Neuroscience Perspective," 83.

92   *For adults* Blakemore, *Inventing Ourselves,* 33; Steinberg, "A Social Neuroscience Perspective," 91.

92   *They took nearly three times* Blakemore, *Inventing Ourselves,* 33; Steinberg, "A Social Neuroscience Perspective," 91.

92   *Ghani notes* Ghani, interview.

92   *In the driving simulation* Blakemore, *Inventing Ourselves,* 33; Steinberg, "A Social Neuroscience Perspective," 91.

92   *Adolescents don't take risks* Blakemore, *Inventing Ourselves,* 44.

92   *In fact, they can be* Blakemore, *Inventing Ourselves,* 44.

92   *That's because they are powerfully shaped* Blakemore, *Inventing Ourselves,* 42–44.

92   *It depends* Blakemore, *Inventing Ourselves,* 42–44.

92   *As Ghani points out* Ghani, interview.

93   *When I asked* Sidney, interview by author, July 1, 2018.

93   *Listening back* Sidney, interview.

93   *The more readily an incident* Amos Tversky and Daniel Kahneman, "Availability: A Heuristic for Judging Frequency and Probability," *Cognitive Psychology* 5, no. 2 (1973): 207–32.

93   *But harms that are more common* Jessica Grose, "Why Covid Has Broken Parents' Sense of Risk," *New York Times,* Sept. 15, 2021.

93   *Yet, the risk* Ashley J. Thomas, P. Kyle Stanford, and Barbara W. Sarnecka, "No Child Left Alone: Moral Judgments About Parents Affect Estimates of Risk to Children," *Collabra* 2, no. 1 (2016): 1.

93   *By contrast, drowning* Nagesh N. Borse et al., *CDC Childhood Injury Report; Patterns of Unintentional Injuries Among 0–19 Year Olds in the United States, 2000–2006,* Centers for Disease Control and Prevention, Dec. 2008, 4.

93   *Because our assessments* Paul Slovic, "Perception of Risk," *Science* 236 (Apr. 17, 1987): 284–85; Grose, "Why Covid Has Broken."

93   *In a national study* Children's Hospital of Philadelphia, "About Half of Parents Use Cell Phones While Driving with Young Children in the Car," *ScienceDaily,* July 12, 2018, https://www.sciencedaily.com/releases/2018

/07/180712100538.htm; Catherine C. McDonald et al., "Factors Associated with Cell Phone Use While Driving: A Survey of Parents and Caregivers of Children Ages 4–10 Years," *Journal of Pediatrics* 201 (Oct. 1, 2018): 208.

94 *That is despite* Children's Hospital of Philadelphia, "Parents Use Cell Phones."

94 *Just as concerning* Children's Hospital of Philadelphia, "Parents Use Cell Phones."

94 *Other significant threats* See, e.g., Sumal Nandasena, Ananda Rajitha Wick-remasinghe, and Nalini Sathiakumar, "Indoor Air Pollution and Respiratory Health of Children in the Developing World," *World Journal of Clinical Pediatrics* 2, no. 2 (May 8, 2013): 6–15.

94 *It's legal pharmaceuticals* See, e.g., *BMJ*, "Nearly Third of US Young People Prescribed Psychoactive Drugs Admit Misusing Them," *ScienceDaily*, Feb. 2, 2021, https://www.sciencedaily.com/releases/2021/02/210202192756.htm; Israel Agaku, Satomi Odani, and Jantel Nelson, "Medical Use and Misuse of Psychoactive Prescription Medications Among US Youth and Young Adults," *Family Medicine and Community Health* 9, no. 1 (Jan. 2021): 1–17; Gopnik, *The Gardener and the Carpenter*, 195.

94 *Roughly one in three teens BMJ*, "Nearly Third of US."

94 *The reason* Teresa W. Wang et al., "E-cigarette Use Among Middle and High School Students—United States, 2020," *Morbidity and Mortality Weekly Report* 69, no. 37 (Sept. 2020): 1310–12; Eunice Park-Lee, "Notes from the Field: E-Cigarette Use Among Middle and High School Students—National Youth Tobacco Survey, United States, 2021," *Morbidity and Mortality Weekly Report* 70, no. 39 (2021): 1387–89; Matt Richtel, "Youth Vaping Declined Sharply for Second Year, New Data Show," *New York Times*, Sept. 30, 2021.

94 *It was that new regulations* Richtel, "Youth Vaping Declined."

94 *Few of us* Cheryl D. Fryar, Margaret D. Carroll, and Cynthia L. Ogden, "Prevalence of Overweight, Obesity, and Severe Obesity Among Children and Adolescents Aged 2–19 Years: United States, 1963–1965 Through 2015–2016," Health E-Stats (Sept. 2018): 1–6; Committee on Communications, "Children, Adolescents, and Advertising," *Pediatrics* 118, no. 6 (Dec. 1, 2006): 2565.

94 *We worry about binoculared perverts* Helen Clark et al., "A Future for the World's Children? A WHO–UNICEF–Lancet Commission," *Lancet* 395, no. 10224 (Feb. 2020): 632.

95 *The average child* Clark et al., "A Future for the World's Children?" 633; Children's Commissioner, *Who Knows What About Me? A Children's Commissioner Report into the Collection and Sharing of Children's Data* (Nov. 2018), https://www.childrenscommissioner.gov.uk/wp-content/uploads/2018/11/cco-who-knows-what-about-me.pdf.

95 *While we may fail* Clark et al., "A Future for the World's Children?" 606, 630; Gabrielle Jenkin et al., "A Systematic Review of Persuasive Marketing Techniques to Promote Food to Children on Television," *Obesity Reviews* 15, no. 4 (2014): 281–93; Matthew A. Lapierre et al., "The Effect of Advertising on Children and Adolescents," *Pediatrics* 140, no. Supplement_2 (Nov. 1, 2017): S152–56.

95 *They are well aware* Clark et al., "A Future for the World's Children?" 630; Sapna Maheshwari, "Online and Making Thousands, at Age 4: Meet the Kidfluencers," *New York Times*, Mar. 1, 2019.

95 *Children's malleability presents* Clark et al., "A Future for the World's Children?" 630.

95 *Given that children* Iowa State University, "Money Spent on Beer Ads Linked to Under-Age Drinking," *ScienceDaily*, Nov. 18, 2019, https://www.sciencedaily.com/releases/2019/11/191118140327.htm; Douglas A. Gentile et al., "Beer Advertisements and Adolescent Drinking Knowledge, Expectancies, and Behavior," *Addictive Behaviors Reports* 10 (Dec. 1, 2019): 1–6.

95 *Recent research shows* Iowa State University, "Money Spent"; Gentile et al., "Beer Advertisements."

96 *Bullying is prevalent* National Academies of Sciences, Engineering, and Medicine, *Preventing Bullying Through Science, Policy, and Practice*, ed., Frederick Rivara and Suzanne Le Menestrel (Washington, D.C.: The National Academies Press, 2016), 2.

96 *Kids often suffer* Katelyn K. Jetelina et al., "Mechanisms and Frequency of Violent Injuries Among Victims and Perpetrators of Bullying," *Journal of Adolescent Health* 64, no. 5 (May 2019): 664–70.

96 *Even when they escape* Lyndal Bond et al., "Does Bullying Cause Emotional Problems? A Prospective Study of Young Teenagers," *BMJ* 323, no. 7311 (Sept. 1, 2001): 480–84; Gianluca Gini and Tiziana Pozzoli, "Association Between Bullying and Psychosomatic Problems: A Meta-Analysis," *Pediatrics* 123, no. 3 (Mar. 1, 2009): 1059–65; Anat Brunstein Klomek et al., "Bullying, Depression, and Suicidality in Adolescents," *Journal of the American Academy of Child & Adolescent Psychiatry* 46, no. 1 (Jan. 2007): 40–49; Tanya N. Beran, Ginger Hughes, and Judy Lupart, "A Model of Achievement and Bullying: Analyses of the Canadian National Longitudinal Survey of Children and Youth Data," *Educational Research* 50, no. 1 (Mar. 1, 2008): 25–39.

96 *Bullying in childhood* David Alejandro González-Chica et al., "Bullying and Sexual Abuse and Their Association with Harmful Behaviours, Antidepressant Use and Health-Related Quality of Life in Adulthood: A Population-Based Study in South Australia," *BMC Public Health* 19, no. 1 (Jan. 7, 2019): 26; University of Adelaide, "Binge Eating and Smoking Linked to Bullying and Sexual Abuse," *ScienceDaily*, Jan. 11, 2019, https://www.sciencedaily.com/releases/2019/01/190111095130.htm.

96 *Moreover, witnessing bullying* Michel Janosz et al., "Witnessing Violence in Early Secondary School Predicts Subsequent Student Impairment," *Journal of Epidemiology and Community Health* 72, no. 12 (Dec. 1, 2018): 1117–23; University of Montreal, "Witnessing Violence in High School as Bad as Being Bullied," *ScienceDaily*, Sept. 17, 2018, https://www.sciencedaily.com/releases/2018/09/180917082442.htm.

96 *In one recent study* Janosz et al., "Witnessing Violence"; University of Montreal, "Bad as Being Bullied."

96 *It didn't matter much* Janosz et al., "Witnessing Violence"; University of Montreal, "Bad as Being Bullied."

97 *One study of American children* David Light Shields et al., "The Sport Be-

havior of Youth, Parents and Coaches; The Good, The Bad, and The Ugly," *Journal of Research in Character Education* 3, no. 1 (2005): 44.

97 *And another study showed* Bradford Strand et al., "Athletes' Recollections of Inappropriate Behaviors by Their High School Sport Coaches," *The International Journal of Sport and Society* 8 (Jan. 1, 2017): 44, 50.

97 *Mary Cain was the fastest girl* Mary Cain, "I Was the Fastest Girl in America, Until I Joined Nike," *New York Times*, Nov. 7, 2019.

97 *Likewise, verbal and emotional abuse* Mitch Weiss and Holbrook Mohr, "US Gymnasts Tell AP Sport Rife with Verbal, Emotional Abuse," AP News, Feb. 24, 2018, https://apnews.com/article/north-america-us-news-ap-top -news-olympic-games-in-state-wire-0c67e962d7524c87a865d3c468bdd521.

97 *He didn't realize* Ghani, interview.

97 *Arriving in Brooklyn* Ghani, interview.

97 *In Trinidad* Ghani, interview.

98 *His voice* Ghani, interview.

98 *He didn't have siblings* Ghani, interview.

98 *His mother's unwavering love* Ghani, interview.

98 *"I got picked on"* Ghani, interview.

98 *He ran away* Ghani, interview.

98 *Sifting through these memories* Ghani, interview.

98 *Ghani is driven* Ghani, interview.

98 *We can help* Kelly Lynn Mulvey et al., "School and Family Factors Predicting Adolescent Cognition Regarding Bystander Intervention in Response to Bullying and Victim Retaliation," *Journal of Youth and Adolescence* 48, no. 3 (Mar. 1, 2019): 581–96; North Carolina State University, "Family, School Support Makes Kids More Likely to Stand Up to Bullying," *ScienceDaily*, Nov. 12, 2018, https://www.sciencedaily.com/releases/2018/11 /181112131527.htm.

98 *Research shows* Megan R. Holmes et al., "Economic Burden of Child Exposure to Intimate Partner Violence in the United States," *Journal of Family Violence* 33, no. 4 (May 1, 2018): 239–49; Case Western Reserve University, "Exposure to Domestic Violence Costs US Government $55 Billion Each Year: Exposure to Domestic Violence Carries Long-Term Consequences for Both Children and Society," *ScienceDaily*, Apr. 25, 2018, https://www.sciencedaily.com/releases/2018/04/180425093846 .htm; Amy D. Marshall, Mark E. Feinberg, and Kelly A. Daly, "Children's Emotional and Behavioral Reactions to Interparental Aggression: The Role of Exposure to Within-incident, Cross-dyad Aggression Spillover," *Journal of Family Psychology* 33, no. 5 (2019): 617–28; Penn State University, "Interparental Aggression Often Co-occurs with Aggression Toward Kids," *ScienceDaily*, Apr. 4, 2019, https://www.sciencedaily.com/releases /2019/04/190404124750.htm; Rebecca Waller et al., "Parenting Is an Environmental Predictor of Callous-Unemotional Traits and Aggression: A Monozygotic Twin Differences Study," *Journal of the American Academy of Child & Adolescent Psychiatry* 57, no. 12 (Dec. 2018): 955–63; University of Pennsylvania, "How Parenting Affects Antisocial Behaviors in Children," *ScienceDaily*, Oct. 11, 2018, https://www.sciencedaily.com /releases/2018/10/181011173131.htm.

98 *But a recent study* Kelly Lynn Mulvey et al., "School and Family Factors Predicting Adolescent Cognition Regarding Bystander Intervention in Response to Bullying and Victim Retaliation," *Journal of Youth and Adolescence* 48, no. 3 (Mar. 1, 2019): 581–96; North Carolina State University, "Family, School Support Makes Kids More Likely."

99 *In a real-world experiment* Elizabeth Levy Paluck, Hana Shepherd, and Peter M. Aronow, "Changing Climates of Conflict: A Social Network Experiment in 56 Schools," *Proceedings of the National Academy of Sciences* 113, no. 3 (Jan. 19, 2016): 566–71; Blakemore, *Inventing Ourselves*, 47–48.

99 *Those small peer interventions* Paluck, Shepherd, and Aronow, "Changing Climates"; Blakemore, *Inventing Ourselves*, 47–48.

99 *And when popular students* Paluck, Shepherd, and Aronow, "Changing Climates"; Blakemore, *Inventing Ourselves*, 47–48.

99 *That justifies R ratings* Amy E. Feldman, "For Teens, Sexting Can Be a Crime," *Wall Street Journal,* Nov. 19, 2020; Steven Petrow, "Teen Sexting Is Definitely a Problem, but a Felony?" *USA Today,* Nov. 14, 2015; Mark Joseph Stern, "Maryland's Unjust Court Decision on Sexting," *Slate,* Aug. 29, 2019, https://slate.com/technology/2019/08/maryland-sk-court-case-teen-sexting-child-pornography.html; Maggie Jones, "What Teenagers Are Learning from Online Porn," *New York Times,* Feb. 7, 2018.

99 *For more than half* Laura M. Padilla-Walker, "Longitudinal Change in Parent-Adolescent Communication About Sexuality," *Journal of Adolescent Health* 63 (June 28, 2019): 754; Dalmacio Flores and Julie Barroso, "21st Century Parent-Child Sex Communication in the U.S.: A Process Review," *Journal of Sex Research* 54, no. 4–5 (May 2017): 532–48.

99 *There is little* John Santelli et al., "Abstinence and Abstinence-Only Education: A Review of U.S. Policies and Programs," *Journal of Adolescent Health* 38, no. 1 (Jan. 2006): 75; Douglas B. Kirby, "The Impact of Abstinence and Comprehensive Sex and STD/HIV Education Programs on Adolescent Sexual Behavior," *Sexuality Research and Social Policy* 5, no. 3 (Sept. 2008): 24; Debra Hauser, *Five Years of Abstinence-Only-Until-Marriage Education: Assessing the Impact* (Washington, D.C.: Advocates for Youth, 2004), 2, https://www.advocatesforyouth.org/wp-content/uploads/storage/advfy/documents/stateevaluations.pdf.

99 *And worryingly* Santelli et al., "Abstinence," 76; Hauser, *Five Years*, 4.

99 *Moreover, the sexual abuse* Dorothy L. Espelage et al., "Understanding Types, Locations, & Perpetrators of Peer-to-Peer Sexual Harassment in U.S. Middle Schools: A Focus on Sex, Racial, and Grade Differences," *Children and Youth Services Review* 71 (Dec. 2016): 174–83; University of Illinois at Urbana-Champaign, "Sexual Harassment Common Among Middle School Children, Study Finds," Phys.org, Dec. 9, 2016, https://phys.org/news/2016-12-sexual-common-middle-school-children.html; Dorothy L. Espelage and Melissa K. Holt, "Dating Violence & Sexual Harassment Across the Bully-Victim Continuum Among Middle and High School Students," *Journal of Youth and Adolescence* 36, no. 6 (June 16, 2007): 799–811.

99 *With parents* Jones, "Online Porn."

100 *The result is a near-endless stream* Jones, "Online Porn."

100 *One recent study* Jones, "Online Porn."

100 *Research shows that* Padilla-Walker, "Longitudinal Change," 754–56; Brigham Young University, "Checked Off 'the Talk' with Your Teen? Not So Fast: Once Isn't Enough: Ongoing Communication About Sex Between Parents and Their Adolescent Children Leads to Safer Sex at Age 21," *ScienceDaily*, Oct. 1, 2018, https://www.sciencedaily.com/releases/2018/10/181001154039.htm; Laura Widman et al., "Adolescent Sexual Health Communication and Condom Use: A Meta-analysis," *Health Psychology: Official Journal of the Division of Health Psychology, American Psychological Association* 33, no. 10 (Oct. 2014): 1113–24; Flores and Barroso, "21st Century," 532–48; M. Katherine Hutchinson et al., "The Role of Mother–Daughter Sexual Risk Communication in Reducing Sexual Risk Behaviors Among Urban Adolescent Females: A Prospective Study," *Journal of Adolescent Health* 33, no. 2 (Aug. 2003): 98–107.

100 *As with anti-bullying efforts* Richard Weissbourd et al., *The Talk: How Adults Can Promote Young People's Healthy Relationships and Prevent Misogyny and Sexual Harassment*, Harvard Making Caring Common Project, May 2017, 3, 6, https://static1.squarespace.com/static/5b7c56e255b02c683659fe43/t/5bd51a0324a69425bd079b59/1540692500558/mcc_the_talk_final.pdf; Peggy Orenstein, "We Can't Just Let Boys Be Boys," *New York Times*, Sept. 29, 2018; Moises Velasquez-Manoff, "Real Men Get Rejected, Too," *New York Times*, Feb. 24, 2018.

100 *Within days* Nicholas Kristof, "The Children of Pornhub," *New York Times*, Dec. 4, 2020; Nicholas Kristof, "An Uplifting Update, on the Terrible World of Pornhub," *New York Times*, Dec. 10, 2020; Associated Press, "Pornhub: Mastercard and Visa to Block Use of Cards on Site After Child Abuse Allegations," *Guardian*, Dec. 10, 2020.

101 *One of the victims* Kristof, "The Children of Pornhub."

101 *The videos ended up* Kristof, "The Children of Pornhub."

101 *"I was dumb"* Kristof, "The Children of Pornhub."

101 *"It was one small thing"* Kristof, "The Children of Pornhub."

101 *Growing up* Elizabeth, interview by author, Mar. 30, 2022.

101 *"We could go anywhere"* Elizabeth, interview.

101 *In the 1970s* Roger Hart, *Children's Experience of Place* (New York: Irvington Publishers, 1979).

101 *When he returned* Lulu Miller and Alix Spiegel, "Fearless," Jan. 18, 2015, in *Invisibilia* (podcast), 57:39, https://www.npr.org/programs/invisibilia/377515477/fearless?showDate=2015-01-16.

101 *A more likely explanation* Thomas, Standford, and Sarnecka, "No Child Left Alone."

101 *That's one of the reasons* Lela Moore, "From Tokyo to Paris, Parents Tell Americans to Chill," *New York Times*, Aug. 2, 2018.

101 *It is a tradition* Ellen Barry, "A Peculiarly Dutch Summer Rite: Children Let Loose in the Night Woods," *New York Times*, July 21, 2019.

101 *They are given a cellphone* Barry, "Dutch Summer Rite."

102 *It's not simply* Thomas, Standford, and Sarnecka, "No Child Left Alone."

102 *Drawing back* Thomas, Standford, and Sarnecka, "No Child Left Alone."

102 *That moral intuition* Thomas, Standford, and Sarnecka, "No Child Left Alone."

102 *The process seems backward* Thomas, Standford, and Sarnecka, "No Child Left Alone."

102 *But, as scientists have discovered* Thomas, Standford, and Sarnecka, "No Child Left Alone."

102 *In a clever set of studies* Thomas, Standford, and Sarnecka, "No Child Left Alone."

102 *The scientists then asked* Thomas, Standford, and Sarnecka, "No Child Left Alone."

102 *When the parent left* Thomas, Standford, and Sarnecka, "No Child Left Alone."

102 *And the more morally objectionable* Thomas, Standford, and Sarnecka, "No Child Left Alone."

102 *Andre is eleven* Andre, interview by Adam Benforado, Sept. 5, 2018.

102 *He gets himself up* Andre, interview.

102 *But he doesn't wait* Andre, interview.

102 *It's a regular city bus* Andre, interview.

102 *Andre explains that the school* Andre, interview.

102 *And he admits* Andre, interview.

102 *"I just went"* Andre, interview.

103 *He laughs* Andre, interview.

103 *He feels bad* Andre, interview.

103 *The other day* Andre, interview.

103 *"I didn't even"* Andre, interview.

103 *"He was like"* Andre, interview.

103 *Andre, though* Andre, interview.

103 *"I asked them"* Andre, interview.

103 *So, in front of the security guard* Andre, interview.

103 *But the guard wouldn't budge* Andre, interview.

103 *The research is clear* Gopnik, *The Gardener and the Carpenter*, 150–51; Michael Yogman et al., "The Power of Play: A Pediatric Role in Enhancing Development in Young Children," *Pediatrics* 142, no. 3 (2018): 1–16.

103 *But somehow* Gopnik, *The Gardener and the Carpenter*, 88–90.

104 *Since the 1970s* Romina Barros, Ellen Johnson Silver, and Ruth E. K. Stein, "School Recess and Group Classroom Behavior," *Pediatrics* 123, no. 2 (Feb. 1, 2009): 434.

104 *Under the guise* Alexandria Hoff, "City Council Passes New, Simplified Curfew for Philadelphia Minors," CBS Philly, June 25, 2021, https://philadelphia.cbslocal.com/2021/06/25/city-council-passes-new-simplified-curfew-for-philadelphia-minors/?fbclid=IwAR2k5BHyfkyzu96LwVFdGUukwhwYSNh68nFzqCJ9rnJ-78ZsnDoNbCy_fbQ.

104 *And if they dare* Michaela Winberg and Max Marin, "Teen-Repelling 'Mosquito' Devices to Stay in Philly Public Parks Indefinitely," Billy Penn, Jan. 24, 2020, https://billypenn.com/2020/01/24/teen-repelling-mosquito-devices-to-stay-in-philly-public-parks-indefinitely/.

104 *We can take inspiration* United Nations Convention on the Rights of the Child, Nov. 20, 1989, 1577 U.N.T.S. 3, art. 31.

104 *We can commit ourselves* Gopnik, *The Gardener and the Carpenter*, 176.

105 *But in all the euphoria* NIH/Eunice Kennedy Shriver National Institute of

Child Health and Human Development, "Teen Crash Risk Highest During First Three Months After Getting Driver's License," *ScienceDaily,* July 10, 2018, https://www.sciencedaily.com/releases/2018/07/180710072026.htm; Pnina Gershon et al., "Crash Risk and Risky Driving Behavior Among Adolescents During Learner and Independent Driving Periods," *Journal of Adolescent Health: Official Publication of the Society for Adolescent Medicine* 63, no. 5 (Nov. 2018): 568–74.

105 *And simply raising* Gopnik, *The Gardener and the Carpenter,* 209.

105 *Gradually phasing out* NIH/Eunice Kennedy Shriver National Institute of Child Health and Human Development, "Teen Crash Risk"; Gershon et al., "Crash Risk."

5. Late Adolescence: The Right to Be Heard

106 *Wylie had worn* Wylie, interview by author, Sept. 26, 2018.

106 *He had added buttons* Wylie, interview.

106 *As a junior* Wylie, interview.

106 *He'd begun* Wylie, interview.

106 *He'd sought* Wylie, interview.

106 *But the most defining* Wylie, interview.

106 *Forty-nine people lost* Kayla Cockrel, "The Lives Lost or Changed Forever in the Pulse Nightclub Attack," *New York Times,* June 12, 2018; Tim Fitzsimons, "What Really Happened That Night at Pulse," NBC News, June 12, 2018, https://www.nbcnews.com/feature/nbc-out/what-really-happened-night-pulse-n882571.

106 *"I'm gay"* Wylie, interview.

106 *The vacuous* Wylie, interview.

106 *The Parkland massacre* Wylie, interview.

106 *Another Floridian* Margaret Kramer and Jennifer Harlan, "Parkland Shooting: Where Gun Control and School Safety Stand Today," *New York Times,* Feb. 13, 2019; Emily Shapiro et al., "Parkland School Shooting 4 Years Later: Remembering the 17 Victims," ABC News, Feb. 14, 2021, https://abcnews.go.com/US/teacher-coach14-year-freshman-florida-high-school-massacre/story?id=53092879.

106 *The "paranoia and fear"* Wylie, interview.

107 *As Wylie suddenly understood* Wylie, interview.

107 *Wylie had hoped* Wylie, interview.

107 *It was a month* Wylie, interview; Tat Bellamy-Walker, "Teens Get 'Corporal Punishment' in Rural Arkansas for Participating in Student Walkout," *Daily Beast,* Mar. 15, 2018, https://www.thedailybeast.com/teens-face-corporal-punishment-in-rural-arkansas-for-participating-in-student-walkout.

107 *He was watching* Wylie, interview; Bellamy-Walker, "Teens Get 'Corporal Punishment.'"

107 *That's when students* Wylie, interview; Vivian Yee and Alan Blinder, "National School Walkout: Thousands Protest Against Gun Violence Across the U.S.," *New York Times,* Mar. 14, 2018.

107   *When time* Wylie, interview.

107   *The rest* Wylie, interview.

107   *One kid said* Wylie, interview.

107   *Wylie said* Wylie, interview.

107   *When he got outside* Wylie, interview.

107   *That, he said* Wylie, interview.

107   *Wylie's hometown* Wylie, interview; Christina Zdanowicz and Ralph Ellis, "Arkansas Student Says He Was Paddled for Gun Control Walkout," CNN, Mar. 17, 2018, https://www.cnn.com/2018/03/17/us/paddling -for-student-protester/index.html.

107   *You head in* Wylie, interview; Satellite view of Greenbrier, Arkansas, Google Maps, accessed Sept. 26, 2021.

107   *It's a tight-knit community* Wylie, interview.

107   *A large American flag* Satellite view of Greenbrier, Arkansas.

107   *A smaller one* Satellite view of Greenbrier, Arkansas.

107   *When the Panthers play* Wylie, interview; Zdanowicz and Ellis, "Arkansas Student."

107   *And, so, it was* Wylie, interview; Satellite view of Greenbrier, Arkansas.

107   *Two police trucks* Wylie, interview.

107   *"We couldn't see"* Wylie, interview.

107   *The boys wondered* Wylie, interview.

107   *But it was the principal* Wylie, interview.

107   *"Boys, what are you doing?"* Wylie, interview.

107   *He warned* Wylie, interview.

107   *Wylie explained* Wylie, interview.

107   *The principal was exasperated* Wylie, interview.

108   *The other students* Wylie, interview.

108   *Wylie was volunteering* Wylie, interview.

108   *The boys were called* Wylie, interview.

108   *To his surprise* Wylie, interview.

108   *Under Greenbrier Public School policy* Bellamy-Walker, "Teens Get 'Corporal Punishment'"; Greenbrier Public Schools, "4.39—Corporal Punishment," in *Student Policies, 2017–2018* (2018), 29, https://s3.amazonaws .com/scschoolfiles/1314/district_student_policy_book_2017-2018.pdf.

108   *Wylie didn't hesitate* Wylie, interview.

108   *It seemed "nobler"* Wylie, interview.

108   *The other boys* Wylie, interview.

108   *Seventeen-year-old Wylie* Wylie, interview.

108   *Wylie describes* Wylie, interview.

108   *It's "all marked up"* Wylie, interview.

108   *There's a ritual* Wylie, interview.

108   *After the dean* Wylie, interview.

108   *Wylie put his hands* Wylie, interview.

108   *Wylie doesn't suppose* Wylie, interview.

108   *Rumors circulated* Cleve R. Wootson, Jr., "NRA Host Taunts Parkland Teens: 'No One Would Know Your Names' If Classmates Were Still Alive," *Washington Post,* Mar. 24, 2018; Mari Uyehara, "The Sliming of David Hogg and Emma Gonzalez," *GQ,* Mar. 30, 2018.

109   *When David* Rebekah Baker, "Flashback: James Woods Points Out Problem with the Hogg Siblings' Twitter Picture," *Western Journal,* Mar. 12, 2018.

109   *Never mind that the actual* Baker, "Flashback"; Bianca Sánchez, "The Young Anti-War Activists Who Fought for Free Speech at School," *Smithsonian Magazine,* Jan. 23, 2019.

109   *Never mind that David* Baker, "Flashback"; Lauren Hogg (@lauren_hoggs), "Inspired by the Supreme Court Landmark case Tinker vs Des Moines I'm starting #armbandsforchange. Make your own and wear it to school or work to protest gun violence," Twitter, Mar. 10, 2018.

109   *According to the conservative* Rebecca Savransky, "Erick Erickson: Florida Shooting Survivor Is 'a High School Bully,'" *The Hill,* Feb. 26, 2018, https://thehill.com/blogs/blog-briefing-room/news/375595-erick -erickson-florida-shooting-survivor-is-a-high-school-bully; Joe Difazio, "Conservative Commentator Erick Erickson Calls Florida Shooting Survivor David Hogg 'a Bully,'" *Newsweek,* Feb. 26, 2018.

109   *As Erickson concluded* Savransky, "Erick Erickson"; Difazio, "Conservative Commentator."

109   *Bill O'Reilly offered* Josh Delk, "O'Reilly Questions If Media Should Interview Fla. Shooting Survivors 'Who Are in an Emotional State,'" *The Hill,* Feb. 20, 2018, https://thehill.com/blogs/blog-briefing-room/374656 -oreilly-questions-media-interviews-with-fla-shooting-survivors-who.

109   *As Parkland students* Andrew Wyrich, "Fox News Host Asks Parents How They'd Feel If Their Kids 'Lectured' a Senator—and Got Completely Owned," *Daily Dot,* Feb. 22, 2018, https://www.dailydot.com/debug /todd-starnes-parents-senators-tweet/.

109   *Emma González came off* Emily Witt, "How the Survivors of Parkland Began the Never Again Movement," *New Yorker,* Feb. 19, 2018; CNN, "Florida Student to NRA and Trump: 'We Call BS,'" YouTube, Feb. 17, 2018, https://www.youtube.com/watch?v=ZxD3o-9H1lY.

109   *On television* Benjamin Hart, "The Parkland Teens Are Winning the Culture War," *Intelligencer,* Mar. 31, 2018; Charlotte Alter, "How Parkland Students Are Taking on Politicians in the Gun Control Battle," *Time,* Mar. 22, 2018; Witt, "How the Survivors."

109   *In conversation, Wylie* Wylie, interview; Bellamy-Walker, "Teens Get 'Corporal Punishment.'"

110   *As he explained* Wylie, interview.

110   *One of the most remarkable things* Witt, "How the Survivors"; Margaret Talbot, "The Extraordinary Inclusiveness of the March for Our Lives," *New Yorker,* Mar. 24, 2018.

110   *Hundreds of thousands* Emily Witt, "From Parkland to Sunrise: A Year of Extraordinary Youth Activism," *New Yorker,* Feb. 13, 2019.

110   *The march* Witt, "From Parkland."

110   *Alongside David Hogg* Talbot, "The Extraordinary Inclusiveness"; Los Angeles Times Staff, "Six of the Most Powerful Young Speakers at March for Our Lives," *Los Angeles Times,* Mar. 24, 2018; NBC News, "11-Year-Old Naomi Wadler's Speech at the March for Our Lives (Full)," YouTube, Mar. 24, 2018, https://www.youtube.com/watch?v=C5ZUDImTIQ8; Community Coalition, "Edna Chavez—March for Our Lives (Full Speech),"

YouTube, Mar. 28, 2018, https://www.youtube.com/watch?v=BinNv KznltA.

110 *"I learned to duck"* Los Angeles Times Staff, "Six of the Most"; Community Coalition, "Edna Chavez."

110 *She asked the crowd* Los Angeles Times Staff, "Six of the Most"; Community Coalition, "Edna Chavez."

110 *In the weeks* See, e.g., Noah Weiland, "At Rallies, Students with a Different View of Gun Violence: As Urban Reality," *New York Times,* Mar. 25, 2018; Quinn Myers, "'Love March' Showcases 'Black Joy' on Chicago's West Side," WTTW News, July 25, 2020, https://news.wttw.com/2020/07/25 /love-march-showcases-black-joy-chicagos-west-side; Ronishlla Maharaj, "Richmond High School Students Speak Out about Protests and Police Brutality," *EdSource,* June 11, 2020, https://edsource.org/2020/richmond -high-school-students-speak-out-about-protests-and-police-brutality /633323.

110 *In Florida* Patricia Mazzei, "Tired of Gang Violence, Students Walked Out of Class. Even That Was Dangerous," *New York Times,* May 3, 2018.

110 *As Ricky Pope, a junior* Mazzei, "Tired of Gang Violence."

110 *In Nashville* Margaret Renkl, "These Kids Are Done Waiting for Change," *New York Times,* June 15, 2020.

111 *"No justice, no peace"* Renkl, "These Kids Are Done"; Natalie Neysa Alund, Brinley Hineman, and Adam Tamburin, "Teenagers Join Pantheon of Nashville Youth Who Harnessed Peaceful Protests to Urge Change," *Tennessean,* June 5, 2020.

111 *"Change is coming"* Alund, Hineman, and Tamburin, "Teenagers Join Pantheon."

111 *These broad efforts* Matt Vasilogambros, "After Parkland, States Pass 50 New Gun-Control Laws," *Stateline,* Aug. 2, 2018, https://pew.org/2MaUDLp.

111 *In the first six months* Vasilogambros, "After Parkland."

111 *For the first time* Catie Edmondson, "House Passes First Major Gun Control Law in Decades," *New York Times,* Feb. 27, 2019.

111 *And lawmakers* Tim Mak, "NRA Facing Most Formidable Opposition Yet, a Year After Parkland," NPR, Feb. 14, 2019, https://www.npr.org/2019/02 /14/693929383/nra-facing-most-formidable-opposition-yet-a-year-after -parkland; Juana Summers, "House Passes Bills to Strengthen Gun Laws, Including Expanding Background Checks," NPR, Mar. 11, 2021, https:// www.npr.org/2021/03/11/976000003/house-passes-bills-to-strengthen -gun-laws-including-expanding-background-checks.

111 *Youth protests* Karina Zaiets, Janie Haseman, and Jennifer Borresen, "Cities and States Across the US Announce Police Reform Following Demands for Change," *USA Today,* June 19, 2020; Orion Rummler, "The Major Police Reforms Enacted Since George Floyd's Death," *Axios,* Oct. 1, 2020, https://www.axios.com/police-reform-george-floyd-protest-2150b2dd -a6dc-4a0c-a1fb-62c2e999a03a.html.

111 *Young environmental activists* Helen Clark et al., "A Future for the World's Children? A WHO–UNICEF–Lancet Commission," *Lancet* 395, no. 10224 (Feb. 2020): 645; Charlotte Alter, Suyin Haynes, and Justin Worland, "Greta Thunberg Is TIME's 2019 Person of the Year," *Time,* Dec. 11, 2019; The

Canadian Press, "Canadian Indigenous Water Activist Autumn Peltier Addresses UN on Clean Water," CBC, Sept. 28, 2019, https://www.cbc.ca/news/world/canadian-indigenous-water-activist-autumn-peltier-addresses-un-on-clean-water-1.5301559.

111 *Youth movements* Clark et al., "A Future for the World's Children?" 618; Samira Sadeque, "Angered by Traffic Deaths, Students Began to Direct Traffic in Bangladesh," NPR, Aug. 7, 2018, https://www.npr.org/sections/goatsandsoda/2018/08/07/635981133/angered-by-traffic-deaths-students-began-to-direct-traffic-in-bangladesh; Global Nonviolent Action Database, Swarthmore College, "Chilean Students Protest for Free Public Education, 2011–13," Mar. 2011, https://nvdatabase.swarthmore.edu/content/chilean-students-protest-free-public-education-2011-13; Cristián Bellei and Cristian Cabalin, "Chilean Student Movements: Sustained Struggle to Transform a Market-Oriented Educational System," *Current Issues in Comparative Education* 15, no. 2 (Spring 2013): 108–23.

111 *Argentinian vice president* Mariela Daby and Mason Moseley, "Argentina Is About to Debate Legalizing Abortion—Despite Being a Very Catholic Country," *Washington Post*, Mar. 6, 2020.

111 *Look back through history* Maggie Astor, "7 Times in History When Students Turned to Activism," *New York Times*, Mar. 5, 2018; Jon Grinspan, *The Virgin Vote: How Young Americans Made Democracy Social, Politics Personal, and Voting Popular in the Nineteenth Century* (Chapel Hill: University of North Carolina Press, 2016); Enrique Krauze, "I Was Part of the Student Movement of '68. We Paid for Freedom with Our Lives," *New York Times*, Oct. 1, 2018.

111 *The members of the Greensboro Four* Astor, "7 Times in History."

112 *A year later* Maurice Berger, "50 Years After Their Mug Shots, Portraits of Mississippi's Freedom Riders," *New York Times*, May 15, 2018.

112 *Mary Beth Tinker* Mary Beth Tinker, interview by author, Aug. 7, 2018; Bianca Sánchez, "The Young Anti-War Activists Who Fought for Free Speech at School," *Smithsonian Magazine*, Jan. 23, 2019.

112 *As she recalls* Tinker, interview.

112 *When I spoke* Tinker, interview.

112 *In 2019* Lois Beckett, "'You Didn't Vote for Me': Senator Dianne Feinstein Responds to Young Green Activists," *Guardian*, Feb. 23, 2019.

112 *When sixteen-year-old* Beckett, "'You Didn't Vote'"; Ashley Boucher, "'We're the Ones Affected': Teen Climate Activist on Her Viral Clash with US Senator," *Guardian*, Feb. 28, 2019.

112 *By his mid-teens* Benjamin Brown Foster, *Down East Diary*, ed. Charles H. Foster (Orono: University of Maine at Orono Press, 1975), 31.

113 *But, as he recorded* Foster, *Down East Diary*, 140–41.

113 *And, so it was* Foster, *Down East Diary*, 141.

113 *As Susan B. Anthony* Daniel Nichanian, "The Case for Allowing Felons to Vote," *New York Times*, Feb. 22, 2018.

113 *"[B]aby boomers"* Jon Kelly, "Brexit: How Much of a Generation Gap Is There?" *BBC News Magazine*, June 24, 2016, https://www.bbc.com/news/magazine-36619342.

113 *On June 23, 2016* Kelly, "Brexit."

113 *And nineteen-year-old* Kelly, "Brexit."

113 *As she told the BBC* Kelly, "Brexit."

113 *Elizabeth, a Staffordshire University student* Kelly, "Brexit."

113 *As a member of the EU* Henry Saker-Clark, "From Jobs to Travel and Study: How Would Brexit Affect Young Britons?" *Guardian*, June 22, 2016.

113 *On a whim* Saker-Clark, "From Jobs to Travel."

113 *She could walk* Saker-Clark, "From Jobs to Travel."

113 *She could take up* Saker-Clark, "From Jobs to Travel."

113 *And as she moved* Saker-Clark, "From Jobs to Travel."

113 *Elizabeth wasn't wrong* Kelly, "Brexit."

114 *Sixty percent* Kelly, "Brexit."

114 *By contrast* Kelly, "Brexit."

114 *They could cheer* NPR Staff, "5 Changes That Could Come from Leaving the Paris Climate Deal," NPR, June 1, 2017, https://www.npr.org/2017/06/01/531056661/5-things-that-could-change-when-the-u-s-leaves-the-paris-climate-deal.

114 *Senator Feinstein's* Beckett, "'You Didn't Vote.'"

114 *It is revealing* Joshua Gans, "Why It's Time to Give Children the Right to Vote," *Forbes*, Apr. 20, 2012.

114 *As one pamphlet* National Association Opposed to Woman Suffrage, *Household Hints* (New York: 1911), available at Jewish Women's Archive, https://jwa.org/media/pamphlet-distributed-by-national-association-opposed-to-woman-suffrage.

115 *"You do not need"* National Association Opposed to Woman Suffrage, *Household Hints*.

115 *California state senator* Constitutional Amendment No. 8 of 1911: Argument Against Senate Constitutional Amendment No. 8 (1911) (statement of JB Sanford, Senator, Chairman of Democratic Caucus), https://sfpl.org/pdf/libraries/main/sfhistory/suffrageagainst.pdf.

115 *Today, the biggest objection* Gans, "Why It's Time."

115 *Once a person reaches* Laurence Steinberg and Elizabeth Scott, "Less Guilty by Reason of Adolescence: Developmental Immaturity, Diminished Responsibility and the Juvenile Death Penalty," *American Psychologist* 58, no. 12 (Dec. 2003): 1011; Vivian E. Hamilton, "Democratic Inclusion, Cognitive Development, and the Age of Electoral Majority," *Brooklyn Law Review* 77, no. 4 (2012): 1447, 1504–10; Joshua A. Douglas, "In Defense of Lowering the Voting Age," *University of Pennsylvania Law Review Online* 165 (Jan. 24, 2017): 69–71; Laurence Steinberg, "Why We Should Lower the Voting Age to 16," *New York Times*, Mar. 2, 2018.

115 *In the voting booth* Laurence Steinberg, "Adolescent Development and Juvenile Justice," *Annual Review of Clinical Psychology* 5, no. 1 (Apr. 27, 2009): 467; Steinberg, "Why We Should Lower."

115 *It's not that once people* Steinberg, "Why We Should Lower."

115 *And neuroimaging studies* Steinberg, "Why We Should Lower"; Steinberg, "Adolescent Development."

115 *Well, these late-blooming* Steinberg, "Why We Should Lower."

115 *In such a "hot" state* Steinberg, "Why We Should Lower."

116 *As we've already discussed* Steinberg, "Adolescent Development," 470–71.

116 *This account* Steinberg, "Why We Should Lower."

116 *It is entirely consistent* Steinberg, "Adolescent Development," 477; Laurence Steinberg et al., "Are Adolescents Less Mature Than Adults? Minors' Access to Abortion, the Juvenile Death Penalty, and the Alleged APA 'Flip-Flop,'" *American Psychologist* 64, no. 7 (2009): 583–94.

116 *Many existing voters* Charles P. Sabatino and Sally Hurme, "Who Has the Capacity to Vote," *Experience* 19, no. 1 (2009): 23–24.

116 *Many others* Pamela S. Karlan, "Framing the Voting Rights Claims of Cognitively Impaired Individuals," *McGeorge Law Review* 38, no. 4 (2016): 917; Rebecca Wiseman, "So You Want to Stay a Judge: Name and Politics of the Moment May Decide Your Future," *Journal of Law & Politics* 18, no. 3 (2002): 663–64; Gordon Patzer, "Marketing U.S. Presidential Candidates: Height Matters," *American Society of Business and Behavioral Sciences* 19, no.1 (Feb. 2012): 693; Jon A. Krosnick, "In the Voting Booth, Bias Starts at the Top," *New York Times*, Nov. 4, 2006; Emma Roller, "What Voters Want," *New York Times*, Jan. 26, 2016.

116 *One in three* Annenberg Public Policy Center, "Americans Are Poorly Informed About Basic Constitutional Provisions," The Annenberg Public Policy Center of the University of Pennsylvania, Sept. 12, 2017, https://www.annenbergpublicpolicycenter.org/americans-are-poorly-informed-about-basic-constitutional-provisions/.

116 *Just one in four* Annenberg Public Policy Center, "Americans Are Poorly Informed."

116 *To remain enfranchised* Jennifer Mathis, "Voting Rights of Older Adults with Cognitive Impairments," *Clearinghouse Review* 42, no. 3 (Sept.–Oct. 2008): 293–94; Sally Balch Hurme and Paul S. Appelbaum, "Defining and Assessing Capacity to Vote: The Effect of Mental Impairment on the Rights of Voters," *McGeorge Law Review* 38, no. 4 (Jan. 2006): 961, 964–65.

116 *A ninety-five-year-old* Hurme and Appelbaum, "Defining and Assessing Capacity," 933, 960.

116 *He may struggle* Hurme and Appelbaum, "Defining and Assessing Capacity," 958–59.

117 *How we should* Gans, "Why It's Time."

117 *Contrast their experiences* Hansi Lo Wang, "Generation Z Is the Most Racially and Ethnically Diverse Yet," NPR, Nov. 15, 2018, https://www.npr.org/2018/11/15/668106376/generation-z-is-the-most-racially-and-ethnically-diverse-yet; Dan Levin, "Generation Z: Who They Are, in Their Own Words," *New York Times*, Mar. 28, 2019.

117 *Ninety-four percent of children* Cecilia Kang, "In Protests of Net Neutrality Repeal, Teenage Voices Stood Out," *New York Times*, Dec. 20, 2017; Amanda Lenhart et al., "Instagram and Snapchat Are Most Popular Social Networks for Teens; Black Teens Are Most Active on Social Media, Messaging Apps," Associated Press–NORC Center for Public Affairs Research, Apr. 2017, https://apnorc.org/projects/instagram-and-snapchat-are-most-popular-social-networks-for-teens-black-teens-are-most-active-on-social-media-messaging-apps/.

117 *So, when the FCC* Cecilia Kang, "In Protests of Net Neutrality Repeal, Teenage Voices Stood Out," *New York Times*, Dec. 20, 2017; Meg McIntyre

Sentinel Staff, "Local High School Students Protest Proposed Rollback of Net Neutrality Rules," SentinelSource.com, Dec. 8, 2017, https://www.sentinelsource.com/news/local/local-high-school-students-protest-proposed-rollback-of-net-neutrality-rules/article_204cec19-3104-58f4-930a-404c65d84e65.html; Patrick Anderson, "Net Neutrality Protest Reaches Sioux Falls, Lincoln Student Takes on the FCC," *Argus Leader,* Dec. 7, 2017.

117 *Maria, a high school sophomore* Maria, interview by author, Sept. 5, 2018.

117 *But Maria knows* Maria, interview.

117 *They'd practiced* Maria, interview.

117 *"You're not supposed to text"* Maria, interview.

118 *When I asked* Andre, interview by author, Aug. 10, 2018.

118 *And while he acknowledged* Andre, interview.

118 *Speaking with him* Andre, interview.

118 *The oft-cited proof* Jewel Jordan, "2020 Presidential Election Voting and Registration Tables Now Available," United States Census Bureau, Apr. 29, 2021, https://www.census.gov/newsroom/press-releases/2021/2020-presidential-election-voting-and-registration-tables-now-available.html.

118 *Eighteen, for example* Zachary Crockett, "The Case for Allowing 16-Year-Olds to Vote," *Vox,* Nov. 7, 2016, https://www.vox.com/policy-and-politics/2016/11/7/13347080/voting-age-election-16; Douglas, "In Defense of Lowering," 67.

118 *If you want more* Douglas, "In Defense of Lowering," 67; Eric Plutzer, "Becoming a Habitual Voter: Inertia, Resources, and Growth in Young Adulthood," *American Political Science Review* 96, no. 1 (Mar. 2002): 41–56; Joshua Douglas, "Parkland Students Show Why 16-Year-Olds Should Be Able to Vote," CNN, Feb. 20, 2018, https://www.cnn.com/2018/02/19/opinions/parkland-shooting-voting-age-opinion-douglas/index.html; Crockett, "The Case for Allowing"; Alexander Coppock and Donald P. Green, "Is Voting Habit Forming? New Evidence from Experiments and Regression Discontinuities," *American Journal of Political Science* 60, no. 4 (2016): 1044, 1060; Alan S. Gerber, Donald P. Green, and Ron Shachar, "Voting May Be Habit-Forming: Evidence from a Randomized Field Experiment," *American Journal of Political Science* 47, no. 3 (2003): 540, 545–48.

118 *Instead, since 2020* Farah Stockman, "How College Campuses Are Trying to Tap Students' Voting Power," *New York Times,* Mar. 3, 2018; David Bornstein, "Getting Student Power into the Voting Booth," *New York Times,* July 4, 2018; Stuart Baum, Brianna Cea, and Alex Cohen, "The 26th Amendment Turns 50 Amid Renewed Voter Suppression," Brennan Center for Justice, June 30, 2021, https://www.brennancenter.org/our-work/analysis-opinion/26th-amendment-turns-50-amid-renewed-voter-suppression.

118 *Young people* Pew Research Center, "Climate Change and Energy: Public Opinions and Views," in *Americans, Politics and Science Issues,* July 1, 2015, https://www.pewresearch.org/science/2015/07/01/chapter-2-climate-change-and-energy-issues/; Frank Newport, "Americans Continue to Say U.S. Wealth Distribution Is Unfair," Gallup, May 4, 2015, https://news.gallup.com/poll/182987/americans-continue-say-wealth-distribution-unfair.aspx.

119 *While 60 percent* Pew Research Center, "Climate Change and Energy."

119 *Likewise, 59 percent* Newport, "Americans Continue to Say."

119 *But it's not simply* Dan Kahan, "How Age and Political Outlooks Interact in Formation of Policy Positions," The Cultural Cognition Project at Yale University, July 26, 2017; Drew DeSilver, "The Politics of American Generations: How Age Affects Attitudes and Voting Behavior," Pew Research Center, July 9, 2014, https://www.pewresearch.org/fact-tank/2014/07/09/the-politics-of-american-generations-how-age-affects-attitudes-and-voting-behavior/; Ilse Cornelis et al., "Age Differences in Conservatism: Evidence on the Mediating Effects of Personality and Cognitive Style," *Journal of Personality* 77, no. 1 (Dec. 29, 2008): 51–88.

119 *So, if you are sixty-five* Kahan, "How Age."

119 *There was a 26 percent gap* Roper Center for Public Opinion Research, "How Groups Voted in 2016," Cornell University, 2016, https://ropercenter.cornell.edu/how-groups-voted-2016.

119 *In the 2018 midterms* K. K. Rebecca Lai and Allison McCann, "Exit Polls: How Voting Blocs Have Shifted from the '80s to Now," *New York Times,* Nov. 7, 2018.

119 *Consistent with all of this* Gans, "Why It's Time."

119 *In the vote* Emma Langman, "Scottish Independence: Research Finds Young Voters 'Don't Copy Parents,'" BBC Scotland News, Mar. 4, 2014, https://www.bbc.com/news/uk-scotland-scotland-politics-26265299.

119 *As Tyler* Tyler, interview by author, Aug. 14, 2018.

119 *He notes* Tyler, interview.

120 *One of the major insights* Adam Benforado and Jon Hanson, "Naive Cynicism: Maintaining False Perceptions in Policy Debates," *Emory Law Journal* 57, no. 3 (2008): 513–14; Lee Ross and Andrew Ward, "Naive Realism in Everyday Life: Implications for Social Conflict and Misunderstanding," in *Values and Knowledge,* ed. Edward S. Reed, Elliot Turiel, and Terrance Brown (New York: Psychology Press, 1996), 103, 106–8.

120 *When they don't* Benforado and Hanson, "Naive Cynicism," 525–33; Ross and Ward, "Naive Realism in Everyday Life," 103, 106–8; Emily Pronin, Carolyn Puccio, and Lee Ross, "Understanding Misunderstanding: Social Psychological Perspectives," in *Heuristics and Biases: The Psychology of Intuitive Judgment,* ed. Thomas Gilovich, Dale Griffin, and Daniel Kahneman (Cambridge: Cambridge University Press, 2002), 647–48.

120 *It's driven* William H. Frey, "Diversity Defines the Millennial Generation," Brookings, June 28, 2016, https://www.brookings.edu/blog/the-avenue/2016/06/28/diversity-defines-the-millennial-generation/; Pew Research Center's Religion & Public Life Project, *Religion in America: U.S. Religious Data, Demographics and Statistics,* Religious Landscape Study at Pew Research Center, 2014, https://www.pewforum.org/religious-landscape-study/.

120 *Research shows* Jonathan J. Rolison et al., "Risk-Taking Differences Across the Adult Life Span: A Question of Age and Domain," *Journals of Gerontology: Series B* 69, no. 6 (Nov. 2014): 870–80; Steven M. Albert and John Duffy, "Differences in Risk Aversion Between Young and Older Adults," *Neuroscience and Neuroeconomics* 2012, no. 1 (Jan. 15, 2012): 7; Nancy

Ammon Jianakoplos and Alexandra Bernasek, "Financial Risk Taking by Age and Birth Cohort," *Southern Economic Journal* 72, no. 4 (2006): 999.

120 *This increased cautiousness* Rolison et al., "Risk-Taking Differences," 870; Mara Mather, "A Review of Decision-Making Processes: Weighing the Risks and Benefits of Aging," in *When I'm 64*, ed. Laura L. Carstensen and Christine R. Hartel (Washington, D.C.: National Academies Press, 2006); Nigel Nicholson et al., "Personality and Domain-Specific Risk Taking," *Journal of Risk Research* 8, no. 2 (Mar. 1, 2005): 157–76; Michael A. Wallach and Nathan Kogan, "Aspects of Judgment and Decision Making: Interrelationships and Changes with Age," *Behavioral Science* 6, no. 1 (1961): 23–36.

120 *Part of the reason* Ian Sample, "Risk Aversion in Old Age Down to Changes in Brain Structure, Scans Suggest," *Guardian*, Dec. 13, 2016; Sharon Gilaie-Dotan et al., "Neuroanatomy Predicts Individual Risk Attitudes," *Journal of Neuroscience* 34, no. 37 (Sept. 10, 2014): 12394–401; Naftali Raz and Karen M. Rodrigue, "Differential Aging of the Brain: Patterns, Cognitive Correlates and Modifiers," *Neuroscience and Biobehavioral Reviews* 30, no. 6 (Jan. 2006): 730–48.

120 *Other studies have linked* Robert Glatter, "Why Older People Take Fewer Risks," *Forbes*, June 6, 2016; Robb B. Rutledge et al., "Risk Taking for Potential Reward Decreases Across the Lifespan," *Current Biology* 26, no. 12 (June 2016): 1634–39; Jennifer R. St. Onge and Stan B. Floresco, "Dopaminergic Modulation of Risk-Based Decision Making," *Neuropsychopharmacology* 34, no. 3 (Feb. 2009): 681–97.

121 *When it comes* David L. Eckles et al., "Risk Attitudes and the Incumbency Advantage," *Political Behavior* 36, no. 4 (Dec. 2014): 734; A. V. Muthukrishnan, "Decision Ambiguity and Incumbent Brand Advantage," *Journal of Consumer Research* 22 (June 1, 1995): 98–109; James N. Druckman, Martin J. Kifer, and Michael Parkin, "Campaign Communications in U.S. Congressional Elections," *American Political Science Review* 103, no. 3 (Aug. 2009): 343–66.

121 *And this irrational privileging* Eckles et al., "Risk Attitudes," 734.

121 *In an era* Eckles et al., "Risk Attitudes," 734.

121 *Andre was quick* Andre, interview.

121 *As he points out* Andre, interview.

121 *"Why do we have"* Andre, interview.

121 *Today, a sixteen-year-old* John Nichols, "Lower the Voting Age to 16," *Nation*, Feb. 23, 2018; *Voting Age Status Report*, National Youth Rights Association, accessed Oct. 21, 2021, https://www.youthrights.org/issues/voting-age/voting-age-status-report/.

121 *And, as predicted* Steinberg, "Why We Should Lower"; Crockett, "The Case for Allowing."

121 *When Scotland lowered* Andy McSmith, "Scottish Referendum Results: Huge Turnout Bolsters Case for Voting at 16," *Independent*, Oct. 6, 2015.

121 *As Tommy Raskin* Lindsay A. Powers, "Takoma Park Grants 16-Year-Olds Right to Vote," *Washington Post*, May 14, 2013. Tommy, the son of Congressman Jamie Raskin, was a model of youth activism, working to combat injustice, until his life was tragically cut short by depression.

121 *Four other municipalities* Alan Greenblatt, "Maryland Suburb Says 16 Is

Old Enough to Vote," NPR, May 15, 2013, https://www.npr.org/2013/05/15/184243993/maryland-suburb-says-16-is-old-enough-to-vote; "Maryland," Vote16USA, accessed Mar. 20, 2022, https://vote16usa.org/project/maryland/.

122 *And a similar measure* "November 3, 2020 Election Results—Summary," City and County of San Francisco Department of Elections, last modified Dec. 1, 2020, https://sfelections.sfgov.org/november-3-2020-election-results-summary; "Yes on G Earns 49.2% and Looks to the Future," Vote 16SF, Nov. 10, 2020, https://www.vote16sf.com/post/prop-g-final-statement.

122 *Today, the march continues* Hannah Grabenstein, "Should 16-year-olds Be Allowed to Vote?" *PBS NewsHour*, Apr. 20, 2018, https://www.pbs.org/newshour/politics/should-16-year-olds-be-allowed-to-vote; "The Movement to Lower the Voting Age: A History," National Youth Rights Association, accessed Oct. 21, 2021, https://www.youthrights.org/issues/voting-age/history-of-the-movement/; "Primary Voting at Age 17," FairVote, accessed Oct. 21, 2021, http://www.fairvote.org/primary_voting_at_age_17#facts_17_year_old_primary_voting.

122 *At the federal level* Maggie Astor, "16-year-olds Want a Vote. Fifty Years Ago, So Did 18-year-olds," *New York Times*, May 19, 2019; Siobhan Hughes, "House Defeats Effort to Expand Voting to 16-year-olds," *Wall Street Journal*, Mar. 3, 2021.

122 *In March 2021* Hughes, "House Defeats Effort."

122 *States and localities* Grabenstein, "Should 16-year-olds"; Douglas, "In Defense of Lowering," 66; Joshua A. Douglas, "The Right to Vote Under Local Law," *George Washington Law Review* 85, no. 4 (2017): 1039–111.

122 *Over the last century* Paul Demeny, "Pronatalist Policies in Low-Fertility Countries: Patterns, Performance, and Prospects," *Population and Development Review* 12 (1986): 335–58; Jenny Gesley, "Family Voting as a Solution to Low Fertility? Experiences from France and Germany," In Custodia Legis (blog), Law Library of Congress, April 19, 2018, https://blogs.loc.gov/law/2018/04/family-voting-as-a-solution-to-low-fertility-experiences-from-france-and-germany/; Reiko Aoki and Rhema Vaithianathan, "Is Demeny Voting the Answer to Low Fertility in Japan?" Centre for Intergenerational Studies Discussion Paper No. 435, Institute of Economic Research, Hitotsubashi University (2009); Paul Demeny et al., "Demeny Voting and Its Impact," Centre for Intergenerational Studies Discussion Paper No. 520, Institute of Economic Research, Hitotsubashi University (2011); Leigh Phillips, "Hungarian Mothers May Get Extra Votes for Their Children in Elections," *Guardian*, Apr. 17, 2011.

122 *As Andre pointed out* Andre, interview.

123 *The proposal introduced* John Wall, "Why Children and Youth Should Have the Right to Vote: An Argument for Proxy-Claim Suffrage," *Children, Youth, and Environments* 24, no. 1 (2014): 119.

123 *Others have suggested* Wall, "Why Children," 118–19.

123 *One of the most* Phillips, "Hungarian Mothers."

123 *The Americans with Disabilities Act* Jennifer Mathis, "Voting Rights of Older

Notes | 285

Adults with Cognitive Impairments," *Clearinghouse Review Journal of Poverty Law and Policy* 42, no. 5–6 (Sept.–Oct. 2008): 299; Pamela S. Karlan, "Framing the Voting Rights Claims of Cognitively Impaired Individuals," *McGeorge Law Review* 38, no. 4 (2017) 923.

124 *If such accommodations* Pendarvis Harsha, "The Passing of Oakland's Measure QQ and the Future of Our Democracy," KQED, Nov. 12, 2020, https://www.kqed.org/arts/13889129/the-passing-of-oaklands-measure-qq-and-the-future-of-our-democracy; Laurence Pevsner, "Let Children Vote. Even 13-year-olds," *Washington Post*, Oct. 27, 2016; Daniel B. Wood, "Should 14-year-olds Vote? OK, How About a Quarter of a Vote?" *The Christian Science Monitor*, Mar. 12, 2004.

124 *California legislators* "The Movement to Lower the Voting Age," National Youth Rights Association.

124 *It was approved* "The Movement to Lower The Voting Age," National Youth Rights Association.

124 *Wylie was firm* Wylie, interview.

124 *Sure, some will be* Wylie, interview.

124 *"If your system fails"* Wylie, interview.

124 *But is it really optimal* Jennifer E. Manning, *Membership of the 116th Congress: A Profile*, Congressional Research Service, Dec. 17, 2020, https://fas.org/sgp/crs/misc/R45583.pdf; Astra Taylor, "Out with the Old, In with the Young," *New York Times*, Oct. 18, 2019.

124 *Are we well served* Alex Pareene, "Congress Needs a Mandatory Retirement Age," *Splinter*, Dec. 21, 2017.

124 *Has it benefited* Niall McCarthy, "Trump Is Set to Become the Oldest President in U.S. History," *Forbes*, Jan. 6, 2017; David Leonhardt, "Life Expectancy Data," *New York Times*, Sept. 27, 2006.

124 *In 2018* Monica Hesse, "Six Teenagers Are Running for Governor in Kansas, and Suddenly This Doesn't Seem So Preposterous," *Washington Post*, Mar. 2, 2018.

125 *So, six teens* Hesse, "Six Teenagers Are Running."

125 *As Monica Hesse* Hesse, "Six Teenagers Are Running."

125 *Legislation was quickly introduced* Amira Vera and Andrea Diaz, "Thanks to a Loophole in Kansas Law, 6 Teens Are Running for Governor," CNN, Feb. 9, 2018, https://www.cnn.com/2018/02/09/politics/kansas-teens-running-for-governor-trnd/index.html.

125 *And the Republican Party of Kansas* Tyler, interview.

125 *But the young candidates* Hesse, "Six Teenagers Are Running."

125 *Democrat Jack Bergeson's* Jack Bergeson, campaign website, last visited Aug. 15, 2018, https://www.jackforkansas.com; "Teens Run for Kansas Governor," *Weekend Edition Sunday*, NPR, Feb. 11, 2018, https://www.npr.org/2018/02/11/584896231/teens-run-for-kansas-governor.

125 *In conversation* Heather Boushey, "Failed Tax-Cut Experiment in Kansas Should Guide National Leaders," *The Hill*, Nov. 29, 2018, https://thehill.com/opinion/finance/418768-kansas-voters-render-final-verdict-on-failed-tax-cut-experiment; Jeremy Hobson, Dean Russell, and Samantha Raphelson, "As Trump Proposes Tax Cuts, Kansas Deals with Aftermath of

Experiment," NPR, Oct. 25, 2017, https://www.npr.org/2017/10/25/560040131/as-trump-proposes-tax-cuts-kansas-deals-with-aftermath-of-experiment.

125 *Brownback had gambled* Cameron Easley, "America's Most and Least Popular Governors," *Morning Consult*, July 18, 2017; Stephen Koranda, "Kansas Governor Ends Tenure as One of Least Popular in Country," NPR, July 27, 2017.

125 *He balanced school* Tyler, interview.

125 *And he'd seen things* Boushey, "Failed Tax-Cut Experiment"; Hobson, Russell, and Raphelson, "As Trump Proposes."

126 *In line with the psychological research* Kahan, "How Age"; Tyler, interview.

126 *As Tyler put it* Tyler, interview.

126 *Tyler admitted* Tyler, interview.

126 *When Tyler appeared* Hesse, "Six Teenagers Are Running."

126 *When she pressed him* Hesse, "Six Teenagers Are Running."

126 *Simple: it's what he believed* Hesse, "Six Teenagers Are Running."

126 *John Adams had it right* John Adams, *Thoughts on Government* (Apr. 1776), in *Papers of John Adams*, vol. 1, ch. 4, ed. Robert J. Taylor, Mary-Jo Kline, and Gregg L. Lint (Cambridge, Mass.: Belknap Press, 1977), 86–93.

126 *The problem* John Seery, *Too Young to Run? A Proposal for an Age Amendment to the U.S. Constitution* (University Park, Pa.: Penn State University Press, 2011); Taylor, "Out with the Old."

127 *In child custody* Rachel Birnbaum et al., "Children's Experiences with Family Justice Professionals in Ontario and Ohio," *International Journal of Law, Policy and the Family* 25, no. 3 (2011): 398–422.

127 *In one multistate survey* Catherine A. Crosby-Currie, "Children's Involvement in Contested Custody Cases: Practices and Experiences of Legal and Mental Health Professionals," *Law and Human Behavior* 20, no. 3 (1996): 289–97.

127 *In another study* Barbara A. Atwood, "The Child's Voice in Custody Litigation: An Empirical Survey and Suggestions for Reform," *Arizona Law Review* 45, no. 3 (2003): 629–90.

127 *As we touched on* Child Welfare Information Gateway, *Consent to Adoption*, U.S. Department of Health and Human Services, Administration for Children and Families, Children's Bureau (2021), 2, https://www.childwelfare.gov/pubpdfs/consent.pdf.

127 *The justifications* Barbara A. Atwood, "The Child's Voice in Custody Litigation: An Empirical Survey and Suggestions for Reform," *Arizona Law Review* 45 (2003): 629–90; Birnbaum et al., "Children's Experiences."

127 *Even young children* Atwood, "The Child's Voice"; Richard Wolman and Keith Taylor, "Psychological Effects of Custody Disputes on Children," *Behavioral Sciences & the Law* 9, no. 4 (Autumn 1991): 399–418.

127 *And they want* Birnbaum et al., "Children's Experiences."

127 *It is painful* Birnbaum et al., "Children's Experiences."

127 *Allowing children to participate* Stephanie Holt, "The Voice of the Child in Family Law: A Discussion Paper," *Children and Youth Services Review* no. 68 (Sept. 2016): 139–45; Atwood, "The Child's Voice"; Wolman and Taylor, "Psychological Effects of Custody."

127 *This is largely* Birnbaum et al., "Children's Experiences"; Nicholas Bala et al. "Rethinking the Role of Lawyers for Children: Child Representation in Canadian Family Relationship Cases," *Cahiers de Droit (Québec)* 59, no. 4 (2018): 787–829; United Nations Convention on the Rights of the Child, Nov. 20, 1989, 1577 U.N.T.S. 3.

127 *And we would do well* Birnbaum et al., "Children's Experiences"; Convention on the Rights of the Child.

127 *A minor* Unif. Probate Code § 2-501 (1969); Lisa Vollendorf Martin, "What's Love Got to Do with It: Securing Access to Justice for Abused Teens," *Catholic University Law Review* 61, no. 2 (Winter 2012): 460–526; Larry Cunningham, "A Question of Capacity: Towards a Comprehensive and Consistent Vision of Children and Their Status Under Law," *UC Davis Journal of Juvenile Law & Policy* 10, no. 2 (Summer 2006): 377; Rhonda Gay Hartman, "Adolescent Autonomy: Clarifying an Ageless Conundrum," *Hastings Law Journal* 51, no. 6 (Aug. 2000): 1305; 42 Am Jur 2d Infants § 148; Jennifer Ann Drobac, "Sex and the Workplace: 'Consenting' Adolescents and a Conflict of Laws," *Washington Law Review* 79, no. 2 (2004): 507.

128 *But, as seventeen-year-old* M.D. v. T.H., No. A-5841-05T1, 2007 N.J. Super. Unpub. LEXIS 277 (N.J. Super. Ct. App. Div. Sep. 10, 2007).

128 *It wasn't M.D.*, 2007 N.J. Super. Unpub. LEXIS 277.

128 *M.D. simply did not have M.D.*, 2007 N.J. Super. Unpub. LEXIS 277.

128 *In New Jersey* M.A. v. E.A., 388 N.J. Super. 612, 909 A.2d 1168 (N.J. Super. Ct. App. Div. 2006); Vollendorf Martin, "What's Love Got to Do with It," 473–74. That said, your mom could get a restraining order if the violence or threats of violence against you were actually meant to terrorize, harass, or coerce her. J.L. v. A.C., 2016 N.J. Super. Unpub. LEXIS 731 (N.J. Super Ct. Ch. Div. Mar. 17, 2016).

128 *When eleven-year-old Sahara* First Amended Complaint at 16-17, 88, 92, Juliana v. United States, 217 F. Supp. 3d 1224 (D. Or. 2016); Juliana v. United States, 947 F.3d 1159, 1164 (9th Cir. 2020); Brady Dennis, "Federal Appeals Court Tosses Landmark Youth Climate Lawsuit Against U.S. Government," *Washington Post,* Jan. 17, 2020.

128 *Sure, they'd Juliana*, 947 F.3d at 1175.

128 *Sahara herself* First Amended Complaint at 16-17.

128 *The efforts Sahara makes* First Amended Complaint at 16.

128 *But, according to the court Juliana*, 947 F. 3d at 1175.

128 *A few recent victories* Ivana Kottasová, "Kids Are Taking Governments to Court Over Climate. And They Are Starting to Win," CNN, May 9, 2021, https://www.cnn.com/2021/05/09/europe/climate-lawsuits-governments-intl-cmd/index.html; Adam Morton, "The Australian Court Finds Government Has Duty to Protect Young People from Climate Crisis," *Guardian,* May 27, 2021.

129 *In 2021* Morton, "The Australian Court Finds"; Sharma by Her Litigation Representative Sister Marie Brigid Arthur v. Minister for the Environment (2021) FCA 560.

129 *But that ruling* Hillary Whiteman, "Australian Court Overturns Teenagers' Landmark Climate Ruling," CNN, Mar. 15, 2022, https://www.cnn.com/2022/03/15/asia/australia-climate-court-appeal-intl-hnk/index.html.

129 *The last ten* Sinéad Baker, "Ruth Bader Ginsburg Celebrates 25 Years in the Supreme Court Today—Here's When She and Her Colleagues Could Retire," *Business Insider*, Aug. 10, 2018, https://www.businessinsider.com /supreme-court-when-ginsberg-other-justices-could-quit-based-on-age -tenure-2018-6; Barry McMillion, *U.S. Circuit and District Court Judges: Profile of Select Characteristics*, Congressional Research Service, Aug. 1, 2017, https://fas.org/sgp/crs/misc/R43426.pdf.

129 *In a recent speech* Eric Holder, "Structure of Federal Courts," C-SPAN, 8:10, Jan. 25, 2021, https://www.c-span.org/video/?508244-1/structure -federal-courts.

129 *In 1975* Taylor v. Louisiana, 419 U.S. 522 (1975).

129 *To apply* Although repeated in *Taylor*, the language comes from Ballard v. United States, 329 U.S. 187 (1946).

129 *Even among adults* Dan M. Kahan, "Culture, Cognition and Consent: Who Perceives What, and Why, in Acquaintance-Rape Cases," *University of Pennsylvania Law Review* 158, no. 729 (2010): 776–77; Dan M. Kahan et al., "Whose Eyes Are You Going to Believe? Scott v. Harris and the Perils of Cognitive Illiberalism," *Harvard Law Review* 122, no. 3 (2009): 867.

130 *The cops* Troy Brown, "Redmond Youth Court Participants Practice Restorative Justice," King County Employees (blog), Feb. 4, 2020, https://kcem ployees.com/2020/02/04/redmond-youth-court-participants-practice -restorative-justice/.

130 *Her headlights* Brown, "Redmond Youth Court."

130 *When they walked up* Brown, "Redmond Youth Court."

130 *Still, they only wrote her up* Brown, "Redmond Youth Court."

130 *In court, though* Brown, "Redmond Youth Court."

130 *Mary's advocate* Brown, "Redmond Youth Court."

130 *It was now left* Brown, "Redmond Youth Court."

130 *In the end* Brown, "Redmond Youth Court."

130 *What was astonishing* Brown, "Redmond Youth Court."

130 *Today, the Redmond Youth Court* Brown, "Redmond Youth Court"; Christina M. Dines, "Minors in the Major Leagues: Youth Courts Hit a Home Run for Juvenile Justice," *Notre Dame Journal of Law, Ethics & Public Policy* 13, no. 1 (2017): 177.

130 *The most ingenious aspect* Gabe Motsinger, "Teen Court Offers Young Misdemeanor Offenders a Path to Redemption," *Sante Fe New Mexican*, Apr. 27, 2017; Tina Rosenberg, "Where Teenagers Find the Jury Isn't Rigged," *New York Times*, Oct. 18, 20211.

130 *As we have discussed* Rosenberg, "Where Teenagers Find"; Katie J. M. Baker, "In Teen Court, Kids Have a Right to a Jury of Their Peers," *BuzzFeed*, Jan. 16, 2015, https://www.buzzfeednews.com/article/katie jmbaker/welcome-to-teen-court#.enPdOPZ8Gv; Jeffrey A. Butts, Janeen Buck, and Mark B. Coggeshall, *The Impact of Teen Court on Young Offenders*, Urban Institute Justice Policy Center (Apr. 2002), https://www.urban .org/sites/default/files/publication/45461/410457-The-Impact-of-Teen -Court-on-Young-Offenders.pdf.

131 *The other notable innovation* Rosenberg, "Where Teenagers Find."

131 *Part of Mary's sentence* Brown, "Redmond Youth Court."

131 *And that experience* Rosenberg, "Where Teenagers Find."

131 *Indeed, those who go through* Rosenberg, "Where Teenagers Find."

131 *At the Newark Youth Court* Center for Court Innovation, *"Welcome to the Newark Youth Court,"* YouTube, Nov. 9, 2018, https://www.youtube.com/watch?v=yirexx-Xfv8&t=1s.

131 *As Tyree* Center for Court Innovation, *Welcome to the Newark Youth Court.*

131 *The rotating group* Brooks Barnes, "PG? NC-17? She Made Such Calls for 30 Years," *New York Times*, Nov. 23, 2018.

131 *In 2021* Spencer Stuart, *2021 U.S. Spencer Stuart Board Index*, Oct. 2021, 5, 9, https://www.spencerstuart.com/-/media/2021/october/ssbi2021/us-spencer-stuart-board-index-2021.pdf.

131 *That ought to concern shareholders* Kenneth MacCrimmon et al., "Characteristics of Risk Taking Executives," *Management Science* 36, no. 4 (1990): 433; Robert Samuelson, "Risk Averse America," *Washington Post*, Oct. 2, 2011.

131 *Indeed, economists have theorized* Norma Cohen, "Ageing Societies Are Becoming More Risk Averse," *Financial Times*, Nov. 17, 2017.

132 *That ended up* Samuelson, "Risk Averse America."

132 *When students* A.C. v. Raimondo, 494 F. Supp. 3d 170, 174-5 (D.R.I. 2020); Valerie Strauss, "Federal Judge Rules Students Have No Constitutional Right to Civics Education—But Warns That 'American Democracy Is in Peril,'" *Washington Post*, Oct. 22, 2020.

132 *But he denied them* A.C., 494 F. Supp. 3d at 175 (D.R.I. 2020); Strauss, "Federal Judge Rules."

132 *It's time* Alina Tugend, "In the Age of Trump, Civics Courses Make a Comeback," *New York Times*, June 5, 2018; Sarah Shapiro and Catherine Brown, "The State of Civics Education," Center for American Progress, Feb. 21, 2018, https://www.americanprogress.org/issues/education-k-12/reports/2018/02/21/446857/state-civics-education/; Ashley Jeffrey and Scott Sargrad, "Strengthening Democracy with a Modern Civics Education," Center for American Progress, Dec. 14, 2019, https://www.americanprogress.org/issues/education-k-12/reports/2019/12/14/478750/strengthening-democracy-modern-civics-education/.

132 *Prompted by the lawsuit* Linda Borg, "General Assembly Passes Civics Education, Black History Curriculum Bills," *Providence Journal*, July 2, 2021; Associated Press, "Rhode Island Passes Civics, Black History Curriculum Bills," AP News, July 2, 2021, https://apnews.com/article/ri-state-wire-rhode-island-race-and-ethnicity-bills-9394efe73110fe040579646db6d8d7e7.

132 *But it's a single course* Borg, "General Assembly Passes"; Associated Press, "Rhode Island Passes."

132 *As Precious Lopez* Linda Borg, "A Bill Would Make Civics Education Mandatory but Some Students Say It Doesn't Go Far Enough," *Providence Journal*, Feb. 2, 2021.

132 *New York's Mamaroneck High* Tugend, "In the Age of Trump."

133 *And at Palo Alto High* Palo Alto High School, "Social Justice Pathway," accessed Mar. 20, 2022, https://www.paly.net/learning/programs-pathways/social-justice-pathway.

133 *A few weeks after* Christina, interview by author, Sept. 7, 2018.

134 *In the first instance* Christina, interview.

134 *She contacted* Christina, interview.

134 *It was what* Christina, interview.

134 *In the second instance* Christina, interview.

134 *They focused on* Christina, interview.

134 *As Christina explains* Christina, interview.

134 *The student reporters* Christina, interview.

134 *On the day of Christina's graduation* Christina, interview.

134 *Their adviser reached out* Christina, interview.

134 *It's upsetting* Christina, interview.

134 *And the adults* Christina, interview.

134 *But we do not protect Christina* Christina, interview.

134 *Christina had her eyes* Christina, interview.

135 *Christina's experience* Christina notes that the newspaper is actually far more independent than most school newspapers, as it is not funded by the school and not censored by the school district. Christina, interview.

135 *If anything* Jaclyn Peiser, "Hard News. Angry Administration. Teenage Journalists Know What It's Like," *New York Times*, July 1, 2018.

135 *The legal ground* Educational Theatre Association, "Recently Banned and Challenged Plays," *EdTA*, Jan. 24, 2016, https://www.schooltheatre.org /advocacy/local/freedomexpression/recentlybannedandchallengedplays; Alyssa Lukpat, "When a Valedictorian Spoke of His Queer Identity, the Principal Cut Off His Speech," *New York Times*, June 28, 2021; Lulabel Seitz, "A Conversation with the Valedictorian Whose Speech Was Censored," interview by Michel Martin, NPR, June 10, 2018, https://www.npr .org/2018/06/10/618738572/a-conversation-with-the-valedictorian -whose-speech-was-censored.

135 *In the middle* Justin Driver, "Do Public School Students Have Constitutional Rights?" *New York Times*, Aug. 31, 2018.

135 *But in recent years* Driver, "Do Public School Students."

135 *Neo-Nazi men* Skokie v. National Socialist Party, 69 Ill. 2d 605 (Ill. 1978); National Socialist Party v. Skokie, 432 U.S. 43 (1977); Morse v. Frederick, 551 U.S. 393, 402 (2007).

135 *The president* New York Times Co. v. United States, 403 U.S. 713 (1971); Hazelwood Sch. Dist. v. Kuhlmeier, 484 U.S. 260, 262 (1988).

135 *In 2021* Mahanoy Area Sch. Dist. v. B.L., 141 U.S. 2038, 2048 (2021); Justin Driver, "A Cheerleader Lands an F on Snapchat, but a B+ in Court," *New York Times*, June 24, 2021; Adam Liptak, "A Cheerleader's Vulgar Message Prompts a First Amendment Showdown," *New York Times*, Dec. 28, 2020.

135 *But the opinion Mahanoy Area Sch. Dist.*, 141 U.S. at 2048; Driver, "A Cheerleader Lands"; Liptak, "A Cheerleader's Vulgar Message."

135 *According to the court Mahanoy Area Sch. Dist.*, 141 U.S. at 2046.

136 *Censors have gotten Hazelwood Sch. Dist.*, 484 U.S. at 271; Jaclyn Peiser, "Hard News. Angry Administration. Teenage Journalists Know What It's Like," *New York Times*, July 1, 2018.

136 *Who gets to decide* Peiser, "Hard News."

136 *She would focus* Maria, interview.

136   If "America's public schools" Mahanoy Area Sch. Dist., 141 U.S. at 2046. Article 12 of the UN's Convention on the Rights of the Child echoes this sentiment: even very young children are capable of having opinions and they ought to have a right not only to express those opinions but also to have those views given serious weight. Gerison Lansdown, Shane R. Jimerson, and Reza Shahroozi, "Children's Rights and School Psychology: Children's Right to Participation," Journal of School Psychology 52, no. 1 (Feb. 2014): 4–5; Convention on the Rights of the Child, art. 12.

136   At the Sudbury Valley School Christine R. Traxler, "The Most Democratic School of Them All: Why the Sudbury Model of Education Should Be Taken Seriously," Schools 12, no. 2 (Sept. 2015): 271–96.

136   At the Brooklyn Free School Heather Schwedel, "The Coolest High Schools Across the Country," Teen Vogue, Nov. 20, 2013.

136   The psychological research Lansdown, Jimerson, and Shahroozi, "Children's Rights and School Psychology," 6; Katherine Covell and R. Brian Howe, "Moral Education Through the 3 Rs: Rights, Respect and Responsibility," Journal of Moral Education 30, no. 1 (Mar. 2001): 29–41; Perpetua Kirby and Sara Bryson, Measuring the Magic? Evaluating and Researching Young People's Participation in Public Decision Making (London: Carnegie Young People Initiative, 2002); Renate Kränzl-Nagl and Ulrike Zartler, "Children's Participation in School and Community; European Perspectives," in A Handbook of Children and Young People's Participation: Perspectives from Theory and Practice, ed. Barry Percy-Smith and Nigel Thomas (London: Routledge, 2010); Liam O'Hare et al., "The Reliability and Validity of a Child and Adolescent Participation in Decision-Making Questionnaire," Child: Care, Health and Development 42, no. 5 (2016): 692–98; Svein Arild Vis et al., "Participation and Health—A Research Review of Child Participation in Planning and Decision-Making," Child & Family Social Work 16, no. 3 (2011): 325–35.

136   And that fits Madeline Levine, "Raising Successful Children," New York Times, Aug. 4, 2012.

137   Authoritative parents Levine, "Raising Successful Children."

137   As Mary Beth Tinker, interview.

137   Her parents Tinker, interview.

137   They didn't hide Tinker, interview.

137   They pointed Tinker, interview.

137   Mary Beth's father Tinker, interview.

137   As she remembers Tinker, interview.

137   Her father "always said" Tinker, interview.

137   As Mary Beth recalls Tinker, interview.

138   Wylie's protest Wylie, interview.

138   Every day Wylie interview.

6. On the Cusp of Adulthood: The Right to Start Fresh

139   "I was an emancipated juvenile" Chris and Tyler, interview by the author, Sept. 16, 2021.

139   "So, ten days" Chris and Tyler, interview.

139 *As Chris explains* Chris and Tyler, interview.

139 *"I'm ninth generation"* Chris and Tyler, interview.

139 *Chris's friend Tyler* Chris and Tyler, interview.

139 *There's a certain personality* Chris and Tyler, interview.

139 *But family history* Chris and Tyler, interview.

139 *"I was, you know"* Chris and Tyler, interview.

139 *There was no sleight of hand* Chris and Tyler, interview.

139 *Tyler wanted infantry* Chris and Tyler, interview.

140 *It didn't matter that combat arms* Chris and Tyler, interview.

140 *"Truth be told"* Chris and Tyler, interview.

140 *"As uncomfortable"* Chris and Tyler, interview.

140 *"They come in with"* Chris and Tyler, interview.

140 *As Tyler puts it* Chris and Tyler, interview.

140 *Recruiters go* Seth Kershner and Scott Harding, "Do Military Recruiters Belong in Schools?" *Education Week,* Oct. 28, 2015, https://www.edweek.org/policy-politics/opinion-do-military-recruiters-belong-in-schools/2015/10.

140 *The Pentagon partners* Rebecca Keegan, "The U.S. Military's Hollywood Connection," *Los Angeles Times,* Aug. 21, 2011; Eric Kiefer, "Black Hawk Helicopter Lands at West Orange High School," *Patch,* Nov. 15, 2021, https://patch.com/new-jersey/westorange/black-hawk-helicopter-lands-west-orange-high-school; Michael Schottey, "The Flag and the Shield: The Long Alliance Between the NFL and US Military," *Bleacher Report,* May 26, 2014, https://bleacherreport.com/articles/2029052-the-flag-and-the-shield-the-long-alliance-between-the-nfl-and-the-us-military; Pat Elder, "Army Vans Equipped for Recruiting," *Military Vehicles Magazine,* July 14, 2008.

140 *In 2021, the army* U.S. Army, "U.S. Army Reveals the People Behind the Uniform in New Animated Film Series," PR Newswire, May 4, 2021, https://www.prnewswire.com/news-releases/us-army-reveals-the-people-behind-the-uniform-in-new-animated-film-series-301282737.html.

140 *"This is the story"* Emma, "The Calling," available at U.S. Army, "Film Series."

140 *Emma, with a blue ribboned ponytail* Emma, "The Calling."

140 *"Although I had"* Emma, "The Calling."

141 *In 2020, the navy partnered* "Sailor VS," VMLY&R, Sept. 23, 2020, https://www.vmlyr.com/en-us/united-states/work/sailor-vs; Matthew Cox, "How the Pandemic Changed Military Recruiting Forever," Military.com, Apr. 13, 2021, https://www.military.com/daily-news/2021/04/13/how-pandemic-changed-military-recruiting-forever.html.

141 *As the marketing* "Sailor VS."

141 *Banner ads* Elizabeth Howe, Elena LoRusso, and Emma Moore, "Esports and the Military," Aug. 3, 2021, https://www.cnas.org/publications/reports/esports-and-the-military; Kim Lyons, "After Impassioned Speech, AOC's Ban on US Military Recruiting via Twitch Fails House Vote," *Verge,* July 30, 2020, https://www.theverge.com/2020/7/30/21348451/military-recruiting-twitch-ban-block-amendment-ocasio-cortez; Jordan Uhl, "The US Military Is Using Online Gaming to Recruit Teens," *Nation,* July 15, 2020.

141 *"What is really"* Matthew Cox, "Army Gambles on Virtual Tools Like Facetime to Make Up Recruiting Shortfall," Military.com, May 3, 2020, https://www.military.com/daily-news/2020/05/01/army-gambles-virtual-tools-facetime-make-recruiting-shortfall.html.

141 *What they leave out* Chris and Tyler, interview.

141 *"You're in high school"* Chris and Tyler, interview.

141 *And you're not even cooking* Chris and Tyler, interview.

141 *"You come back"* Chris and Tyler, interview.

141 *"Oh, you have"* Chris and Tyler, interview.

141 *"You really lose"* Chris and Tyler, interview.

142 *Growing research* Chris R. Brewin, Bernice Andrews, and John D. Valentine, "Meta-analysis of Risk Factors for Posttraumatic Stress Disorder in Trauma-Exposed Adults," *Journal of Consulting and Clinical Psychology* 68, no. 5 (2000): 751, 755.

142 *In one study* Bruce P. Dohrenwend et al., "The Roles of Combat Exposure, Personal Vulnerability, and Involvement in Harm to Civilians or Prisoners in Vietnam-War-Related Posttraumatic Stress Disorder," *Clinical Psychological Science* 1, no. 3 (July 2013): 230.

142 *Similarly, a study* Karen H. Seal, "Bringing the War Back Home: Mental Health Disorders Among 103,788 US Veterans Returning from Iraq and Afghanistan Seen at Department of Veterans Affairs Facilities," *Archives of Internal Medicine* 167, no. 5 (Mar. 12, 2007): 480.

142 *Although it can be challenging* Seal, "Bringing the War Back," 476; Christopher Bergland, "Why Is the Teen Brain So Vulnerable?" *Psychology Today,* Dec. 19, 2013; Colleen Manitt et al., "Dcc Orchestrates the Development of the Prefrontal Cortex During Adolescence and Is Altered in Psychiatric Patients," *Translational Psychiatry* 3, no. 12 (Dec. 2013): e338.

142 *A twenty-year-old's prefrontal cortex* Bergland, "Teen Brain"; Manitt et al., "Prefrontal Cortex."

142 *And alterations* Bergland, "Teen Brain"; Manitt et al., "Prefrontal Cortex."

142 *The youngest cohort* U.S. Department of Veterans Affairs, Office of Suicide Prevention, *Suicide Among Veterans and Other Americans 2001–2014,* Aug. 3, 2016, 19, https://www.mentalhealth.va.gov/docs/2016suicidedatareport.pdf.

142 *The repercussions* Fianna Sogomonyan and Janice L. Cooper, "Trauma Faced by Children of Military Families: What Every Policymaker Should Know," National Center for Children in Poverty, Mailman School of Public Health, Columbia University, May 2010, 4, https://www.nccp.org/wp-content/uploads/2010/05/text_938.pdf.

142 *One study of American children* Tom Vanden Brook and Ray Locker, "Study Finds More Child Abuse in Homes of Returning Vets," *USA Today,* Nov. 12, 2015; Christine M. Taylor et al., "Differential Child Maltreatment Risk Across Deployment Periods of US Army Soldiers," *American Journal of Public Health* 106, no. 1 (Jan. 2016): 153.

142 *And even for children* Sogomonyan and Cooper, "Military Families," 4; Alan Lincoln, Erika Swift, and Mia Shorteno-Fraser, "Psychological Adjustment and Treatment of Children and Families with Parents Deployed in Military Combat," *Journal of Clinical Psychology* 64, no. 8 (Aug. 2008): 984–92; An-

gela J. Huebner et al., "Parental Deployment and Youth in Military Families: Exploring Uncertainty and Ambiguous Loss," *Family Relations* 56, no. 2 (2007): 112–22.

143   *In another study* Eric M. Flake et al., "The Psychosocial Effects of Deployment on Military Children," *Journal of Developmental & Behavioral Pediatrics* 30, no. 4 (Aug. 2009): 271.

143   *The unemployment rate* James V. Marrone, "Debt and Delinquency After Military Service: A Study of the Credit Records of Young Veterans in the First Year After Separation," Consumer Financial Protection Bureau (Nov. 2020): 19, https://files.consumerfinance.gov/f/documents/cfpb_debt-and -delinquency-after-military-service_report_2020-11.pdf.

143   *The median income* Marrone, "Debt and Delinquency," 19.

143   *As Tyler points out* Chris and Tyler, interview.

143   *You may be on patrol* Chris and Tyler, interview.

143   *"You're back"* Chris and Tyler, interview; Simone Weichselbaum, "Officers with Military Experience More Likely to Shoot, Study Says," Marshall Project, Oct. 15, 2018, https://www.themarshallproject.org/2018/10/15 /police-with-military-experience-more-likely-to-shoot.

143   *In one recent study of Dallas* Weichselbaum, "Likely to Shoot"; Jennifer M. Reingle Gonzalez et al., "Does Military Veteran Status and Deployment History Impact Officer Involved Shootings? A Case–Control Study," *Journal of Public Health* 41, no. 3 (Sept. 30, 2019): e245–52.

143   *A separate study* Weichselbaum, "Likely to Shoot"; Simone Weichselbaum and Beth Schwartzapfel, "When Warriors Put on the Badge," Marshall Project, Mar. 30, 2017, https://www.themarshallproject.org/2017/03/30 /when-warriors-put-on-the-badge.

143   *Chris told me* Chris and Tyler, interview.

143   *When he finally* Chris and Tyler, interview.

144   *"I remember"* Chris and Tyler, interview.

144   *"Because it ain't"* Chris and Tyler, interview.

144   *We blame them* Julie Beck, "When Do You Become an Adult?" *The Atlantic*, Jan. 5, 2016; Laurence Steinberg, *Age of Opportunity: Lessons from the New Science of Adolescence* (Boston: First Mariner Book, 2015).

144   *In contrast to previous conflicts* Paulina Cachero, "US Taxpayers Have Reportedly Paid an Average of $8,000 Each and Over $2 Trillion Total for the Iraq War Alone," *Business Insider*, Feb. 6, 2020, https://www.businessinsider .com/us-taxpayers-spent-8000-each-2-trillion-iraq-war-study-2020-2; Uri Friedman, "Fighting Terrorism with a Credit Card," *The Atlantic*, Sept. 12, 2016.

144   *Instead, they gave themselves* Cachero, "US Taxpayers Have Reportedly Paid an Average of $8,000 Each"; Friedman, "Fighting Terrorism with a Credit Card."

145   *As the navy's recruitment* "Enlistment Bonuses and Incentives," America's Navy, https://www.navy.com/joining-the-navy/enlistment-bonuses.

145   *"The Navy can help"* "Enlistment Bonuses and Incentives," America's Navy.

145   *Roughly two* Emma Kerr and Sarah Wood, "See 10 Years of Average Total Student Loan Debt," *U.S. News*, Sept. 14, 2021.

145   *In 2022, 43.4 million* Melanie Hanson, "Student Loan Debt Statistics,"

Education Data Initiative, Mar. 1, 2022, https://educationdata.org/student
-loan-debt-statistics.

145 *Most colleges* Michael R. Bloomberg, "Why I'm Giving $1.8 Billion for Col-
lege Financial Aid," *New York Times*, Nov. 18, 2018.

145 *That was the situation* Christina, interview by author, Sept. 7, 2018.

145 *She wanted* Christina, interview.

145 *In Christina's case* Christina, interview.

145 *Students who go* "Some Colleges Have More Students from the Top 1 Percent Than the Bottom 60," *New York Times*, Jan. 18, 2017.

146 *When these talented* Bill Gates, "Help Wanted: 11 Million College Grads,"
GatesNotes (blog), June 3, 2015, https://www.gatesnotes.com/Education
/11-Million-College-Grads; Anneken Tappe, "Nearly Half of American
Companies Say They Are Short on Skilled Workers," CNN Business,
Oct. 25, 2021, https://www.cnn.com/2021/10/25/economy/business
-conditions-worker-shortage/index.html; Bloomberg, "Why I'm Giving
$1.8 Billion for College Financial Aid."

146 *By 2025* Gates, "Help Wanted"; Tappe, "Nearly Half."

146 *Almost a third* Alex Baumhardt and Emily Hanford, "Overwhelmed by Student Debt, Many Low-Income Students Drop Out," APM Reports,
Feb. 12, 2018, https://www.apmreports.org/story/2018/02/12/student
-debt-low-income-drop-out.

146 *Five years into repayment* Ben Miller, "The Student Debt Problem Is Worse
Than We Imagined," *New York Times*, Aug. 25, 2018.

146 *For-profit colleges* Miller, "The Student Debt Problem."

146 *And unlike other kinds of debt* Abbye Atkinson, "Race, Educational Loans, &
Bankruptcy," *Michigan Journal of Race and Law* 16, no. 1 (2010): 4.

146 *Even when a lender* Fenaba R. Addo, Jason N. Houle, and Sharon Sassler,
"The Changing Nature of the Association Between Student Loan Debt and
Marital Behavior in Young Adulthood," *Journal of Family and Economic Is-
sues* 40, no. 4 (2018): 86–101.

146 *To provide some perspective* Matt Phillips and Karl Russell, "The Next Financial Calamity Is Coming. Here's What to Watch," *New York Times*,
Sept. 12, 2018.

146 *Emerging research suggests* Addo, Houle, and Sassler, "The Changing Nature."

146 *People put off* RTI International, "New Report Details Experiences of
Graduates with Student Loan Debt During the Great Recession,"
ScienceDaily, May 2, 2018, https://www.sciencedaily.com/releases/2018
/05/180502104040.htm; Fenaba R. Addo, "Debt, Cohabitation, and Marriage in Young Adulthood," *Duke University Press* 51, no. 5 (2014): 1677–
1701.

146 *They delay* RTI International, "New Report Details"; Addo, "Debt, Cohabitation, and Marriage."

146 *They wait* Michael Nau, Rachel E. Dwyer, and Randy Hodson, "Can't Afford a Baby? Debt and Young Americans," *Research in Social Stratification
and Mobility* 42 (2015): 114–22.

146 *They live* Jason N. Houle and Cody Warner, "Into the Red and Back to the
Nest? Student Debt, College Completion, and Returning to the Parental

Home Among Young Adults," *Sociology of Education* 90, no. 1 (2017): 89–108.

146 *In July 2020* Richard Fry, Jeffrey S. Passel, and D'Vera Cohn, "A Majority of Young Adults in the U.S. Live with Their Parents for the First Time Since the Great Depression," Pew Research Center, Sept. 4, 2020, https://www.pewresearch.org/fact-tank/2020/09/04/a-majority-of-young-adults-in-the-u-s-live-with-their-parents-for-the-first-time-since-the-great-depression/.

146 *That's greater* Fry, Passel, and Cohn, "A Majority of Young Adults."

147 *These dynamics* Matt Phillips and Karl Russell, "The Next Financial Calamity Is Coming. Here's What to Watch," *New York Times*, Sept. 12, 2018; Tara Siegel Bernard and Karl Russell, "The New Toll of American Student Debt in 3 Charts," *New York Times*, July 11, 2018.

147 *Parents often dip* Bernard and Russell, "The New Toll."

147 *Good luck* M. H. Miller, "I Came of Age During the 2008 Financial Crisis," *New York Times*, Sept. 15, 2018.

147 *With interest accruing* RTI International, "New Report Details."

147 *It is awful* Miller, "The Student Debt Problem."

147 *At the 2019 Morehouse College* Shannon Van Sant, "Robert Smith Pledges to Pay Off Student Loans for Morehouse College's Class of 2019," NPR, May 19, 2019, https://www.npr.org/2019/05/19/724836836/robert-smith-pledges-to-pay-off-student-loans-for-morehouse-colleges-class-of-20.

148 *From a man* Zack Friedman, "Billionaire Robert Smith Pays Student Loans for Morehouse Parents," *Forbes*, Sept. 26, 2019; Matthew Goldstein, "A Buyout Fund C.E.O. Got in Tax Evasion Trouble. Here's Why Investors Shrugged," *New York Times*, Mar. 12, 2021.

148 *But then Smith* Van Sant, "Robert Smith Pledges."

148 *As Kamal Medlock* Van Sant, "Robert Smith Pledges."

148 *The faculty* Van Sant, "Robert Smith Pledges."

148 *Chants of "MVP"* Van Sant, "Robert Smith Pledges."

148 *The president of Morehouse* Friedman, "Billionaire Robert Smith."

148 *For Kamal* Van Sant, "Robert Smith Pledges."

148 *A year earlier* Alissa Quart, "What Billionaires Don't Understand About College Debt," *New York Times*, Dec. 23, 2019.

148 *This giving* Van Sant, "Robert Smith Pledges."

148 *But Daniel Edwards* Quart, "What Billionaires Don't Understand."

148 *And he has a point* Quart, "What Billionaires Don't Understand."

149 *A year later* Jordan Williams, "Billionaire Who Said He Would Pay Off Morehouse Student Debt Admits to Tax Fraud," *The Hill*, Oct. 16, 2020, https://thehill.com/policy/finance/521389-billionaire-who-said-he-would-pay-off-morehouse-student-debt-admits-to-tax; Goldstein, "A Buyout Fund C.E.O."

149 *That is just* Quart, "What Billionaires Don't Understand."

149 *In the near term* Erica L. Green and Madeleine Ngo, "Plans for Free Pre-K and Community College Could Provide a 'Ladder into the Middle Class,'" *New York Times*, Oct. 16, 2021; Celeste K. Carruthers et al., "Promise Kept? Free Community College, Attainment, and Earnings in Tennessee,"

Dec. 2020, https://volweb.utk.edu/~ccarrut1/Carruthers_Fox_Jepsen%20 2020-12-07.pdf; David L. Kirp, "Community College Should Be More Than Just Free," *New York Times*, May 25, 2021.

149 *That means forgiving* Green and Ngo, "Plans for Free Pre-K and Community College"; Astra Taylor, "Make Americans' Crushing Debt Disappear," *New York Times*, July 2, 2021.

149 *In fact, there is a strong argument* Taylor, "Make Americans' Crushing Debt Disappear."

149 *Tyler describes* Chris and Tyler, interview.

149 *"You drive around"* Chris and Tyler, interview.

149 *Young enlisted servicemembers* James V. Marrone, "Debt and Delinquency After Military Service," Consumer Financial Protection Bureau (Nov. 2020): 3, https://files.consumerfinance.gov/f/documents/cfpb_debt-and -delinquency-after-military-service_report_2020-11.pdf.

149 *"A lot of these kids"* Chris and Tyler, interview.

150 *A third of all soldiers* Marrone, "Debt and Delinquency After Military Service," 3.

150 *But if we allow* Marrone, "Debt and Delinquency After Military Service," 4.

150 *New Jersey has shown* Katrina L. Goodjoint, "New Jersey Just Eliminated Fines for Youth in the Juvenile System," NJ.com, Jan. 22, 2020, https://www.nj.com/opinion/2020/01/new-jersey-just-eliminated-fines-for -youth-in-the-juvenile-system-and-thats-a-good-thing-opinion.html.

150 *Before the state* Goodjoint, "New Jersey Just Eliminated Fines."

150 *But the research* Goodjoint, "New Jersey Just Eliminated Fines"; Alex R. Piquero and Wesley G. Jennings, "Justice System–Imposed Financial Penalties Increase the Likelihood of Recidivism," *Youth Violence and Juvenile Justice*, 2016, https://debtorsprison.jlc.org/documents/JLC-Debtors -Prison-criminology-study-2016.pdf; Jessica Feierman et al., *Debtors' Prison for Kids?* Juvenile Law Center (2016): 6, https://debtorsprison.jlc .org/documents/JLC-Debtors-Prison.pdf.

150 *For example, although millennials'* Josh Zumbrun, "Younger Generation Faces a Savings Deficit," *Wall Street Journal*, Nov. 9, 2014; Christopher Kurz, Geng Li, and Daniel J. Vine, "Are Millennials Different," *Finance and Economics Discussion Series* (Nov. 2018), https://www.federalreserve.gov /econres/feds/files/2018080pap.pdf.

150 *What's different* Kurz et al., "Are Millennials Different."

150 *They make less* Kurz et al., "Are Millennials Different."

150 *They have less* Kurz et al., "Are Millennials Different."

150 *They own fewer* Kurz et al., "Are Millennials Different."

150 *Courtney's name* The Race, "The Race E14 Housing Part 1 of 4," YouTube, Dec. 6, 2019, https://www.youtube.com/watch?v=1PNQPyQlFUI.

150 *She has* The Race, "Housing," 2:37.

151 *A red towel* The Race, "Housing," 2:37.

151 *At PodShare* The Race, "Housing," 1:50.

151 *There's not much privacy* Catharine Smith, "Bunk Beds Are Renting for $1,000 as the Housing Crisis Spins Out of Control," *HuffPost*, Sept. 27, 2019, https://www.huffpost.com/entry/renting-bunk-beds-instead-apartment _n_5d8d135be4b0019647a592e2.

151 *"I'm not going"* The Race, "Housing," 2:33.

151 *"A year and a half ago"* The Race, "Housing," 2:46.

151 *Her health insurance* Nita Lelyveld, "Why Are These L.A. People Sleeping in Stacked Pods? It's Not Just the Cost of Housing," *Los Angeles Times*, Oct. 12, 2019.

151 *"I was about ready"* The Race, "Housing," 3:02.

151 *It doesn't matter* Lelyveld, "Stacked Pods."

151 *We've pursued policies* Astra Taylor, "Out with the Old, In with the Young," *New York Times*, Oct. 18, 2019.

151 *We are covering* Katie Lobosco, "Social Security Won't Be Able to Pay Full Benefits by 2034," CNN, Sept. 1, 2021, https://www.cnn.com/2021/08 /31/politics/social-security-medicare-report/index.html.

151 *During the pandemic* Richard Fry, Jeffrey S. Passel, and D'vera Cohn, "A Majority of Young Adults in the U.S. Live with Their Parents for the First Time Since the Great Depression," Pew Research Center, Sept. 4, 2020, https://www.pewresearch.org/fact-tank/2020/09/04/a-majority-of -young-adults-in-the-u-s-live-with-their-parents-for-the-first-time-since -the-great-depression/.

151 *In many industries* OECD, *OECD Skills Outlook 2015 Youth, Skills and Employability: Youth, Skills and Employability* (OECD Publishing, 2015), 105.

151 *And rather than standing up* Derek Thompson, "'Unnecessary' and 'Political': Why Unions Are Bad for America," *The Atlantic*, June 12, 2012.

151 *When the pandemic* Lori Weisberg, "San Diego Hotels Must Rehire Laid-Off Workers by Seniority, City Council Says," *San Diego Union-Tribune*, Sept. 8, 2020; Martha J. Keon and Paul J. Sopher, "Philadelphia Hotel, Airport Hospitality, and Event Center Businesses Face Significant New Recall and Retention Obligations," Littler Mendelson P.C., Apr. 12, 2021, https://www.littler.com/publication-press/publication/philadelphia -hotel-airport-hospitality-and-event-center-businesses.

152 *As San Diego* Weisberg, "San Diego Hotels."

152 *Law firms* Bryce Engelland, "Leverage Is Everything: Archimedean Lessons in Law Firm Finances," Thomson Reuters, Sept. 29, 2021, https:// www.thomsonreuters.com/en-us/posts/legal/leverage-law-firm -finances/; Karen Sloan, "Proposed Cap on Lawyer Hours a Tough Sell in Legal Business Boom," Reuters, Nov. 4, 2021, https://www.reuters.com /legal/legalindustry/proposed-cap-lawyer-hours-tough-sell-legal -business-boom-2021-11-04/; Xiumei Dong, "The Path to Law Firm Partnership Just Keeps Getting Longer," Reuters, Jan. 31, 2022, https://www .reuters.com/legal/legalindustry/path-law-firm-partnership-just-keeps -getting-longer-2022-01-31/.

152 *In business* Noam Scheiber, "Despite Labor Shortages, Workers See Few Gains in Economic Security," *New York Times*, Feb. 1, 2022.

152 *The privileging* David Cyranoski et al., "Education: The PhD Factory," *Nature* 472, no. 7343 (Apr. 1, 2011): 276–79; Staša Milojević, Filippo Radicchi, and John P. Walsh, "Changing Demographics of Scientific Careers: The Rise of the Temporary Workforce," *Proceedings of the National Academy of Sciences* 115, no. 50 (Dec. 11, 2018): 12616–23.

152 *A recent study* Milojević, Radicchi, and Walsh, "Changing Demographics."

152　*In 1960* Milojević, Radicchi, and Walsh, "Changing Demographics."

152　*While just a quarter* Milojević, Radicchi, and Walsh, "Changing Demographics."

152　*More than ten million* Greg Iacurci, "16 Million People 65 and Older Will Be in the Workforce by 2030," CNBC, Oct. 15, 2021, https://www.cnbc.com/2021/10/15/these-are-the-best-and-worst-states-for-older-workers.html; Marc Freedman, *Encore: Finding Work That Matters in the Second Half of Life* (New York: PublicAffairs, 2018), 111; Alicia H. Munnell and Steven A. Sass, *Working Longer: The Solution to the Retirement Income Challenge* (Washington, D.C.: Brookings Institution Press, 2008).

152　*That limits opportunities* TIAA-CREF, *An Age of Opportunity: Taking a Strategic Approach to Longevity, Retirement and Job Satisfaction in Higher Education* (Apr. 2012), 2–3.

152　*In legal academia* Jon Marcus, "Aging Faculty Who Won't Leave Thwart Universities' Attempts to Cut Costs," *The Hechinger Report,* Oct. 9, 2015, http://hechingerreport.org/aging-faculty-who-wont-leave-thwart-universities-attempts-to-cut-costs/.

153　*Between 2000 and 2010* Alexia Fernández Campbell, "The Workforce That Won't Retire," *The Atlantic,* June 17, 2016.

153　*Under federal law* "Age Discrimination—FAQs," U.S. Equal Employment Opportunity Commission, United States Government, accessed Mar. 24, 2022, https://www.eeoc.gov/youth/age-discrimination-faqs; "Age Discrimination," U.S. Equal Employment Opportunity Commission, United States Government, accessed Mar. 24, 2022, https://www.eeoc.gov/youth/age-discrimination.

153　*There is no such protection* "Age Discrimination—FAQs"; "Age Discrimination"; Manfred Liebel, "Discrimination Against Being Children: A Blind Spot in the Human Rights Arena," in *Children's Rights from Below: Cross-Cultural Perspectives,* ed. Manfred Liebel et al. (New York: Palgrave Macmillan, 2012), 95.

153　*Quips by co-workers* "Age Discrimination—FAQs."

153　*You might assume* Lisa A. Marchiondo, Ernest Gonzales, and Shan Ran, "Development and Validation of the Workplace Age Discrimination Scale," *Journal of Business and Psychology* 31, no. 4 (Dec. 2016): 493–513; Ed Snape and Tom Redman, "Too Old or Too Young? The Impact of Perceived Age Discrimination," *Human Resource Management Journal* 13, no. 1 (2003): 78–89.

153　*They are the target* Marchiondo, Gonzales, and Ran, "Workplace Age Discrimination," 494; Lisa M. Finkelstein, Katherine M. Ryan, and Eden B. King, "What Do the Young (Old) People Think of Me? Content and Accuracy of Age-Based Metastereotypes," *European Journal of Work and Organizational Psychology* 22, no. 6 (2013): 633–57; Snape and Redman, "Too Old."

153　*In comparison* Marchiondo, Gonzales, and Ran, "Workplace Age Discrimination," 495; Marilena Bertolino, Donald M. Truxillo, and Franco Fraccaroli, "Age Effects on Perceived Personality and Job Performance," *Journal of Managerial Psychology* 28, no. 7/8 (Nov. 4, 2013): 867–85, https://doi.org/10.1108/JMP-07-2013-0222; Kevin J. Gibson, Wilfred J. Zerbe, and

R. E. Franken, "The Influence of Rater and Ratee Age on Judgments of Work-Related Attributes," *Journal of Psychology* 127, no. 3 (1993): 271–80.

153 *And these negative perceptions* Marchiondo, Gonzales, and Ran, "Workplace Age Discrimination," 495; Snape and Redman, "Too Old"; Colin Duncan and Wendy Loretto, "Never the Right Age? Gender and Age-Based Discrimination in Employment," *Gender, Work & Organization* 11, no. 1 (2004): 95–115.

153 *Young Americans* Janet Adamy and Paul Overberg, "Struggling Americans Once Sought Greener Pastures—Now They're Stuck," *Wall Street Journal*, Aug. 2, 2017.

153 *But no more* Adamy and Overberg, "Struggling Americans."

154 *It's not that half* Adamy and Overberg, "Struggling Americans."

154 *Tightly regulated land use* David Schleicher, "Stuck! The Law and Economics of Residential Stagnation," *Yale Law Journal* 127, no. 1 (Oct. 2017): 84; Adamy and Overberg, "Struggling Americans."

154 *The average rent* "Los Angeles, CA Rental Market Trends," RentCafe, last modified Oct. 2021, https://www.rentcafe.com/average-rent-market-trends/us/ca/los-angeles/.

154 *The spartan pod* The Race, "Housing," 2:10.

154 *Moreover, since public benefits* Schleicher, "Stuck!" 84.

154 *Even for those* Schleicher, "Stuck!" 78; Adamy and Overberg, "Struggling Americans."

154 *A quarter of Americans* Adamy and Overberg, "Struggling Americans,"

154 *Why these legal barriers* Schleicher, "Stuck!" 113.

154 *And that may itself* Schleicher, "Stuck!" 111.

154 *The older professional* Schleicher, "Stuck!" 119.

154 *That makes* Schleicher, "Stuck!" 119.

154 *He also likes* Schleicher, "Stuck!" 124.

154 *After all* Schleicher, "Stuck!" 124.

155 *And, like many* Michael Kolomatsky, "Baby Boomers: Rich with Real Estate and Not Letting Go," *New York Times*, July 8, 2021.

155 *Politically, he is more likely* Schleicher, "Stuck!" 132–49.

155 *Whatever the cause* Schleicher, "Stuck!" 84–85.

155 *A hundred years ago* Samuel R. Bagenstos, "Racism Didn't Stop at Jim Crow," *Democracy Journal*, Oct. 12, 2017, https://democracyjournal.org/magazine/46/racism-didnt-stop-at-jim-crow/.

155 *But on the ground* Bagenstos, "Racism Didn't Stop"; Otto Kerner et al., *Report of the National Advisory Commission on Civil Disorders* (Washington, D.C.: U.S. Government Printing Office, 1968), 1.

155 *In 2010* Bagenstos, "Racism Didn't Stop."

155 *The conventional story* Bagenstos, "Racism Didn't Stop."

155 *In such a light* Bagenstos, "Racism Didn't Stop."

156 *But that perspective* Richard Rothstein, *The Color of Law: A Forgotten History of How Our Government Segregated America* (New York: Liveright, 2017), xvii.

156 *Because public housing* Rothstein, *The Color of Law;* Bagenstos, "Racism Didn't Stop."

156 *And it turned out* Rothstein, *The Color of Law;* Bagenstos, "Racism Didn't Stop."

156 *The federal government* Rothstein, *The Color of Law;* Bagenstos, "Racism Didn't Stop."

156 *And the neighborhood* Rothstein, *The Color of Law;* Bagenstos, "Racism Didn't Stop"; Dorothy A. Brown, *The Whiteness of Wealth: How the Tax System Impoverishes Black Americans—and How We Can Fix It* (New York: Crown, 2021): 68–69.

156 *It is likely to be* Rod K. Brunson, "Protests Focus on Over-Policing. But Under-Policing Is Also Deadly," *Washington Post,* June 12, 2020.

156 *In American cities* Brad Plumer, Nadja Popovich, and Brian Palmer, "How Decades of Racist Housing Policy Left Neighborhoods Sweltering," *New York Times,* Aug. 24, 2020; Jeremy S. Hoffman, Vivek Shandas, and Nicholas Pendleton, "The Effects of Historical Housing Policies on Resident Exposure to Intra-Urban Heat: A Study of 108 US Urban Areas," *Climate* 8, no. 1 (Jan. 2020): 12.

156 *For decades, trees* Plumer, Popovich, and Palmer, "How Decades of Racist Housing."

157 *In a recent empirical study* Stanford University, "Stanford Professor's Study Finds Gentrification Disproportionately Affects Minorities," *Stanford News,* Dec. 1, 2020, https://news.stanford.edu/2020/12/01/gentrification-disproportionately-affects-minorities/; Jackelyn Hwang and Lei Ding, "Unequal Displacement: Gentrification, Racial Stratification, and Residential Destinations in Philadelphia," *American Journal of Sociology* 126, no. 2 (Sept. 2020): 357–58.

157 *But residents moving* Hwang and Ding, "Unequal Displacement," 357–58.

157 *In other words* Hwang and Ding, "Unequal Displacement," 357–58, 393.

157 *That's, in part* Hwang and Ding, "Unequal Displacement," 394; Megan Leonhardt, "Black and Hispanic Americans Often Have Lower Credit Scores—Here's Why They're Hit Harder," CNBC, Jan. 28, 2021, https://www.cnbc.com/2021/01/28/black-and-hispanic-americans-often-have-lower-credit-scores.html.

157 *They may also get* Hwang and Ding, "Unequal Displacement," 394.

157 *For people of color* Rothstein, *The Color of Law;* Bagenstos, "Racism Didn't Stop."

157 *Many of our restrictions* Adamy and Overberg, "Struggling Americans"; Schleicher, "Stuck!" 78.

157 *Economies thrive* Adamy and Overberg, "Struggling Americans."

157 *Prevent people* Schleicher, "Stuck!" 78.

157 *In recent times* Schleicher, "Stuck!" 96–104.

157 *One study estimated* Schleicher, "Stuck!" 103; Chang-Tai Hsieh and Enrico Moretti, "Housing Constraints and Spatial Misallocation," *American Economic Journal: Macroeconomics* 11, no. 2 (Apr. 1, 2019): 25–26.

158 *Moreover, stymying the ability* Schleicher, "Stuck!" 104–7.

158 *Not only are more people* Schleicher, "Stuck!" 104–7.

158 *One place to start* Schleicher, "Stuck!" 118, 151.

158 *Our legal forebears* Schleicher, "Stuck!" 111; Jide Nzelibe, "Free Movement:

A Federalist Reinterpretation," *American University Law Review* 49, no. 2 (Dec. 1999): 433–69.

158 *Lawyers, psychologists* Schleicher, "Stuck!" 151. Such positive reforms are already in motion. See, e.g., Karen Sloan, "Michigan Opts for Universal Bar Exam as States Shun Patchwork Tests," Reuters, Oct. 19, 2021, https://www.reuters.com/legal/legalindustry/michigan-opts-universal-bar-exam-states-shun-patchwork-tests-2021-10-18/.

158 *Core benefits* Schleicher, "Stuck!" 152–53; Rothstein, *The Color of Law;* Richard D. Kahlenberg, "The 'New Redlining' Is Deciding Who Lives in Your Neighborhood," *New York Times*, Apr. 19, 2021.

158 *Again, zoning laws* Kahlenberg, "The 'New Redlining.'"

159 *One of the reasons* Laura Bliss, "Oregon's Single-Family Zoning Ban Was a 'Long Time Coming,'" Bloomberg, July 2, 2019, https://www.bloomberg.com/news/articles/2019-07-02/upzoning-rising-oregon-bans-single-family-zoning.

159 *In 2018, Minneapolis got rid* "San Francisco to End Parking Requirements for New Developments," CBS San Francisco, Dec. 5, 2018, https://sanfrancisco.cbslocal.com/2018/12/05/san-francisco-end-parking-requirements-new-developments/; Henry Grabar, "San Francisco Legalizes Itself," *Slate*, Dec. 18, 2018, https://slate.com/business/2018/12/san-francisco-eliminates-parking-minimums-its-a-trend.html; Kahlenberg, "The 'New Redlining'"; Richard D. Kahlenberg, "How Minneapolis Ended Single-Family Zoning," The Century Foundation, Oct. 24, 2019, https://tcf.org/content/report/minneapolis-ended-single-family-zoning/; Bliss, "Oregon's Single-Family Zoning."

159 *In 2019, Oregon ended* Tim Gruver, "Oregon Bill Builds on State's Ongoing Quest to 'Upzone' Neighborhoods," *The Center Square*, May 18, 2021, https://www.thecentersquare.com/oregon/oregon-bill-builds-on-states-ongoing-quest-to-upzone-neighborhoods/article_33e4e4dc-b81c-11eb-8678-bf487c397de7.html.

159 *We might also* Schleicher, "Stuck!" 152–53; Matias Busso, Jesse Gregory, and Patrick Kline, "Assessing the Incidence and Efficiency of a Prominent Place Based Policy," *American Economic Review* 103, no. 2 (Apr. 1, 2013): 897–947; Rothstein, *The Color of Law.*

159 *Embarking on adulthood* Patrick Sharkey, "To Avoid Integration, Americans Built Barricades in Urban Space," *The Atlantic,* June 20, 2020.

159 *By failing to ensure* Gopnik, *The Gardener and the Carpenter,* 239.

160 *A few blocks* Roberta Smith, "Art Review; A Museum, Reborn, Remains True to Its Old Self, Only Better," *New York Times*, May 18, 2012.

160 *Worth more* Julia Hatmaker, "The Barnes Foundation Is Home to Billions of Dollars' Worth of Artwork: Cool Spaces," PennLive, Jan. 5, 2019, https://www.pennlive.com/life/2017/08/barnes_foundation_cool_spaces.html; The Barnes Foundation, "The Barnes Collection: A Story Behind Every Object," 2022, https://www.barnesfoundation.org/whats-on/collection.

160 *The art is housed* Smith, "Art Review."

160 *Albert C. Barnes made his fortune* Sylvia Karasu, "Albert C. Barnes, MD: The Physician Who Spun Silver into Gold," *Hektoen International Journal,*

2009, https://hekint.org/2020/08/18/albert-c-barnes-md-the-physician
-who-spun-silver-into-gold/.

160 *Barnes had a particular vision* Carol Vogel, "Judge Rules the Barnes Can
Move to Philadelphia," *New York Times,* Dec. 14, 2004; Roberta Smith,
"Art Review; A Museum, Reborn, Remains True to Its Old Self, Only Bet-
ter," *New York Times,* May 18, 2012.

160 *As he set down* Vogel, "Judge Rules"; Smith, "Art Review"; Ilana H. Eisen-
stein, "Keeping Charity in Charitable Trust Law: The Barnes Foundation
and the Case for Consideration of Public Interest in Administration of
Charitable Trusts," *University of Pennsylvania Law Review* 151, no. 5
(2003): 1747–86.

161 *Only twelve hundred people* Vogel, "Judge Rules."

161 *Had Barnes left* Vogel, "Judge Rules."

161 *No matter* Smith, "Art Review."

161 *It was only pending bankruptcy* Vogel, "Judge Rules."

161 *And, though, I can say* Smith, "Art Review."

161 *We need to understand* Aaron H. Kaplan, "The Jewish Clause and Public
Policy: Preserving the Testamentary Right to Oppose Religious Intermar-
riage Note," *Georgetown Journal of Law & Public Policy* 8, no. 1 (2010):
295–99; Emalee G. Popoff, "Testamentary Conditions in Restraint of the
Marriage of Homosexual Donees," *Drexel Law Review* 7, no. 1 (Fall 2014):
163–67; Eva Subotnik, "Artistic Control After Death," *Washington Law Review* 92, no. 16 (May 13, 2017): 299; The Barnes Foundation's Bylaws
(Apr. 30, 1946), 30, https://www.barneswatch.org/main_bylaws.html.

161 *In the Pacific Northwest* Blue Mountain Land Trust, "Connecting People to
the Land: Our Story," 2022, https://bmlt.org/our-story.

162 *In fact, in many ways* Restatement (Third) of Property: Wills & Other Do-
native Transfers § 10.1 cmt. c (2003); Subotnik, "Artistic Control After
Death," 299.

162 *We ought to care* Richard C. Ausness, "Sherlock Holmes and the Problem of
the Dead Hand: The Modification and Termination of 'Irrevocable' Trusts,"
Quinnipiac Law Journal 28, no. 3 (2015): 295.

162 *We ought to privilege* Tanya K. Hernandez, "The Property of Death," *University of Pittsburgh Law Review* 60 (1999): 971, 976–77.

7. The Invisible Kid: What Holds Us Back

166 *He assured me* That is also explained in the materials that Philadelphia Water
provides to the public. "Lead Programs and Initiatives," Philadelphia Water
Department, 2016–17.

166 *The tests results showed* Lorenzo Lucia, Philadelphia Water, letter to author,
Aug. 19, 2016.

166 *As the technician wrote* Lucia, letter.

167 *Indeed, my initial response* Donovan Hohn, "Flint's Water Crisis and the
'Troublemaker' Scientist," *New York Times,* Aug. 16, 2016; Marc Edwards,
letter to author, Apr. 21, 2017.

167   *The first sample* Edwards, letter; Lucia, letter.

167   *We had* Edwards, letter.

167   *As I discovered* Edwards, letter; Lucia, letter.

167   *Instead, they tested* Lucia, letter.

167   *Measure the pipes* Nicola Horscroft, letter to author, June 22, 2017.

167   *That's exactly what* Horscroft, letter.

167   *And, in the sectors* Horscroft, letter. What is particularly revealing is that the new draws from the faucet and the main were identical to those taken at the first visit—"non-detects." Lucia, letter. If the second Philadelphia Water team had used the same method as the first technician, the problem would have been hidden once again.

168   *The EPA's Lead* "Drinking Water Requirements for States and Public Water Systems," United States Environmental Protection Agency, accessed July 20, 2021, https://www.epa.gov/dwreginfo/lead-and-copper-rule.

168   *By instructing its technicians* It is important to note that the Water Department denies that it tested the water in my house "in a manner to avoid finding lead." Eleanor N. Ewing, letter to author, July 13, 2017. Its support for this denial is that "it properly conducted all testing and accurately reported what the results indicated at the time of sampling," that it "abides by all applicable laws and regulations," and that "its sampling techniques are consistent with standard practices." Ewing, letter; Eleanor N. Ewing, letter to author, July 26, 2017. That said, using protocols that under-detect contaminants as a means of avoiding additional governmental oversight appears to be common in the United States. Oliver Milman and Jessica Glenza, "At Least 33 US Cities Used Water Testing 'Cheats' over Lead Concerns," *Guardian*, June 2, 2016.

168   *In fact, Philadelphia* Jessica Glenza, "Philadelphia Water Department Faces Class Action Lawsuit over Water Testing," *Guardian*, June 3, 2016; Jessica Glenza, "Philadelphia Reforms Its Water Testing After Investigation into Lead Levels," *Guardian*, July 13, 2016.

168   *Before being forced* Glenza, "Philadelphia Water Department Faces"; Glenza, "Philadelphia Reforms."

168   *Often, technicians* Glenza, "Philadelphia Water Department Faces"; Glenza, "Philadelphia Reforms."

168   *Both actions were flagged* Glenza, "Philadelphia Water Department Faces"; Glenza, "Philadelphia Reforms."

168   *The department mails out* Philadelphia Water Department, postcard sent to author, 2017.

168   *Download the department's* Philadelphia Water Department, *2017 Drinking Water Quality Report*, Spring 2018, https://water.phila.gov/pool/files/2017-pwd-water-quality-report.pdf.

168   *The people in the photographs* Philadelphia Water Department, *2017 Drinking Water Quality Report*.

168   *And it doesn't matter* Philadelphia Water Department, postcard.

169   *It would be quite reasonable* "Basic Information About Lead in Drinking Water," United States Environmental Protection Agency, accessed July 20, 2021, https://www.epa.gov/ground-water-and-drinking-water/basic-information-about-lead-drinking-water.

169   *Under the 1974* "Basic Information," United States Environmental Protection Agency.

169   *For lead* "Basic Information," United States Environmental Protection Agency.

169   *When fetuses and children* Elise Gould, "Childhood Lead Poisoning: Conservative Estimates of the Social and Economic Benefits of Lead Hazard Control," *Environmental Health Perspectives* 117, no. 7 (July 2009): 1162–67.

169   *Lead has been linked* Gould, "Childhood Lead Poisoning," 1163–65.

169   *Indeed, there is a particularly troubling* Gould, "Childhood Lead Poisoning," 1165.

169   *The problem for the EPA* "Basic Information," United States Environmental Protection Agency; Jessica Pupovac, "Lead Levels Below EPA Limits Can Still Impact Your Health," NPR, Aug. 13, 2016, https://www.npr.org /sections/thetwo-way/2016/08/13/489825051/lead-levels-below-epa -limits-can-still-impact-your-health.

169   *At fifteen parts* "Basic Information," United States Environmental Protection Agency.

170   *I was going up* Craig Lambert, "Black, White, and Many Shades of Gray," *Harvard Magazine,* Apr. 15, 2013; Jennifer Steinhauer, "A First Lady at 50, Finding Her Own Path," *New York Times,* Jan. 16, 2014.

171   *We demand that* Katrina Jackson and Alexis Mayer, *Demanding a More Mature Miranda for Kids,* Georgetown Juvenile Justice Initiative (Oct. 2020), https://www.law.georgetown.edu/wp-content/uploads/2020/10/More MatureMiranda-1.pdf; Lorelei Laird, *"Miranda* for Youngsters: Police Routinely Read Juveniles Their Miranda Rights, But Do Kids Really Understand Them?" *ABA Journal,* June 2016; Kenneth J. King, "Waiving Childhood Goodbye: How Juvenile Courts Fail to Protect Children from Unknowing, Unintelligent, and Involuntary Waivers of Miranda Rights," *Wisconsin Law Review* 2006, no. 2 (2006): 431–78.

171   *In immigration court* Astrid Galvan, "Kids as Young as 1 in US Court, Awaiting Reunion with Family," AP News, July 8, 2018, https://apnews.com /article/occasions-north-america-us-news-ap-top-news-reunions-4cb60fc 06ca34160bf7445fdc1f47eed.

171   *The only thing* Galvan, "Kids as Young as 1."

171   *Migrant children* Misyrlena Egkolfopoulou, "The Thousands of Children Who Go to Immigration Court Alone," *The Atlantic,* Aug. 21, 2018; Christina Jewett and Shefali Luthra, "Immigrant Toddlers Ordered to Appear in Court Alone," *Texas Tribune,* June 28, 2018; Marie Solis, "Toddlers Appearing Unaccompanied in Immigration Court Is Nothing New," *Vice,* July 9, 2018, https://www.vice.com/en/article/43py3d/toddlers -appearing-unaccompanied-in-immigration-court-is-nothing-new.

171   *As Jack H. Weil* Jerry Markon, "Can a 3-Year-Old Represent Herself in Immigration Court? This Judge Thinks So," *Washington Post,* Mar. 5, 2016. We leave it to someone else to change the protocol, cruel and nonsensical as it might be. When the 9th Circuit had the opportunity to ensure that all immigrant children at least have a right to a government-appointed attorney, the court shrugged its shoulders: the law and precedent said no. Brandon Conradis, "Court Rules Children Facing Deportation Have No Right to

Court-Appointed Lawyer," *The Hill*, Jan. 29, 2018, https://thehill.com/latino/371253-court-rules-children-facing-deportation-have-no-right-to-court-appointed-lawyer. Never mind that a deportation order can be a death sentence and children without an attorney are more than five times as likely to be deported. Egkolfopoulou, "The Thousands of Children."

172 *Rather than act* United States Environmental Protection Agency, *Protect Your Family from Lead in Your Home*, Mar. 2021, https://www.epa.gov/sites/production/files/2020-04/documents/lead-in-your-home-portrait-color-2020-508.pdf.

172 *Instead of paying* Philadelphia Water, *Cleaning Faucet Aerators*, Aug. 30, 2016, https://water.phila.gov/wu/lead%20information/dailycleaning_faucetaerators.pdf; American Water Works Association, *Clean Water Clean Tap Brochure*, 2013, https://www.awwa.org/Portals/0/AWWA/ETS/Resources/TEC2012CleanWaterCleanTapBrochure.pdf?ver=2013-01-17-153232-490; American Water Works Association, *Meter to Tap Brochure*, 2013, https://www.awwa.org/Portals/0/AWWA/ETS/Resources/TEC2012MeterToTapBrochure.pdf?ver=2013-01-17-153232-863.

172 *Rather than giving up* Trisha Korioth, "Parent Plus: Button Batteries Can Cause Injuries, Death If Swallowed," *American Academy of Pediatrics News*, May 6, 2016, http://publications.aap.org/aapnews/news/12468/Parent-Plus-Button-batteries-can-cause-injuries; "Industry Code on Consumer Goods That Contain Button Batteries," Product Safety Australia, Australian Competition & Consumer Commission (July 2016), 7.

172 *Rather than hiring* Eric Lipton, "How the Trump Administration Pulled Back on Regulating Toxic Chemicals," *Yale Environment 360*, Feb. 12, 2019, https://e360.yale.edu/features/how-trump-administration-has-pulled-back-on-regulating-toxic-chemicals; Dave Goulson, "Pesticides, Corporate Irresponsibility, and the Fate of Our Planet," *One Earth* 2, no. 4 (Apr. 2020): 302–5; Pesticide Action Network, "Corporate Science & Spin," http://www.panna.org/gmos-pesticides-profit/corporate-science-spin.

172 *With a waiver* "How Water Parks Can Avoid Customer Injuries and Liability," OMAG, July 28, 2016, https://www.omag.org/news/2016/7/28/how-water-parks-can-avoid-customer-injuries-and-liability.

172 *With a nondisclosure agreement* Annie Hill, "Nondisclosure Agreements: Sexual Harassment and the Contract of Silence," *Gender Policy Report*, Nov. 14, 2017, https://genderpolicyreport.umn.edu/nondisclosure-agreements-sexual-harassment-and-the-contract-of-silence/.

172 *Detectives have figured out* Naomi E. S. Goldstein et al., "Waving Good-Bye to Waiver: A Developmental Argument Against Youths' Waiver of Miranda Rights," *Legislation and Public Policy* 21, no. 1 (2018): 35–39.

172 *The multimillionaire Jeffrey Epstein's lawyers* Julie K. Brown, "How a Future Trump Cabinet Member Gave a Serial Sex Abuser the Deal of a Lifetime," *Miami Herald*, Nov. 28, 2018.

172 *And they set to work* Brown, "How a Future Trump"; Connie Bruck, "Alan Dershowitz, Devil's Advocate," *New Yorker*, June 29, 2019; Patricia Mazzei, "Prosecutors Broke Law in Agreement Not to Prosecute Jeffrey Epstein, Judge Rules," *New York Times*, Feb. 21, 2019; David Von Drehle, "It Pays to

Be Rich. Just Look at the Lurid Case of Jeffrey Epstein," *Washington Post*, Dec. 4, 2018.

173   *Epstein's attorney* Von Drehle, "It Pays to Be Rich."

173   *When you tell someone* Lucia, letter.

173   *Instead, I got a letter* Ewing, letter, July 13, 2017.

174   *They drink contaminated water* American Academy of Pediatrics, "With No Amount of Lead Exposure Safe for Children, AAP Calls for Stricter Regulations," HealthyChildren.org, June 20, 2016; Council on Environmental Health, "Prevention of Childhood Lead Toxicity," *Pediatrics* 138, no. 1 (July 1, 2016): e20161493; Eliza Barclay, "Lead in Soil May Be an Overlooked Threat to Kids' Health," NPR, Apr. 5, 2013, https://www.npr.org/sections/health-shots/2013/04/04/176257595/soil-lead-may-be-an-overlooked-threat-to-kids-health.

174   *They live in cities* M. B. Pell and Joshua Schneyer, "Thousands of U.S. Areas Afflicted with Lead Poisoning Beyond Flint's," *Scientific American*, Dec. 19, 2016; Dr. Mona Hanna-Attisha, "Déjà Vu: Flint Pediatrician Speaks About the Newark Water Crisis," interview by NRDC, Sept. 3, 2019, https://www.nrdc.org/stories/deja-vu-flint-pediatrician-speaks-about-newark-water-crisis.

174   *In 2019, as Philadelphia* Jake Blumgart, " 'Universal' Lead Bill Passes, Making Philly the Biggest U.S. City to Require Landlords to Test for Lead," WHYY, Sept. 26, 2019, https://whyy.org/articles/universal-lead-bill-passes-making-philly-the-biggest-u-s-city-to-require-landlords-to-test-for-lead/; Nick Corasaniti, Corey Kilgannon, and John Schwartz, "Lead Crisis in Newark Grows, as Bottled Water Distribution Is Bungled," *New York Times*, Aug. 14, 2019.

174   *In the five years* Erica L. Green, "Flint's Children Suffer in Class After Years of Drinking the Lead-Poisoned Water," *New York Times*, Nov. 6, 2019.

174   *It is embodied* Gillian Jones, "Legislative Update: Parental Rights Amendment," *Children's Legal Rights Journal* 32, no. 2 (2012): 75–77.

174   *Of course, the "what about me?"* Heather McGhee, *The Sum of Us: What Racism Costs Everyone and How We Can Prosper Together* (New York: One World, 2021).

174   *Gay marriage was derided* Patrick Busch, "Is Same-Sex Marriage a Threat to Traditional Marriages? How Courts Struggle with the Question," *Washington University Global Studies Law Review* 11, no. 1 (Jan. 2011): 144.

175   *If we sanction lawyers* Johnny Edwards, "Alleged Victims Say Powerful Georgia Lawmaker Repeatedly Delays Cases," *Atlanta Journal-Constitution*, Feb. 19, 2019.

175   *Red flag laws* Timothy Williams, "What Are 'Red Flag' Gun Laws, and How Do They Work?" *New York Times*, Aug. 6, 2019; Matt Vasilogambros, "Red Flag Laws Spur Debate over Due Process," Pew Charitable Trusts, accessed June 30, 2021, https://www.pewtrusts.org/en/research-and-analysis/blogs/stateline/2019/09/04/red-flag-laws-spur-debate-over-due-process.

175   *Barring those who are pregnant* Angela Spivey, "The Weight of Lead: Effects

Add Up in Adults," *Environmental Health Perspectives* 115, no. 1 (Jan. 2007): 35–36; Automobile Workers v. Johnson Controls, Inc., 499 U.S. 187 (1991).

175 *Allowing kids* Dennis Owens, "State Senator Pushing Bill to Let Pa. Teens Get Vaccines Without Parental Consent," ABC 27 News, June 2, 2021, https://www.abc27.com/news/this-week-in-pennsylvania/state-senator-pushing-bill-to-let-pa-teens-get-vaccines-without-parental-consent/; "Model Legislation for 'Mature Minor' Consent to Vaccinations," American Medical Association, https://www.ama-assn.org/system/files/2019-05/a19-yps-resolution-01.pdf; Jan Hoffman, "As Parents Forbid Covid Shots, Defiant Teenagers Seek Ways to Get Them," *New York Times*, June 26, 2021.

176 *The first-year casebook* Two examples are *Oxendine v. State* and *Midget v. State. Criminal Law: Cases and Materials*, 8th ed., ed. Joshua Dressler and Stephen P. Garvey (St. Paul, Minn.: West Academic, 2019), 228, 275.

176 *In* Oxendine v. State Oxendine v. State, 528 A.2d 870, 874 (Del., 1987).

176 *While a lay person Oxendine,* 528 A.2d at 870–71.

176 *The anger a non-lawyer Oxendine,* 528 A.2d at 871.

176 *What's most important Oxendine,* 528 A.2d at 873–74.

176 *The notion* Scholars have also argued that a focus on children can be a "diverter of attention" and "useful for masking selfishness," and a means "to achieve a result that would be difficult to achieve otherwise." Martin Guggenheim, *What's Wrong with Children's Rights* (Cambridge, Mass.: Harvard University Press, 2005), xii.

176 *Using Sandy Hook* Paul Waldman, "Why the Parkland Students Have Made Pro-Gun Conservatives So Mad," *Washington Post*, Feb. 21, 2018; Josh Feldman, "Tucker Carlson: The Media Is 'Using' FL Student Survivors 'in a Kind of Moral Blackmail,'" *Mediaite*, accessed June 25, 2021.

176 *Highlighting birth defects* Carl-Gustaf Bornehag et al., "Prenatal Phthalate Exposures and Anogenital Distance in Swedish Boys," *Environmental Health Perspectives* 123, no. 1 (Jan. 1, 2015): 101–7.

176 *As one woman put it* Simon Romero, "Militia in New Mexico Detains Asylum Seekers at Gunpoint," *New York Times*, Apr. 18, 2019.

176 *As a conservative friend* Joseph, email to author, Oct. 1, 2018.

177 *A couple of weeks later* Irwin Redlener, "Tear Gas Should Never Be Used on Children. Period.," *Washington Post*, Nov. 28, 2018.

177 *It is not a coincidence* Patricia McCormick, "The Girl in the Kent State Photo and the Lifelong Burden of Being a National Symbol," *Washington Post*, Apr. 19, 2021.

177 *The widely circulated picture* Kim Kyung Hoon, "Children Fleeing Tear Gas at Border in Mexico," Nov. 25, 2018, Photograph, *Washington Post;* Redlener, "Tear Gas Should Never."

177 *Every parent has held* Redlener, "Tear Gas Should Never."

177 *And there is Saira* Redlener, "Tear Gas Should Never."

177 *And there is Cheili* Redlener, "Tear Gas Should Never."

177 *You notice* Redlener, "Tear Gas Should Never."

177 *Migrant mothers* Erica Anderson, "Migrants Who Want Better for Their Children Aren't Bad Parents. They're the Best," *Washington Post*, Aug. 26, 2019.

177 *They have brought* Dan Restrepo, Trevor Sutton, and Joel Martinez, "Get-

ting Migration in the Americas Right," Center for American Progress, June 24, 2019, https://www.americanprogress.org/issues/security/reports /2019/06/24/471322/getting-migration-americas-right/.

177 *Policing the border* Redlener, "Tear Gas Should Never."

177 *When you see Saira* Redlener, "Tear Gas Should Never"; Jeremy Leung, "Build Central America, Not a Wall," *New York Times,* Feb. 25, 2019.

178 *New psychological research* University of Bath, "Being Around Children Makes Adults More Generous," *ScienceDaily,* May 4, 2021, https://www .sciencedaily.com/releases/2021/05/210504191559.htm; Lukas J. Wolf et al., "The Salience of Children Increases Adult Prosocial Values," *Social Psychological and Personality Science* 13, no. 1 (Apr. 16, 2021): 160–69.

178 *In a series of experiments* University of Bath, "Being Around Children"; Wolf et al., "The Salience of Children."

178 *In fact, when researchers* University of Bath, "Being Around Children"; Wolf et al., "The Salience of Children."

178 *The "child salience effect"* University of Bath, "Being Around Children"; Wolf et al., "The Salience of Children."

178 *Focusing on children* University of Bath, "Being Around Children"; Wolf et al., "The Salience of Children."

178 *And it didn't matter* University of Bath, "Being Around Children"; Wolf et al., "The Salience of Children."

178 *As the psychologists concluded* University of Bath, "Being Around Children"; Wolf et al., "The Salience of Children."

178 *The things that harm kids* Air pollution, for instance, poses a threat to everyone, but it is children who are most vulnerable to the lifelong effects. Helen Clark et al., "A Future for the World's Children? A WHO–UNICEF– Lancet Commission," *Lancet* 395, no. 10224 (Feb. 2020): 609; M. J. Friedrich, "Global Impact of Air Pollution on Children's Health," *Journal of the American Medical Association* 320, no. 23 (Dec. 18, 2018): 2412; Joel Schwartz, "Air Pollution and Children's Health," *Pediatrics* 113, no. 4 (Dec. 26, 2005): 1037–43; Marissa Hauptman and Alan D. Woolf, "Childhood Ingestions of Environmental Toxins: What Are the Risks?" *Pediatric Annals* 46, no. 12 (Dec. 1, 2017): e466–71.

178 *Take tear gas* Redlener, "Tear Gas Should Never."

178 *An infant might take* Redlener, "Tear Gas Should Never."

178 *And infants' and preschoolers'* Redlener, "Tear Gas Should Never"; Joseph D. Lyons, "What Tear Gas Does to Children Like Those at the Border, According to an Expert," *Bustle,* Nov. 26, 2018, https://www.bustle.com/p/ tear-gas-can-affect-children-more-than-adults-border-agents-used-it-near -them-anyway-13195244.

179 *The asthma rates* Redlener, "Tear Gas Should Never."

179 *How did we decide* Craig Rothenberg et al., "Tear Gas: An Epidemiological and Mechanistic Reassessment," *Annals of the New York Academy of Sciences* 1378, no. 1 (Aug. 2016): 97.

179 *Arguably the most influential* Rothenberg et al., "Tear Gas," 100; F. W. Beswick, P. Holland, and K. H. Kemp, "Acute Effects of Exposure to Orthochlorobenzylidene Malononitrile (CS) and the Development of Tolerance," *British Journal of Industrial Medicine* 29, no. 3 (July 1972): 298–306.

179   *Now, though, police* Rothenberg et al., "Tear Gas," 96–97, 99–100.

179   *A ten-pound preemie* Environmental Working Group, "Drinking Water and Children's Health," July 26, 2017, https://www.ewg.org/research /drinking-water-and-childrens-health.

179   *The eight-year-old takes* American Academy of Child and Adolescent Psychiatry, *A Guide for Community Child Serving Agencies on Psychotropic Medications for Children and Adolescents,* Feb. 2012, 11, https://www.aacap.org /app_themes/aacap/docs/press/guide_for_community_child_serving _agencies_on_psychotropic_medications_for_children_and_adolescents _2012.pdf; Ajit Ninan et al., "Adverse Effects of Psychotropic Medications in Children: Predictive Factors," *Journal of the Canadian Academy of Child and Adolescent Psychiatry* 23, no. 3 (June 9, 2014): 219.

179   *She was writing fiction* Alice Walker, *Possessing the Secret of Joy* (New York: Washington Square Press, 1992), 165.

8. Stop and Give a Thought: What Change Looks Like

180   *But the result* Nancy Gertner and Chiraag Bains, "Mandatory Minimum Sentences Are Cruel and Ineffective. Sessions Wants Them Back," *Washington Post,* May 15, 2017; David Murphey and P. Mae Cooper, "Parents Behind Bars," *Child Trends,* Oct. 2015, 1.

180   *A majority of people* Stephanos Bibas, "The Truth About Mass Incarceration," *National Review,* Sept. 16, 2015; "Parents in Prison," The Sentencing Project, accessed July 6, 2021, http://www.sentencingproject.org /publications/parents-in-prison/.

181   *Kirstjen Nielsen* Sarah Stillman, "America's Other Family-Separation Crisis," *New Yorker,* Oct. 29, 2018.

181   *The shocking answer* Cary Aspinwall, "Overlooked," *Dallas Morning News,* June 22, 2017; *Safeguarding Children of Arrested Parents,* International Association of Chiefs of Police, Aug. 2014, https://bja.ojp.gov/sites/g/files /xyckuh186/files/Publications/IACP-SafeguardingChildren.pdf; "Arrest," Legal Services for Prisoners with Children, http://www.prisonerswithchil dren.org/pubs/ipm/arrest.htm.

181   *In 2012, a mail carrier* Mike Glenn and John Rigg, "Siblings Found Living in Abandoned School Bus in Splendora," *Houston Chronicle,* Mar. 7, 2012.

181   *"The little girl's hair"* "Texas Children Found Living in School Bus, While Parents Imprisoned for Embezzlement," Fox News, Mar. 9, 2012, https:// www.foxnews.com/us/texas-children-found-living-in-school-bus-while -parents-imprisoned-for-embezzlement.

181   *The kids were living* "Texas Children Found."

181   *Their clothes were dirty* "Texas Children Found."

181   *Toys and trash* "Texas Children Found."

181   *When authorities checked* "Texas Children Found."

181   *Months earlier* "Texas Children Found."

181   *An aunt was supposed* "Texas Children Found."

181   *Meticulous attention* Michael Grczyk, "Texas Parents Get Custody of Kids Living in Bus," *San Diego Union-Tribune,* Jan. 22, 2012.

181   *Sarah and Jen were four* Sarah, interview by author, Sept. 10, 2018.

182   *She would eventually* Tina, interview by author, Aug. 22, 2018.

182   *Early childhood for the girls* Tina, interview.

182   *Sarah does have one* Sarah, interview.

182   *No one intervened* Sarah, interview.

182   *And then, improbably* Sarah, interview.

182   *They welcomed Sarah* Sarah, interview.

182   *As Sarah explains* Sarah, interview.

182   *For years, Sarah and Jen* Sarah, interview.

182   *The only reason* Sarah, interview.

182   *Because we locked up* Sarah, interview.

182   *With Jen incarcerated* Sarah, interview.

183   *Tina's youngest grandchild* Sarah, interview.

183   *He's in a group home* Sarah, interview.

183   *He's on Prozac* Sarah, interview.

183   *Think back to Adam and Ariel* Ariel, interview by author, Aug. 22, 2018.

183   *They "were kept very far"* Adam, interview by author, Aug. 23, 2018.

183   *"The jury"* Ariel, interview.

183   *And, if you are a judge* Adam, interview.

183   *The* United States Amy B. Cyphert, "Prisoners of Fate: The Challenges of Creating Change for Children of Incarcerated Parents," *Maryland Law Review* 77, no. 2 (2018): 385.

183   *And so, the prosecutor* U.S. v. Kubinski, 91 F.3d 135, 1996 U.S. App. LEXIS 16700, at *4–5 (1996).

183   *Three judges on the Fourth Circuit* Kubinski, 1996 U.S. App. LEXIS 16700, at *5. Other federal judges were similarly dismissive of the notion that Adam and Ariel's deprivation and suffering should have any bearing on the sentencing of their father. In his 2011 order, the district court judge overseeing the case noted that he had "carefully reviewed" "the poignant letters" from Adam and Ariel, but then went on to explain that "petitioner has provided no legal basis for a change in his sentence." Kubinski v. U.S., 2011 WL 13176803, at *1 (E.D.N.C. May 31, 2011) (order denying motion for relief from judgment pursuant to Rule 60[b]).

184   *While the guidelines* Cyphert, "Prisoners of Fate," 385.

184   *In 2015, a downward departure* U.S. Sentencing Commission, "Reasons Given by Sentencing Courts for Downward Departures from the Guideline Range," Table 25 (2015), http://www.ussc.gov/sites/default/files/pdf /research-and-publications/annual-reports-and-sourcebooks/2015 /Table25.pdf.

184   *If you look* Cyphert, "Prisoners of Fate," 400; Ilene H. Nagel and Barry L. Johnson, "The Role of Gender in a Structured Sentencing System: Equal Treatment, Policy Choices, and the Sentencing of Female Offenders Under the United States Sentencing Guidelines," *Journal of Criminal Law and Criminology* 85, no. 1 (1994): 201.

184   *Similarly, when the First Circuit* U.S. v. Pozzy, 902 F. 2d 133, 139 (1st Cir. 1990).

185   *It becomes easy* Overton v. Bazetta, 539 U.S. 126, 131 (2003).

185   *The cruelty becomes routine* Pozzy, 902 F. 2d at 139.

185 *We'd listen to Tina* Tina, interview.
185 *Tina is smart* Tina, interview.
185 *She loved her daughters* Tina, interview.
185 *She'd completed rehab* Tina, interview.
185 *"They gave me a timeline"* Tina, interview.
186 *When you focus* Seth Stoughton, "Law Enforcements 'Warrior' Problem," *Harvard Law Review Forum* 128 (Apr. 10, 2015), https://harvardlawreview .org/2015/04/law-enforcements-warrior-problem/.
186 *You can no longer ignore* Sarah Maslin Nir, "Furor in Rochester After Police Pepper Spray Mother with Toddler," *New York Times*, Mar. 5, 2021; Janet McConnaughey, "Suit: Cops Killed Autistic Teen by Sitting on Him, Chokehold," ABC News, Jan. 14, 2021, https://abcnews.go.com/US /wireStory/suit-cops-killed-autistic-teen-sitting-chokehold-75259124.
186 *You must face* Bryan Stole and Grace Toohey, "The City Where Police Unleash Dogs on Black Teens," Marshall Project, Feb. 12, 2021, https://www .themarshallproject.org/2021/02/12/the-city-where-police-unleash-dogs -on-black-teens.
186 *We have begun to limit* Nicole Scialabba, "Making the Case to End Solitary Confinement for Juveniles," American Bar Association, June 27, 2016, https://www.americanbar.org/groups/litigation/committees/childrens -rights/articles/2016/making-case-end-solitary-confinement-juveniles/; Jessica Feierman, Karen U. Lindell, and Natane Eaddy, *Unlocking Youth: Legal Strategies to End Solitary Confinement in Juvenile Facilities*, Juvenile Law Center, 2017, https://jlc.org/sites/default/files/publication_pdfs /JLC_Solitary_Report-FINAL.pdf; Amy Fettig, "The Movement to Stop Youth Solitary Confinement: Drivers of Success & Remaining Challenges," *South Dakota Law Review* 62, no. 3 (2017): 776–96.
186 *We have begun to prohibit* Michael Levenson, "Illinois Lawmakers Bar Police from Using Deception When Interrogating Minors," *New York Times*, June 1, 2021; Saul Kassin, "It's Time for Police to Stop Lying to Suspects," *New York Times*, Jan. 29, 2021.
186 *We abolished the death penalty* Roper v. Simmons, 543 U.S. 551, 578 (2005); Miller v. Alabama, 567 U.S. 460, 489 (2012); Graham v. Florida, 560 U.S. 48, 82 (2010); Montgomery v. Louisiana, 577 U.S. 190, 193 (2016). Unfortunately, the Supreme Court's opinion in *Jones v. Mississippi* in 2021 is a reminder that the trend toward limiting the application of the harshest penalties to those who commit their crimes as juveniles can be reversed. Jones v. Mississippi, 593 U.S. 1307 (2021).
187 *Imagine that the dominant approach* It is, of course, open to debate whether originalism is *the* dominant approach or *a* dominant approach, but a majority of the current Supreme Court appear to view themselves as primarily adopting this approach. John O. McGinnis, "Which Justices Are Originalists?" *Law & Liberty*, Nov. 9, 2018, https://lawliberty.org/which-justices -are-originalists/; Eric J. Segall, "Does Originalism Matter Anymore?" *New York Times*, Sept. 10, 2018. Even Elena Kagan conceded at her own confirmation, "We are all originalists." Brandon J. Murrill, *Modes of Constitutional Interpretation*, Congressional Research Service, Mar. 15, 2018, 9, https://fas.org/sgp/crs/misc/R45129.pdf.

187 *Does it really* U.S. Const. amend. II; Christopher Ingraham, "What 'Arms' Looked Like When the 2nd Amendment Was Written," *Washington Post*, June 13, 2016; David B. Kopel and Joseph Greenlee, "The Second Amendment Rights of Young Adults," *Southern Illinois University Law Journal* 43 (2019): 495–613.

187 *States, for example* Leo E. Strine, Jr., "The Dangers of Denial: The Need for a Clear-Eyed Understanding of the Power and Accountability Structure Established by the Delaware General Corporation Law," *Wake Forest Law Review* 50, no. 3 (2015): 761.

187 *That might seem* Moreover, as some scholars have pointed out, although the widely held perception is that the law requires corporate leaders to focus solely on shareholder profit, in practice, the law already allows directors to deviate from maximizing wealth. Jonathan R. Macey, "Corporate Law Myths," *Southern California Law Review* 93, no. 923 (Dec. 2020): 923–85; Murray, J. Haskell, "Choose Your Own Master: Social Enterprise, Certifications, and Benefit Corporation Statutes," *American University Business Law Review* 2, no. 1 (2012): 1–54; Lynn A. Stout, *The Shareholder Value Myth: How Putting Shareholders First Harms Investors, Corporations, and the Public* (San Francisco: Berrett-Koehler, 2012). It is market forces—not legal duties—that keep America's corporate leaders laser focused on shareholder profit. Macey, "Corporate Law Myths," 943–52. In other countries, the customs and rules are different and so directors prioritize other interests. Macey, "Corporate Law Myths," 951–53.

187 *We've seen what happens* Helen Clark et al., "A Future for the World's Children? A WHO-UNICEF-Lancet Commission," *Lancet* 395, no. 10224 (Feb. 2020): 633; Christine Woodrow and Frances Press, "(Re)positioning the Child in the Policy/Politics of Early Childhood," *Educational Philosophy and Theory* 39, no. 3 (2007): 312–25.

187 *At the birth* "Fisher-Price® Deluxe Newborn Auto Rock 'n Play™ Sleeper in Safari Dreams," Buybuy BABY, accessed July 9, 2021, https://www .buybuybaby.com/store/product/fisher-price-reg-deluxe-newborn-auto -rock-39-n-play-trade-sleeper-in-safari-dreams/1043103737.

188 *After all, sleep-related deaths* "About 3,500 Babies in the US Are Lost to Sleep-Related Deaths Each Year," CDC Online Newsroom, Apr. 16, 2019, https://www.cdc.gov/media/releases/2018/p0109-sleep-related-deaths .html.

188 *And this was a product* Todd Frankel, "Fisher-Price Invented a Popular Baby Sleeper Without Medical Safety Tests and Kept Selling It, Even as Babies Died," *Washington Post*, May 30, 2019; Jessica Winter, "The Life and Death of Fisher-Price's Recalled Rock 'n Play, a Wildly Popular Baby Sleeper," *New Yorker*, Apr. 15, 2019.

188 *Just how wrong* Frankel, "Fisher-Price Invented."

188 *Not only* Frankel, "Fisher-Price Invented."

188 *No one apparently checked* Frankel, "Fisher-Price Invented."

188 *A two-minute search* Frankel, "Fisher-Price Invented."

188 *Inclined sleep is dangerous* Winter, "The Life and Death."

188 *In fact, it appears* Winter, "The Life and Death."

188 *When the Consumer* Winter, "The Life and Death."

189 *More than half* Winter, "The Life and Death."

189 *When there was an initial lawsuit* Winter, "The Life and Death."

189 *And, even with the millions* Winter, "The Life and Death."

189 *For decades* Clark et al., "A Future for the World's Children?" 630; Nigel C. Rollins et al., "Why Invest, and What It Will Take to Improve Breastfeeding Practices?" *Lancet* 387, no. 10017 (2016): 491–504; Roni Caryn Rabin, "Trump Stance on Breast-Feeding and Formula Criticized by Medical Experts," *New York Times*, July 9, 2018.

189 *In a single year* Rabin, "Trump Stance on Breast-Feeding."

189 *If you don't have clean water* Rollins et al., "Why Invest"; Rabin, "Trump Stance on Breast-Feeding."

189 *It would be nice to think* Subcommittee on Economic and Consumer Policy, Committee on Oversight and Reform, *Baby Foods Are Tainted with Dangerous Levels of Arsenic, Lead, Cadmium, and Mercury*, 117th Cong., at 4 (Feb. 4, 2021).

189 *With a new product* Consumer Product Safety Commission, "Recall List" (2021), https://www.cpsc.gov/Recalls/.

189 *And any company* Ernesto Dal Bo, "Regulatory Capture: A Review," *Oxford Review of Economic Policy* 22, no. 2 (2006): 203–25; Daniel Carpenter and David A. Moss, *Preventing Regulatory Capture: Special Interest Influence and How to Limit It* (Cambridge: Cambridge University Press, 2014).

190 *In 2018* Andrew Jacobs, "Opposition to Breast Feeding Resolution by U.S. Stuns World Health Officials," *New York Times*, July 8, 2018.

190 *When the Trump administration* Subcommittee on Economic and Consumer Policy, *Baby Foods Are Tainted*, at 4–5, 53–56.

190 *For most baby foods* Subcommittee on Economic and Consumer Policy, *Baby Foods Are Tainted*, at 6.

190 *With their eye trained on profit* See, e.g., Blythe v. Bumbo Int'l Tr., 634 F. App'x 944 (5th Cir. 2015).

190 *If, against the odds* Frank B. Cross, "In Praise of Irrational Plaintiffs," *Cornell Law Review* 86, no. 1 (2000): 6–8; Maureen A. Weston, "Buying Secrecy: Non-Disclosure Agreements, Arbitration, and Professional Ethics in the #METOO Era," *University of Illinois Law Review* 507, no. 2 (2021): 507–44.

190 *If journalists* Marion Nestle, *Unsavory Truth: How Food Companies Skew the Science of What We Eat* (New York: Basic Books, 2018); Jon D. Hanson and Douglas A. Kysar, "Taking Behavioralism Seriously: Some Evidence of Market Manipulation," *Harvard Law Review* 112, no. 7 (1999): 1483–96; Clark et al., "A Future for the World's Children?" 634.

190 *You understand* Nestle, *Unsavory Truth;* Hanson and Kysar, "Taking Behavioralism Seriously." A Trump administration spokesman explained the opposition to the 2018 WHO resolution promoting breastfeeding in just such "consumer-choice" language: "The resolution as originally drafted placed unnecessary hurdles for mothers seeking to provide nutrition to their children. We recognize not all women are able to breast-feed for a variety of reasons. These women should have the choice and access to alternatives for the health of their babies, and not be stigmatized for the ways in which

they are able to do so." Andrew Jacobs, "Opposition to Breast Feeding Resolution by U.S. Stuns World Health Officials," *New York Times*, July 8, 2018.

190 *In the unlikely event* Alex Bogusky, "How Big Tobacco Got a New Generation Hooked," *New York Times*, May 3, 2019.

190 *You trade off* Cross, "In Praise of Irrational Plaintiffs," 8.

190 *Big tobacco didn't die* Bogusky, "How Big Tobacco."

191 *When anti-cigarette efforts* Bogusky, "How Big Tobacco"; Andrea S. Gentzke, Robin Koval, and Laura Oliven, "Surge in Youth Tobacco Product Use: Causes and Public Health Implications," Centers for Disease Control and Prevention, Office for State, Tribal, Local, and Territorial Support, Feb. 12, 2019, https://stacks.cdc.gov/view/cdc/76046.

191 *Time and time again* Clark et al., "A Future for the World's Children?" 634.

191 *But self-regulation* Clark et al., "A Future for the World's Children?" 632–33.

191 *Voluntary guidelines* Clark et al., "A Future for the World's Children?" 632–33.

191 *Today, many companies* Clark et al., "A Future for the World's Children?" 633; Tara M. Collins, "The Relationship Between Children's Rights and Business," *International Journal of Human Rights* 18, no. 6 (2014): 582–633.

191 *There was much fanfare* "Business Roundtable Redefines the Purpose of a Corporation to Promote 'An Economy That Serves All Americans,'" *Business Roundtable*, Aug. 19, 2019, https://www.businessroundtable.org /business-roundtable-redefines-the-purpose-of-a-corporation-to-promote -an-economy-that-serves-all-americans; Peter Goodman, "Stakeholder Capitalism Gets a Report Card. It's Not Good," *New York Times*, Sept. 22, 2020; Bronagh Ward et al., "COVID-19 and Inequality: A Test of Corporate Purpose," KKS Advisors and Test of Corporate Purpose (Sept. 2020), 20.

191 *But when researchers looked* Goodman, "Stakeholder Capitalism"; Ward et al., "COVID-19 and Inequality," 24.

191 *As a WHO-UNICEF-Lancet Commission* Clark et al., "A Future for the World's Children?" 633.

191 *Roughly two out of three* Cydney Posner, "So Long to Shareholder Primacy," *Harvard Law School Forum on Corporate Governance*, Aug. 22, 2019, https://corpgov.law.harvard.edu/2019/08/22/so-long-to-shareholder -primacy/; Alan Murray, "A New Purpose for the Corporation," *Fortune*, Aug. 19, 2019.

192 *In early 2018* Niraj Chokshi, "Apple Investors Warn iPhones and Other Technology May Be Hurting Children," *New York Times*, Jan. 8, 2018.

192 *The investors emphasized* Chokshi, "Apple Investors Warn."

192 *Most notably* Chokshi, "Apple Investors Warn."

192 *Apple's response* David Gelles, "Tech Backlash Grows as Investors Press Apple to Act on Children's Use," *New York Times*, Jan. 8, 2018.

192 *We need to use* It is worth pointing out that there have already been changes to state laws that formally permit—or even require—directors and officers to consider things other than the bottom line for shareholders in making decisions, as with the development of the "benefit corporation," which is organized for the purpose of creating a positive impact on society and the

environment. Leslie Guevarra, "How California Companies Can Turn a Deeper Shade of Green," GreenBiz, Dec. 6, 2011, https://www.green biz.com/article/how-california-companies-can-turn-deeper-shade -green.

192 *In making a decision* Natasha Singer, "Mark Zuckerberg Is Urged to Scrap Plans for an Instagram for Children," *New York Times,* Apr. 15, 2021; Daniel Victor, "Peloton Recalls Treadmills After Injuries and a Child's Death," *New York Times,* May 5, 2021; Michael Forsythe et al., "Consulting Firms Keep Lucrative Saudi Alliance, Shaping Crown Prince's Vision," *New York Times,* Nov. 4, 2018. The UN and other groups have already begun to develop tools to help businesses ensure that their products, marketing, and practices do not harm children. Clark et al., "A Future for the World's Children?" 633; Catherine Rutgers, ed., *Child Safeguarding Toolkit for Business: A Step-by-Step Guide to Identifying and Preventing Risks to Children Who Interact with Your Business,* UNICEF, May 2018, https://www.unicef.ca /sites/default/files/2020-12/UNICEF_ChildSafeguardingToolkit _FINAL.pdf; *Guiding Principles on Business and Human Rights: Implementing the United Nations "Protect, Respect and Remedy"* (New York: United Nations Human Rights Office of the High Commissioner, 2011), https:// www.ohchr.org/sites/default/files/Documents/Publications /GuidingPrinciplesBusinessHR_EN.pdf; *Children's Rights and Business Principles,* UNICEF, The Global Compact, and Save the Children, 2012, https://www.unicef.org/media/96136/file/Childrens-Rights-Business -Principles-2012.pdf.

192 *A child primacy norm* Clark et al., "A Future for the World's Children?" 634; Carolyn Raffensperger and Joel Tickner, eds., *Protecting Public Health & the Environment: Implementing the Precautionary Principle* (Washington, D.C.: Island Press, 1999); Gary E. Marchant, "From General Policy to Legal Rule: Aspirations and Limitations of the Precautionary Principle," *Environmental Health Perspectives* 111, no. 14 (Nov. 2003): 1799–1803.

192 *And the burden of proof* Clark et al., "A Future for the World's Children?" 634; Adam Briand, "Reverse Onus: An Effective and Efficient Risk Management Strategy for Chemical Regulation," *Canadian Public Administration* 53, no. 4 (Nov. 2010): 489–508.

192 *When corporate executives* Subcommittee on Economic and Consumer Policy, *Baby Foods Are Tainted.*

193 *The annual drain* "The Lancet: Increasing Breastfeeding Worldwide Could Prevent over 800,000 Child Deaths Every Year," United Kingdom Committee for UNICEF, https://www.unicef.org.uk/babyfriendly/lancet -increasing-breastfeeding-worldwide-prevent-800000-child-deaths-every -year/; Rollins et al., "Why Invest," 491.

193 *It's a prompt* Rachel Metz, "A Phone That Says 'No' to Little Kid Fingers," *MIT Technology Review,* Feb. 9, 2018.

193 *Indeed, there is tremendous new profit* The economic naysayers are similar to those who have warned of the negative effects of instituting restrictions on fossil fuel use to combat climate change. Joel Jaeger and Devashree Saha, "10 Charts Show the Economic Benefits of US Climate Change," World

Resources Institute, July 28, 2020, https://www.wri.org/insights/10 -charts-show-economic-benefits-us-climate-action.

193 *Requiring companies* Some child advocates have proposed adding an Optional Protocol to the Convention on the Rights of the Child that would require ratifying countries to prohibit or regulate certain marketing, products, and data collection harmful to children. Clark et al., "A Future for the World's Children?" 630, 634. That would be an important step forward, but we are now well acquainted with the limits of a model premised on government monitoring and enforcement: much of the time, the regulatory state ends up captured and businesses, with far greater resources than the regulators, are able to evade the law. Clark et al., "A Future for the World's Children?" 634.

194 *The aim would be* Kirsten Hanna and Nic Mason, "Putting Children at the Center of Policy Development," *First Focus,* Sept. 9, 2010, 1, https://first focus.org/wp-content/uploads/2010/09/Putting-Children-at-the-Center -of-Policy-Development.pdf.

194 *Well, when researchers* Douglas A. Wolf, Shannon M. Monnat, and Jennifer Karas Montez, "Effects of US State Preemption Laws on Infant Mortality," *Preventive Medicine* 145 (Apr. 2021): 4.

194 *Sometimes the driest* Wolf, Monnat, and Montez, "Effects of US State Preemption," 4; Margot L. Crandall-Hollick, Gene Falk, and Jameson A. Carter, *The Impact of the Federal Income Tax Code on Poverty,* Congressional Research Project, Oct. 19, 2020, 6, https://www.everycrsreport.com/files /2020-10-19_R45971_1551e2dfb0739782b0fc17bf3b8992a595444816.pdf; Aron Levin and Irwin Levin, "Packaging of Healthy and Unhealthy Food Products for Children and Parents: The Relative Influence of Licensed Characters and Brand Names," *Journal of Consumer Behaviour* 9 (Sept. 1, 2010): 393–402.

194 *Faced with America's worst* American Civil Liberties Union, "Gov. Christie Signs Historic Bill Requiring Criminal Justice Policies to Project Racial Impact," ACLU, Jan. 16, 2018, https://www.aclu.org/press-releases/gov -christie-signs-historic-bill-requiring-criminal-justice-policies-project -racial; Corinne Ramey, "New Jersey Requires Racial-Impact Statements for Crime-Law Changes," *Wall Street Journal,* Jan. 16, 2018; New Jersey Senate 677, 217th Leg. (N.J. 2016).

194 *The law acknowledges* New Jersey Senate 677.

194 *And it explicitly endorses* New Jersey Senate 677.

194 *While racial impact statements* Rabel J. Burdge, "A Brief History and Major Trends in the Field of Impact Assessment," *Impact Assessment* 9, no. 4 (Dec. 1991): 93–104; Stephanie N. T. Landim and Luis E. Sánchez, "The Contents and Scope of Environmental Impact Statements: How Do They Evolve over Time?" *Impact Assessment and Project Appraisal* 30, no. 4 (Oct. 6, 2012): 217–28; Samina Raja and Niraj Verma, "Got Perspective? A Theoretical View of Fiscal Impact Analysis," *Planning Theory* 9, no. 2 (2019): 127.

194 *The 1970 National Environmental Policy Act* Environmental Protection Agency, "What Is the National Environmental Policy Act," NEPA, Sept. 17, 2020, https://www.epa.gov/nepa/what-national-environmental-policy-act;

National Preservation Institute, "Environmental Impact Statement," NPI, 2021, https://www.npi.org/environmental-impact-statement; *The National Environmental Policy Act (NEPA): Background and Implementation,* Congressional Research Service, Jan. 10, 2011, 1–2, https://www.everycrsreport.com/files/20110110_RL33152_69b27c980f2b1121fd078e3982ac47e9c48d7111.pdf; Thomas O. McGarity, "Courts, the Agencies, and NEPA Threshold Issues," *Texas Law Review* 55, no. 5 (May 1977): 801–88; Meir Rinde, "Richard Nixon and the Rise of American Environmentalism," Science History Institute, June 2, 2017, https://www.sciencehistory.org/distillations/richard-nixon-and-the-rise-of-american-environmentalism; Eliza Griswold, "How 'Silent Spring' Ignited the Environmental Movement," *New York Times,* Sept. 21, 2012.

194 *And there are many aspects* The NEPA Task Force, *Modernizing NEPA Implementation,* Sept. 2003, 70–71, https://ceq.doe.gov/docs/ceq-publications/report/finalreport.pdf; Kevin DeGood, "The Benefits of NEPA: How Environmental Review Empowers Communities and Produces Better Projects," Center for American Progress, Jan. 16, 2018, https://www.americanprogress.org/issues/green/reports/2018/01/16/444899/benefits-nepa-environmental-review-empowers-communities-produces-better-projects/.

195 *In contrast* Linda Luther, *The National Environmental Policy Act: Background and Implementation,* Congressional Research Service, Feb. 29, 2008, 2–3, https://fas.org/sgp/crs/misc/RL33152.pdf; Lynton K. Caldwell, "Is NEPA Inherently Self-Defeating?" *Environmental Law Reporter* 9 (1979). In addition, in some cases, the auditing processes in the environmental context have been subject to manipulation designed to exclude important costs and benefits to reach a desired end. Under the Trump administration, for instance, in assessing the value of new mercury regulations, the EPA was ordered to only consider the comparatively modest health benefits to adults and children that came from reduced mercury exposure—and to ignore the very great health benefits produced when power plants necessarily had to reduce other pollutants to meet the mercury requirements. Cass R Sunstein, "Weaken Mercury Regulations? It's Scarier Than It Sounds," Bloomberg, Oct. 4, 2018, https://www.bloomberg.com/opinion/articles/2018-10-03/epa-mercury-regulations-should-reflect-all-benefits-and-all-costs. Ignoring these "co-benefits"—11,000 deaths, 4,700 nonfatal heart attacks, 130,000 asthma attacks each year—is absurd, wrong, and immoral. Sunstein, "Weaken Mercury Regulations?" And it results in terrible economic waste for our country—to the tune of tens of billions of dollars. Sunstein, "Weaken Mercury Regulations?" But it's just the kind of thing industry lobbyists and political operatives think they can get away with. We must set in place standard mechanisms to ensure that all costs and benefits to children are captured. Moreover, we should recognize that while impact statements can be quite effective as limitations on engaging in harmful actions, they often function only indirectly to promote beneficial actions. That need not be the case and we should develop strategies to encourage positive use, too.

195 *And we should require* Bradley C. Karkkainen, "Toward a Smarter NEPA:

Monitoring and Managing Government's Environmental Performance," *Columbia Law Review* 102, no. 4 (May 2002): 903, 908.

195 *Spurred by the UN's* Hanna and Mason, "Putting Children at the Center," 2–3; Rachel Hodgkin, Peter Newell, and UNICEF, eds., *Implementation Handbook for the Convention on the Rights of the Child,* 3rd ed. (Geneva: UNICEF, 2007), 35–37; European Union Agency for Fundamental Rights, "Child Rights Impact Assessment," Nov. 24, 2014, https://fra.europa.eu/en/publication/2015/mapping-child-protection-systems-eu/impact-assessment; Carmel Corrigan, "Child Impact Statements: Protecting Children's Interests in Policy and Provision?" *Journal of Children's Services* 2, no. 4 (Jan. 1, 2007): 30–33.

195 *We don't have to invent* Clark et al., "A Future for the World's Children?" 626; Rachel Marcus et al., "Integrating a Child Focus into Poverty and Social Impact Analysis," UNICEF and the World Bank Guidance (Washington, D.C.: World Bank, 2011), 13, https://childimpact.unicef-irc.org/documents/view/id/130/lang/en; Raúl Mercer et al., "Promoting Equity from the Start Through Early Child Development and Health in All Policies," in *Health in All Policies: Seizing Opportunities, Implementing Policies,* ed. Kimmo Leppo et al. (Finland: Ministry of Social Affairs and Health, 2013), 105–22.

195 *In 2008* Michael Schmidt and Julie Coffey, "Change in Sight: Child Well-Being as a Policy Development Framework," *First Focus* (Oct. 5, 2010): 50–51, https://firstfocus.org/wp-content/uploads/2010/10/Big-Ideas-2010-Schmidt-Coffey.pdf.

195 *For decades* Schmidt and Coffey, "Change in Sight," 52–53.

195 *When manufacturing plants* Schmidt and Coffey, "Change in Sight," 52–53.

195 *When funding cuts* Yvonne Abraham, "Consider the Children," *Boston Globe,* June 26, 2014.

195 *Reformers aimed* Schmidt and Coffey, "Change in Sight," 50–59.

195 *The effort was limited* Michael Schmidt and Julie Coffey, "SHELBY Child Impact Assessment," Oct. 28, 2015, http://criacommunity.org/knowledge-base/shelby-child-impact-assessment-web-app/; Schmidt and Coffey, "Change in Sight," 54–55.

196 *But, in the interests* Clark et al., "A Future for the World's Children?" 606.

196 *You can't adequately tackle* Our disjointed, sectoral approach organized around facets of children's needs and experience—health, education, adoption, and the like—is also emblematic of international organizations. Clark et al., "A Future for the World's Children?" 606.

196 *Much as we did* "The Origins of the EPA," United States Environmental Protection Agency, accessed July 14, 2021, https://www.epa.gov/history/origins-epa.

196 *Today, the bureau* "ACF History," Administration for Children and Families, accessed July 14, 2021, https://www.acf.hhs.gov/about/history.

197 *It was no progressive* Richard N. L. Andrews, "The EPA at 40: A Historical Perspective," *Duke Environmental Law & Policy Forum* 31, no. 2 (Spring 2011): 24; Lily Rothman, "Here's Why the Environmental Protection Agency Was Created," *Time,* Mar. 22, 2017.

197 *Do we inherit the world* For similar sentiments, see, e.g., Lloyd Lewis and

Henry Justin Smith, *Oscar Wilde Discovers America* (New York: Harcourt, Brace, 1936), 350; Wendell Berry, "The One-Inch Journey," in *The Unforeseen Wilderness: An Essay on Kentucky's Red River Gorge* (New York: National Audubon Society, 1971), 26; Dennis Hall, "The Land Is Borrowed from Our Children," *Michigan Natural Resources* 44, no. 4 (1975): 3.

198 *It can put us* Our egocentric bias has been—and is—incredibly damaging, in part because it is so obvious to us that we should come first. Of course, people from other countries should have no say on American policy. Of course, economists should discount the welfare of future people. Of course, animal lives should be counted less than human lives. But those are dubious positions and may reflect nothing more than, in the words of the philosopher Frank Ramsey, "the weakness of the imagination." F. P. Ramsey, "A Mathematical Theory of Saving," *Economic Journal* 38, no. 152 (Dec. 1928): 543. When I talk to people about children's rights, they often bring up the danger of the slippery slope. For example, doesn't your argument that a twelve-year-old should have a vote also suggest that a bear should get a vote? My response is that I welcome those thoughts. If this book makes you consider our failure to ensure the rights of other animals, future generations, or those living outside of the United States who are profoundly affected by our decisions, I see that as a good thing. There are other entities whose interests we have long ignored to their detriment and ours. There are boundaries we have long-marked and policed—between the deserving, us, and the underserving, them—that have little or no justification in the actual landscape.

198 *Giving a thought* Clark et al., "A Future for the World's Children?" 605.

INDEX

ABOUT THE AUTHOR

Adam Benforado is a professor of law at Drexel University. A graduate of Yale College and Harvard Law School, he served as a federal appellate law clerk and an attorney at Jenner & Block. He is the author of the award-winning *New York Times* bestseller *Unfair* and numerous scholarly articles and popular essays. He lives in Philadelphia with his wife and two children.

ABOUT THE TYPE

This book was set in Ehrhardt, a typeface based on the original design of Nicholas Kis, a seventeenth-century Hungarian type designer. Ehrhardt was first released in 1937 by the Monotype Corporation of London.